Genealogical Abstracts of Wood County, Texas Newspapers Before 1920

Wood County Genealogical Society

HERITAGE BOOKS
2012

HERITAGE BOOKS
AN IMPRINT OF HERITAGE BOOKS, INC.

Books, CDs, and more—Worldwide

For our listing of thousands of titles see our website
at
www.HeritageBooks.com

Published 2012 by
HERITAGE BOOKS, INC.
Publishing Division
100 Railroad Ave. #104
Westminster, Maryland 21157

Copyright © 1995
The Wood County Genealogical Society

All rights reserved. No part of this book may be reproduced or transmitted in any form or by any means, electronic or mechanical, including photocopying, recording or by any information storage and retrieval system without written permission from the author, except for the inclusion of brief quotations in a review.

International Standard Book Numbers
Paperbound: 978-0-7884-0237-1
Clothbound: 978-0-7884-8963-1

Introduction

Weekly newspapers were published in at least four communities in Wood County, Texas before the turn of the century. Original copies and/or microfilm are known to survive for only two of these communities: Winnsboro (*Winnsboro Wide Awake*, *Winnsboro Weekly News*, and *Winnsboro News*) and Quitman (*Wood County Democrat*). Quitman is the county seat of Wood County, Texas.

The Wood County Genealogical Society has extracted items of genealogical interest from all available papers published before 1920 plus two later issues of the *Wood County Democrat* that contained significant genealogical and historical information related to the nineteenth century.

The extractions include, in addition to the usual births, deaths, and marriages, short notices and personal column items when these items included possible clues to family relationships. The choice of items to include/exclude was purely subjective and based solely on the extractor's feeling for the importance of the item.

Insofar as possible, items are extracted exactly as they appeared in the paper. No attempt has been made to correct spelling, punctuation, or any other feature of the material that might be considered incorrect or inappropriate by contemporary standards. The character of the original material was considered of maximum importance. However, considerable liberty was exercised in abstracting the genealogical content. Many obituaries and family history sketches contained lengthy paragraphs of praise for persons and families which have not been included in these extractions.

When text of non-genealogical interest was excluded, we have placed dots (. . .) to indicate omissions. Researchers should, of course, consult the original records for additional text of interest.

These being newspaper items, the newspaper editors occasionally inserted personal comments, usually of the form: (comment - Ed.) In order to distinguish additional comments made

Introduction

by the Wood County Genealogical Society, we have put our additions in square brackets such as: [Society comment - Ed.].

Since every attempt was made to extract the material verbatum, researchers should check every possible alternate spelling of surnames in the index. Remember that the early newspaper editors were largely dealing with oral reports and frequently spelled the names phonetically.

The Society wishes particularly to thank The Quitman Public Library; The Ima Hogg Museum in Quitman, Texas; and Mrs. Valetta Ramsour of Winnsboro, Texas for providing access to the source materials.

Every work of this type is subject to errors of both omission and commission, and this document is likely to contain both, despite all efforts to remove them. For any and all errors contained herein, we apologize in advance.

Early Officials

WOOD COUNTY OFFICIALS
1850 - 1880

[The following material listing all of the county officials elected to office between county organization in 1850 and just beyond the burning of the county courthouse in 1878 was taken from the *Wood County Democrat* issue of August 13, 1924. - Ed.]

EARLY EVENTS IN WOOD COUNTY
The "Missing Link" Between Organization of County and Burning of the Court House

Our county, (Wood) was organized in 1850, and in 1878 the Court House with all of our records were burned, and so we are anxious to get to the missing link for those twenty-eight years, and hence this write up in the Democrat.

Reminiscences of the Early Days of Wood County

Up to the year of 1848, this country was included in Nacogdoches County, when Van Zandt County was segregated from Nacogdoches, which territory covered the present counties of Van Zandt, Wood and Rains.

In 1850 our State Legislature incorporated Wood County, which covered the territory more fully described by the following metes and bounds.

Beginning at the southwest corner of Upshur County, on the Sabine River, thence up Sabine River with its meanderings in a southwesterly direction to the southeast corner of Hunt County; thence north with the east boundry line of the said Hunt County, to the southwest corner of Hopkins County; thence east with the southern boundry line of said Hopkins County, to its southeast corner, which is also the southwest corner of Titus County; continuing east with the south boundry line of Titus County, to the northwest corner

1

of Upshsur County; thence south with the west boundry line of Upshur County to place of beginning.

It will be remembered that Gregg County was taken off the southern part of Upshur County, and that Camp County was taken off the North end of Upshur County and that Rains County was taken off the Northwestern portion of Wood County.

Of course after the organization of the county, it was necessary to select the County Seat, and in order to make it as convenient as possible to the inhabitants of the county, by agreement, the people met at the residence of George **Greer**, four miles east of where Mineola is now situated, and held that election under the shade of a large Post Oak tree, which stood in the yard of Mr. Greer. There were probably twenty-five votes polled at said election, and a beautiful oak grove, where the town of Quitman is now situated, was selected as the Capital site.

It was, of course, necessary for the county to have officers, and under the law they had to be appointed, and the following officers were appointed in 1850:

Chief Justice (Now known as County Judge), D. O. **Norton**

County Clerk, Ambrose **Fitzgerald**.

District Clerk, Jessie **Rupell**.

Co. Treasurer, Henry W. **Norton**.

Sheriff, Henry **Stout**.

Tax Assessor and Collector, Gilbert **Yarbrough**.

County Commissioners:

William **Rice** (of Rice's Point)

Daniel **Center**

Peter **Rozell**

P. M. **Gunstream**

Justice of Peace:

Precinct No. 1. Jacob R. **Lacy**

Precinct No. 1. James O. **Clark**

Precinct No. 3. Robert **Duncan**

Precinct No. 4. P. M. **Gunstream**

Officers elected in Year 1851

Chief Justice, Reuben **Elledge**.

County Clerk, Ambrose **Fitzgerald**.

County Treasurer, Ezekiel **Boone**.

Early Officials

County Surveyor, Charles L. **Stanley**.
Sheriff, Peter **Rozell**.
Tax Assessor and Collector, Gilbert **Yarbrough**.
County Commissioners: Same as in 1850.
Justice of Peace:
Precinct No. 1. Abraham **Payne**.
Precinct No. 2. Arabian **Fitzgerald**.
Precinct No. 3. F. G. **Barden**.
Precinct No. 4. Hillary **Davis**.

Elected in the Year 1852
County Judge, Reuben **Elledge**.
County Clerk, Ambrose **Fitzgerald**.
County Treasurer, Ezekiel **Boone**.
County Surveyor, Charles L. **Stanley**.
Sheriff, Henry **Stout**.
Tax Assessor and Collector, Gilbert **Yarbrough**.
County Commissioners:
  William **Rice**.
  Samuel M. **Flournoy**,
  P. M. **Gunstream**.
  Gaines W. **Greer**.
Justice of Peace:
Precinct No. 1. R. W. **Spradling**.
Precinct No. 2. James O. **Clark**
Precinct No. 3. A. H. **Farrington**.
Precinct No. 4. Isom **Stevens**.

Elected in the Year 1853
County Judge, Same as in 1852.
Other officers the same, with the exception of County Surveyor, Phineas P. **Woodbury**.
Justice of Peace:
Precinct No. 1. _____
Precinct No. 2. James O. **Clark**
Precinct No. 3. John W. **Drennan**
Precinct No. 4. William M. **Webb**

Elected in the Year 1854
County Judge, Reuben **Elledge**.
County Clerk, Ambrose **Fitzgerald**.
District Clerk, John E. **Lemon**.
County Treasurer, Ed G. **Carter**.
County Surveyor, Phineas P. **Woodbury**.
Sheriff, Thomas H. **Norton**.
Tax Assessor and Collector, Gilbert **Yarbrough**.
Coroner (Our first Coroner) M. K. **Courtney**.

County Commissioners:
  James **Spradling**.
  Benjamin **Lee**.
  Isaac P. **Richey**.
  Gaines W. **Greer**.
Justice of Peace:
  Precinct No. 1. R. W **Spradling**.
  Precinct No. 2. James O. **Clark**.
  Precinct No. 3. Abner **Gunter**.
  Precinct No. 4. P. P. **Woodbury**.
  Precinct No. 5. Harmon **Husbands**.
  Precinct No. 6. William **Byrom**.
  Precinct No. 7. H. W. **Hester**.
  Precinct No. 8. Nathan **Warren**.
  Precinct No. 9. James **Pierce**.

   Elected in the Year 1855
  Chief Justice, Reuben **Elledge**.
  County Clerk, Ambrose **Fitzgerald**.
  County Treasurer, L. S. **Wright**.
  County Surveyor, William S. **Harris**.
  Sheriff, John M. **Boyd**.
  Tax Assessor and Collector, Gilbert **Yarbrough**.
County Commissioners:
  Jesse S. **Montgomery**.
  Gaines W. **Greer**.
  A. L. **Adams**.
  Isaac P. **Ritchey**.
Justice of Peace:
  Precinct No. 1. John **Essary**.
  Precinct No. 2. _____
  Precinct No. 3. _____
  Precinct No. 4. H. F. **Davis**.
  Precinct No. 5. Henry **Grogan**.

   Elected in the Year 1856
  County Officers same as 1855.
Justice of Peace:
  Precinct No. 1. R. W. **Spradling**.
  Precinct No. 2. James O. **Clark**.
  Precinct No. 3. C. H. **Haines**.
  Precinct No. 4. Joel **Mabry**.
  Precinct No. 5. Silas **Williams**.
  Precinct No. 6. W. L. **White**.
  Precinct No. 7. J. P. **Elder**.
  Precinct No. 8. Andrew **Vanney**.

   Elected in the Year 1857
  Chief Justice, Reuben **Elledge**.
  County Clerk, A. **Fitzgerald**.

Early Officials

District Clerk, W. I. **McGee**.
County Treasurer, W. R. **Fitzgerald**.
County Surveyor, Hiram **McMillan**.
Sheriff, John M. **Boyd**.
Tax Assessor and Collector, Gilbert **Yarbrough**.
County Commissioners:
Richard **McGee**.
E. J. **Ward**.
P. J. **Hardigree**.
T. J. **Turman**.
Justice of Peace:
Same as in 1856.
Elected for the Year 1858
County Officers same as in 1857, and same for 1859.
Justice of Peace:
Precinct No. 1. William **Rice**.
Precinct Ho. 2. James O. **Clark**.
Precinct No. 3. C. H. **Haines**.
Precinct No. 4. R. B. **Graves**.
Precinct No. 6. W. J. **Richards**.
Precinct No. 7. O. S. **Forbis**.
Precinct No. 8. W. S. **White**.
Precinct No. 9. M. **Lasator**.
Precinct No. 10. J. M. **Starnes**.
Precinct No. 11. G. Y. **Chambliss**.
Elected in the Year 1860
Chief Justice, J. E. **Stevens**.
County Clerk, Ambrose **Fitzgerald**.
District Clerk, Jessie R. **Wright**.
County Treasurer, C. H. **Haines**.
County Surveyor, Hiram **McMillan**.
Sheriff, W. M. **McCord**.
Tax Assessor and Collector, Gilbert **Yarbrough**.
County Commissioners:
C. B. **Willingham**.
Gaines W. **Greer**.
William **Cooke**.
B. S. **Watts**.
Justice of Peace:
Precinct No. 1. Q. W. **Byers**.
Precinct No. 2. James O. **Clark**.
Precinct No. 3. H. O. **Hedrick**.
Precinct No. 4. H. **Davis**.
Precinct No. 6. J. M. **Hay**.
Precinct No. 7. H. R. **Rhone**.
Precinct No. 8. John **Bailey**.
Precinct No. 9. J. W. **Reagan**.

5

Precinct No. 10. J. M. **Starnes**.

Elected in the Year 1861

Officers same as in 1860, excepting:

Sheriff, W. M. **McCord**.

Tax Assessor and Collector, W. W. **Doyle**.

County Commissioners:

W. D. **McKnight**.

W. M. **Webb**.

Justice of Peace:

Precinct No. 1. P. T. **Taylor**.

Precinct No. 4. C. **Lankford**.

Precinct No. 5. F. G. **Wells**.

Precinct No. 11. J. **Harry**.

Precinct No. 12. J. M. **Dennis**.

Elected in the Year 1862

Chief Justice, Gilbert S. **Mathews**.

County Clerk, Ambrose **Fitzgerald**.

District Clerk, James G. **Brown**.

County Treasurer, Samuel L. **Houston**.

County Surveyor, Hiram **McMillan**.

Sheriff, John M. **Boyd**.

Tax Assessor and Collector, Joseph W. **Greer**.

Coroner, William **Lair**.

County Commissioners:

William **Cooke**.

James M. **Lloyd**.

Hiram Y. **Lively**.

William R. **Thorpe** (Died) David L. **Ray** appointed.

Justice of Peace:

Precinct No. 1. John M. **Vincent**.

Precinct No. 2. High R. **Rhone**.

Precinct No. 3. Eli R. **Shuford**.

Precinct No. 4. Henry **Graham**.

Precinct No. 6. James M. **Hay**.

Precinct No. 7. W. T. **Pond**.

Precinct No. 8. J. W. **Northcut**.

Precinct No. 9. G. W. **Gravirr**.

Precinct No. 10. John M. **Starnes**.

Precinct No. 12. A. H. **Farrington**.

Precinct No. 13. Jesse **Mezzles**.

Elected in the Year 1863

Chief Justice, James J. **Jarvis**.

County Clerk, Ambrose **Fitzgerald**.

Sheriff, John M. **Boyd**.

County Assessor and Collector, J. W. **Greer**.

Coroner, William **Lair**.

Early Officials

County Commissioners:
  C. H. **Haines**.
  Miles **Morris**.
  David L. **Ray**.
Justice of Peace:
  Same as 1862.
  Elected in the Year 1864
  County Officials same as 1863 with the exception of:
  County Treasurer, Andrew J. **Farthing**.
  County Surveyor, Albert P. **Shuford**.
  Coroner, Joseph **Rainwater**.
County Commissioners:
  The same as previous year except:
  Jessie R. **Wright** and Hiram Y. **Lively**.
Justice of Peace:
  Precinct No. 1. James **Watson**.
  Precinct No. 2. James O. **Clark**.
  Precinct No. 3. John A. **Alred**.
  Precinct No. 4. Willis J. **Richard**.
  Precinct No. 5. Thomas B. **Wells**.
  Precinct No. 6. Robert C. **Hall**.
  Precinct No. 7. William **Bynum**.
  Precinct No. 8. James W. **Northcut**.
  Precinct No. 9. John B. **Mousell**.
  Precinct No. 10. Louis **Starr**.
  Precinct No. 11. S. J. **Coker**.
  Precinct No. 12. Andrew H. **Farrington**.
  Precinct No. 13. C. W. **Cox**.
  Elected in the Year 1865
  Chief Justice, John D. **Rains**.
  County Clerk, Ambrose **Fitzgerald**.
  District Clerk, Mercer W. **Flournoy** (resigned) James **Collins** appointed Feb. 1866.
  County Treasurer, A. J. **Farthing**.
  County Surveyor, P. P. **Woodbury**.
  Sheriff, Eli **Bibb**.
  Tax Assessor and Collector, W. S. **Scroggins**.
  J. J. **Jarvis** appointed District Attorney Sixth Judicial District.
County Commissioners:
  H. Y. **Lively**.
  C. H. **Haines**.
  Miles **Morris**.
  D. L. **Ray**.
Justice of Peace:
  Precinct No. 1. Eli **Shuford**.

7

Precinct No. 2. James O. **Clark**.
Precinct No. 3. Perry **Taylor**.
Precinct No. 4. R. **Reed**.
Precinct No. 5. Thompson **Wells**.
Precinct No. 6. R. C. **Huie**.
Precinct No. 7. O. S. **Forbis**.
Precinct No. 8. J. W. **Lawrence**.
Precinct No. 9. Joel **Maberry**.
Precinct No. 10. Z. **Alvis**.
Precinct No. 11. John C. **Greer**.
Precinct No. 12. Joseph E. **Ray**.
Precinct No. 13. J. W. **Reagan**.

Elected in the Year 1866

(Now we come to County Judge)

County Judge, Jacob **Zeigler** a captain in the Confederate War (Removed by order 195 by Alexander **Hamilton**.)

County Clerk, A. **Fitzgerald**.

District Clerk, J. W. **Greer**.

County Treasurer, Dr. A. L. **Patten**.

County Surveyor, J. L. **Ray**.

Sheriff, John P. **Williams**.

Tax Assessor and Collector, John F. **Baxter** (But disqualified)

Coroner, I. W. **McCullough**.

County Commissioners:
  Giles **Harris**.

Justice of Peace:
  Precinct No. 2. Isaac **Ship**, vice, James O. **Clark** appointed by Major Gen. **Reynolds** by special order 195. Did not qualify. Record does not show anyone else appointed.

Elected in the Year 1867

Officers appointed by Gov. **Hamilton** by order 195 by the authority of the U. S. Government.

County Judge, William **Grogan**.

County Clerk, George W. **Haines**.

District Clerk, B. B. **Hart**.

County Treasurer, J. H. **Morrow**.

County Surveyor, R. H. **Doyle**.

Sheriff, B. J. **Harris**.

Tax Assessor and Collector Thomas **Jackson**, Vice, John F. **Baxter**.

County Commissioners:
  George M. **Shearer**.
  J. H. **Newsom**.
  Mark **Rushing**.

Early Officials

Justice of Peace:
Precinct No. 2. T. M. **Baggett**.
Precinct No. 3. Samuel **Roe**.
Precinct No. 5. E. P. **Gibbs**.
Precinct No. 8. John **Bagley**.
Precinct No. 10. R. F. **Stokes**.

Elected in the Year 1868

Registor, E. R. **Shuford** (with whom the voters had to register and pay 25¢ for the privilege of voting)
District Clerk, William **Fitzgerald**.
County Treasurer, P. T. **Shuford**.
County Surveyor, R. H. **Doyle**.
Sheriff, John P. **Williams** (Removed from office) by order of our Military Governor.
Board of Appeals
(In lieu of County Commissioners)
  W. A. **Grogan**.
  J. M. **Brock**.
  Giles **Harris**.
  J. H. **Newsom**.
Justice of Peace:
Precinct No. 1. E. R. **Shuford**.
Precinct No. 2. T. M. **Baggett**.
Precinct No. 3. R. W. **Spradling**.
Precinct No. 4. R. F. **Stokes**.
Precinct No. 5. William P. **Brown**.

No Changes in 1869

Year 1870

Sheriff, J. H. **Newsome** appointed failed to qualify. A. H. **Jones** appointed, failed to qualify, J. T. **Holbert** appointed.
Registrator, E. R. **Shuford**.
District Clerk, J. F. **Baxter**.
County Surveyor, N. T. **Dickerson**.
Board of Appeals:
(In lieu of County Commissioners)
  W. M. **Lamb**.
  W. A. **Grogan**.
  J. H. **Newsom**.
  J. S. **Bell**.
Justice of Peace:
Precinct No. 3. Joseph E. **Ray**.
(No election in 1871 recorded in the Sec. State's office)

Elected in the Year 1872

We are now clear of Military Rule.
No change in office except:
District Clerk, Thomas J. **Worthy**.

Sheriff, John P. **Williams**.
County Treasurer, Dave **Price**.

Elected in the Year 1873

No change in County officials except:

County Treasurer, W. I. C. **Awtry**.

Justice of Peace:

Precinct No. 1. James S. **Hogg**.

Precinct No. 2. L. Z. **Wright**.

Precinct No. 3. Joseph W. **Bird**.

Precinct No. 4. R. C. **Huie**.

Precinct No. 5. E. B. **Wells**.

Elected for the Year 1874

No changes except:

Justice of Peace:

Precinct No. 4. John H. **Newsom**.

We find no changes in the Year 1875

Elected in the Year 1876

County Judge, W. J. **Jones**.

County Clerk, T. J. **Worthy**.

District Clerk, F. P. **Dowell**.

County Attorney, J. C. **Buchanan** (First Elected in Wood County.)

County Treasurer, G. W. **Haines**.

County Surveyor, J. H. **Sanders**.

Sheriff and Tax Collector, J. P. **Williams**.

Tax Assessor, Mercer W. **Flournoy**.

County Commissioners:

J. W. **Bird**.

J. R. **Wright**.

P. M. **Gunstream**.

Justice of Peace:

Precinct No. 1. Asa **Weems**.

Precinct No. 2. J. E. **Ward**.

Precinct No. 3. J. C. **Mapes**.

Precinct No. 4. J. J. **Kennedy**.

Precinct No. 6. A. **Morrison**.

Elected in the Year 1877

No change on record in 1877 escept:

County Attorney, D. W. **Crow**.

County Surveyor, John R. **Craddock** (Resigned, C. **Rainwater** appointed in his place.)

Justice of Peace:

Precinct No. 1. M. T. **Harris**.

Elected in the Year 1878

County Judge, W. J. **Jones**.

County Clerk, M. D. **Lankford**.

Early Officials

District Clerk, F. P. **Dowell**.

County Attorney, James S. **Hogg**.

County Treasurer, G. W. **Haines**.

County Surveyor, J. L. **Ray**.

Sheriff and Tax Collector, J. P. **Williams**.

Tax Assessor, M. W. **Flournoy**.

County Commissioners:
 J. L. **Galt**.
 D. T. **Lipscomb**.
 J. R. **Wright**.
 R. G. **Reed**.

Justice of Peace:
 Precinct No. 1. T. J. **Goodwin**.
 Precinct No. 2. D. S. **Lankford**.
 Precinct No. 3. M. A. **Moore**.
 Precinct No. 4. J. J. **Kennedy**.
 Precinct No. 5. T. B. **Wells**.
 Precince No. 6. A. A. **Morrison**.

No Changes on Record for 1879 Elected in the Year 1880

County Judge, W. J. **Jones**.

County Clerk, John T. **Craddock**.

District Clerk, I. W. **Robins**.

County Attorney, R. N. **Stafford**.

Sheriff, F. P. **Dowell**

County Treasurer, Daniel **Wright**.

County Surveyor, G. W. **Cowan**.

Tax Assessor, M. W. **Flournoy**.

Tax Collector, B. F. **Young**.

County Commissioners:
 T. W. **Wren**.
 F. M. **Dyer**.
 W. J. **Craddock**.
 R. D. T. **Stapler**.

Justice of Peace:
 Precinct No. 1. T. J. **Goodwin**.
 Precinct No. 2. D. S. **Lankford**.
 Precinct No. 3. L. F. **Lloyd**.
 Precinct No. 4. R. C. **Huie**.
 Precinct No. 5. T. B. **Wells**.
 Precinct No. 6. J. C. **Shields**.

It will be noticed that in the early days of the county, we had no need of a County Assessor - one man would do the assessing and collecting of taxes.

In the spring of the year, Uncle Gilbert **Yarbrough**

would get on his clay-bank pony, light his clay pipe, and start out over the county assessing taxes. Then in the fall of the year, he would mount this same clay-bank pony and ride over the county collecting the taxes. After he was through collecting, he would hunt up his saddle bags, place the taxes due the state in them, an extra clean shirt and pair of socks, prepare a lot of well-baked biscuits and jerked venison, put that in his poke bag with a good supply of coffee, a tin cup attached to his saddle and a stake-rope tied to his pony's neck and fastened to the horn of his saddle, and would mount that same clay-bank pony, light his same old clay pipe, and start for Austin, Texas. With the addition of a blanket for his bedding, he was well prepared to camp out every night on his way. The tax money was strictly gold and silver, as we had no paper money at that time. Of course, now on the way, he would meet with other county assessors and collectors, and by the time they would reach Austin, it was usually a pretty lively crowd. While we are on the subject -- this same man held the office of Assessor and Collector from the time of the organization of the county until 1860.

Another noted charactor I wish to mention is Ambrose **Fitzgerald**, who was the first County Clerk, and who held the office until 1865. He was also first County Clerk of Van Zandt County, and held the office until he was transferred to Wood. After Rains County was segregated from wood County, he moved back to his old home, where he originally settled when he first came to Texas, and was the first County Clerk of Rains County.

ROSTER OF COMPANY B, 19TH TEXAS CAVALRY

[The following letter to the editor appeared in the *Wood County Democrat*, issue of August 13, 1924. The author of the letter refers to a previous Democrat issue which gave the roster of Company A, but a copy of that previous issue, unfortunately, has not been located. -Ed.]

Organization of Second Company In Wood County, 1861

Editor Democrat:

Noticing a Roster of Co. A. organized in Quitman in 1861, published in the Democrat, I am sending you a list of Co. B. organized in 1861. I see two names in Roster of Co. A. that belongs in Co. B. viz: T. E. **Conger** and W. J. **Sparks**. At the reorganization of the Army W. J. Sparks was elected Leiut. of C. B. and afterward promoted to Adj. under J. J. **Jarvis**. I will give two names that belong to Co. A. that I did not see in the Roster as published, viz: Bill **Shamburger**, whose parents sleep in the Quitman cemetery, and the other an Irishman who was Howard **Keys'** substitute. I have forgotten the Irishman's name. He was Co's. A. & B. blacksmith. Howard Keys, by hiring a substitute stayed at home.

I have given from memory this data and I am 83 years old and it may contain some errors. All of this Company were volunteers except Pat, the Irishman blacksmith of this company.

I know of but two members of this Co. now living, myself and J. D. **Hataway** of Campbell, Texas.

Following is the Roster of Co. B. 19th Texas Cavelry, **Lock**'s Reg. sworn into service Sept. 16, 1861, with John **Wilson** as Capt., and the names

Wood County Newspapers

of the Co. so far as I recall them, follows:

Austin, Jim
Attaway, J. D.
Attaway, Bird
Azbell, Virg
Azbell, Nick
Apel, Billie
Benton, F. M.
Benton, Tony
Blalock, John
Brown, (Little John of Quitman)
Bell, Bill
Bell, Frank
Brown, J. P.
Brown, Sil
Cannon, Joe, 1st Lieut.
Coats, Henry
Cook, Joe
Conley, Pope
Crumpler, Berry
Conger, T. E.
Coker, Tom
Collier, J. C.
Clayton, John
Davis, J. D. J. (Baptist Preacher).
Duncan, John
Duncan, Silas
Davis, (Little Jim)
Fowler, Bill
Garrett, Ben
Garrett, Andy
Grant, Andy
Guy, Jim
Greer, John
Hoyle, Roy
Huggins, Jack, 3rd Leuit.
Howard, Jess
Harris, Dave, Flag Bearer
Hay, George
Hay, Levi
Huggin, Newt
Jones, Willie
Kinchelo, E. B.
King, Frank
Lyles, Wash, (Christian Preacher)
Lyles, Ben, (Fiddler)
Lyles, Jim
Linley, R. A.
McClarin, George
McClarin, C. J.
McFarland, Jim
Mansell, Socrates
Paine, John
Paine, Bill (who married him a wife near Lauderdale, Miss.)
Paine, John
Price, John
Price, Dave
Rozell, George
Rozell, Jim (2nd Leiut.)
Rozell, Pete
Rozell, Wes
Rheinhart, M. A.
Rheinhart, Bro. to M. A.
Rogers, Will
Redding, Tom
Redding, Bob

Shamburger, S. L.
Smith, Joe
Setzler, Jake
Setzler, Lee
Setzler, Tip
Simpson, Lum (Bugler)
Sparks, W. J. (Appointed adj. under J. J. **Jarvis**)
Taylor, Nemrod
Tompson, Frank
Usselton, Bob
Webster, Abb
Willingham, Ed
Wilson, Jim
Wilson, Cris
Zeigler, Jake, (Baptist Preacher Orderly Sargent)

Yours truly,
S. L. **Shamburger**,

Winnsboro, Texas

P.S. If my memory serves me right the name of O. B. **Forbes** should be added to Co. A. 10th Texas Cavelry, who lived at Emory in Rains county. Jim **Patrick** Sr. of Winnsboro, should be added to Co. B. and also J. M. **Richards** of Stout. Two Doctors Reg. Surgeons should also be added, but I am not sure which Co. They were Dr. T. N. **Skeen** and Dr. W. S. **Mimms** of Winnsboro, both of whom belonged to old 10th.

S. L. **Shamburger**.

Wood County News - 1900

August 3, 1900

Arlie Henry Hurt

Arlie **Henry** fell from a derrick at the new electric light plant Tuesday evening, a distance of about 25 feet, and had his arm badly dislocated and bruised at the shoulder joint. He was assisting Mr. **Lestarjette** with the work of boring the deep well for the plant.

Purely Personal

Miss Mamie **Smith**, of Natchitoches, La., is visiting in the city, the guest of her uncle, J. H. Cox and family.

Mr. and Mrs. Jesse W. **Smith** are rejoicing on account of the appearance of a fine baby boy at their new home.

Directory

District Judge, J. G. **Russell**.
District Attorney, R. W. **Simpson**
State Senator, R. N. **Stafford**.
Representative, D. F. **Sutherland**.

COUNTY OFFICERS.

Judge, D. W. **Crow**.
Attorney, V. B. **Harris**.
Sheriff, Hiram **Apel**.
Clerk, W. H. **Holley**.
Tax Collector, E. W. **Montgomery**.
Tax Assessor, S. J. **Benton**.
Treasurer, R. P. **Mayo**.
District Clerk, M. H. **Morrison**.

COUNTY COMMISSIONERS.

Ambrose **Coker**, Yantis.
John T. **Morse**, Alba.
G. W. **McIntosh**, Hawkins.
Henry **Douglass**, Quitman.

PRECINCT OFFICERS.

No. 1, Quitman - P. N. **Thomas**, justice; Frank **Cobb**, constable.
No. 2, Mineola - Jeff **Dowell**, justice; Lee **Mabry**, constable.
No. 3, Yantis - J. L. **Ross**, justice; A. J. **Reddy**, constable.
No. 4, Winsboro - W. S. **McAfee**, justice; O. E. **Thompson**, constable.
No. 5, Hawkins - Frank **Mabry**, justice; C. E. **Thompson**, constable.
No. 6, Pine Mills - A. **Morrison**, justice; J. E. **Burkett**, constable.
No. 7, Alba - D. J. **Spurlock**, justice; Z. T. **Howard**, constable.
No. 8, Coke - W. H. **Galloway**, justice, ?. ?. **Bateman**, constable.

Mineola City Directory
OFFICERS

Mayor and Recorder, I. H. **Huffmaster**.
Attorney, Ernest L. **Bruce**.
Marshal, A. **Baird**.
Treasurer, H. H. **Howell**.
Secretary, J. H. **Cox**.
Assessor and Collector, W. D. **Williams**.
Aldermen - W. W. **Blasingame**, Aaron **Munzesheimer**, B. F. **Read**, John **Walker**, L. D. **Callaway**, J. W. **Jennings**.

CITY SCHOOLS

President, J. W. **McMurry**; Treasurer, D. S. **Lankford**; Secretary, A. B. **Terry**, F. L. **Jones**, L. R. **Graham**, J. H. **Cofield**, S. C. **Forman**.
Superintendent, Johnson **Walker**.

CHURCHES

Methodist - W. J. **Owens**, pastor. . . . Sam J. **Smith**, superintendent.
Baptist - A. A. **Duncan**, pastor. . . . L. D. **Callaway**, superintendent.
Christian Church - . . . W. E. **Lott**, superintendent.
Episcopal - . . . W. D. **Christian**. Terrell, rector.
Presbyterian - . . . W. H. **Johnston**, Pastor.

LODGE MEETINGS

K. of P., Mineola . . . C. E. **Kine**, C.C.; Geo C. **Reeves**, K. of R. & S.

Woodmen of the World. . . C. E. **Kine**, C.C.; W. D. **Williams**, clerk.

Mineola Lodge No. 502, A.F. & A.M. . . . E. C. **Revelle**, W.M.; I. H. **Huffmaster**, secretary.

MISCELLANEOUS.

First National Bank - H. M. **Cate**, president; H. H. **Howell**, cashier; S. R. **Bruce**, assistant cashier.

Mineola Furniture Works - R. J. **Smith**, President and general manager; Will B. **Hicks**, secretary and treasurer.

Mineola Cotton and Compress Company - C. S. **Meridith**, president; Chas T. **Bonner**, secretary and Treasurer, C. H. **Lucy**, manager cotton department; S. W. **Neill**, superintendent.

Wood County Democrat - 1901

[The few issues of the Wood County Democrat for 1901, 1902, and 1906 are located in the Miss Ima Hogg Museum in the Gov. Hogg Shrine State Park in Quitman, Texas. These issues have not been microfilmed and only the front page of each issue was extracted to avoid damaging the fragile sheets. - Ed]

January 24, 1901

In Memory of Prof. Ollie **Thompson**, Who Died at His Home, Near Pleasant Grove, Saturday, January 12th, 1901.[Long Eulogy - Ed.]

In Memory of A. Morrison
. . . At his home near Pine Mills on the evening of Wednesday 16th. inst. after a painful illness of some weeks, Esq A **Morrison** calmly fell asleep. . . . For more than forty years he has been a citizen of Wood county . . . In about 1858 he was happily married to Miss M. J. **Jones**. Six sons and two daughters blessed their union.

In Memorium.
Mrs. Fannie **Long**: . . . death . . . occured at her home three miles east of Quitman on the evening of Jan 16. Her maiden name was **Deharp**. She was born Dec. 31, 1858, was married to Mr. J. H. Long, Dec. 30th, 1877.

. . . the death of Jim **Dickey**. . . For years he had lived near Pleasant Grove, last fall he was elected Constable of the Winsboro precinct and moved to that city. . . . buried . . . Monday evening in the Hopewell cemetery.

DIED.

Mrs. J. W. **Bogan** died at her home in Mineola Sunday morning, Jan. 13, at 6 o'clock. . . . in the city cemetery. - Mineola Courier.

Fines Taylor Dead.

Fines **Taylor**, a brother to the lamented Wallace Taylor, died at his home, near Pleasant Grove, Saturday and was buried Sunday.

. . .This time we have laid to rest our very dear friend, James **Bateman**, of the Rock Hill community. . . . He was with on Monday night, Dec. 31. and was so full of life . . . He was taken with a chill Tuesday night and pneumonia set up at once, and at 1 o'clock p.m. he closed his eyes . . .

February 7, 1901

Death's Harvest

Mrs. Nellie **Jones**: . . . at her home 4 miles northeast of town at 3 o'clock Wednesday morning . . . Interment at Quitman cemetery today, Thursday.

Mrs. Mollie **Wingard**: The wife of our friend, J. E. Wingard, died at the family residence in Winsboro on the 30th. inst, and was buried the following day at Pleasant Grove beside her two brothers, Wallace and Fines **Taylor**. . . .

C. S. **Jackson**: . . . citizen of the Oak Grove community died Monday night and was buried the following day at Ebenezer. . .

Mr. **Hartsfield**: The father of Prof. J. B. Hartsfield, whose death was reported in last week's issue, died at his home near Pine Mills Friday last and was buried at Mt. Pisga the following day. . .

Amy **Parrish**: The baby girl of W. A. Parrish, died at the home three miles east of town, Thursday night, and was buried at Mr. Pisga the following day. Friend Al, and the sister and little brother . . .

Sam **Weems**: The eldest son of Mrs. Joe **Sarver**, died at the family residence three miles east of town and was buried the next evening at Clover Hill. . . .

Democrat - 1901

The babe of Mrs. **Perrin**, widow of the late J. H. Perrin, died at the home of her brother, Sam Johnson, and was buried at Myrtle Springs.

The youngest son of Mr. and Mrs. Joe **Peret**, died at their home, one mile north of town, Tuesday evening and was buried the following day at Myrtle Springs.

The New House
Mineola, Tex. Feb 4th, 1901

I am now opening up a large stock of general merchandise in Mineola. [Long article.] I am yours very truly, Aaron **Munzesheimer**.

Marriage License Issued.

Earl **Voorhees** - Ollie **Wood**
J. R. **Shipes** - Alma **Reese**
J. C. **Smith** - Lula **King**
T. J. **Coburn** - Thedicia **Crow**
Gus **McGee** - Isabela **Davis**
T. L. **Martin** - Lizzie **Rogers**

Mrs. Drew Dead.

Mrs. **Drew**, the aged mother of Mr. Joe Drew, died at her son's home a few miles east of town Monday night, and was buried Tuesday. . . . - Mineola News.

March 7, 1901

Mr. J. E. **Wren** and Miss Eunice **Butler**, of Mineola were married in the office of the County Clerk at 3 o'clock by the Democrat editor. . . . the bride is a daughter of George W. Butler. . . . the bridal couple were accompanied to Quitman by Mr. Geo. F. **Dillard** and Mrs. **Kay**, both of Mineola.

Mr. J. S. **McCoy** and Mrs. Rosa **Sims** - nee **Newman** - of Mineola were married in the County Clerk's office Thursday of last week, the Democrat editor performing the ceremony. McCoy is in the employ of the I. & G.N. railroad at Mineola, the bride is a daughter of Mr. J. P. Newman who resided for years 5 miles north of Quitman, . . .

Mrs. J. G. **Mosely** was in town Monday soliciting aid for Rev. **Lumans** who had the misfortune of losing his house and contents by fire on Sunday.

H. L. **Herring** left this County some weeks ago for Henderson County to spend the summer, but last Friday he came back . . .

J. W. **Low** and family moved to Winsboro Wednesday. . . .

Miss Pearl **Hays** accompanied Miss Alice **Parrish** home from her school at Bellefonte. . .

Dr. **Goldsmith** and Sheriff **Apel** returned Tuesday from New Orleans. . . .

Mesdames W. H. and A. R. **Low** are visiting Mrs Artie **Taylor** at Winsboro.

Robert **Low** was down from Winsboro Sunday.

April 25, 1901

District Court

. . .Judge **Russell** arrived at 4 o'clock. . . . The following is the personnel of the [Grand] Jury: T. J. **Goodwin**, foreman, Z. T. **Brittain**, Tom **Daniels**, Joe **Perret**, Bud **Puckett**, W. C. **Hollinshed**, Bud **Lloyd**, John **Jarred**, Dow **Amason**, Drew **Cox**, Webb **Faulk** and Bob **Cain**.

George **Lindley**, George **Whitehurst** and John **Welch** were appointed commissioners of partition to partition the estate of the late C. H. **Haines**.

Habeas Corpus hearing of D. D. **Suddeth**, charged with the murder of J. C. **Stewart** at Canton last week . . .

Billie Rogers Dead.

. . . Billie **Rogers'** death, at his home near Pleasant Grove, which occured on Tuesday, the 16th inst. at 5 o'clock p.m. . . . left to mourn the loss . . . the wife of his youth and a lovely daughter of 18 years . . .

August 29, 1901

Information Wanted.

Miss Lizzie **Langston** wants to know the whereabouts of her father, M. D. Langston and her brother William P. Langston, who left her at Paris, Texas, some three years ago last March, since which time she has not heard from them. If living, her father is 60 years old and her brother 12 years old. Lizzie is 15 years old . . . Write her at Cooper, Texas, in care of Miss Mattie **Cooper**.

James Marvin.

In the death notice of the babe of Rev. and Mrs. J. M. **McCarter** we made a mistake in the name. The name was James Marvin instead of James Warren, as we made it appear.

September 5, 1901

Brought From Yantis.

Sheriff **Apel**, accompanied by Drs. **Goldsmith** and **Lipscomb**, went to Yantis Thursday of last week and brought Levi and Walter **Sharp**, who were so seriously wounded in the Sharp-**Harrington** fight on August 9th, to Quitman. They stood the trip very well and are both improving.

J. A. **Nixon** has opened a new saloon in the house occupied by **Willingham** as a restaurant, the restaurant having been moved into the rear of the house. Mr. Nixon has bought the house from W. C. **Benton,** had it repapered, weatherboarded, and otherwise repaired.

Winsboro Wide-Awake - 1901

Friday, December 20, 1901

Death of Mrs. J. R. Smith.

Mrs. Sallie **Smith**, wife of Mr. J. R. Smith, died at their home in this city, at 11:20 o'clock Tuesday evening, December 17, 1901. The funeral took place at the residence at 2:30 p.m. Wednesday, after which the remains were conveyed to the city cemetery for interment. . . .

The maiden name of deceased was Sallie **McLendon**, and she was born in Sulphur Springs, where she grew up to young womanhood and was married there 18 years ago to Mr. Smith, who removed to Winsboro about that time, and has resided here ever since. . . . leaving motherless a daughter of tender years and a little baby boy. . . .

Personal Paragraphs.

Mrs. Artie **Taylor** and children left Wednesday for Quitman where they will reside in the future.

Mrs. Annie **Mauney** and little daughter, of Grapevine, are visiting their relatives in this city, Mr. and Mrs. J. R. **Wright**.

Roberts - Flournoy.

Mr. Walter **Roberts**, of this place, and Miss Pearl **Flournoy**, of Greenville, were married in Pittsburg Tuesday evening . . .

Wood County Democrat - 1902

January 16, 1902

Difficulty at Mineola.

On last Friday a difficulty occured in Mineola between Aaron and S. **Munzesheimer**, two well known business men of that place. We have not been able to get the full particulars, but it seems they had a dispute over a bale of cotton, which dispute resulted in the death of S. Munzesheimer. Three shots were fired, two of which took effect, one in the side of the neck, which passed out, breaking the jaw; the other in the back, near the spine. The third shot struck one of Mr. Hinson's mules in the leg.

Mr. Munzesheimer died Saturday night and was buried Monday morning with Jewish ceremonies.

Mrs. Butler Dead.

. . . Mrs. Ella **Butler** was dead. . . .

Mrs. Butler was the daughter of Mr. J. C. **Holley** and sister of County Clerk W. H. Holley. She had been married only a few years to Bob Butler, . . .

The funeral took place Wednesday at noon at Clover Hill.

Wood County Democrat - 1906

January 4, 1906

Morrison - Jackson

Thursday of last week M. H. **Morrison** and Miss Ethel **Jackson** were united in marriage at the home of the bride's parents, Mr. and Mrs. D. S. Jackson, at Golden, Rev. E. G. **Sharp** officiating.

Prof. Idas Wood Weds.

Thursday, December 21, 1905, Prof Idas **Wood** and Miss Belle **Smith** drove to Quitman and were married at the **Grogan** House, Judge J. O. **Rouse** officiating. . . .

Prof. Wood is one of the most prominent teachers in the county and is also joint owner with Hon. A. D. **Jackson** of the Mineola Monitor. . . His bride is a daughter of ex-County Commissioner Green **Smith**, . . .

Walker - Holley.

J. B. **Walker** and Miss Sallie **Holley** were married at the residence of Rev. G. M. **Fletcher** Christmas day, that gentleman officiating. Mr. Walker is a son of Simp Walker, a prominent citizen of the Pleasant Grove country . . . the bride is the accomplished daughter of Mr. and Mrs. J. C. Holley of Alba.

Married Sunday.

Judge J. O. **Rouse** united in marriage last Sunday afternoon Oscar **Pevler** and Miss Mary **Ramey**, at the home of the bride's parents, Mr. and Mrs. R. F. Ramey, 2 miles west of town.

Attempted Assault.

. . . the attempt of a negro to assault Mrs. Claud **Bateman**, at the home of her father, Hon. W. R. Blalock. The negro accused is named Earnest **Turman**. . . .

Eason - Lloyd

Christmas-eve day Rev. A. B. **Jenkins** united in marriage Mr. W. W. **Eason** and Miss Elsie **Lloyd** at the home of John **Scoggins** near Pleasant Grove. . . . the bride is the youngest daughter of County Treasurer L. F. Lloyd.

Cowan - Ingram

Geo H. **Cowan** and Miss Maud **Ingram** were married Sunday before Christmas in front of Esq. **Goodwin**'s residence that gentleman performing the ceremony. The contracting parties live near Stormville, the bride being a daughter of the late Carrol Ingram.

Black - Lindley.

. . . Dr. W. T. **Black** and Miss Amanda **Lindley** . . were married at the residence of the bride's parents, Mr. and Mrs. G. W. Lindley, near Hainesville, Sunday, Dec. 24, Judge J. O. **Rouse** officiating. . . Miss Amanda is the youngest daughter of "Uncle George" and Mrs. Lindley. . . .

Patton - Perrin

J. H. **Patton** and Mrs. Sis **Perrin**, of Alba, were married Sunday before Christmas. . . . Mrs. Perrin is a sister of Mrs. J. **Rainwater**, of our town . . .

May 17, 1906

To Marry Sunday.

Mr. Jno. W. **Smart** and Miss Lillie **Apel** will be married at the residence of Mr. and Mrs. Hiram Apel, parents of the bride-to-be, at 4 o'clock next Sunday afternoon, May 20.

The Winnsboro Free Press and Wide Awake - 1909

Thursday, June 24, 1909

[This issue is framed in the office of *The Winnsboro News*. Only the front page was available for extraction. - Ed.]

A crowd of young people spent several days last week at Stinson Lake fishing. The following girls and boys composed the crowd. Mrs. __ __ and children. Misses Jessie **Baird**, Lucille **Cole**, Mammie **Knight** and Byrtha **Ponder**, of Sulphur Spgs.
Messrs. John **Craddock**, Shelton **Brock**, Richard **Smith** and Bert **Knight** . . .

Coke Dots

Aunt Mary **Robinson** is very sick at present.
Marion **Martin** is on the sick list this week.
Mr. and Mrs. Hardee **McCrary** visited John **Scoggins** and family at Pleasant Grove Sunday.
Mrs. Dr. **Hyde** and Mrs. Dink **Busset** of Reily Springs visited their mother, Mrs. M. E. **Hunt** last week.
Mr. and Mrs. Sam **Glenn** of Black Oak visited Mrs. Glenn's parents, Uncle Henry and Aunt Mary **Robinson** Sunday.
Mrs. Effie **Green** of Winnsboro visited her sister, Mrs. Hardee **McCrary** last week.
Mrs. Ella **Hargrove** and daughter Topsp . . .
Monroe **Turner** and family of Winnsboro . . .
At the residence of the bride's parents, one mile west of Coke, Sunday afternoon at 3 o'clock, Ocia **Scoggins** led to hymen's alter Miss Minnie **Turner** . . .

Resolutions.

. . . lodge No. 146, A. F. & A. M. . . . death of our beloved brother, J. F. **Stivers** . . .
- R. R. **Alvis**, W. D. **Suiter**, J. H. **Rhodes**, Committee.

(Advertisement) Merchants & Planters State Bank. R. G. **Andrews**, President; J. F. **Turner**, Vice President; S. M. **Woodard**, Vice President; S. J. **McFarland**, Vice President; Alf **Morris**, Cashier.

Winnsboro Weekly News - 1910

Friday, June 10, 1910

R. G. Andrews for Congress.

. . . Mr. **Andrews** was born in the state of Tennessee in 1867, moved to Texas in 1883 and located at Winnsboro with his mother, his father having died in 1879. He attended the schools at this place for several terms and completed his education at Lebanon, Tenn., returning to Winnsboro and entering the mercantile business with a small capital. He is the head of the largest mercantile establishment in the city and has large farming, lumber milling and banking interests.

Miss Kay Married.

H. L. **Crosby** returned yesterday from Big Sandy, where he and Mrs. Crosby went to be present at the marriage of Miss Mary **Kay** to Mr. Loeb **Perdue**, Tuesday afternoon at 2:30.. . .Mr. Perdue is cashier of the bank at Big Sandy.

Mrs. S. O. **Ashberry** is entertaining her mother, Mrs. A. E. **Dickey**, and sister, Mrs. J. E. **Moore**, of Blossom.

J. F. Berry Dead.

John F. **Berry** died at his home in the city Friday, June 3, of cancer of the stomach . . .

Death of Mrs. Gibson.

Monday morning, Mrs. Frank **Gibson** died at the family residence in East Winnsboro. .. . Deceased was a daughter of Mr. and Mrs. J. H. **Patrick**, of this city, and leaves a husband and several children . . .

Wood County Democrat - 1914

Thursday, July 23, 1914

Death at the Jail

H. C. **Johnson** an ex-Confederate soldier, who was tried and adjudged insane some six months ago, and who has been in charge of Sheriff **Williams** since that time, died at the jail last Sunday afternoon. The remains were buried in the Quitman cemetery Monday morning.

Death from Kick of Horse

The little son of Mr. J. E. **Powell**, who lives on Will **White**'s place near Rock Hill, was kicked by a horse some four or five weeks ago, the kick crushing the skull in. The little fellow lingered until Saturday night last and died. Mr. White and a brother of the little boy were here Sunday morning after a coffin for the deceased. Interment was had at Rock Hill Sunday afternoon.

Death of J. M. **Weeks**

Another good man has filled his mission and passed to his reward. The subject of this sketch was born in Alabama, near Winfield, October 15, 1853; was married in 1870 to Miss Nancy Jane **Franks**, in Marion county, Alabama. To this union were born thirteen children, nine of whom survive him. His wife, Mrs. N. J. Weeks, preceded him March 7, 1907, at Valley View, Cook County, Texas. The children who survive him are: J. W. Weeks, Cement, Okla; Mrs. Normer **Patrick**, W. T. Weeks, M. E. Weeks and Eugene Weeks, Golden, Texas; Albert Weeks, Pauls Valley, Okla; I. F. Weeks, Wichita, Kan; Mrs. Pearl **Woods**, Alba; Mrs. Ida **Ayer**, Golden. . . . He and his family came to Wood county in January 1894, and continuously lived here, with the exception of two or three years spent in northwest Texas, settling near Golden about 4 years ago and remained there until his death. Bro. Weeks was a member of Pilgrims Rest church at the time of his death. . . . The remains were laid to rest in the Sand Springs cemetery. . . .

Thursday, July 30, 1914

Local and Personal

Misses Willie Maye and Lona **Apel** visited . . .

Misses Haskie, Lillie, and Lema **Hartsfield** visited Miss Inez **Mounts** Monday.

Miss Beulah **Conger** came in last week from Dallas . . .

Miss Katie **Wright** . . .

C. M. **Goodwin**, the only and original Clarence, came in from Houston Friday and remained over with his parents, Mr. and Mrs. T. J. Goodwin . . .

Mrs. Lydia C. **Wright**, of Lamesa, Texas is visiting her daughter, Mrs. W. T. **Williams**.   Messers **Pope** and **Carter** were over from Golden . . .

Card of Thanks

. . . during the illness and death of our dear mother Mrs. B. T. **Jones**, also Drs. **Shelton** and **Coleman** for their unflagging efforts in her behalf. . . .- The Children.

D. G. **Cummins**, living on the Charlie **McCain** place 3 miles south of town, showed us a sample of his corn Monday . . .

Local and Personal (Delayed from last week)

Mrs. R. E. **Bozeman** and children visited relates at Alba Saturday.

Charlie **Dixson** was down from Winnsboro . . .

H. J. **Wilder** has added a new "Ford" to his Garage . . .

Mrs. **Clark**, of Grand Saline . . . visited with her brother, H. J. **Wilder** and family . . .

Mr. and Mrs. A. **Murck**, Mrs. **Grogan** and her brother Charlie **Cox** motored over to Alba . . .in Mr. Murck's "Hupp."

Ulys **Butts** and wife returned home Monday from Calvary . . .

Edgar **Goodwin** came in Saturday to join his wife and boy . . . Edgar is still holding his job as mail clerk on the railroad, running from Ft. Worth to Caldwell, Kan.

J. B. **Mounts** carried his little boy over to Greenville last week and had an operation performed on him for some nose trouble. . . . getting along fine.

Mr. Bob **Taylor** and babe visited her parents near Rock Hill . . .

Jno. F. **Smart** came in from Kaufman . . . his wife and boy are visiting her parents at Sherman . . .

O. A. **Floyd**, of Yantis, . . .

Earl **Jones** and family, of Winnsboro, spent last week with his father, Jno. D. Jones and family . . .

. . . Mr. **Jarman**, of Lindale, who is here visiting his sister, Mrs. D. M. **Maynor**.

The "**Dodgen** boys" were here Monday, at least a part of them, Claud, Hardee and Barney. Claud and Barney were accompanied by their wives and children . . .

G. W. **Ely**, who was called to Dallas Sunday a week ago on account of the serious illness of his brother, Chas. A. Ely. He returned home Thursday of last week, his brother having died before he reached his bedside. The remains were carried to Myrkle for burial where the parents, four brothers and five sisters reside. Deceased was 22 years of age and his death was caused from an operation of several years ago from which he never entirely recovered. He was attending school at Denton . . .

A. J. **Conger** returned . . . his daughter Mrs. Wylie **Williams**, at Rockwall . . .

Jno. W. **Smart** was here from Winnsboro a short while Monday. We understand that Walter has sold his interest in the First National Bank at Winnsboro, also his home in that town, and bought the interests of two of the principal stockholders in the First State Bank of Mineola and will move to Mineola in the course of a few days and be associated with that institution.

Democrat - 1914

Local and Personal

Richard **Smith** and wife went to Dallas Monday.

B. F. **Smart** made a business trip to Marshall Monday.

R. C. **Brittain** made a business trip to Dallas first of this week.

Miss Donnie **Smith**, of Tampa, Texas, is visiting Mrs. A. J. **Britton** this week.

Mrs. J. M. **Lloyd** and children . . .

Mrs. W. G. **McCrary** and children returned . . . relatives in Titus county.

Dr. **Black** and Rip **Wood** went over to Greenville Wednesday with little Veta Wood to have an operation performed for throat trouble.

Miss Nannie **Allman**, of Ranger, Texas, . , . her uncle, Dr. J. B. **Goldsmsith** and fmaily.

D. S. **Armstrong** and wife, Clyde **Jorday** and wife and Miss Ramah **Morrow**, of Alba.

E. F. **Wilder** and family left last week for Kingston, Okla., where they will make their future home. . . .

W. J. **King**, with the Southwestern Paper Co., Dallas . . .Mr. King's parents at Pleasant Grove. . .

Mr. A. **Murck** has his home 2 miles out, about ready for occupancy . . .

Thursday, August 6, 1914

D. Z. **Johnson**, H. C. **Dourglas**, W. L. **Johnson**, R. M. **Deas**, J. B. **Brogden**, R. S. **Posey**, P. E. **Harrison**, G. A. **Lloyd**, E. J. **McCrary**, W. J. **Hale**, W. L. **Moody** and J. C. **Price** were the out of town Masons in attendance on the Lodge Saturday night.

County Socialists Meet

The Socialists of Wood county met at the courthouse in Quitman, Saturday August 1st, 1914, with R. F. **Blackmon**, chairman and Jobe **Holbrook** secty, protem.

The following list of delegates were present from the various precincts of the county: E. U. **Phillips**, A. I. **Browning**, T. J.

Hamrick, P. **Mitchan**, A. J. **Weems**, W. S. **Baker**, S. B. **Whitley**, A. E. **Smith**, J. C. **Ford**, W. A. **Wright**, H. C. **Wood**, W. H. **Gable**, George **Barnett**, C. B. **Watkins**, E. F. **Busby**, Joseph R. **White**, L. W. **Murphy**, J. S. **Vandiver**, R. F. **Blackmon**, Jobe **Holbrook**.

Death of Mrs. Steele

Mrs. Mary **Steele** was born in Tenn., July 23, 1825. When a child, her parents moved to Kentucky where she was married to J. J. V. Steele in 1848, to which union nine children were born, 4 of whom, Mrs. May **Smith**, of Tyler, W. A. **Steele**, of Quitman, A. J. Steele, of Tyler, and H. F. Steele, of Lindale, survive. After the war, Mr. Steele with his family moved to Miss., where he died in 1869, and 1877, the widow with her children moved to Smith county where she has continued to reside, for the past 4 years in Tyler with her daughter, Mrs. Smith. Mrs. Steele died at that place Sunday June 26, at 4 o'clock in the afternoon, and was buried the following day at Liberty Hill, near Tyler. The funeral services were conducted by Rev. W. E. **Stamps**, of Tyler. . . .

H. M. **Craig** and Miss Grace **Miller** were married at the home of the bride's parents, Mr. and Mrs. J. D. Miller, in Quitman, last Sunday evening at 4 o'clock, Rev. W. M. **Bass** officiating .

Saturday evening at the home of the bride's parents, Mr. and Mrs. W. H. **Stokes**, Rev. Jno. **Finch** joined the lives of Miss Fannie Stokes and Mr. Will **Turner** in the holy bonds of matrimony. . . . Miss Fannie is one of Winnsboro's most popular young ladies . . . and Mr. Turner who is one of our most enterprising young business men . . . Mr. and Mrs. Turner are at home in the Cassel cottage on east Broadway. -Winnsboro Free Press.

The County Convention

The County Convention held at Quitman last Saturday . . .Hon W. P. **Jones**, County Chairman. . . . B. H. **Toney** . . secretary and Z. C. **Alvis** was chosen temporary charman.

Democrat - 1914

... committee on credentials ... C. W. **Moore**, J. B. **Lee**, J. A. **Thompson**, E. Q. **Shamburger** and **B. G. Dickey**. ... duly accredited delegates and entitled to seats in the convention:

Quitman. W. R. **Blalock**, Jepp **Wright**, A. P. **Porter**, A. D. **Rape**, A. J. **Horton**, L. C. **Saxon**, W. M. **Lloyd**, E. T. **Hartsfield**, Dr. J. D. **Conger**, Henry **Chreitzber** ...

Mineola. W. N. **Jones**, E. A. **Tharp**, D. S. **Lankford**, T. E. **Wylie**, L. F. **Hamilton**, R. T. **Jones**, E. Q. **Hearn**, J. E. **Moore**, T. A. **Browning**, W. J. **Ray**, Prof. **Jones**, Henry **Speights**, M. H. **Landers**, J. L. **Beckham**, J. S. **Reese**, L. B. **Hart** Sr., W. B. **Dixon**, Gardner **Mansell**, Will **Moore**, J. D. **Dowell** ...

Alba. T. M. **Reneau**, J. W. **McKinzie**, W. W. **Campbell**, W. W. **Williams**, L. H. **Patten**, R. E. **Terry**, A. S. **Cain**, J. E. **Kilgore**, W. B. **Gilliend** ...

Yantis. Cade **Masset**, J. C. **Mapes**, W. H. **Britton**, J. A. **Thompson**, W. A. **Robinson**.

Rock Hill. J. V. **White**, T. **Gilbreath** ...

Pleasant Grove. B. G. **Dickey**, W. H. **Carter**, J. G. **Wilson**, H. A. **Richburg**, W. D. **Hinson**, J. W. **Holley**, A. J. **Harris**, H. B. **Wilson**, A. H. **McElroy**, T. E. **Raley**, W. T. **Smith**.

Stout. R. L. **Simons**, B. B. **Raley**, J. R. **Reid**, R. E. **Noles** ...

Winnsboro. Z. C. **Alvis**, Dr. G. L. **Baber**, Dr. R. A. **Harals**, J. F. **Brock**, G. W. **Green**, C. W. **Moore**, R. R. **Alvis**, C. M. **Browning**, R. H. **Martin**, Bert **Roberts** ...

Pine Mills. J. E. **Burkett**, E. Q. **Shamburger** ...

Stinson. Joe **Rogers**, H. J. **Kirkland** ...

Hawkins. J. L. **Hartsfield**, J. M. **McLain**, B. H. **Toney**, W. R. **Parrish**, J. P. **Crisman**, H. F. **Browning**, A. T. **Carlile**, R. W. **Faulk**, C. C. **Dodson** ...

Coke. R. C. **McCrary**, A. H. **Hunt**, H. A. **Robinson**, E. J. **McCrary**, J. D. **Benton** ...

Golden. J. P. **Sullivan**, A. J. **Perkins**, H. V. **Johnson**, S. K. **Crenshaw**, J. H. **Vandiver**, J. R. **Clark** ...

Hainesville. Frank **Haines**, A. C. **Wood**, W. E. **Veach**, J. W. **Carlile**, Mat **Hobbs** ...

Wood County Newspapers

Cartwright. C. S. **Vickers**, J. B. **Lee**, I. T. **Roundtree**, G. W. **Miller**, T. A. **Wright** . .
Oak Grove. J. H. **Moore**, Emmett **Awtry**, W. B. **Black**, Jno. M. **Caldwell**, T. H. **Winkle**, J. H. **Brewer** . . .
Peach. W. E. **Roberts**, E. S. **Roberts**, J. R. **Hinson**, A. L. **Moore**, J. L. **Pogue**, J. M. **Roberts**, T. J. **Pogue** . . .
Ogburn. J. W. **Ogburn**, J. P. **Baker** . . .

Local and Personal

Whit **Dubose** was up from Mineola last week . . .

R. R. **Alvis** and wife spent Saturday and Sunday with Supt. T. O. **Craddock** and wife.

Jim **Chappell**, of Lindale, . . .

Miss Nettie **Higgins** left Sinday to visit her sister at Vernon, in Wilbarger county.

Mr. and Mrs. Dan **Graham** spent Sunday with the latters brother, J. T. **Harris** and wife.

Mrs. Howard **Lott**, of Mineola, is visiting her uncle, Sheriff **Williams** and family this week.

Roy **Ramey** came in from Italy last Thursday and will dispense cold drinks at the reunion grounds this week.

Clough **Robbins** wife and babe of Newsome visited his parents, Mr. and Mrs. I. W. Robbins Saturday until Tuesday.

Cashier Earl **Falkner**, of the People's Bank, Mineola . . .

Misses Vennie and Mattie **Ware**, of Edgewood, came in Monday to spend the week with their sister Mrs. W. M. **Bass**.

Miss Lois **Robbins** has returned home from Denton where she has been attending the Denton Normal for the past two months.

Prof. Bruce **Edwards** came in from Denton Saturday where he has been attending the Denton Normal for the past two months.

Rev. W. M. **Bates** left Monday for Smith county . . .

The **Guin** heirs have sold the old home place 4 miles out on the Hainesville road, to G. R. **Cherry**, consideration $2,140.

Mrs. J. B. **Price** . . . returned from the home of her sister, Mrs. L. E. **Lewis**, near Greenville, where she was called the week before to

Democrat - 1914

attend the burial of her sister's six year old daughter. Mrs. Price says she left her mother quite sick thought somewhat improved.

J. L. **Shoemaker** and wife spent several days here last week with his father O. W. Shoemaker. Uncle Wes, as we all call him, was getting along very well and able to sit up some until last Sunday when he fell and fractured or dislocated his hip since which time he has been suffering quite a lot.

Ocal, the little daughter of Bro. and Mrs. W. M. **Bass**, jumped on an old rake while playing in the yard . . . now all right.

Mrs. Charlie **Green** and the boys came in from Gilmer Sunday . . . will locate here . .

Elmore **Wright** and wife and his son Tobe, of Cartwright . . . Mrs. **Chapell**, who has been visiting her son, Barnie and wife and their new boy . . .

Prof. G. E. **Jones**, of Sulphur Springs . . . his brother, J. F. Jones . . .

A. S. **Kennimer** was in . . . team ran away with him and Sol Turner . . .

C. J. **Smart** and wife visited their daughter Mrs. Shaw D. **Ray** at Winnsboro . . .

W. P. **Lawrence** and family and Miss Shellie **Horton** attended closing services . . .

Mrs. Harriet **Williams** and two daughters and Miss Hallie **Dickerman**, of Gainesville, came in . . .

Duge **Lindley** was here a short while Friday visiting his sister, Mrs. Dr. W. T. **Black** . . . Duge is saw milling at Crow . . .

Luther **Johnson** was down from Cartwright Saturday . . . his Uncle S. J. **Benton** and family.

H. J. **Williams** came in from his home at Mr. Enterprise, Texas . . .

W. N. **Wier**, a newspaper man of Paduka, Ky., is spending a few days in Quitman, the guest of his old time friend and co-worker, G. L. **Higgins**.

George **Lloyd** and family of Coke . . .

Rev. Charlie **Hughes** and family came in from Rusk . . .

Mrs. W. H. **Low** and daughter, Miss Mattie, of Alba, are here for the reunion.

Mrs. Ector **Kilgore** and babe, of Alba, are here for the reunion.

Blalock-Kirkland Marriage

Through an oversight the past week we failed to mention the marriage of Mr. Johny **Blalock** and Miss Nora **Kirkland** which occurred the week before, Rev. R. J. Martin officiating . . . [See also issue of August 13, 1914 for correction of this entry. -Ed.]

Thursday, August 13, 1914

In Memory of Little Louise

Last Tuesday night August 4, 1914, the home of Mr. George **Patrick** was made to mourn and to weep for the spirit of their little daughter Louise took flight and flew back to God who gave it. She was one of their little twin girls and was sick a short time. She only stayed in this world of sin and suffering sixteen months . . . [eulogy] . . . Her little body was laid in its last resting place about five o'clock Wednesday evening in the Sand Springs Cemetery . . .

Having tendered my resignation as Judge of the Seventh Judicial District of Texas to the Govenor . . . Mrs. **Simpson** at San Antonio . . . for her health. . . R. W. Simpson

Old Settlers Reunion

W. (Will) M. **Pierson** . . . was here and the committee got him to make a speech . . .

Uncle Bill **Williams** and his daughter, Miss Ora, were also with us. Uncle Bill is one of the oldest of the old settlers.

Russ **Blount** and his son, Clyde, were here also and spent the three days . . .

Bob **Watkins** came down from Ft. Worth just to attend . . .

Jim and Burnie **Denton** and their sister, Miss Myrtle, came down from Dallas . . .

Democrat - 1914

J. A. **Giles**, who lived in Wood County 40 years ago . . . He lived in the Hawkins country and is distantly related to the lamented Capt. Bill Giles and Dick and Jeff Giles, who still reside in this county.

Rev. G. E. **Alexander** and wife, of Ada, Okla, were here . . . Mrs. Alexander's father, Jno. D. **Jones** . . . "Sweety" Jones, the baby boy of Mr. and Mrs. J. H. Jones . . . his real name, Earl.

Editor **Billings**, of the Pickton Star, and his wife . . . accompanied by Bura **Cain** and wife.

John **Storms** and family came in from Lampassas county . . . Mrs. Storms' mother, Mrs. Georgia **Wright**.

Miss Odeal **Reeves** of Emory . . . the guest of Mrs. Jno. R. **Elmonds**

. . . Grandma **Horton** . . . her daughter and husband, Mr. and Mrs. A. D. **Harper** of Heflin, Ala. . . . Ace Horton, as big and ugly as he is, just hopped around and laughed and cried by turns.

Prof. Perry **Jeter** and his brother, Tyre were in from their Oklahoma home . . .

Miss Ora **Williams**, after spending a few weeks with relatives and friends at Winnsboro and Oak Grove, is visiting relatives and friends in Quitman this week.

J. J. **Love**, the Ogburn Agent, was in . . .

Gov. **Colquitt** has appointed Hon. M. B. **Briggs**, of Gilmer, to the district judgeship made vacant by the resignation of Judge **Simpson**.

Mr. I. W. **Roundtree** and Miss Averil **Hinson** were married Wednesday evening, August 5th, near the reunion grounds, the Democrat man officiating. This popular young couple live at Pleasant Grove, and were accompanied by Mr. and Mrs. J. H. Roundtree, Mr. L. **Douglas** and Miss Emma Roundtree.

Local and Personal

Cashier R. W. **Low**, of the Farmers & Merchants Bank, spent Sunday in Dallas.

S. J. **Benton**, wife and Elyse visited his son, Frank, and wife at Alba Saturday and Sunday.

J. T. **Rowsey** left Sunday for Tennessee to spend a couple of weeks . . .

Rev. C. W. **Hughes**, of Rusk . . .

Miss Bessie **Ellis**, of Mineola, is visiting her uncle, M. J. **Benton** and family and her aunt, Mrs. Jas D. **Harris**, this week.

Mrs. T. J. **Goodwin** returned Saturday from Greenville . . .

Mrs. N. A. **McKnight** and Miss Annie Wallace **Taylor** of Winnsboro . . . visiting relatives . . . in Quitman.

Rev. W. M. **Bass** returned Saturday from Smith county . . .

Rev. W. S. **Hopkins** was in a meeting a White Oak, near Yantis, the past week . . .

C. V. **Wallis**, who has been conducting a repair shop in Quitman for some months, left us Wednesday for Alba where he will engage in a like business.

Mrs. F. W. **Denney** and the "Boy" are visiting at the home of A. J. **Conger** this week.

J. L. **Pogue** was here Monday . . .

George **Britton**, of the firm of **McKee** & Britton, Yantis, was in Monday . . .

The Cathey-Russell Vickery Land Co., of Quitman, is another new enterprise for our town.

. . . The mistake this time regards the marriage of Mr. Johny **Blalock**. We reported him having married Miss Nora **Kirkland**, when in truth and in fact he has married Miss Myrtie **Wright**.

Death of Thos. H. Napier

. . . occured the past week at Texas City, at which place he had been for several weeks in the hope of regaining his health. . . . He was for years a citizen of Winnsboro at which place he established and published for years the Winnsboro Wide Awake. He also represented Wood and Rains counties in the Texas Legislature for four years . . . Later he was appointed State Printer by Governor **Colquitt** which position he held for nearly two years and resigned and returned to Dallas and accepted his former position with the Dallas Times-

Herald as Telegraph Editor of that paper. . . . He leaves the wife by a second marriage and a son by his first marriage together with two sisters, one being Mrs. Charlie **Vickers**, of Cartwright . . . The remains were buried at Dallas the day following his demise, the last sad rites being under the auspices of the Knights of Pythias, of which order he was an honored member.

Yantis News. (By Old Maid)

Hance **Gilbreath** is very sick with slow fever.

G. M. C. **Massey** made a flying trip to your town Saturday.

Miss Annie **Seawright** returned home from Childress last week.

. . . Miss Alma **Newsome** who has been very low with slow fever improving.

Miss Pearl **Rippy** left last week for Oklahoma for a visit with her sister Mrs. Barney **Taylor** . . .

Bob Lee **Young** of Oklahoma is here for a visit.

Miss Evelyn **Apel** who has been visiting her sister Mrs. G. A. **McCreight**, returned home Saturday.

Mrs. Sarah **Crossland** of Naples Texas and her sister Mrs. **Clayton** of Winnsboro visited relatives here last week.

Mrs. Jess **Sharp** of Grubbs community visited her parents Mr. and Mrs. **Seawright** Saturday.

Mrs. Mollie **Britton** and Miss Mattie **Kirkpatrick** attended the Holiness meeting at Arbala Monday and Tuesday.

Jno. **Moore** and family visited his parents W. A. Moore of Center Point Sunday.

W. R. **Hickmon** and Gus **Kirkpatrick** have sold their restaurant to Floyd and J. B. **Rose**.

Vernon **Stevenson** and wife have moved in the house with Dr. **White**.

We are sorry to report Mrs. **McDonel** no better.

Lightning Sets Fire to the Livery Barn

About 1 o'clock this (Thursday) afternoon during a heavy rain, lightning struck the livery barn here belonging to Tom **Reese** and set it on fire.

When the lightning struck, Tom **Reese**, Leslie **Thorn**, Roy **Allen**, Oilin **Poole** (of Smith county) and Uncle Jack **Brown** (colored) were all in the hallway of the barn near the front. The stroke knocked all of them down and dazed them so that they hardly know what did take place. However, in a few seconds they were all on their feet and able to get about except Leslie. Uncle Jack Brown found that Leslie was still lying on the ground and Tom was throwing burning hay from the feed house on Leslie's body. Leslie was removed to Thorn-Page's and altho burned about the bodyt, is not seriously injured. Both of Tom's hands were severely burned while fighting the fire. None of the others were injured more than numbed and frightened.   - Hawkins Enterprise.

Thursday, August 20, 1914

Last Saturday evening, August 15, at 1 o'clock, O. W. **Shoemaker** breathed his last. He was at the home of his daughter, Mrs. Bettie **Kendrick** where he had been confined to his bed for several weeks. . . . His grandson, Roger **Williams**, . . . "Uncle Wes" as he was most familiarly known and called by almost everyone, was among the first settlers of the county. . . . He married and raised a large family . . . Since the death of his wife which occured something over a year ago, he had made his home most of the time with his son, J. L. Shoemaker, at Alba although they would often come and stay for weeks with his daughter, Mrs. Bettie Kendrick, living one mile out from town. . . . funeral Sunday afternoon . . . interment in Quitman cemetery . . .

Mr. L. F. **Todd** and Miss **E. B. Reid**, daughter of W. T. Reid, living out one mile north of town, were married Monday at noon while sitting in their buggy at the Democrat home, the Democrat man [P. N. **Thomas**] officiating. Mr. Todd lives at Winfield, Texas, for which place they left immediately . . .

Democrat - 1914

Bro. R. J. **Martin** officiated at the marriage of Mr. Edgar **Clanton** and Miss Mattie **Roman** at his home last Sunday afternoon. The contracting parties live out east of town about four miles.

Mr. Robt. J. **Edmonds** and Miss Mozelle **Harris** will be married this Thursday evening at the home of Judge and Mrs. V. B. Harris, parents of the bride to be.

Notice to the churches of Wood County Association: . . . Bro. **Woodfin** having moved to Alabama, Bro. J. T. **Williams** is assigned to open query No. 2. Bro. **Patton** Pastor of Pilgrims Rest, No. 2 alternate. -- J. R. **Reid**, Pastor.

Bro. **Phillips**, who is assisting Bro. **Hopkins** in his meeting at Myrtle Springs, has our thanks for renewal subscription for his brother, J. L. Phillips, at Milam, Texas.

Local and Personal

Miss Mattie **Morrow**, of Alba, is visiting her aunt, Mrs. Preistley **Grogan** and other relatives and friends in Quitman.

V. G. **Fields**, of the Alba country, has been here this week as a juror in county court . .

Jno. W. **Low** spent several days here the past week with his son, R. W. Low, and family, returning to his home at Alba Saturday.

R. W. **Galloway** and wife left the past week for a visit with Mrs. Galloway's brother, Russ **Blount**, and family in west Texas

Mrs. S. F. **Green** . . . was looking for a residence in Quitman, having rented her farm out for another year.

S. S. **Moore**, of Pleasant Grove, accompanied his daughter, Mrs. C. C. **Mansell**, of Mineola . . . this far on her return home.

J. L. **Black** went to Hawkins Saturday after his wife and they returned home Monday, being accompanied by their daughter, Mrs. C. A. **Peacock**. Mrs. Black is improved some but is still quite feeble.

C. F. **Parker** and W. P. **Lawrence** are having the old blacksmith shop at the rear of the **Gilbreath** brick torn down . . .

Milton **Parrish** was up from his farm near Mr. Pisga Saturday. . .

Uncle Sam **Hart** says he has been having a time with a carbunkle on his toe . . . Now his daughter, Miss Ronda, is suffering with a like trouble, having a carbunkle on her face, and has been quite sick from the effects of same.

We understand the Hon. R. B. **Howell**, of Winnsboro, is a condidate for District Judge to fill out the unexpired term of Judge **Simpson** resigned. . . .

Marriage License permits, Aug 1 thru Aug 18, 1914
H. M. **Craig**, Grace **Miller**
Clem **Brown**, Hattie **Walton**
J. A. **Culpepper**, Ola **Mars**
Ocie **Beardon**, Pearl **Pollard**
I. W. **Roundtree**, Averil **Hinson**
Anthony **Grant**, Johy May **Lee**
J. B. **Cannon**, Vesta **Gore**
Walter **Mount**, Oleva **Richardson**
L. L. **Blackmon**, Edith **Jones**
Green **Monroe**, Minnie **Perritt**
E. L. **Wren**, Alta Ione **James**
A. D. **Collin**, Joel **Brooks**
Albert **Amons**, Ellie Mae **Patrick**
Jess **Williams**, Alma **Sykes**
Edgar **Clanton**, Mattie **Boman**
Tim **Kelly**, Lissie **Roten**
L. F. **Todd**, E. B. **Reid**
Robt. J. **Edmonds**, Mozelle **Harris**

Thursday, August 27, 1914

Mr. H. J. **Craddock**, better known and familiarly called "Uncle Hint," died at his home in Winnsboro Friday evening of last week and was buried Saturday at Lee grave yard. Uncle Hint had been a sufferer for over a year with cancer . . . the last of the older set of Craddocks pass into history. Since our day in Wood County four of them have

Democrat - 1914

(Uncle Amos) and now the last, Uncle Hint. . . . County Commissioner of the Winnsboro precinct several years ago . . . bereaved wife and children and other relatives.

Quitman Odd Fellow Lodge

A charter was granted for the organization of a Odd Fellow's Lodge in Quitman in 1851, and continued in existance till the fall of 1861. It was known as Orphans Friends Lodge No. 26, one of the early charters. In 1854 the lodge hall burned, destroying all the effects including the charter. From 1855 to 1861 we have the minute books and finance records of this early lodge. Several lodges contributed liberally to a fund to rebuild the lodge hall as did also the grand lodge of Texas at its session at Galveston the same year. This was the first Odd Fellow hall to burn in Texas. We have letters written during these years from the grand secretary of the order, letters from widows desiring to take the Rebekah degree, and other old papers of the rime. During war time the lodge became inactive but was resuscitated in 1872. In 1873 J. S. **Hogg** (ex-Gov) made application for membership to this lodge and was initiated April 12, 1873, afterward receiving all the 5 degrees. We will give a list of early names on the rolls both in 1855 and in the 70's thinking probably some of their relatives are still living in this community. Odd fellowship in Wood county, therefore, is not new.

. . . Odd Fellow Lodges are already organized and working at Winnsboro, Mineola, Golden, Alba and Yantis in Wood county.

- Contributed.

Local and Personal

Mrs. **Ely** and children visited relatives in Fannin county the past week.

John **Moore** and his sister-in-law, Miss Jewel **Seymore**, of Yantis, were Quitman visitors Monday.

W. M. **Taylor** and the Democrat man made a business trip to Dallas .. .

E. M. **Burkett**, the Hainesville gin man . . .

Rev. Charlie **Hughes** wife and boys left for their home at Rusk . . . relatives in Quitman.

J. W. **Tucker** was down from Cartwright Saturday to meet his daughter, Miss Callie, who returned from a visit with her grand parents at Lindale.

Miss Lonnie **Smart**, of Dallas, visited her father, C. H. Smart and family, the past week. . . . Miss Lonnie has a position with the Dorsey Printing Co. at Dallas.

Uncle Dick **Clanton** and his wife spent Sunday night with their daughter, Mrs. J. R. **Mayo**, and Uncle Dick called in Monday . . . he told us that day was his birthday, he being 79 years old . . .

G. A. **McCreight**, Democratic nominee for County Clerk, accompanied by his wife, is spending a few days in Quitman and will visit Mrs. McCreight's parents, Mr. and Mrs. Hiram **Apel**, at Mineola. . . .

Hon. A. M. **Billings** came in from Dallas Friday to join his wife who has been visiting her parents, Mr. and Mrs. S. H. **Hart**.

R. W. **Galloway** and wife returned Tuesday from a two weeks visit with Russ **Blount** and family at Rotan, Texas.

Miss Maye **Lake** is visiting relatives and friends at Gilmer this week.

Miss Annie **Mattox** left Saturday for Winnsboro after spending a week with her sister, Mrs. R. W. **Low**.

Bob **Butler**, Pat **Conger** and the Democrat man went over to Winnsboro Saturday with Wiley **Williams** in his Michigan.

S. G. **Lipscomb** wife and child visited Mrs. Lipscomb's mother, Mrs. **James**, at Winnsboro.

J. H. **Knight**, executive committeeman from Hainesville, . . .

The **Conger** family went to Mineola Sunday in Mr. **Williams**' car, returning . . . accompanied by Mr. Conger's niece, Mrs. S. L. **Bradford** . . .

B. A. and F. G. **Browning**, of the Stout country, accompanied by Messers Joe **Lester** and Jim **Hickman**, friends of theirs of Okla., were in Quitman Monday . . .

J. L. **Cassel** and wife and Mrs. Cassel's mother, Mrs. **Beck**, came down from Cartwright Sunday . . .

Jno. L. **Pogue** was here Tuesday and sold a bill of lumber to S. H. **Hart** for the remodeling of his residence.

T. B. **Breedlove**, of the firm of Breedlove Bros., lumber dealers at Alba, was here Tuesday.

Miss Pearl **Marler** . . . one day last week . . . her hands severely burned. She was burning some powder in the room to kill mesquitos [sic] and her clothes caught fire and in extinguishing the flames she burned her hands very badly . . .

Miss Sallie **Hughes**, who has been in the employ of Mr. **Macon**, the phone man, left Saturday for Wichita Falls where she will accept a position in the central phone office at that place. Miss Mary **Robbins** takes the place vacated by Miss Sallie and is now the central "Hello girl" . . .

Mrs. L. L. **McLeod** and children and Miss Nettie **Higgins**, daughters of Mrs. G. L. Higgins came in from Vernon Tuesday in answer to a message announcing the illness of Mr. Higgins.

F. L. **Turner**, the "Squash Hollow" merchant . . .

Mr. Alva **Smith** and Miss Lois **Cox**, of Alba, were married Friday of last week, the Democrat man performing the ceremony.

Mr. Robt. J. **Edmonds** and Miss Mozelle **Harris** were married Thursday evening, August 20th, 1914, at the hoome of the bride's parents in Quitman, Rev. R. J. **Martin** performing. . . . The marriage of this popular young couple unite two of our oldest and best families. Robert is the only son of Hon. Jno. R. Edmonds and wife. . . . Miss Mozelle is the youngest daughter of Judge and Mrs. V. B. Harris, she was born and has been raised in Quitman. . . . Mr. and Mrs. Edmonds are now at home with the parents of the groom.

Thursday, September 3, 1914

Local and Personal

Mrs. D. M. **Maynor** is visiting her parents at Lindale.

Miss Ronda **Hart** is visiting her sister, Mrs. M. B. **Briggs**, at Gilmer.

Mrs. Jas. D. **Harris** has returned from a visit with her mother at Mineola.

Mesdames S. J. **Benton** and R. C. **Brittain** visited relatives at Winnsboro . . .

Mr. **Alcott**, with the Jesse French Piano Co., Dallas, was here last week.

Prof. R. J. **King** passed thru town Tuesday enroute to Aspermont where he will teach the coming session of school.

S. J. **Benton** and wife and Mesdames R. C. Brittain and Hall Benton spent Tuesday at the **Jones** home west of town.

Mrs. W. F. **Burrow** came in from Stamford the past week to visit her parents, Mr. and Mrs. G. L. **Higgins**, for a few weeks.

Cashiers Bob **Low** and Jim **Harris**, T. L. Harris and Dr. C. D. **Lipscomb** made a business trip to Winnsboro .. .

Capt. Bob **Neeland**, who was visiting his daughter, Mrs. R. J. **Martin**, the past week, .

Pat **Conger** is going on crutches this week, caused from sticking a stag in his foot last Sunday.

Mrs. Judge **Bozeman** and children visited her parents at Ginger last week while Judge Bozeman was attending the District Conference at Emory.

R. D. **Adrain**, . . . subscriber at Mineola . . .

Artemus **McCreight** has bought a residence lot on the Rainwater block, just east of the **Shoemaker** place . . .

. . . Dick **Lindley** of Redland . . .

Misses Ruth **Price** and Alene **Barker**, of Yantis, visited Miss Ascha **Moseley** Monday and Tuesday . . .

Clyde **Robinson** and wife, of Dallas, spent a couple of days here last week with his brother, Tobe Robinson and family.

Miss Edie **Rainwater** left Tuesday for Marshall where she goes to take a business course under the direction of Mrs. **Shamburger**.

. . . moved the old barber shop building out of the lot recently purchased by Judge **Briggs**, from W. M. **Lloyd**, just east of the **Goodwin** brick.

Democrat - 1914

Bro. **Bass** returned Friday from Emory where he with Judge **Bozeman**, Andrew **Harbin** and Tom **Posey** attend the District Conference of their church.

Uncle Bill **Blalock** and his wife returned Friday from a visit with their daughter and son-in-law, Mr. and Mrs. Jack **Killough** at Demitt, Texas.

J. A. **Nixon** is having a new building erected on the site where the old law office formerly stood, the old building having been purchased by John **Rainwater** who has had it moved out on his home lot and will convert it into a residence.

W. A. **Spencer**, M. B. **Peppers**, of Yantis, have bought the **Hartsfield** and **Mounts** sawmill south of town and have moved to Quitman to the Rainwater place just west of town recently vacated by Mr. **Ely**.

Mr. and Mrs. E. E. **Graham**, of Caro, were called here last week on account of the serious illness of the latter's mother, Mrs. W. S. **Grice**.

Judge **Heath**, of Pittsburg, candidate for District Judge of this district . . .

D. O. **Price**, of Hemphill, Texas, was here last week being enroute to Yantis to visit his mother and other relatives. He spent the night with his brother, Ciem and the two went to Yantis where they witnessed the marriage of their mother to Dr. **White**, Sunday.

D. D. **Rusk** and family have moved to Quitman, and occupy the new residence recently erected by **Mounts** & **Horton** at their gin place.

Mr. and Mrs. W. F. **Denney** and babe visited Mrs. Denney's father, A. J. **Conger** and family Saturday . . . returned to their home at Winnsboro accompanied by her sister, Miss Mattie Conger.

Messrs. Bill **Stokes**; Alf. **Morris**, --. **Pate**, and Wick **Worthington** came down froom Winnsboro . . .

Mrs. E. M. **Fowler** and babe returned to her home at Lindale Saturday accompanied by her sister Mrs. Dr. **Black** and W. T. Jr. who will spend the week there.

Mrs. **James**, Dr. and Mrs. J. A. **Hightower** and their little boy came down from Winnsboro . . . spent the day with Mr. and Mrs. S. G. **Lipscomb**.

Grandma **Smith** has returned home from a visit with her son, Dr. E. M. Smith at Garland.

Miss Rosa **Moseley**, of Oak Grove, is visiting Miss Lena Mosley this week.

Will **Moore** was up from Mineola . . .

R. B. **Smith**, manager of the J. B. Smith & Son general merchandise store at Hawkins

Prof. H. M. **Johnson**, secretary of the Cypress Baptist Association . . .

C. J. **Smart** left Tuesday morning . . . Uncle Sam **Kendrick**, Ben **Cathey**, and Tode **Robinson** . . .

Bryan **Cathey** has been compelled to return to his home, his health being such that he was forced to quit school at Winnsboro

Mrs. Margaret **Price**, wife of the late "Uncle John" Price died at the home of her son, B. G. Price, Friday evening of last week and was buried at the family graveyard Saturday afternoon. Seven children, a sister, and numbers of relatives are left . . .

County Atty. **Maynor** has bought him a home in Quitman . . . the "corner lot" of the **Smith** home from Judge Smith . . . consideration being $500.00, cash, . . . "Dunk" and his excellent wife are to stay with us.

The 16th annual reunion of the "Old Settlers" of Wood county . . . Aug 5, 6, and 7. . . [speakers] M. H. **Vandiver** of Mineola and Jno. R. **Edmonds** of Quitman. . . . Mr. Geo. C. **Reeves** . . . Hon Ben **Cathey** . . . We are especially indebted to Misses **Barnett** and Donna **Ray**, of Mineola, Odeal **Reeves** of Emory and Lela **Lipscomb**, Laverne **Powers**, Winona **Martin**, Elise **Benton**, Eloise **Macon** and Moy **Edmonds** for their readings and recitations. . . . officers elected for the next year. R. E. **Bozeman**, W. M. **Lloyd** and B. F. **Smart**, directors. S. J. **Benton**, Secty.

Democrat - 1914

Dan **Graham**, living 4 miles west of town, . . .Jim **Kennedy**, living 2 miles north of town. . . [cotton] bought by W. M. **Taylor** for 9 cents per pound.

New shingle mill, 7 miles southeast of Quitman, half mile south of Wayside church, on Pine Mills road . . . W. I. & W. S. **Conally**.

G. L. **Higgins** moved Tuesday to the residence vacated the past week by Ulys **Butts**, who moved to his father's farm west of town, and Hall **Benton** and wife are moving to the residence vacated by Mr. Higgins.

H. L. **Denton** sold his farm, known as the county farm, the past week to J. D. **Moore**, of Hanlett Okla., consideration $3936.00. Mr. Moore is a brother of Mrs. E. L. **Horton**, of the Lone Star community. . . . Mr. Denton tells us that he will likely move back to "the old home place" near Clover Hill. We regret to lose Lemuel and his good wife from our community . . .

Mrs. W. C. **Dowell** requests us to announce that the monument of Mrs. Lillie **Leanard** will be unveiled at Sand Springs cemetery next Sunday at 3 o'clock . . .

Local and Personal
Rev. J. P. **Thompson** and his daughter, Miss Minnie, of near Mineola, spent several days with his son, Bud **Thompson**, north of town last week . . .
W. H. **Pittman** and J. L. **Rountree**, of Pleasant Grove,. . .
Judge T. R. **Yantis**, of Canton, candidate for District Judge of this judicial district . . .
Hon. A. J. **Britton** made a business trip to Dallas . . .
L. C. **Gunstream**, of Orange, Texas, is her visiting relatives this week.
George **Britton** and Artemus **McCreight** were down from Yantis.
Mr. and Mrs. L. L. **Lipscomb** left Tuesday for Dallas to spend a few days.

Mrs. M. E. **Fowler** and babe, of Lindale, is visiting her sister, Mrs. W. T. **Black**, this week.

Miss Beulah **Conger** left for Dallas the past week after a few weeks spent with relatives here.

Miss Francis **Marshall**, of Dallas, came Saturday for a visit with Mesdames Jon. **Russell** and Van **Wood**.

Miss Ida **White**, of Myrtle Springs, visited Miss Eviline **Black** . . .

Miss Bonnie Maye **Sutherland**, of Winnsboro, has accepted a position with **Harris & Britton** in their office in Quitman.

Miss Myrtle **Brewer**, of Oak Grove, visited Miss Myrtle **Black** . . . accompanied Mrs. C. A. **Peacock** to her home at Hawkins . . .

Hon. B. F. **Cathey** moved his family to Winnsboro Wednesday of last week where they will make their home in the future.

C. C. **Ferguson** left Monday for Dallas on a business trip. . .

J. B. **Kay** and wife from near Alba, spent several days here the past week with Mr. and Mrs. J. T. **Power**.

Hon. A. B. **Rhodes** was down from Coke Saturday . . .

Bill **McCrary** is having his residence repaired and repainted . . .

Mr. **Garvin** and his brother the former of Como and the latter of Arizona, were here last week visiting with their relatives, the **Lipscombs** and Mrs. Olga **Wright**.

Cashier Jas. D. **Harris** was in Dallas the first of the week on business, his wife accompanying him as far as Mineola where she visited her mother, Mrs. **Hall** . . .

Wallace **Wilcox** left Sunday for Scurry county where he says he will make his home "until he gets ready to come back to Quitman," which we opine will not be many moons.

Jess **Hartsfield** came up from Hawkins Saturday . . . assistant ticket agent with the T. & P at Hawkins.

Sam **Johnson** and family, of Myrtle Springs, spent Saturday night and Sunday with Mrs. Johnson's brother, I. W. **Robbins**, and family . . .

J. L. **Corley** . . . his daughter Mrs. **Taylor** . . . her home at Dallas. . . .

Democrat - 1914

H. C. **Williams** and wife and daughter, of near Grand Saline, visited relatives here last week. . . . Mr. [sic] Williams is a sister of Mrs. S. H. **Smart** and J. M. **Brummett**, and an aunt of Mrs. J. F. **Crofford** whom they visited when here.

Editor **Small**, of the Alba News, . . .

After spending a month with Jno. D. **Jones** and family, "Sweety," the youngest son of Mr. and Mrs. J. H. Jones, Ada, Okla., left for his home Friday of last week.

Dr. Roy **Harris** was up from Oak Grove Friday . . .

Rev. **Alexander** and wife, after a few weeks visit with the later's father, Jno. D. **Jones**, and family, at Forrest Hill; left for their home at Ada, Okla., the past week.

R. W. **Dykes** and wife and their little daughter, of the Vernon community, passed through Quitman Tuesday enroute to Golden to visit J. I. C. **Haygood** and family, who is a brother to Mrs. Dykes.

On Monday, August 17, 1914, Ben **Ingram**, an old time slave negro, died at his late home 5 miles southeast of Quitman, at the age of 75 years. Ben was brought to Texas by his late master, John S. Ingram, in 1849, with whom he lived until freed. In spite of his freedom, Ben remained loyal to his former Mistress, Mrs. Julia Ingram. . . . Ben leaves a wife and seven children, three boys and four girls . . .

Local and Personal

Miss Margaret **Johnson**, of Tyler, is visiting Mrs. H. H. **Macon** this week.

Capt. Bob **Neeland** and wife, of Como, are visiting his daughter, Mrs. R. J. **Martin**.

Mrs. R. E. **Bozeman** and children are visiting relatives at Alba this week.

W. T. **Coleman**, of Ft. Worth, came in Tuesday to spend a few days with his friend, A. **Murck**, and family.

W. T. **Baggett**, of Austin, an old time resident of Wood county who left here 36 years ago, spent Tuesday in Quitman.

Dr. W. L. **Baber**, of Winnsboro, was called here Tuesday to see Mrs. J. T. **Hamrick** in consultation with Dr. W. T. **Black**.

Prof. Xylander **Carson** and family, of Tyler, spent Friday until Sunday with Mrs. Carson's parents, Mr. and Mrs. J. T. **Hamrick**, two miles north of town.

Mesdames Alex **Mingle**, of Chattanooga, Tenn, and Sanford **Apple**, of Little Rock, sisters of the **Cathey**'s are visiting with their brothers and sisters here this week.

Sul **Smith**, who has been with the Mineola Monitor for the past several months, came in Tuesday with his wife and babe to spend a few weeks with his parents, Judge and Mrs. R. M. Smith.

Van **Wood** went to Como Tuesday to meet his brother, Rev. A. C. Wood and brought Miss Ovilla, daughter of the latter, home with him . . .

Reuline **Thomas**, our nephew, . . . left for his home at Lott, Texas Tuesday. . . .

Thursday, September 10, 1914

Local and Personal:

Dr. N. D. **Lipscomb** and wife were called to Pleasant Grove Friday evening last to see Mrs. Lipscomb's father, Mr. A. J. **Harris**, who had fallen from a wagon that evening and was pretty badly hurt. They returned Saturday and report Uncle Abb getting along fairly well.

Miss Maye **Cagul** . . . leave for Palacios, Texas . . . winter in school.

W. A. **Moody** . . . was here Saturday.

Mr. J. T. **Rowsey** tells us this is his last week in Quitman. . . . sold his home to L. **Horton** and will leave next week for Rule, Haskell county . . .

Mrs. F. P. **Russell** and daughter, Miss Bessie, of Golden spent last week with her son, County Clerk Jon. Russell and family. Mrs. Russell has been in poor health . . .

Miss Maye **Lake** visited Mrs. B. F. **Cathey** at Winnsboro . . .

Democrat - 1914

Miss Dora **Blackwell**, of Hainesville, visited her sister, Mrs. C. W. **Vickery**, this week.

Mrs. Alex **Mingle**, of Chattanooga, Tenn., is visiting her sister, Mrs. J. P. **Marlow** this week.

Rose **Brittain** and wife visited his parents, Mr. and Mrs. Z. T. **Brittain**, at Golden.

Pat **Murphy** was up from home near Stinson . . .

Ed **Cathey**, of Golden, visited his uncle and aunt, Mr. and Mrs. J. P. **Marlowe** . . .

Joe **French** and wife, of the Cartwright country, spent Sunday with Mr. and Mrs. W. P. **Lawrence**.

Mrs. J. A. **Thomas** of Mineola, and little son, Master Bill, visited Mrs. G. L. **Higgins** .

Atty. Max **Newsome** was here Monday . . .

Ben **Stokes** and Bob **Sage** were down from Winnsboro Monday . . .

T. L. **Harris** left Monday on a business trip to Harrisburg, Ill . .

Atty. Walter **Russell** came down from Winnsboro Sunday . . .

Mr. and Mrs. Addie **Booth** and babe of Edgewood, visited Rev. and Mrs. W. M. **Bass** . . . Mrs. Booth is a sister of Mrs. Bass.

J. H. **Taylor**, one of the Pleasant Grove merchants . . .

Mr. A. **Murck** . . drove over to Alba Sunday morning in his Hupp and brought W. H. **Low** and wife over to spend the day with Mrs. **Grogan** . . .

Master Austin **Moreland**, of Lubbock, Texas, who has been visiting his uncle, Jess **Marlowe** . . .

Rev. W. M. **Bass** preached . . .three members . . received . . Bryan **Williams** by experience and baptism and Mr. and Mrs. **Ely** by transfer from Mineola church.

Mrs. **Ford**, living out on route 3 from Winnsboro was here last week looking for a home. . . . comes to Quitman to school her children.

Lon **Chreitsberg** and his deputy, Gordon **Wilson** . . .

Miss Maggie **Smart** is teaching a kindergarden school in the building recently vacated by Mr. C. V. **Wallis** . . .

Sheriff **Williams** went to Sulphur Springs Tuesday as a witness in the **Ray** case, wherein Ray is charged with killing Bob **Murdock**, but the case was continued .. .

Col. **Bluett**, the popular life insurance agent . . .

Artemus **McCreight** and wife came down from Yantis Tuesday . . . her parents in Mineola.

Dr. E. M. **Smith**, of Garland, visited his sister, Mrs. H. H. **Macon** . . .his nephew Hunter Macon . . .

Wm. **Morgan** and Bud **Wilson** of the Yantis country . . .

Miss Bonnie Maye **Sutherland** left Tuesday for Winnsboro.. .

Mrs. Milner **Cain**, of Alba, is visiting her mother, Mrs. S. W. **Gilbreath** . .

Dink **Kennimer** and wife, of Coke, are visiting Jim **Lloyd** . . John **Pogue** was up from Peach . . .

Monroe **Peppers**, of Yantis . . .

Geo. W. **Green** was here from Winnsboro . . .

Judge **Smith** was a Mineola visitor Monday.

Quitman school opened Monday with 91 pupils. . . Prof. **Cox**, Supt **Craddock**, C. W. **Vickery**, Judge **Harris**, Judge **Bozeman** and Dr. **Lipscomb** [made talks] . . . faculty consists of Prof. W. E. **Cox**, principal, Miss Myrtle **Black**, intermediate, Miss Ascha **Moseley**, primary, and Mrs. D. M. **Maynor**, music.

Local and Personal:

C. J. **Smart** received a letter last week from Rev. **Blackmon**, . . . underwent an operation for appendicitis at the Baptist sanitarium at Dallas.

Mr. **Murphy**, mail carrier on the morning route from Mineola has bought the restaurant next door to the post office.

The work on S. H. **Hart**'s home is progressing . .

Miss Bettie **Greer** . . . erection of residence . . Smart addition . .

The home of Henry **Chreitzberg** is nearing completion.

Work is progressing . . . home of County Clerk-elect Artemus **McCreight**.

Andrew **Harbin** . . . home in the Smart addition.

Sam **Benton** is having his barn built . . . residence in the near future . . . **Lloyd** addition.

Thursday, September 17, 1914

Dr. L. **Werblun**, optician of Dallas. . .will be in Quitman, at Dr. **Black'**s office Sept 24 and in Mineola, at Dr. **Hart'**s office Sept 25 and 26. . . .

. . . Tiliett S. **Teddlie**, recently of Golden, now a citizen of Alba, and has a position with S. E. **Howard'**s grocery store . . .Teddlie has bought a home in the suburbs of Alba and will engage in truck farming . . .

. . . Dr. and Mrs. F. V. **McKnight** and regret to note that the Doctor is confined to his room with typhoid fever. He has had fever for 35 days, but is holding up first class. Mrs. McKnight and their daughter, Miss Mildred, are also sick.

Mrs. Margarett L. **Price**, widow of the late John R. Price, was born Dec. 29th, 1838, age at the time of her death 75 years, 5 months and five days. Was married to John R. Price Jan. 6, 1859, her husband having preceded her to the world beyond Jan. 28, 1904. To this union 11 children were born, 7 of whom lived to the age of maturity, four having died in infancy. Of the 11 children, only two are living, B.G. and J. D. Price. Deceased had lived a devoted christian life for 60 years. Her native state was Mississippi, moved to Texas with her parents when about 13 years of age. After the death of her husband she made her home at the old home place with her son, B. G. Price, until her death. In addition to the rearing of her own children, she raised an orphan boy, Homer **Thompson**, and had started to raise a second grandson but owing to bad health she had to give him up. [Additional Eulogy followed].

J. F. **Wilson** succeeds **Patton & Wilson** at one of the Alba gins.

J. T. **Tucker** has bought an interest in the **Layton** gin at Oak Grove.

F. H. **Bridges** has bought the **Bridges & Suiter** gin at Coke and his son, C. A. Bridges operating it.

T. J. **Vines** & Son have bought the Golden Gin & Lumber Co. outfit at Golden and consolidated the two establishments.

S. K. **Crenshaw** succeeds W. R. **Butts** as manager of the **Bellefont** Gin Co.

V. S. **Cassel** has bought the gin at Stout from T. W. **Liles** and is operating it.

Wiley & Baker, of Smith County, have bought the **Kay & Atkins** gin at Hawkins and T. W. Wiley is operating it.

Mrs. B. A. **Brooks** succeeds R. D. **Adrian** as manager of the Mineola Gin Co.

The Hardie **Russell** gin at Winnsboro has been sold to the Farmers Gin Co., of that city and A. A. **Snow** is the manager.

Dick **Lindley** has bought the C. A. **Peacock** gin at Redland and is operating it.

W. A. **Boyd** has bought the interest of the **Jared**s in the Merrimac gin and is operating it.

A. C. **Hagan** has bought the interest of his former partner, Mr. **Fox**, in the Fox & Hagan gin 5 miles east of Winnsboro.

. . . in the case of Wiley **Kitchens** versus J. W. **Moseley** and J. Q. **Parkerson** . . .Levied on the 2 day of September, 1914, as the property of J. Q. Parkerson to satisfy a judgement amounting to

Democrat - 1914

$35.77 in favor of Wiley Kitchens and costs of suit. . . . J. D. **Williams**, Sheriff.

Dr. J. B. **Goldsmith**, president of The Quitman & Northern Railroad . . .

. . . Judge **Bozeman** . . . meeting to discuss the distressed cotton situation. J. A. **Thomas**, of Mineola, was chosen chairman and Jon. **Russell** secretary. . . . B. F. **Cathey** . . a delegate to the meeting at Austin and J. S. **Newman** and W. H. **Carter** as delegates to the Dallas meeting.

Mr. J. H. **Hill** and Miss Sallie **Nugent** were married Sunday morning in front of the Democrat office, the Democrat man performing the marriage ceremony. The parties live on the Quince **Shamburger** place near Pine Mills, Mr. Hill being in the employ of Mr. Shamburger at his saw mill.

The 29th annual session of the Wood County Sacred Harp Convention convened at Pleasant Grove, Wood County, Texas, August 28, 1914. . . . W. B. **McAllister**, J. C. **Reese**, J. W. **Cain**, T. L. **Bryant**, D. M. **Pines**, J. P. **Thompson**, D. G. **Webb**, P. G. **Webb**, Dr. **Askew**, J. H. **Jordan**, E. T. **Dozier**, J. E. **Gibbins**, Lee **Rhods**, Mc **Rhods**, Charlie **Rhods**, N. Keith, E. E. **Hinson**, G. M. **Sellers**, A. J. **Harris**, J. B. **Kimbro**, Jim **Turner**, Jim **Darden**, O. F. **Dykes**, J. L. **Roundtree**, H. B. **Turner**, G. A. **Pilley**, H. D. **Richardson**, J. E. **Kay**, S. C. **Davenport**, J. J. **Rouse**, Bro. **Bartlett**, Joe **Darden**, H. W. **Smith**, E. N. **Hamrick**, J. F. **Johnson**, Homer **Darden**, S. L. **Phillips**, Mrs. G. M. **Benton** of Eldorado Texas, E. J. **Leonard**, T. B. **Moore**, H. B. **Turner**, S. L. **Phillips**, J. T. **Darden**, J. W. **Wood**.

Mrs. Ollie **Dodgen** was born and reared in this county near Oak Grove. Mrs. Dodgen's death was expected by all, but it is indeed sad to part with those whom we love. Mrs. Dodgen was 24 years of age the 12th day of January, 1914. She professed faith in Christ at the age of 15 and joined the Baptist church at Ebenezer and was baptized by

Rev. **Awtry** who was serving this church at that time. She lived by her faith until death overtook her on September 13, 1914, at half past six o'clock in the morning. Mrs. Dodgen was confined to her room for three or four months and she was not the one to murmur or complain. Mrs. Dodgen was married to A. D. Dodgen on the 22 of December, 1912, her maiden name was Harris, daughter of Mr. and Mrs. Judson **Harris**, who were old settlers of this county. Deceased leaves to mourn their loss a husband, one child about four months old, four sisters and two brothers, all of whom were present at her death except one sister. Her remains were laid to rest the same day at Hopewell . . . Rev. John **Finch**, of Winnsboro. . .

Bro. A. C. **Wood** began a meeting here Monday night, August 31, and closed Thursday night, September 10, 1914. There were 6 men heads of families baptized, as follows: R. D. **Kennemer**, R. C. **McCrary**, Perry **Wilson**, Harrison **Smith**, Claud **Kennemer** and Mike **Lloyd**. The others were: Mrs. Lottie **Kennemer**, Claudie **Lloyd**, Effie **Lloyd**, Dollie **French**, Mrs. **McDonald**, Mrs. Carl **Phillips**, Grady **Suiter**, Eva **Galoway** and Maggie **Goldsmith**.

Friday evening at 9:25 at the home of A. W. **Formby** in Brashear, occurred the death of little Zelma Love Formby, the three and a half months old baby of Mr. and Mrs. Andrew Formby. The cause of the death was a severe attack of cholera infantum from which the baby suffered only a short time. Funeral services were held at the home at 10:30 Saturday morning with Brother **Bentley** officiating. The remains . . . Woodland cemetery that afternoon . . . Brother Jack **Alford** in charge. . . . Little Zelma Love was a granddaughter of Mrs. Georgia **Wright** of Quitman . .

Local and Personal:
Tom **Butler** and Bruce **Daniels** were down from Winnsboro last week and spent the night with the Butler family south of town. Tom . . goes to Ft. Worth to take charge of a drug store that belonged to Mr. W. H. **Kendrick**, brother of I. J. Kendrick, of Winnsboro, who was drowned a few weeks ago. . . .

Democrat - 1914

Miss Emma **Roundtree**, who has been attending Tyler Commerical College . . . her diploma. She, with her grand-mother, Mrs. **Adams**, and her sister, Miss Lula May, and her brother, R. L. Roundtree and wife, passed through town Thursday enroute to her home at Pleasant Grove. . .

Miss Ora **Williams** . . . left for her home at Malakoff.

Cleveland **Williams** and wife, of Dallas, spent Sunday with his brother, Sheriff Williams and family and went to Oak Grove to visit the **Awtry** and **Moore** families Sunday night . . . and then to Mineola where they will visit his parents.

County Clerk **Russell** and wife have moved to their new home on Mineola street, which is the prettiest home in Quitman. Van **Wood** and wife will make their home with Mr. and Mrs. Russell.

C. F. **Alston** . . . just returned from Lone Oak where he and his wife visited the latters daughter and her husband, Mr. and Mrs. Steve **Wood**.

Oscar **Baker** and family have moved to Hoyt . . .

Our friend Bob **Cain**, of Mathis . . .

Lucius **Hart** . . .

A. B. **Black** . . . his brother, E. L. Black, Tallassee, Ala. . . .

Miss Mary **Robbins** is visiting her brother, Clough Robbins and family, at Newsome.

Buck **Low** and Frank **Jones** were over from Alba . . .

Miss Maggie **Smart** . . .her sister, Mrs. Shaw D. **Ray**, at Winnsboro.

W. B. **Irving**, of Texarkanna, with his family is visiting his father-in-law, Emmett **Awtry** and family at Oak Grove.

C. M. **Hughes**, Peach, route 1 . . . his mother, Mrs. H. G. Hughes . . .

Hon. Max **Newsome** . . from Winnsboro . .

Luther and Jess **Hartsfield** were up from Hawkins Tuesday . . .

Reese & **Falkner**, the Big 4, of Mineola . . .

Editor Jess **Thomas** was over from Mineola . . .

Bob **Low** and family . . . Joe **Sarver** and family . . .

Mrs. N. A. **McKnight** . . . relatives in Quitman . . .

Mrs. M. E. **Bagby** . . . out on route 5, from Quitman . . .

Mrs. R. M. **Smith** . . . Mineola . . relatives . . . Tyler and McKinney . . .

M. D. **Carlock** was down from Winnsboro . . . The case of L. L. **Winterbaur** vs. Ben **Johnson** et al, for recovery of a horse, was tried, judgement being rendered for plaintiff.

Editor **Smith** of the Alba News . . . former townsman, C. V. **Wallis** was glad to see old Quitman again.

Dr. J. M. **Puckett** was in from Hainesville .. .reports the arrival recently of a fine girl at the home of Joe **Hasten** and at Erk **Bradshaw**.

Wylie **Williams** and wife . . left for their home at Rockwall. . . Miss Marrie **Conger**, sister of Mrs. Williams . . will attend school at Rockwall this fall and winter.

Prof. and Mrs. W. E. **Cox** . . .

Shaw **Ray**, wife and babes came down from Winnsboro Tuesday accompanied by Mr. and Mrs. Wallace **Daniels**. . . . Mrs. Ray parents, Mr. and Mrs. C. J. **Smart**.

Misses Idella **Moseley** and Evilene **Black** are learning the switchboard at central station.

Pleasant Ridge Grove will unveil the monument of Mrs. Arie **Reese** next Sunday, Sept 20, at Sand Springs, at 3 o'clock in the afternoon.

Thursday, September 24, 1914

Sunday School: Judge **Bozeman**, Supt; R. W. **Low**, assistant; Miss Myrtle **Black**, secretary; Miss Rubie **Thomas**, Organist; Mrs. H. H. **Macon**, assistant organist. Teachers: T. O. **Cradick**, C. W. **Vickery**, Mrs. S. J. **Benton**, R. J. **Low**, Miss Vernon **Smart**, Mrs. R. W. **Low**, Mrs. H. H. **Macon**, Mrs. J. T. **Power**.

Pat **Conger** has demonstrated . . he is some pumpkin grower.

Democrat - 1914

From Ichang, China:
I enlisted in the navy June 18, 1912, in Olkahoma City, Okla. I was then sent to Dallas for medical examination; on the 24 I was sent to San Francisco, Cal., to Goat Island Training Station; I served five months there, then our company was ordered to China. . . .I will be a free man in 1916, then I am coming to see you all. William R. **Attaway**.

List of County Court Jurors for the October term, 1914:

First Week

I. W. **Suiter**
W. E. **McGuire**
W. T. **Curl**
M. K. **Cain**
J. D. **Benton**
J. F. **Adrain**
B. A. **Shirey**

I. W. **Wilbanks**
C. C. **Smith**
J. H. **McGee**
Jno. M. **Caldwell**
B. J. **Mansell**
J. M. **Sarver**
T. A. **Cartwright**

Second Week

P. A. **Carrington**
J. K. **Deas**
N. E. **Bullock**
R. A. **Reinhardt**
G. W. **Britton**
C. R. **White**
B. D. **McRae**

J. M. **Wright**
Claud **Bateman**
Joe **Williamson**
Jim **Strange**
J. M. **Blount**
B. L. **Johnson**
W. F. **Browning**

The Election: . .of a District Judge. . . . Judge **Heath**, of Pittsburg seems to have won over Judge Yantis. Chairman Wiley **Jones** . . .

J. B. **Hathcox** of Black Oak was in Como Saturday . . .

The Wood County Singing Convention (at Coke, September 12 and 13).
President T. J. **Shaw**. Az **Robertson**, Early **Cartwright**, M. J. **Kennemer** and Jack **Hamrick**, committee on arrangements. . . following to render music: V. O. **Tedlie**, V. O. **Stamps**, Abb **Fowler**,

and S. D. **Simon**. Officers for the following year: H. H. **McAllister** President, V. O. **Tedlie** Vice President, and Genie **Giles** Secretary. Music by Steve **Whitley**, Edd **Goldsmith**, Nath **Hollond**; E. N. **Hamrick**, Tom **Wheeler**, and Arch **Lyle**. Music led by Bruce **Edwards**, Theo **Shaw**, Jim **Floyd**, B. B. **Bateman**, S. D. **Simon**, Robt. **Lloyd**, E. N. **Hamrick** and V. O. **Stamps**. Arrangement committee reported leaders: Otis **Deaton**, Marshal **Yandall**, R. C. **Brittain**, G. M. **Bateman**. Two nice readings by Miss Annie May **Darymple**. S. D. **Somin**, V. O. **Stamps**, B. B. **Bateman** and Bruce **Edwards** rendered music; S. D. **Simon** . . . an intellectual speech.

NOMINEES
DEMOCRATIC PARTY

For Congress, 3rd District
   James **Young**
For State Senator, 7th Dist
   W. D. **Suiter** of Wood Co.
For Representative, Wood & Rains
   W. C. **Middleton**
For District Attorney, 7th Dist
   M. G. **Sanders**
   of Van Zandt County
For County Judge
   R. E. **Bozeman**
For County Atty. (Second term)
   Duncan M. **Maynor**
For Sheriff, (Second term)
   Floyd **Williams**
For County Supt. (Second term)
   T. O. **Craddock**
For County Treas. (Second term)
   Mrs. Lillie **Leath**
For District Clerk
   Julius R. **Taylor**

THE SOCIALIST
NOMINEES

For Representative
   Tom **Cross**
For County Judge
   J. L. **Scoggin**
For Sheriff
   O. J. **Blackmon**, Jr.
For County Treasurer
   Claude **Vandiver**
For County Clerk
   F. O. **Hilburn**
For District Clerk
   M. W. **Coleman**
For Tax Assessor
   A. M. **Shelton**
For Tax Collector
   A. J. **Weems**
For Commissioner,
   Precinct 1 F. L. **Garrett**
For Commissioner,
   Prcnt 2 Jobe **Holbrook**
For Commissioner, Precnt 3
   J. M. **Wilson**

For County Clerk
  G. A. **McCreight**
For Tax Assessor
  W. R. **Caldwell**
For Tax Collector
  S. J. **Benton**
For Commissioner, Precinct 1
  Virgil **Blalock**
For Commissioner, Precinct 2
  J. C. **Russell**
For Commissioner, Precinct 3
  W. J. **Cowley**
For Commissioner, Precinct 4
  W. H. **Carter**
For Justice Peace, Precinct 1
  P. N. **Thomas**
For Justice Peace at Yantis
  J. L. **Ross**
For Justice Peace at Golden
  Sam **Ayres**
For Constable, Precinct 1
  R. H. **Welsh**
For Constable at Yantis
  W. A. **Rushing**
For Constable at Golden
  T. **Pemberton**
For Commissioner, Precnt 4
  J. R. **Scoggin**
For Justice Peace, Precinct 1
  W. H. **Gable**
For Justice Peace, Precinct 2
  A **Perry**
For Justice Peace, Precinct 3
  J. Q. **Parkinson**
For Justice Peace, Precinct 4
  S. B. **Whitley**
For Justice Peace, Precinct 6
  Ike **Taylor**
For Justice Peace, Precinct 7
  R. L. **Rhodes**
For Justice Peace, Precinct 8
  Henry **Dickey**
For Constable, Precinct 1
  Jim **Hamrick**
For Constable, Precinct 2
  George **Barnette**
For Constable, Precinct 4
  E. U. **Phillips**
For Constable, Precinct 7
  P. A. **Stovall**
For Constable, Precinct 8
  John H. **Chappell**

Thursday, October 1, 1914

Roy **Power** and Oliver **Wright** united with the church.

Baptism was administered to Joe **Ivey**, Roy **Power** and Oliver **Wright**, the baptism taking place at the Mount & Horton pool.

Brother **Hopkins** preached his farewell sermon as Pastor . . .

... letters of dismission were granted Mrs. Milner **Cain** and Frank **Benton** who have united with Alba church.

C. W. **Vickery**, ... church clerk for the past two years, tendered his resignation and R. W. **Low** was elected to the position by acclimation.

Local and Personal:

Miss Inez **Mount** left Saturday for Dallas to visit relatives ..
Miss Maye **Lake** spent several days in Winnsboro ..
A. H. **McElroy**, the Pleasant Grove gin man, ...
Rev. J. H. **Baker** and wife attended church here ...
Elmore **Wright**, the Cartwright live wire merchant ...
See Dr. S. C. **Noble**, the Mineola Dentist, at **Wright**'s drug store next Monday and Tuesday ... if you need dental work.
B. F. **Smart**, Judge **Bozeman**, Pink **Lawrence** ... business trip to Winnsboro ...
E. Q. **Shamburger**, the saw mill man, was in town Saturday ...
Frank **Morris** ... has formed a partnership with Mr. Lee **Pierson**, recently of Dallas, for the practice of law at Winnsboro and they have their office over **Hill** & Son drug store ...
S. F. **Nelson**, the old reliable wholesale man, of Winnsboro, ...
Henry **Green** and wife and Boss **Craddock**, wife and children came down from Winnsboro Sunday and spent the day with B. F. **Smart** and family. Henry has recently had his arm amputated ... getting along fine.
Miss Pearl **Power** returned from Edgewood Saturday to which place she went the past week and secured a position as music teacher in the public school at that place.
D. S. **Lankford**, one of the old residenters of the county, was here from Mineola Monday.
Mrs. E. A. **Nichols**, of Timpson, Texas, is visiting Mrs. Dr. **Conger** and Mrs. H. L. **Denton** this week and incidently selling pianos.
Rev. J. M. **Cagul** ... returned from Palacios to which place he accompanied his daughter, Miss Maye ...

Democrat - 1914

J. B. **Matheson**, of Hawkins, and his brother, W. S., of Pine Mills, were Quitman visitors Monday and the former tells us he has sold his farm near Hawkins and bought a home in central Louisiana, to which he will move about the first of the new year.

That hustling fellow over Golden way, the irrepressible George **Jones**, . . .

County Atty. and Mrs. **Maynor** motored over to Lindale Sunday afternoon and spent a few hours with Mrs. Maynor's parents . . .

. . . in Yantis . . . **Bird & Warren, McKey & Britton** and J. H. **Craver** . . .

Lee **Wilcox**, wife and children, of Mineola, Sundayed with Mrs. Ollie **Perrin** . . .

G. L. **Higgins** was a Mineola visitor Sunday.

Jim **Galt**, the Winnsboro horse man, was here Monday . . .

Bro. **Hopkins** made a business trip to Greenville Tuesday . . .

. . . Mr. A. **Murck** . . .

W. O. **Zeigler** . . . in town Monday.

John **Cassel**, of Cartwright, . . .

J. M. **Welch** was up from Hainesville Monday . . .

Deputy Maje **Harris** went to Tyler Monday after a negro wanted in this county on a charge of cattle theft.

R. H. **McCrary** and J. M. **Beard**, of Winnsboro, . . .

. . . Uncle John **Harris**, was up from Oak Grove . . .

The babe of Mr. and Mrs. T. L. **Denton** is quite sick with scarlet fever . . .

D. W. **Harry** . . . his son, Ben, who is at Kirkville, Mo., attending medical school. . .

Mrs. R. M. **Smith** returned Saturday from an extended visit . . .

O.L. **Vickers**, of Cartwright, . . .

W. B. **McAllister** was up from Shady Grove Monday . . . sold his tract of the **Rowsey** land on Cana, to Charlie **Neill**.

Barnie **Denton** and wife came down today to be with his brother, Leanard and wife during the illness of their babe, and Barney is carrying the mail for Leanard.

Commissioner **Cowley** was up from Hainesville Wednesday . . . his son, Irvin, has his store building about completed . . .

... District Clerk **Vickery** has recently had a new roof put on his house and his house painted ...

Prayer meeting last Thursday ... Walter **Crofford** was the leader ... Hall **Benton** is leader for tonight ...

J. R. **Mayo**, doing a general merchandise business in Quitman, filed an assignment Tuesday of this week, naming Hill **Robbins** as assignee. ... The many friends of Jim ...

"Aunt Julia Ann" **Burton**, possibly one of the oldest negro women in this section of the country, died last Saturday night. "Aunt Julia Ann" was the widow of "Uncle Josh" Burton who preceded her to the other side several months ago. She was a mighty good old negro, one of those old time slave negroes, and as we have before stated, this kind is fast passing away. They, as a rule, are good, law abiding negroes and have the respect of all, both white and black.

... Farmers Cotton Oil Co., ... B. F. **Campbell**, the gentlemanly manager, and J. E. **Petty**, the genial secretary and treasurer ... Judge **Snow** is manager of the gins connected with the oil mill ... company bought the Hardee **Russell** gin plant and this gin is under the supervision of Pig **Craddock**.

Thursday, October 8, 1914

Mrs. R. W. **Low** and her guests, Mesdames Earnest **Ashberry** and W. H. **Gorman**, of Winnsboro honored the Democrat office with their presence Saturday ...

[Advertisement] First State Bank. W. M. **Lloyd**, Pres.; R. L. **Butler**, Active V. Pres.; Jas D. **Harris**, Cashier; **J. M. Lloyd**, Asst. Cash.

Democrat - 1914

Fire at Winnsboro, 3 a.m. Oct. 4: W. M. **Rhone**'s two buildings, The Free Press printing plant owned by Al **Thomas**, Otto **Veltel**'s bakery, R. C. **Halbrook** barber shop, J. W. **Taylor** tailor shop.

Rev. W. M. **Bass** announces his fourth quarterly conference . .

The Democrat and A. J. **Britton** accepted a seat in County Atty. **Maynor**'s car Saturday and went over to Yantis. . . . Subscribers J. H. **Craver**, Luther **King**, W. R. **Hickman**. N. B. **Pickett** left Yantis some months ago and went to Nevada. S. M. **Peppers** and J. H. **Floyd** each favored us with an order for some job work. W. R. **Hickman** . . . will not . . open the market.

Mrs. B. F. **Saxon** whose death occured at the family home in Dallas the 22nd of Sept. . . sister of J. H. **Chappell** of Golden and of Mrs. A. D. **Rape**, living near Quitman.

Dovie **Williams** is plaintiff and Robert **Williams** is Defendant . . . divorce. . . . were married on or about the 25th day of March, 1913. . . to marriage . . was born a girl, Ruby **Williams**, now 30 months old.   - C. W. **Vickery**, Clerk, District Court, Wood County

From Prof. T. J. **Shaw**, we learn of the death of our friend, Uncle Jim **Wheeler**, which occured at his home near Pine Mills Tuesday last . . burial taking place at Mt. Pisga the day following, Rev. J. H. **Floyd**, of Gilmer, conducting . .

M. A. **Reinhardt** was born in Mississippi July 2, 1842; moved with his parents to Texas in 1858 and settled near Quitman. When about 17 years of age he went to west Texas and served under Captains **Ross** and **Young** in the Indian uprising. When the South seceded, he came back to Quitman and enlisted in Jno. **Wilson**'s company, and was sent across the Mississippi River where he remained during the 4 years struggle. After the war closed he returned to Quitman and in January, 1867, was married to Miss H. J. **Ussery**. The balance of his life was spent in and near Wood county. In 1883 he settled on a farm about 13 miles east of Quitman where he lived until December 1912, he sold out and moved to Peach, Texas where he lived until death claimed him September 23, 1914, at about 5 o'clock p.m.

City Marshal **Willingham** and Whit **DuBose** of Mineola . . .

Lee **Blalock** is putting the finishing touches on the **McCreight** home this week with his paint brush . . .

The co-partnership between A. M. **Shelton** and M. J. **Ziegler** doing business at Golden . . . Golden Drug Co., was disolved . . June 15th, 1914. A. M. Shelton retiring.

J. T. **Brown,** of the Klondyke community . . reported the death of Miss Lela **Johnson**, only daughter of Mr. and Mrs. Ed **Johnson** . . which occured Thursday of last week. Interment at Sand Springs Friday, Rev. J. P. **Padgett** . .

For sale:
40 acres adjoining the town site of Quitman. Dr. J. D. **Conger**
120 acres 4 mikes east of Quitman. J. H. **Long**
My home in Quitman. T. J. **Goodwin.**

Local and Personal:
Mrs. J. H. **Jarman** of Lindale visited her daughter, Mrs. D. M. **Maynor** a few days.
Constable Rube **Rucker** was up from Mineola . .
H. J. **Caldwell**, principal Cana school . . .
Miss Mattie **Conger**, who went to Rockwall to attend school some weeks ago, returned home the past week on account of being sick . .

M. K. **Cain,** one of our Cartwright subscribers . . .
Esq. **Blackburn** was here from Mineola Monday attending county court as a witness . .   W. R. **Vickery** is spending the week with his brother, District Clerk **Vickery,** and family

Democrat - 1914

Julius **Taylor**, our next District Clerk . . . to move with his sisters . . .

J. W. **Low** came over from Alba Sunday to visit his son, Robert, and family . .

Sid **Pope** and wife and babe, of Alba visited with Mr. and Mrs. P. J. **Hendrix** the past week while the latter were both sick.

Esq. **Ross** was here from Yantis Monday . . .

Uncle John **Calloway** called in Monday . . .

M. J. **Kennimer** was in Tuesday . . .Mose . . .

J. T. **Rowsey** loaded his effect on wagons Monday and carried them to Mineola to be loaded on a chartered car for Rule, Haskell county, where he will make his home. Mrs. **Rowsey** and the girls left today . . .

Jim **Bullock**, who has been with Lucius **Hart** for several months . . .

Mrs. C. F. **Parker** has been quite sick for several days with an attack of appendicitis, and being some better she was carried to the home of her parents, Mr. and Mrs. W. G. **Burford** . .

Mrs. R. J. **Martin** visited her mother, Mrs. **Neyland**, near Como, last week . . . mother quite sick with typhoid fever . . .

J. H. **Rhodes** was here from Winnsboro Monday . . .

C. J. **Smart**, Dr. **Lipscomb**, Herb **Wilder**, Jon. **Russell**, J. B. **Mount**, Ace **Horton**, Sam **Benton**, and the Democrat man went to Mineola Tuesday night to hear Gov. **Noel** speak on the cotton proposition.

J. L. **Pogue**, the saw mill man was here Monday . . .

Mrs. W. P. **Lawrence** visited her mother, Mrs. E. J. **Highnote** near Winnsboro, Sunday.

Grandma **Lipscomb** came in Tuesday from Gainsville for an indefinite visit with her daughter, Mrs. I. W. **Robbins**.

[Issues after October 8, 1914 but before June 24, 1915 have not been located. -Ed.]

Wood County Democrat - 1915

Thursday, June 24, 1915

They Stole a March on Us

Wednesday of last week our daughter Ruby went to Dallas under pretense that she wanted to spend a week or two visiting her friend, Mrs. Clarence **Goodwin**. Sunday morning Dr. Virgil **Robbins** left town under pretense, we were told, of attending a meeting of the State Board of Health at Austin. Monday morning about 7:30 we received a phone message froom Dr. Robbins stating that he and Ruby were married at 7:30 o'clock Sunday evening, the ceremony being performed by Rev. S. A. **Barnes** at the home of Mrs. and Mrs. Clarence Goodwin. They came home Tuesday, arriving here about the noon hour.

Dr. Robbins is the eldest son of Mr. and Mrs. I. W. Robbins and was born and raised in Quitman. He is a graduate of the Baylor Medical College and is making good as a physician. Ruby was also born and raised in Quitman. Modesty forbids us saying more than that she is a good cook and housekeeper.

Monday's Dallas News contained the following announcement of the event:

"Dr. V. E. Robbins of Quitman and Mess Ruby Lee **Thomas**, daughter of P.N. Thomas, editor of the Wood County Democrat, were married last evening at 7:30 o'clock at the home of Mrs. and Mrs. Clarence Goodwin, 4024 Colonial avenue, the Rev. S. A. Barnes officiating. . . .

In Memory of Mrs. Neyland.

Mrs. **Neyland**, whose maiden name was Helen **Johnson**, was born near Coke, in this county, June 27, 1856, and moved with her parents to Hopkins county, settling near Black Oak, where she lived the remainder of her days, her husband, Capt. Bob Neyland, having bought the old home place after his marriage to the daughter, in 1875. . . .

Ten children were born to her and her husband, two of which died when small, the others still survive her, they being A. F. Neyland, Mrs. R. J. **Martin**, Mrs. S. M. **Turner**, Mrs. O. Z. **Smith**, Mrs. Jude **Wilson**, and three daughters who are still under the family roof, the youngest two being twin sisters.

Mrs. Neyland died June 4, 1915, and was buried the following day at Black Oak.

Mrs. Dr. Shelton Badly Burned

Dr. W. T. **Black** was called to Golden Friday of last week to attend Mrs. Dr. **Shelton** who was badly burned about the face and neck by explosion of gasoline while she was filling a gasoline iron. Dr. Black says the burns are deep, especially on the face, and quite painful, but he apprehends no serious results from them.

Local and Personal

Judge **Harris** and Mrs. T. L. **Denton** went to Winnsboro last Thursday to visit their relative, Charlie Harris, who is at the home of his brother, Jim Dave Harris. Charlie has been a member of the army for the past sixteen years, but had to give up the work and come home on account of failing health. . . . suffering with tuberculosis and Bright's disease . . .

W. M. **Lloyd** and wife and Mrs. Robt. **Conger** accompanied the former's mother, Grandma **Stephens**, to Mineola Friday of last week where she took the T.&P. for Sweetwater to spend the summer with relatives. Mr. Lloyd tells us his mother is nearing her 90th birthday and is enjoying good health. Her son, J. V. Lloyd and wife of Coke, accompanied her . . .

Constable **Whitter** was here from Winnsboro Thursday of last week having brought a Mr. **Johnson**, who lives a few miles east of Winnsboro, who is charged with insanity. . . .

Tax Collector and Mrs. W. R. **Caldwell** . . .

Mrs. W. P. **Lawrence** and children visited her mother near Shady Grove the past week.

W. B. **McAllister** of the Merrimac country was a Quitman visitor last Friday.

Master Hollis **Green** of Tyler is visiting her aunt, Mrs. P. A. **Carrington**.

G. W. **Shirey**, living three miles east of town . . .did not sow wheat this year but his son did.

Miss Ronda **Hart** has returned from Baylor county, near Seymore, where she taught . . . the fifth term that Miss Ronda taught at that place . . .

Dr. J. B. **Goldsmith**, wife and son, Bury . . .

C. R. **White**, the "Squash Hollow" merchant . . .

Counts **Benton**, District and County Clerk of Schleicher county . . . his daughter, Miss Olga, is visiting her grandmother, Mrs. **Holley**, at Cartwright.

Miss Ione **Blackstone**, of Maypearl, Texas . . . visit with her aunt, Mrs. D. T. **Koonce**.

T. H. **Winkle**, of Oak Grove, . . . his daughter, Miss Maye, at Tyler . . .

Buck **Low** and his son, Master Joe Becton, came over from Alba . . .

. . . the new residence of T. L. **Harris** and is progressing rapidly.

J. J. **Rouse** and J. B. **Roberts**, the latter of the firm of Roberts & **Baber**, of Winnsboro . .

Mrs. J. M. **White**, of Myrtle Springs community, is visiting her daughters, Mesdames W. M., E. J. and R. F. **Taylor**, this week.

Mrs. D. M. **Maynor** accompanied her husband to Ft. Worth . . . visited her brother and sister . . . accompanied home by her sister, Miss Rilla **Jarman**.

T. L. **Bird**, a former citizen of our town . . . practicing law at Sulphur Springs . . .

Geo. **Collins**, one of the progressive farmers of the Hainesville country . . .

Thursday, July 1, 1915

Our Apology

The Democrat is not up to the standard this week owing to the fact that one of our little grandchildren, little Mary Elizabeth **Hart**, has been dangerously sick since Thursday night of last week . . . is in quite a critical condition.

Burglarizes Denton Home

Tuesday of this week while Mrs. T. L. **Denton** was in Mineola and T.L. was out on his route, a young fellow giving his name as John **Stone** entered the Denton home, secured quite a number of articles . . . Denton and (Sheriff) **Butler** started in pursuit of the young man whom they overtook near Mineola . . . now in jail.

Lots Sold to the State or Reported Delinquent in Former Years Not Redeemed and Are Also Delinquent for 1914, Wood County

Name of Owner	Orig. Grantee	City or Town
Bozeman, T.U.	G. B. **King**	
Bruce, Mrs. S. R	G. W. **Terrell**	Mineola
Flowellen, Fannie	S. **Yarborough**	
Fry, R.	W. P. **Gentry**	
"	J. J. **Pemberton**	
Graham, L. R.	"	
Grissett, D. F.	"	
Hall, A. Q.	F. H. **Davis**	
Hooft, H. H.	"	
Morrison, Lee	Wm. **Page**	
Mosely, L. L.	J. **Hardcastle**	
Painter, H. J.	H. M. **McKnight**	
Palmer, Mollie	G. B. **King**	
Pogues, Mrs. D. E.	"	
Reeves, Mrs. Dora	"	
Richards, J. L.	B. A. **Miller**	
Richard, Alex col	"	
Rucker, J. H.	G. W. **Terrell**	
Rucker, J. K.	Wm **Page**	
Sasser, Mrs. E. F.	Geo **Brewer**	Hawkins
Smith, B. S.	G. B. **King**	
Taytum, A. L.	G. W. **Terrell**	
Wingard, J. E.	G. B. **King**	

Wood County Newspapers

Wood & **Pyle**
"
Jones, T. N.
"
"
"
Blagge, Maggie
Bullard, Freeman
Compton, Matilda
Ellis, Mandy est
Haney, D. M.
UNRENDERED ROLL
Anderson, Ed
Colquitt, D. M.
"
"
"
Bruce, E. L.
Swingle, Julia
 UNKNOWN

J. J. **Pemberton**
W. C. **Barfield**
T. J. **Griffin**
Sam **Houston**
C. **Wicker**
S. **Yarborough**
G. B. **King**
"
"

G. W. **Mathews**   Mineola

T. J. **Rusk**
Charles **Duncomby**
Jesse **Tezzle**
John W. **Reagan**
Wesley **Reid**

J. E. **White**   Mineola

A. **Calderon**
J. M. **Servantes**
Mary **Arochy**
J. A. **Booth**
T. T. **Brown**
Jane **Bean**
Mary **Caruthers**
S. **Calderon**
N. B. **Charlton**
J. C. **Clark**
P. **Dillsworth**
H. **Dixson**
Charles **Duncomby**
S. **English**
J. S. **Ewell**
Charles **Epps**

J. H. **Farrington**
H. V. **Fowler**
A. **Gonsales**
J. A. **Greer**
A. J. **Gilbreth**
Harvey **Hall**
E. E. **Hamilton**
H. **Herneger**
Wm **Hendrix**
Travis **Harris**
John **Hamby**
James **Hunt**
A. **Howington**
A. **Houston**
A. **Joseph**
K. **Keaton**
M. **Putnam**
S. W. **Vickery**
Wm **Whittaker**
A. C. **Walters**
J. H. **White**
A. J. **Ward**
Charles **White**
Charles **Williams**
Wm **Wallace**
M. Y. **Barbo**
S. **Yarborough**
G. W. **Greer**
M. **Kuykendall**
G. W. **Smith**
Thomas **Lee**

SUPPLEMENTAL

W. F. **King**
Benj **Lee**
W. D. **Langham**
J. M. **Moore**

H. M. **McKnight**
D. **McGrane**
Jas **Pollock**
Mary **Pollock**
B. D. **Po_ter**
J. J. **Pemberton**
Jas **Rowe**
Jno **Rudble**
R. **Sunigas**
Berry **Smith**
J. H. **Speer**
Polly **Tier**
G. W. **Terrell**
Benj **Thomas**

Local and Personal

Cashier R. W. **Lowe** has moved to his new home on Winnsboro street, has erected a fine barn . . .

M. A. **Richburg** was in from Cartwright . . . his brother J. W. at Goshen, Ala.

Mrs. Lydia C. **Wright** left last week to visit her son, Mark Francis, in Montana, . . .

. . . A. **Murck** able to be on our streets, after his long seige of illness.

Mrs. Sul **Smith** and little Gladys Ross left Tuesday for Brinkley, Ark., for a six weeks visit with her parents.

Miss Ronda **Hart** left Sunday in answer to a message announcing the illness of her sister, Mrs. M. B. **Briggs** at Gilmer.

Grandma **Smith** is home with her daughter, Mrs. H. H. **Macon**, after an extended visit with her son, Dr. E. M. Smith, at Garland.

Ex-County Commissioner R. H. **Galloway**, "Uncle Dick," as he is best known . . . his home near Rock Hill . . .Mr. **Young**, who recently lost his wife and now has four children sick with typhoid fever, . . .

Democrat - 1915

County Court Jurors, July Term

First Week	Second Week	Third Week
George **Chreitzberg**	Pink **Johnson**	T. R. **Lloyd**
J. D. **Cade**	G. W. **Adair**	George **Blalock**
R. E. **Carter**	H. M. **Mansell**	Jack **Lloyd**
R. M. **Black**	R. W. **Galloway**	E. L. **Foster**
G. W. **Oxford**	Lee **Hays**	J. M. **Gilbreath**
L. M. **French**	J. C. **Futrell**	W. Z. **English**
J. H. **Newby**	Emmett **Awtrey**	Dave **Kimbrell**
B. Q. **Lee**	T. U. **Carter**	A. J. **Peddy**
I. J. **Bradshaw**	J. M. **McLain**	T. L. **Deas**
W. H. **Apel**	T. H. **Penix**	J. L. **Raley**
J. A. **Harris**	M. H. **Lawrence**	L. L. **Layton**
W. H. **Darby**	W. B. **Kirby**	R. A. **Perdue**
J. C. **Edelin**	T. L. **Johnson**	R. F. **Gibson**
R. H. **Jones**	Martin **Ledbetter**	L. B. **Hart**

Local and Personal

Postmaster Shaw D. **Ray** . . . from Winnsboro . ..Miss Maggie **Smart** will visit with her sister, Mrs. Ray . . .

Hon. A. B. **Rhodes** was here froom Coke . . . County School Board . . . deed to Messrs Jon. **Russell** and R. M. **Smith** to the old school buildling and lands, the consideration being $800.00.

Mrs. Jno. R. **Edmonds** has returned from Greenville where she visited her mother, Mrs. N. J. **Holcomb**, and her brother. She was accompanied home by her little neice, Miss Mabel Holcomb . . .

Rev. I. E. **Thomas** came down from Lone Oak .. .

Jack **Denton** has sold his one-third interest in the Denton home place at Clover Hill to his brother, H. L. Denton, consideration $1,500 cash.

Miss Effie **Rainwater** came in Tuesday from Mt. Vernon for a few weeks visit with her parents Mr. and Mrs. J. Rainwater.

Dr. J. S. **Paschal** and his son, Beleher, were here from Stout . . .

Henry **Willingham** was here from Mineola . . .

John **Gilbreath** and wife were over from Alba . . .

Mrs. R. M. **Smith** left Sunday for a visit with her sisters, Mesdames **Sims** and **Cox**, at Mineola.

Miss Bessie **Hall** is here from Mineola this week visiting with her sister, Mrs. Jas. D. **Harris**.

Mrs. Clyde **Jordan** came over from Alba . . . attend the bedside of her little neice, Mary Elizabeth **Hart**.

. . . J. H. **Knight** . . . farm near Hainesville . . .

Dr. L. **Faulk**, W. H. **Low** and his daughter, Miss Mattie **Morrow**, were here froom Alba Tuesday.

Simp **Walker** was in . . . his daughter, Miss Fleta, has been engaged as one of the teachers in the College of Industrial Arts at Denton for the coming year.

J. H. **Gleaton** brought the first wagon load of watermelons of the season to Quitman Tuesday. . . .

Shady Grove

Mrs. **Simons** who has been ill for eight weeks is still in a dangerous condition. . . .

L. C. **Browning** visited relatives and friends in Titus and Camp county last week.

Jim **Thomas** and Herman **Puckett** of Hainesville attended singing here Sunday afternoon.

Mrs. Lula **Williams** spent Friday night with her cousins, Messes Kate and Minnie Lee **Browning**.

Ben **Turner** and Lee **Browning** visited Aron **Little** Sunday.

Mrs. Lucy **Lyles** and family . . . her son Will Lyles.

Mrs. Della **Rutledge** of Ft. Worth is visiting her aunt, Mrs. Ben **Browning** this week.

Lunacy Trials

Judge **Bozeman**, County Atty. **Maynor** and Sheriff **Williams**. . . in the trial of lunacy cases, their being four cases . . .

Monday Willis **Hammonds** . . . acquitted, the proof in the case showed Willis to be about the best farmer in the county . .

I. **Johnson**, who lives a few miles out of Winnsboro . . . was judged insane . . .

A negro . . . also judged insane . . .

Sid **Asbel**, an old time and prominent citizen of Winnsboro, . . . adjudging him insane.

. . . awaiting admission to the hospital for the insane at Terrell.

Death of Mrs. Hart

Mrs. Laura G., wife of J. P. **Hart**, after a protracted illness of several months, died at the family residence in Big Sandy Saturday evening, 12 inst. Mrs. Hart was raised in Upshur county. She was the daughter of G. E. **Warren**, one of the earliest settlers of the county. He served two terms in the Texas legislature, and was the first county court clerk of Upshur county. Mrs. Hart was one of a family of nine children, three boys and six girls, all of whom except her still survive. These are Judge J. R. of Gilmer; W. E. of Almagordo, N.M.; G. E. of Shreveport, La.; Mrs. L. C. **Christian** of Naples; Mrs. S. B. **Stapp**, Mrs. Hugh **McClellen** and Mrs. W. C. **Barnwell** of Gilmer, and Mrs. Lula **Anderson** of Winnsboro. All attended the funeral here Sunday except Mrs. Anderson, who was sick.

Of her own immediate family, she leaves a husband, three daughters -- Misses Cress and Arretta, grown young ladies, and Lorine, a child of about ten years of age -- and one grown son, Warren, who is connected with a bank at Shreveport, La.

--Big Sandy Times.

Mrs. Sam Paschal Dead.

Mrs. Amanda **Paschal**, wife of Mr. Sam Paschal, died at her home in Mabank Monday, June 21, at 3 o'clock p.m. The remains were brought to Winnsboro and funeral services held in the Methodist church at 1:20 Tuesday afternoon, and buried at the Lee cemetery at 3 o'clock. Mrs. Paschal had been in bad health for several months. A short time ago she was taken to the Baptist sanitarium in Dallas and an operation performed for appendicitis. . . . Besides her husband she leaves two sons and three daughters.   -- Winnsboro News.

Judge and Mrs. W. R. **Heath** and son passed through Winnsboro Tuesday afternoon enroute to Philadelphia, Pa., where the Judge will undergo an operation by a specialist for a throat trouble. .

Wood County Newspapers

Thursday, July 8, 1915

Editor Thomas Dangerously Ill

The Democrat is pained indeed to learn of the serious illness of Editor J. A. **Thomas** of the Mineola Monitor. He is reported to be very low with pheumonia in typhoid form.

List of Land and Lots Delinquent on March 31, 1915, for the Taxes of 1914 Only, In Wood County, Texas

Name of Owner	Original Grantee	Acres Delinquent	City or Town	Total Taxes
Adams, J. W.	M. A. **Esparsia**	2		$
Adams, J. W.	M. A. **Esparsia**	6-1/4		
Adams, J. W.	Willis **Parker**	88		16.98
Adams, W. H.	M. **Monteith**	10		2.90
Allen, Solomon (Col.)	S. **Castleberry**	51-3/4		2.99
Allen, Linus B.			Mineola	7.70
Amos, J. S.	Wesley **Tollett**	129		11.68
Anderson, Susan	C. E. **Rivers**	100		8.19
Arthur, Mrs. Jennie	J. **Simpkins**	1		
Arthur, Mrs. Jennie	J. **Simpkins**	1/2		7.83
Aswell, S. J.	M. **Dial**	67	Winnsboro	
Aswell, S. J.			Winnsboro	31.71
Bailey, J. A.	S. **Yarbrough**	42-1/2		
Bailey, J. A.	B. **Jordan**	11-1/2		10.21
Bailey, E. L.	W. W. **Frizzell**	43		4.91
Baker, J. P.	Chas. **Epps**	75		
Baker, J. P.	W. W. **Frizzell**	22		
Baker, J. P.	W. W. **Frizzell**	39		12.57
Baker, Mrs. C. L.	John B. **Lapp**	1/2		5.90
Bass, C. C.	J. **Simpkins**	1		3.36
Beck, T. J.			Mineola	4.83
Bender, Joe	F. **Holland**	89		9.44
Bell, Louis Est.			Mineola	2.50

Democrat - 1915

Name of Owner	Original Grantee	Acres Delinquent	City or Town	Total Taxes
Berry, H. B.	J. A. Greer	50		6.45
Beeville, E. V.	S. **McDonald**	50		10.12
Binford, J. H.	H. **Dickson**	120		9.63
Benard, Will	Jessie **Walker**	67		12.33
Blundell, T. N.	Polly **Tier**	43-3/4		3.60
Bowden, B. S.	William **Cater**	40		5.52
Boyd, J. A.	Daniel **Fuller**	66		6.86
Brinkley, Oscar	F. **Hollon**	104-1/2		11.01
Brown, Mrs. J. S.	Benjamin **Lee**	56		8.08
Brown, W. B.	Benjamin **Lee**	39		8.71
Browning, C. M.	G. B. **King**	1-2		21.78
Bryant, J. B.	Mary **Ward**	2		2.40
Burley, Jake	Travis **Haris**	20		2.31
Burnett, C. W.	J. M. **Chandler**	25		4.33
Bynum, Mollie	J. E. **White**	5		5.51
Byrd, A. S.	S. T. **Belt**	120		
Byrd, A. S.	William **Birch**	20		14.06
Cameron, C. G.	J. **Gross**	30		
Cameron, C. G.	J. **Gross**	30		5.32
Cantaloo, J. V.	G. B. **King**	18-1/2		23.60
Cantaloo, J. V.	G. B. **King**	37-1/2		8.52
Carlile, H. H.	I. **Ivey**	89		
Carter, T. U.	F. L. **Smith**	105		14.50
Carter, T. U.	F. L. **Smith**	10		
Cassell, W. W.	J. H. **McLarty**	57-1/4		
Cassell, W. W.	Berry **West**	63		12.62
Cassell, V. P.	A. **Caldron**	137-3/4		16.04
Chamrod, Roman	S. **Yarbrough**	82		13.57
Chandler, Henry (Col.)	Jessie **Walker**	40		8.17
Childress, H. B.	D. **Gilliland**	67		6.49
Chism, Planco	E. **Weidman**	11		1.64
Christian, Bob	C. B. **King**	1/2		5.37
Cleveland, G. W.	S. **Gonzales**	30		

Name of Owner	Original Grantee	Acres Delinquent	City or Town	Total Taxes
Cleveland, G. W.	William **Clark**	69		15.30
Crabb, C. B.	C. B. **King**	1/2		7.40
Crandford, C. R.	J. **Sherman**	1/2		6.71
Crenshaw, M. E.	J. E. **White**	24		
Crenshaw, M. E.	J. E. **White**	20		13.73
Cyrus, H. C.	L. W. **Gillum**	58		6.63
Davis, W. H.	H. **Anderson**	50		7.45
Davis, W. E.	John **Delapp**	1/4		3.85
Derry, E. (Col.)			Mineola	3.22
Dewitt, C. D.	J. **Simpkins**	2	Alba	
Dewitt,	J. **Florees**	41	Alba	
Dewitt, C. D.	J. **Simpkins**	2	Alba	
Dewitt, C. D.	J. **Simpkins**	3/4	Alba	
Dewitt, C. D.			Alba	
Dewitt, C. D.			Alba	
Dewitt, C. D.				135.14
Dowell, H. G.	S. **Yarborough**	37		275.22
Dowell, Floyd	S. **Yarborough**	37-1/2		6.45
Dykes, O. F.	F. L. **Smith**	44		7.20
Eddington, S. E.(Col.)	J. M. **Moore**	56		12.17
Ecans, L. R.			Alba	5.95
Evans, F. L.	J. **Crofford**	3/4		6.92
Fannin, B. F.	R. E. **Neill**	51		
Fannin, B. F.	R. E. **Neill**	105		12.38
Farrington, Dr. R. A.	F. **McMahon**	50		
Farringron, Dr. R. A.	J. **Crofford**	1-1/2		
Farrington, Dr. R. A.	J. **Crofford**	1		
Farrington, Dr. R. A.	J. **Simpkins**	1/8		
Farrington, Dr. R. A.	J. **Simpkins**	1/12		
Farrington, Dr. R. A.	J. **Simpkins**	1/16		
Farrington, Dr. R. A.	J. **Sherman**	1/8		98.89
Folmer, J. E.	Benj. **Lee**	100-3/4		15.22
French, J. F.	W. H. **Sepurest**	80		8.19

Democrat - 1915

Name of Owner	Original Grantee	Acres Delinquent	City or Town	Total Taxes
Fulong, E. R.	H. M. C. **Hall**	65		11.08
Garrison, S. C. Est.	Allan **Billard**	186		
Garrison, S. C.	L W **Gillum**	1299-8/10		
Garrison, S. C.	E. **Rehorse**	366		
Garrison, S. C.	E. **Rehorse**	91-2/10		
Garrison, S. C.	Mary **Ward**	37-1/2		
Garrison, S. C.	Mary **Ward**	120		
Garrison, S. C.	Mary **Ward**	50		
Garrison, S. C.	Mary **Ward**	111		
Garrison, S. C.	Mary **Ward**	346		109.07
Gibson, A. C.	A. **Barsenas**	103-1/2		5.89
Giles, J. D.	Geo. **Brewer**	1/2		2.59
Gilliland, J. V.	W. C. **Barfield**	72		7.62
Gilliland, B. T.			Alba	8.51
Glenn, W. B. Est.			Hawkins	.49
Grady, J. E.	S. T. **Belt**	100		5.75
Graham, E. D.			Mineola	4.07
Green, J. F.	S. **Yarbrough**	35		6.96
Green, O. D.	Bailey **Martin**	86		4.46
Green, L. V.	M. H. **Ussery**	60		7.16
Grimm, Mrs. J. F.	G. B. **King**	38		3.84
Gunter, A. G.	H. **Anderson**	40		5.22
Gregory, D. W.	G. B. **King**	8		
Gregory, D. W.	C. B. **Gentry**	16		
Gregory, D. W.	J. B. **Cherino**	111-1/2		
Gregory, D. W.	J. B. **Cherino**	24-6/10		
Gregory, D. W.	J. B. **Cherino**	30		21.48
Hall, J. D.	J. A. **Greer**	42		5.07
Hamilton, Mrs. K.			Hawkins	4.80
Hamilton, L. F.	William **Page**	1/4	Mineola	18.28
Ham, H. C.	J. **Sherman**	1		
Ham, H. C.	J. **Sherman**	1-1/2		6.83
Haines, John (Col.)	E. A. **Evans**	1/2		3.86

Wood County Newspapers

Name of Owner	Original Grantee	Acres Delinquent	City or Town	Total Taxes
Haines, Bettie (Col.)			Mineola	1.48
Harris, E. H. & O.	Thomas Brumry	3		
Harris, E. H. & O.	John Craig	97		6.71
Harry, J. B.	J. Swift	61		
Harry, J. B.	C. Hardeman	3-1/3		7.29
Head, J. E.	H. E. Watson	80		8.17
Hemm, J. C.	J. E. White	20-2/10		20.21
Henry, S. B.			Mineola	1.45
Hill, Daniel (Col.)			Mineola	.73
Hill, W. H.	G. B. King	1/4		12.52
Hines, J. A.	J. Crofford	1	Alba	10.40
Hines, G. C.			Alba	5.91
Hogan, W. H.	Reece Reed	220		13.72
Holder, J. T.	G. S. Howard			8.62
Holmes, J. D.	A. M. Ellis	50	Hawkins	
Holmes, J. D.	E. Weidman	46-2/3	Hawkins	
Holmes, J. D.			Hawkins	27.76
Hopkins, W. S.	H. Anderson	130		8.14
Ingram, Robert	Joel P. Wood	35		10.32
Jackson, Sam (Col.)			Mineola	15.32
Johnson, Major (Col.)	Jessie Walker	95		9.81
Johnson, Frank (Col.)			Mineola	3.84
Jones, J. R.	W. H. Crofford	1/3		3.86
Jones, Mariah (Col.)	J. Stark	18		1.26
Jones, J. T.	J. Simpkins	7/10		5.61
Jones, E. W.			Alba	6.71
Jones, Will			Mineola	4.81
Jones, Will (Col.)	J. E. White	16-2/3		9.42
Kilpatrick, J. J.	F. Mahon	20		
Kilpatrick, J. J.	N. Gilbert	45-5/7		7.11
King, Mrs. E. F.	G. B. King	77		7.70
Knight, J. H.	Walker Four	58		5.19
Lattimore, C. L.(Col.)	Sam Burch	100		11.74

Name of Owner	Original Grantee	Acres Delinquent	City or Town	Total Taxes
Lawrence, R. O.	S. H. **Davis**	12-1/2		5.04
Leibrook, E. A.	H. **Payne**	75		
Leibrook, E. A.	Geo. **Brewer**	1		9.11
Lewis, J. T.	H. **Payne**	100		4.80
Lyles & Keith	J. H. **Chereno**	1/4		4.80
Lindley, J. H.	Mary **Rocher**	91-1/4		8.26
Lockett, B.	G. B. **King**	1/4		.48
Lundon, Joe			Mineola	
Lundon, Joe				3.79
Lovelady, L. C.	G. B. **King**	1/2		4.13
Letonsty, Torey	T. E. **White**	51-1/2		
Lutonsty, Torey	David **Williams**	3-3/4		6.57
Mabrey, Mrs. Drank	M. A. **Esparsia**	104	Hawkins	17.71
Mangam, G. W.	S. **English**	57-1/2		15.84
Madison, J. T.	Sam **Brooks**	97-3/4		
Maxfield,			Mineola	13.06
Mitchell, Fed			Mineola	2.06
Molnair, John			Mineola	2.36
Mosely, S. J.	S. **Hartfield**	40		7.30
Murphy, A. (Col.)				3.15
McDonald, W. L.	John **Delapp**	18-9/10		4.34
McDonald, Roxie (Col.)	C. E. **Rivers**	27		
McDonald, Roxie (Col.)	J. E. **White**	1-1/4		2.86
McKern, W. S.	E. **Rehorse**	80		7.20
Northington, M. F.	J. O. **Young**	21-1/5		3.95
Ogburn Orchard Co.	E. **Rehorse**	1000		
Ogburn Orchard Co.	M. H. **Ussery**	515		
Ogburn Orchard Co.	John **Delapp**	586		
Ogburn Orchard Co.	John **Delapp**	25		281.19
Oshields, R. W.	Mary **Ward**	232-1/2		
Oshields, R. W.	Mary **Arocah**	50		36.13
Parker, John (Col.)			Mineola	1.93
Phillips, S. L.	J. M. **Moore**	64-1/2		

Wood County Newspapers

Name of Owner	Original Grantee	Acres Delinquent	City or Town	Total Taxes
Phillips, S. L.	J. M. **Moore**	62-1/2		19.20
Pierce, J. Max	B. **Gray**	22-2/10		
Pierce, J. Max	E. A. **Evans**	8		
Pierce, J. Max	B. **Gray**	110-3/10		
Pierce, J. Max	J. **Hardessale**	55		
Pierce, J. Max	B. **Gray**	31		
Pierce, J. Max	J. **Hardessale**	25-1/3		40.59
Pierce, J. Max	S. **Yarbrough**	68-1/2		
Paschal, Dr. J. S.	J M **Servantes**	249-1/2		
Paschal, Dr. J. S.	J M **Servantes**	18-1/2		
Paschal, Dr. J. S.	J M **Servantes**	60		
Paschal, Dr. J. S.	J M **Servantes**	35		
Paschal, Dr. J. S.	J M **Servantes**	149-1/2		
Paschal, Dr. J. S.	J M **Servantes**	46-1/2		
Paschal, Dr. J. S.	A. **Calderon**	190-1/2		
Paschal, Dr. J. S.	B. **Smith**	23-1/2		
Paschal, Dr. J. S.	J. D. **Ramires**	1/2		
Paschal, Dr. J. S.	J. B. **Cherino**	262/3		
Paschal, Dr. J. S.	J. B. **Cherino**	107		
Paschal, Dr. J. S.	J. B. **Cherino**	146-1/2		
Paschal, Dr. J. S.	J. B. **Cherino**	40		
Paschal, Dr. J. S.	J. B. **Cherino**	60		
Paschal, Dr. J. S.	J. B. **Cherino**	60		
Paschal, Dr. J. S.	J. B. **Cherino**	42		
Paschal, Dr. J. S.	J. B. **Cherino**	76		133.71
Pierce, Prince (Col.)			Mineola	2.40
Pinto, T. J.	John **Sparks**	90		14.79
Porterfield, G. H.	G. B. **King**	2		7.20
Powell, H. H.	F. L. **Smith**	54-9/10		5.29
Pierce, W. H.	H. **Gilbert**	45-5/7		6.20
Pritchett, J. W.	G. W. **Tosrell**	1/4		5.77
Pruitt, Mrs. Mayo			Mineola	14.45
Reese, Albert (Col.)			Mineola	6.10

Democrat - 1915

Name of Owner	Original Grantee	Acres Delinquent	City or Town	Total Taxes
Reed, W. L.	A. J. **Jaco**		Crow	2.90
Reese, J. S.			Mineola	25.41
Reeves, E. A.	Wesley **Tollett**	19		
Reeves, E. A.	J. H. Keaton	106-3/4		
Reeves, E. A.	John **Sparks**	100	Mineola	35.08
Richey, J. H.	A. J. **Jaco**	1		4.72
Robinson, D. M.	H. **Nelson**	3/4		3.84
Roberts, Chaney (Col.)			Mineola	1.68
Roberts, Newt	E. A. **Evans**	1/4		4.80
Roberts, Henry			Mineola	5.77
Romine, Richard	E. **Rehorse**	1		1.59
Rainsy, John (Col.)			Mineola	4.23
Rushing, W. A.	**Berry** Est.	94		11.36
Russell, Cally	James **Richards**	16		.97
Russell, Wilson	James **Richards**	30		
Russell, Wilson	J. **Stark**	30		14.64
Russell, Wilson	R. **Crofford**	106-1/4		6.00
Sanders, E. W.	A. **Campbell**	53-1/2		
Sanders, J. R.	H. **Dickson**	?0		
Sanders, J. R.	H. **Dickson**	38		5.29
Sanford, L. F.	M. **Rentorez**	125		6.24
Sessions, Mrs. Jim (Col.)	R. E. **Neill**	158		
Sessions, Mrs. Jim	H. **Anderson**	66		
Sessions, Allen (Col.)	R. E. **Neill**	134		
Sessions, Allen (Col.)	R. E. **Neill**	42		
Sessions, Allen (Col.)	R. E. **Neill**	25		12.96
Sims, A. L.	Jessie **Walker**	100		13.58
Sims, A. C.	M. H. **Dubose**	100		
Sims, A. C.	M. H. **Dubose**	50		15.84
Singleton, C. S.	Isaac **Reed**	32-4/10		4.33
Smart, C. M.			Hawkins	.97
Smith, E. S.	G. W. **Gay**	199		18.83
Sorey, Henry			Mineola	4.66

Wood County Newspapers

Name of Owner	Original Grantee	Acres Delinquent	City or Town	Total Taxes
Sparkman, W. R.	W. H. Crofford	10	Mineola	12.37
Spivey, E. L.	L. W. Gillum	46-1/2		6.04
Spivey, E. L.	L. W. Gillum	101-1/2		11.16
Stanley, R. H.	Mary Ward	17		
Stanley, R. H.	Mary Ward	40		10.03
Stevens, J. D. (Col.)			Mineola	5.19
Stevenson, W. C.	G. B. King	1/2		8.08
Stennett, W. A.	E. Esparsia	59-6/10		8.68
Stokes, B. L.	Wm. Barnhill	4		
Stokes, B. L.	Wm. Barnhill	21		11.65
Suiter, J. W.	L. W. Gillum	81		7.88
Sutton, J. M.	John Polp	50-1/2		8.25
Sweeten, A. G.	Daniel Fuller	2		1.21
Taylor, I. F.	M. Renderez	150		27.61
Taylor, J. F. (Col.)	J. Robbins	34		
Taylor, J. T	J. Robbins	100		11.74
Tocle & Hattaway	L. Rose	220		10.35
Templeton, J. P.	G. B. King	105-1/4		
Templeton, J. P.	G. B. King	28		13.58
Terry, R. L.	J. E. White	15		15.21
Thatcher, G. W.	Daniel Fuller	22		5.00
Thedford, J. H.	Sam Brooks	17		7.96
Thomas, W. H.	William Hurt	20		4.99
Thompson, Barney (Col)	J. Yarbrough	7-1/4		
Thompson, Barney (Col)	J. Yarbrough	41-1/3		6.58
Thurman Est.	G. B. King	100		9.63
Underwood, J. A.	L. Johnson	24		
Underwood, J. A.	H. Nelson	40		8.47
Ussery, A. M.	H. Nelson	45		8.45
Virt, Thomas	William Fisher	46		7.44
Waddleton, J. D. (Col.)	J. M. Moore	30		6.24
Vehle, Otto	G. B. King	1/2		25.52
Waldrop, C. P.	John Elledge	100		8.69

Democrat - 1915

Name of Owner	Original Grantee	Acres Delinquent	City or Town	Total Taxes
Walton, Mrs. S.W. (Col)	R. E. **Neill**	65		
Walton, Mrs. S.W. (Col)	R. E. **Neill**	125		14.36
Walsh, J. R.	A. J. **Jaco**	1		4.42
Watson, G. A.	M. A. **Meeser**	60		9.04
Weems, G. W.	G. B. **King**	1/2		3.90
Welse, J. W.	H. **Arnold**	70		8.12
Weise, J. J.	G. **Flores**	41		7.07
Weise, E. E.	John **Pullen**	55-1/2		8.51
Wesley, Catherine (Col.)			Mineola	2.8
Wesley, Joe (Col.)	C. A. **Telaferro**	17-1/2		
Wesley, Joe	J. **Knight**	160		10.77
Wesley, William	J. **Knight**	193-1/2		14.93
White, M. L.	J. **Simpkins**	1		7.40
Whitus, I. W.	F. **McMahon**	85-1/2		8.19
Whitworth, N. A.	Buckner **Smith**	75		11.50
Wilburn, Antony	G. B. **King**	1/2		2.40
Williams, Jno. E. (Col.)			Mineola	
Williams, Jno. E. (Col.)			Mineola	8.28
Williams, J. F.	A. B. **Foster**	180		16.12
Wilson, A. A.			Mineola	29.63
Wingo, G. H.	J. **Simpkins**	1/2		3.38
Wood, J. B.	A. **Gonzales**	60		
Wood, J. B.	J. J. **Pemberton**	40		
Wood, J. B.	W. B. **Lacy**	100		
Wood, J. B.	S. P. **Alpino**	102-1/2		
Wood, J. B.	S. P. **Alpino**	50		26.52
Wren, B. L.			Mineola	3.45
Wyley, Mrs. T. E.			Mineola	14.45
Young, W.	Berry **West**	1		4.42
SUPPLEMENT ROLL				
Moore, R. H. & W. A.	R. C. **Burnett**	232		
Moore, R. H. & W. A.	John **Delapp**	1		12.09
Noble, Dr. S. C.			Mineola	42.55

NON-RESIDENT ROLL

Name of Owner	Original Grantee	Acres Delinquent	City or Town	Total Taxes
Armstrong, Susan			Mineola	1.54
Armstrong, Joe (Col.)			Mineola	.97
Barnes, Mrs. Ida	W. H. **Sumerland**	1/2		4.79
Bankston, E. S.	J. **Crofford**	1/2		.59
Booker, Mary (Col.)	Mm. **Benton**	22-1/6		2.12
Browning, W. B.	G. B. **King**	1/2		1.94
Butler, A. G. & A. J.	G. B. **King**	12		1.16
Cain, W. D.	S. **Yarbrough**	150		11.55
Castleman, J. H.			Mineola	2.89
Cate, Mrs. C. B.	F. **Herniger**	377		
Cate, Mrs. C. B.	S. **English**	792		
Cate, Mrs. C. B.	J. E. **White**	21		47.06
Cate, Billie	J. **Simpkins**	2		1.92
Consumers Lignite Co.	F. **McMahon**	30		
Consumers Lignite Co.	S. P. **Alpine**	42		
Consumers Lignite Co.	P. **Vendervile**	63-1/2		
Consumers Lignite Co.	J. J. **Pemberton**	39		
Consumers Lignite Co.	S. P. **Alpine**	39		
Consumers Lignite Co.	J. **Crofford**	7-77/100		101.83
Crosby, J. W.	A. **Houston**	50		4.83
Eastridge, Mrs. J. E.			Winnsboro	7.70
Hayney, Coolar	John **Lammon**	60		2.89
Head, S. P. Est.	L. **Johnson**	10-1/7		.77
Hyde, Mrs. J. H.	J. M. **Urutia**	50		4.80
Lindsey, A. A.	S. **McDonald**	92-1/2		8.86
Munzesheimer, Julia			Mineola	19.25
Hall, Mrs. Mattie	G. B. **King**	1		7.20
Nicholson, J. H.	J. H. **Blackstock**	50		4.80
Ogburn Canning Co.	G. B. **King**	2-3/4		48.??
Pennington, S. P.	Francis **Hill**	18		.87
Pierce, Hattie	G. B. **King**	15-1/2		1.59
Reynolds, A. B.	G. **Jones**	10		.77

Democrat - 1915

Name of Owner	Original Grantee	Acres Delinquent	City or Town	Total Taxes
Sneed, B. T.	John **Delapp**	72		2.40
Still, Hoire	L. **Johnson**	10-9/10		.77
Texas Lignite Co.	J. **Crofford**	360-8/18		18.05
Hansell, Susie			Mineola	1.54
Texas Lignite & Oil Co.	J. **Crofford** & others			248.52
Leon&H **Blum** Land Co	Jessie **Walker**	60		2.88
Thrailkill, John	P. **Gonzales**	50		4.79
Veasey, John (Col.)	J. E. **White**	39-3/4	Mineola	12.32
Vining, E.	H. **Nelson**	5		5.75
Ward, Lottie	G. B. **King**	16-1/2		1.59
Weems, A. W.	J. H. **Blackstock**	15		1.45
White, Jno. W.	H. **Nelson**	8-3/4		5.75
Williams, Jane (Col.)	Chas. **Despalier**	72		
Williams, Jane (Col.)	J. B. **Grant**	40		7.70
Wright, J. M.	J. **Sherman**	3-1/2		
Wright, J. M.	Isaac **McMahon**	2-3/4		
Wright, J. M.	Isaac **McMahon**	24		6.63
	UNRENDERED ROLL			
Acker, R. L.	Sam **Brooks**	43		2.79
Adams, Mrs.R. C.			Hawkins	4.80
Alexander, J. D.	Jessie **Walker**	32		
Alexander, J. D.	Jessie **Walker**	138		14.17
Anderson, ?. B.	W. H. **Crofford**	1-2/3		5.75
Baggett, W. T.	T. G. **Smith**	80		2.31
Baker, J. F.	S. **English**	32-7/10		3.84
Beaty, J. B.	G. B. **King**	32-1/2		3.84
Bessinger, Jake	O. **Engledow**	68		6.52
Beulah, James	Daniel **Fuller**	12		1.16
Borger, Margaret	E. **Weidman**	40		2.40
Chris. Bd. of Missions	Wm. **Burch**	456		26.28
Clausell, Mrs. M. A.			Winnsboro	4.32
Clayton, Mrs. S. E.	W. A. **Clayton**	40		2.31
Color, J. W.	G. B. **King**	1		7.20

Wood County Newspapers

Name of Owner	Original Grantee	Acres Delinquent	City or Town	Total Taxes
Cranford, L. B.	J. **Sherman**	1-1/2		3.83
Crider, E. L.	J. C. **Mosley**	40		2.88
Davenport, Mrs. M. H.	M. **Cartemas**	65		4.37
Davis, Aaron (Col.)	W. B. **Thomas**	106		6.71
Davis, Jake	J. **Sherman**	1		2.40
Boyd, Mrs. E. D.	Sam **Brooks**	103-8/10		9.92
Boyd, E. E.	Wm. **Whittaker**	104		5.95
Butler, Mrs. Mattie	O. **Engledow**	93-3/4		8.96
Carrol, W. J.	H. **Payne**	406		19.54
Carter, C. H.	M. **Cartemas**	10		.68
Cartwright, W. H.	C. G. **Bullard**	50-7/10		.87
Cartwright, L.	M. **McNutt**	60-1/2		4.08
Cate, R. N.	W. H. **Crofford**	6		6.71
Gee, R. H.	J. **Sherman**	7/8		7.70
Green, S. L.	G. B. **King**	3/4		4.08
Hala, A.	F. **Holland**	95-3/5		5.47
Hall, Peter	L. G. **Powell**	110		5.29
Defee, F.	J. **Simpkins**	35-3/10		6.71
Dement, Joe (Col.)	G. B. **King**	1/3		.49
Eddis, E. D.	J. B. **Crane**	50		3.84
Eddins, J. A., Sr.	John **Styres**	160		7.70
Evans, L. R.	J. **Sherman**	1/3		6.71
Fitzgerald, A. H.	J. **Crofford**	20		1.93
Fletcher, E. M.	B. S. **Coy**	35-1/2		3.41
Flowellen, Tom	G. W. **Terrell**	1/2		7.70
Florence, L. O.	Sam **Brooks**	96-6/10		9.04
Folmar, W. O.			Alba	7.70
Fowler, W. L.			Hawkins	1.45
James, R. J.	R. G. **Ramsell**	20		2.40
Jobe, S. E.	J. M. **Harris**	277-1/2		
Jobe, S. E.	C. R. **Patton**	160		23.29
Jones & Hill	J. **Simpkins**	4-7/10		9.63
Justice, S. L.	David **Rose**	40		3.07

Democrat - 1915

Name of Owner	Original Grantee	Acres Delinquent	City or Town	Total Taxes
Kimberlan, J. S. Est.	J. **Simpkins**	1/2		1.45
Lee, B. B.	G. B. **King**	1-3/4		5.75
Lindley, J. A.	Thomas **Walker**	100		5.75
Lindsey, J. H.	Geo. **Nagan**	80		6.14
Hargett, Mrs. C. A.	Geo. **Brewer**	106	Hawkins	12.04
Harris, Mary	G. B. **King**	3		1.45
Harrison, Edw. P.	Joel **Robbins**	320		15.40
Hollon, W. J. (Col.)	T. J. **Rusk**	61-1/4		4.80
Huff, J. B.	S. **English**	60		3.36
Hunter, Ned (Col.)	Wm. **Benton**	30		2.88
Irby, Mrs. P. S.	G. B. **King**	2		3.84
Netzorg, Mrs. E. M.			Mineola	8.67
Newton, Jess	Benj. **Anderson**	91		9.86
Nichols, J. C.	T. J. **Curl**	53-2/3		1.64
Nicholson, J. K.	W. H. **Crofford**	1/2		4.80
Odom, T. J.	J. **Knight**	10		.97
Oliver, J. A.	J. **Simpkins**	1		.30
Page, J. W.	J. **Simpkins**	1		4.32
Parrish, W. R.			Hawkins	1.93
Patrick, J. W.	S. G. **Howard**	80		5.3?
Molton, Mrs. C. O.	G. B. **King**	1/2		3.84
Milliron, A. H.	J. **Simpkins**	1/2		1.93
Miller, B. A.	M. **Gause**	260		12.52
Mitchell, Dr. J. J.	J. M. **Chandler**	103		5.95
Moore, J. W.	C. A. **Dove**	58		1.93
Morgan, M. C. Est.	Nac University	94		
Morgan, M. C. Est.	Nac University	89		8.81
Mosely, Ellis G.	E. A. **Adams**	1-3/4		5.75
Murphy, B. F.	Mary **Ward**	24-1/2		1.21
McGee, L. H.	W. H. **Crofford**	1-3/4		3.84
McGee, Mrs. M. S.	G. B. **King**	3/4		4.80
McGee, A. F.	R. E. **Neill**	100		6.71
Sallas, J. B.	Chas. **Despalier**	177		9.63

Wood County Newspapers

Name of Owner	Original Grantee	Acres Delinquent	City or Town	Total Taxes
Scarborough, Mrs. D.E.	J. **Simpkins**	1/2		3.84
Schrumm, Miss Arie			Ogburn	.49
Sharigk, J. W.	C. L. **Cannon**	320		18.48
Sharp, W. G.	O. **Engledow**	88-1/2		8.47
Shropshire, G. C.	Braun **Vetan**	214		9.63
Shirtliff, J. R.	Geo. **Nagan**	46-1/2		
Shirtliff, J. R.	W. H. **Flannigan**	160		11.27
Sparks, Geo. W.	David **Rose**	100		5.75
Sparkman, L. H.	L. W. **Gillum**	30		1.72
Spaulding, Mrs. Ida	M. J. **Nunes**	141-1/2		13.57
Penney, J. T.	H. **Arnold**	70		5.27
Porter, J. T.	W. A. **Sumerland**	2		2.78
Pruit[?], A.	E. **Alverado**	35		3.35
Putman[?], J. S.	Sam **Brooks**	66		5.09
Redden, Zeb	M. J. **Nunes**	27-1/4		3.61
Reeves, Geo. C.	Daniel **Fuller**	31	Mineola	
Reeves, Geo. C.	John **Layman**	20	Mineola	
Geo. C. **Reeves**	Esley **Tollett**	78	Mineola	
Geo. C. **Reeves**	Esley **Tollett**	20	Mineola	
Reeves, Geo. C.	J. E. **White**	1/2	Mineola	27.25
Richburg, J. W.	J. **Simpkins**	1/2		7.70
Robertson, M. D.	J. **Sherman**	6-2/3		2.88
Rogers, W. B.	I. V. **Fowler**	42		
Rogers, W. B.	J. H. **Kendrick**	58		6.87
Rotan, Julia Est.	Buckner **Smith**	114		10.58
Rigley, W. E.	E. A. **Evans**	4-1/2		1.22
Woodard, R. P.	S. **Greer**	222-6/10		
Woodard, R. P.	J. E. **White**	16		
Woodard, R. P.	R. **Sonigas**	77-4/10		31.57
Tarver, E. T.	J. **Robbins**	72-1/2		4.80
Taylor, E. J.	Mary **Caruthers**	4		7.70
Tedder, J. A.	J. M. **Chandler**	51-1/2		2.94
Testerman, W. O.	Geo. **Skull**	25		1.21

Democrat - 1915

Name of Owner	Original Grantee	Acres Delinquent	City or Town	Total Taxes
Thacher, E. M. Est.	Daniel **Fuller**	61		3.22
Thompson, G. M.	G. B. **King**	1/2		2.88
Tillery, S. M.	Sam **Brooks**	72-1/2		5.99
Upchurch, G. W.	**Brooks-Burleson**	420		12.13
Vaughn, J. L.	J. **Simpkins**	1/2		5.75
Wallen, W. S. Est.	M. J. **Nunes**	42-1/2		
Webb, A. S.	H. **Nelson**	15		3.84
	SUPPLEMENT			
Ramsey, J. A.	T. H. **Rogers**	20		3.46
Ramond, Jno.	John **Gregg**	40		7.40
Ramsey, H. H.	Polly **Tiest**	20		.77
Ballard, E. D.	G. B. **King**	3/4		2.02
Jones, Bob			Mineola	1.93
Jones, Earl			Winnsboro	10.83
Moore, J. W.	G. W. **Terrell**	41-3/10		14.68
Williams, B. W.	W. R. **Buckley**	13-1/5		5.03

Doings in County Court

... the following cases disposed of: Lee **McBride**, Lou **Sells**, J. E. **Head**, Cliff **Boyd**, Lee **Wilson**, Harry **Allen**, Sam **Franklin**, Eck **Underwood** and Henry **Kirkpatrick** dismissed.

Geo. **Ellis**, jury trial, guilty, fine $50.00 and two days in jail.

Almer and Tinnie **Byars**, bonds forfeited and alias capias ordered.

George **Washington**, fine $100.

Sam **Jackson**, jury trial, not guilty.

A. C. **Paul**, appeal dismissed and defendant remanded to proper officers.

Clyde **Williams**, fine $1.00 and 1 day in jail.

Willie **Jones**, fine $5.00 and 1 day in jail.

District Clerk Julius **Taylor** and his sisters moved Thursday to the new residence erected for them by John **Rainwater**, just north of the Rainwater home.

Local and Personal

Mrs. D. F. **Sutherland** is visiting her daughter, Mrs. Claude **Dodgen**, at Winnsboro.

Jake **Wingard** was down from Winnsboro . . .

Tom **Posey** was down from the Coke country . . .

"Shug" **Robinson** came in from Sulphur Springs . . . his brother Tobe Robinson.

Mrs. Puss **Conger** of Greenville . . . her brother Jno. D. **Jones** .

Miss Bonnie Maye **Sutherland** . . . her sister, Mrs. B. A. **Dodgen**, at Mount Pleasant.

Walker **Garrison**, one of the trustees of the school at Musgrove

C. J. **Smart** accompanied his daughter, Miss Lucille, to Coldwater, southeast of Winnsboro, Tuesday where she contracted to the school for the coming term.

Tip **McIntosh** was in . . . best crop for years . . .

J. H. **Newby** . . . his brother, W. F. Newby, Vienna, Ga. Joe . . . living at Yantis.

An Old Landmark Gone

Ed **Foster** of Alba began tearing away the old **McKnight** residence Wednesday morning and will erect a modern residence on the site for Mrs. McKnight.

Local and Personal

Ebb **Faulk** dropped in . . . his uncle, Tobe Faulk, and family near Hawkins. . . .

Jim **Head** was here from Hawkins . . . tells us he has entered the Ministry. . . .

E. L. **Foster** was over from Alba. Ed lost his wife a week or ten days ago and tells us he has placed his children with relatives and broke up housekeeping.

Hon. D. M. **Reedy** was here from Tyler . . .

J. B. **Wallace** . . . his mother, Mrs. H. A. Wallace, Sulphur Springs . . .

. . . J. T. **Morse** and J. W. **Setzler** of the Pleasant Ridge community . . .

Uncle Pate and Aunt Sallie **Hendrix** spent several days with Mr. and Mrs. Phil **Butler** south of town the past week . . .

D. M. **Macoy**, who tried Wood county for a short time and returned to his old Alabama home.

Mrs. W. T. **Williams** . . . her mother, Mrs. Lydia C. **Wright**, at Paso Robles, Cal. to which place Mrs. Wright went the past week to be with her son, Mark Francis, during the illness of his wife.

Mrs. M. B. **Briggs** came over from Gilmer . . . her parents, Mr. and Mrs. Sam **Smart**, and other relatives here.

Mrs. Ollie **Leath** and little Miss Louise . . .visit with her sister, Mrs. W. M. **Britton**, at Hollister, Ok.

Jim **Craver** of Yantis . . . he and his mother are moving to Alba, where they have bought a home and will reside . . .

Lightning's Freaks

During the rain early last Friday morning lightning struck a large oak in Mrs. **Leath**'s pasture, just in front of her residence, tearing the huge tree all to pieces. The tree was only 75 or 80 ft. from the residence of J. P. **Marlow** and his daughter, Miss Mabel, was in the yard . . . not harmed.

Near the same hour a cow belonging to Uncle Pate **Hendrix**, a mile north of town, was killed by lightning, and Pink **Lawrence** tells us that two fine cows belonging to Ben **Browning**, living near Stout, were also killed near the same hour.

The Threshing Outfit

Ase **Horton**, of the firm of **Mount** & Horton, the threshing machine men, . . .

Thursday, July 15, 1915

Died At Mineola Thursday, July 8th
J. A. Thomas [photo]
Biographical Sketch

Jesse A. **Thomas** was born in Pickens county, Alabama, Dec. 23, 1868. He lost his father at the age of 6. He moved with his mother to Texas in 1885 and settled on a farm in Hunt county. Young Thomas, by hard and determined efforts, acquired an education such as few boys circumstanced as he was would acquire amid such hardships. Following this he taught school in Kaufman and Hunt counties. He acquired the Leonard Graphic in 1894, retaining that publication until 1896, at which time he sold it and purchased the Mineola Monitor. In 1895 he was married to Miss Mollie **Caylor** of Tulia, Swisher county, who survives him with their two sons, Hubert, aged 19, and William Sterett, aged 10.

Editor Thomas served in the Twenty-Ninth and Thirtieth Legislature as a Representative of Fannin county. He served as president of the School Board of Leonard and of Mineola . . .

Editor Thomas was appointed postmaster of Mineola and assumed the duties of the office on April 1.

He was a member of the knights of Phthias and an enthusiastic Mason, having attained to the degree of the Royal Arch, and served Mineola chapter as high priest since its organization.

Death of J. W. McMurry

J. W. **McMurry**, an old and highly respected citizen of Mineola, died at a sanitarium in Dallas Thursday of last week and the remains were brought to Mineola on the Friday morning T. & P. train and interment had in the Mineola cemetery immediately upon arrival of the corpse.

Local and Personal

John **Sanders** and family passed through town Tuesday morning enroute to their home in west Texas after a visit with his brother, W. B. Sanders, and other relatives east of town.

Mrs. R. A. **Mingle** of Chattanooga, Tenn., is here for the summer with her brothers, Hon. B. F., Will, John Cathey, and sisters, Mesdames Jess **Marlowe** and Virgil **Blalock**, of Quitman, and J. H. **McGee** and S. B. **Pope** of Golden.

Luther **Tackett** of Ada, Okla., . . .

Mrs. I. J. Bradshaw Dead

From W. P. **Lawrence** we learn of the death of Mrs. I. J. **Bradshaw**, which occurred at the family home hear Shady Grove Saturday and interment was had at Shady Grove Monday.

Thursday, July 22, 1915

Another Landmark Gone

Workmen began the tearing down of the old corner store building known as the "Alliance Old Store" Monday morning of this week. Young **Wright** will use the lumber in the erection of a residence just east of the town limit on the Pine Mills road.

This building was erected in 1887, and was under construction when this writer came to Quitman. It was erected by the Farmers Alliance. Jim **Gregory** was manager and John **Wheelis** was foreman on the work. . . .

Dr. **Goldsmith**, who owns the lot, tells us his plans are to have a brick building erected on the site in the course of a few months.

Stockholders Meeting of Farmers Cotton Oil Co.

. . . directors were elected for the ensuing year:

E. C. **Mitchell**, J. V. **Attaway**, A. A. **Snow**, C. W. **Moore**, J. M. **Craddock**, R. H. **McCrary**, J. P. **Stanley**, W. H. **Attaway**, C. P. **Newman**, Elmore **Wright**, Jno. D. **Jones**, A. R. **Cruce**, I. J. **Bradshaw**, Q. B. **Morris**, Walter **Crumpler**, A. T. **Winkle**, J. C. **Gibson**, Claude **Sharp**.

Doings in County Court

T. A. **Browning** vs. A. P. **Sayers**, jury trial, verdict for defendant.

L. L. **Winterbaur** vs. Ben **Johnson** et al, set for first Monday in September, 1915. . .

R. A. **Farrington** vs. Mrs. M. A. **Holly**, T. D. **Bonner** trustee in bankruptcy permitted to intervene.

Mit **Cox** vs. J. C. **Clinton**, plea to jurisduction sustained, appeal dismissed.

G. C. **Hopkins** vs. N. H. **Spearman**, jury trial, verdict for plaintiff for $750, and against defendant on plea of homestead exemption and counter claim.

The National Supply Co. of Kansas vs. Howard W. **Wright** et al, dismissed by plaintiff, all costs having been paid.

Jones of Binghampton Owners of Osgood Scale Co. vs. J. R. **Culberson**, judgment rendered by the Court for defendant.

First National Bank of Mineola vs. R. R. **Rucker** et al, judgement for plaintiff for $750 . .

Roberts, Johnson, Rand Shoe Co. vs Mrs. Minnie L. **Cobb**, judgment for plaintiff in the sum of $780.31.

First State Bank of Alba vs. H. N. **Dorrough**, jury trial, judgment for defendant.

H. S. **Wilson** vs. T. & P. Rwy. Co., jury trial, judgment for plaintiff for $42.00.

On the state docket the cases against John **Martin** and Grover **Cassel** were dismissed.

Local and Personal

Emmett **Awtry** and wife . . . enroute to Mineola to visit the latter's parents, Mr. and Mrs. J. H. **Williams**. Emmett's son John . . . is some better but still has some fever. He recently had the heel bone of one foot removed and will likely be a cripple for life. . . .

Dr. **Black** reports the arrival of a fine girl at the home of Prof. and Mrs. Geo. **McAllister**.

W. R. **Hickman** of Yantis is with J. R. **Mayo** in the ice and market business . . .

Edgar **Goodwin** came down from Ft. Worth . . .

Sheriff **Williams** . . . his son Bryan acted as sheriff . . .

Attorney Edgar **Tharp** . . .

J. H. **Gleaton**, the man who sometimes sells watermelons - and good ones at that - . . .

Mr. **Mangrum**, conductor on the morning Mineola mail hack, left Saturday for a visit with relatives at his old home, Trenton.

Mr. and Mrs. I. W. **Robbins** and "Buster" visited H. V. **Johnson** and family near Golden Sunday.

Gus **Hodges** and Jim **Robinson** were over from Alba . . .

W. F. **Bartlett** of Pine Mills .. .

Mr. and Mrs. Tobe **Benton** are the proud parents of a fine baby girl, born Wednesday, the 8th.

F. G. **Estes** and J. W. **McKinzie**, two trustees of the Pleasant Ridge school . . .

Jno. R. **Edmonds**, agricultural agent . . .

Cullen **Price**, the little son of our friend Ben Price, living north of town, . . .

Mrs. J. A. **Brewer** and Miss Naomi **Johnson** of Arcadia, La., are visiting the former's brothers, Esq. **Goodwin**, J. A. and J. L. **Ivey** and their families.

Postmaster **McWhorter** was here from Rhonesboro . . .

Spencer **Horton** and Reagan **Turner** are opening up a tailor shop and pressing outfit in the Goodwin brick.

Charley **Sims** has returned to Mineola and accepted a position with A. J. **Falkner** at the Big 4, . . .

Mrs. H. **Hedick** and children of Sulphur Springs . . . her sister, Mrs. A. J. **Britton**.

Ben **Stinson**, the Winnsboro photographer, . . .

Death of Fine Young Man

Robert **Kennedy**, son of Mr. and Mrs. Jas. Kennedy, died at the family home last Saturday evening after a week's illness with appendicitis. He was taken sick at Myrtle Springs at the all-day singing Sunday before his death and continued to grow worse until death relieved him of his suffering Saturday evening.

Robert was 21 years old Oct. 8, 1914. . . .

He is survived by his parents, four brothers and three sisters, and host of other relatives and friends.

The funeral service was conducted by Rev. R. J. **Blackmon** at Myrtle Springs at 3 p.m. Sunday and interment made in the cemetery nearby immediately following the service. . . .

Fatal Auto Wreck

Friday night of last week as Prof G. E. **Jones** and other parties were returning from Dallas, and in passing through Rockwall county they ran onto a small bridge, which gave way, overturning their auto. Mr. Jones was caught under the car, which caught fire, and he was so badly injured that he died at his home in Sulphur Springs Sunday afternoon. His brother, J. F. Jones of our town, was notified . . . [Prof. Jones] was buried Monday at Reiley Springs. . . .

New School at Quitman

A dispatch from Quitman dated July 2, says: "Contractor Clarence **Ray**, with a full crew, has begun laying brick on Quitman's $10,000 school building . . . E. E. **Ramsey** for the past several years principal of the Lone Oak high school, will teach this year in the new school . . .   - Lone Oak News.

Our Sick

Dr. **Black** reports the daughter of Mr. and Mrs. W. J. **Ussery**, west of town, who has had a severe attack of appendicitis, getting along nicely . . .

Mrs. C. A. **Green**, who has been quite sick, is getting along nicely. . . .

Dr. C. D. **Lipscomb** reports his neice, Miss Georgia Lipscomb, who has typhoid fever, getting along as well as could be expected at this stage of the disease.

Dr. **Robbins** reports Miss **Monroe,** who has been sick so long with typhoid fever and who took a backset last week, as getting along reasonably well. . . . Her condition continues critical. He also reports Roy **Ramey** getting along nicely and the little daughter of Mrs. Ollie **Perrin** doing reasonably well.

Thursday, July 29, 1915

Lodge Meeting

... Flora Lodge No. 119, A. F. & A.M. . . . Alba Lodge was also well represented, R. E. **Wright**, V. G. **Fields**, Sid **Pope**, F. G. **Estes**, Clyde **Jordan**, Joe **Patton**, J. C. **Lambert** and R. H. **Franks** being over from the Lignite city.

... Charlie **Goldsmith** to the sublime degree of Master Mason, and the election of Pink **Lawrence** to take the degree ...

Local and Personal

Master Norman **Wright** has been quite sick again this week but his father, Clem Wright, . . . he is some better.

Cecil **Sims**, assistant cashier of First National Bank, Mineola, came up Tuesday with his sister, Miss Euzela who came for a visit with her aunt, Mrs. R. M. **Smith**, . . .

. . . Roy **Ramey** able to on our streets Monday after his siege of fever. He and little Lucille, daughter of Mrs. Ollie **Perrin**, are both able to be up . . .

Mrs. N. A. **McKnight** returned from Alba Sunday where she has been visiting with her daughter, Mrs. R. W. **Low**, . . . Mr. Low, or Buck, as all call him, has bought a big ranch in west Texas and will go there for an indefinite time to improve same, after which he will either return here or his wife will join him on the ranch.

Bridges - White Marriage

. . . the marriage of two of the popular Rock Hill People in the person of Roy **Bridges** and Miss Era **White**. They were married Sunday evening, the 18th inst. while sitting in their buggy in front of the courthouse, Judge R. E. **Bozeman** officiating.

Roy is a son of Mr. and Mrs. Robert Bridges of the Rock Hill country, and Miss Era is a daughter of Mr. and Mrs. John White, of the same community.

B. I. **Whitworth** was over from Klondyke . . . tell us that the 2 year old babe of Mr. and Mrs. Duge **Russom** died Tuesday morning and that interment will be had today. . . .quite a lot if sickness in his neighborhood . . . one of the children of Mr. and Mrs. Woody **Caldwell** who is quite sick with dyptheria. . . .

Doings in County Court

W. M. **Taylor** vs. Boston **McDonald**, dismissed at plaintiff's cost. Commercial Jewelry Co., vs. Mit **Cox**, same order.

Lindsey & Smith vs. First National Bank of Mineola, same order.

Tarver **Steele** Co. vs. L. H. **Reese** Sons & Co., judgment for plaintiff in the sum $570.30.

Pat **Dixon** et al vs. Andrew **Smith** et al, judgment for plaintiff against Andrew Smith with writ of inquiry.

Crescent Bed Co., vs. C. D. **Dewitt**, dismissed at plaintiff's cost.

R. A. **Farrington** vs. First National Bank of Alba, garnashee, dismissed at cost of Intervenor, Thos. D. **Bonner**.

J. M. **Puckett** vs. Hartford Fire Insurance Co., judgment for plaintiff in the sum of $70.00, and cost of suit.

Moore Grocery Co. vs. J. R. **Mayo**, dismissed at plaintiff's cost.

A. L. **Tarrant** vs. Henry **Carpenter** and A. J. **Henry**, judgment for plaintiff with foreclosure of mortgage lein.

T. A. **Browning** vs. L. E. **Goodloe**, dismissed at defendant's cost.

Johnson-Setzler Marriage

Wednesday evening of last week sometime between the hours of 4 and 6, Mr. Earnest **Johnson** and Miss Kate **Setzler** "happened" to meet Rev. J. H. **Baker** and wife in the road between Quitman and Alba, just this side of the Chaney bridge on Lake Fork, and in a very short time Bro. Baker said the words . . .

Earnest is a son of Mr. and Mrs. S. L. Johnson, of the Myrtle Springs community . . . Miss Kate is a daughter of Mr. and Mrs. J. W. Setzler of the Pleasant Ridge community; however, she too, was born and principally reared in the Myrtle Springs community.

Democrat - 1915

Residence Burned

... the residence of our friend, J. L. **Pullen** was burned Tuesday morning, the fire originating from the stove flue. ... complete loss. .. carried no insurance. Mr. Pullen ... a leading farmer of the Oak Grove country ...

C. W. **Vickery** has sold his home to Judge R. E. **Bozeman**, consideration $1,550.00. Mr. Vickery tells us that he will leave us about Sept. 1st, for Celina, Collin county, where he will locate for the practice of his profession. ... Charlie Vickery and his excellant wife ... have been in our midst practically all their lives ...

Local and Personal

Our handsome young friend, Ben **Taylor** left Monday for his old home in Alabama. Madam Rumor has it that Ben bought a round-trip ticket for one and a return ticket for two ...

W. A. **Howard**, wife and babe of Brookeland ... enroute to the **Jones** home west of town to visit her sister, and his grandparents, Mr. and Mrs. J. P. **Butler**, south of town.

Prof. W. H. **Barnes** was in from Redland ...

Commissioner **Cowley** ... tell us that work on the new steel bridge at the Belzora crossing on Sabine below Hawkins is progressing nicely ...

John **Pogue**, the only and original, and his son, Tom ...

W. H. **Ayer**, our popular barber, ...

Will **Shelton**, the Oak Grove merchant, ...

C. O. **Goldsmith** has installed an underground gasoline tank in front of his store and wants to sell you your gasoline.

W. R. **Vickery** who has been at Tioga Wells for several months, has returned home ... somewhat improved in health.

Dr. **Black**, wife and children went over to Lindale Thursday to visit his brother-in-law, W. E. **Fowler** and family, ...

Richard **Smith**, wife and son Malcomb, ...

Tom **Lindley**, the accomodating carrier on Yantis Rt. 2 ...

Dr. **Puckett**, Ellis **Burkett** and the **Lindley** boys were here from Hainesville ...

Belcher **Paschal** was in from Stout . . .

A. J. **Britton** and his two boys . . . his uncle, W. H. Britton, of Yantis, . . .

S. **Parker** and J. B. **Moore** and wife, brother-in-law and son-in-law respectively of J. H. **Long** came in Thursday from Dallas to spend a few weeks at the Long home east of town.

Bro. **Martin** and his daughter, Miss Winona . . .

Jas. D. **Harris** has bought the new residence, recently completed, from the **Taylor** boys, consideration $1250. . . . as an investment . .

G. W. **Cowan** and his little boy were up from Mineola . . .

J. W. **Corley** of Fresno, Calif., . . . says that his wife and babe are at Klamoth Falls, Oregon,

List of Jurors for Special Term of Court

. . . petit jurors for the special term of District Court to be begun and holden on the first Monday in August, 1915 . . .no jury drawn for the third week of the court . . .

First Week

T. F. **Dodgen**	T. J. **Morgan**	W. W. **Chanman**
N. B. **Mansell**	J. G. **Bailey**	H. **Tuggle**
W. J. **Goldsmith**	J. H. **Harvey**	C. E. **Shoemaker**
E. L. **Foster**	R. H. **Covington**	T. J. **Azbell**
C. A. **McLarty**	J. E. **McBride**	T. G. **Goswick**
O. A. **Cain**	D. V. **Wagoner**	W. B. **West**
B. F. **Campbell**	J. H. **English**	J. A. **Thompson**
W. W. **Smith**	A. R. **Culverhouse**	W. P. **Blackwell**
C. A. **Crumpler**	R. M. **Deas**	D. A. **Dollar**
G. W. **Denney**	Vernon **Lankford**	J. P. **Sullivan**
J. J. **French**	J. H. **Moore**	J. D. **Hill**
T. J. **Boyd**	P. E. **Harrison**	W. J. **Slatter**
J. C. **Turbeville**	J. L. **Black**	Edd **Goldsmith**
J. G. **Cathey**	J. S. **Bird**	W. M. **Morgan**
J. H. **Taylor**	T. V. **Hair**	R. W. **Faulk**

Second Week

D. W. **Crumpler**	J. M. **Roberts**	A. B. **Rhodes**
W. N. **Moss**	A. J. **Harbin**	L. J. **Dismuke**

P. Hopkins
J. E. Coats
R. C. Campbell
J. M. Blount
W. M. Lloyd
J. M. Buckner
J. A. Monroe
A. C. Beard
J. W. McKenzie
Will McFarland
C. H. Dykes
V. O. Teddlie
W. J. Hines

A. A. Snow
W. H. Mooring
W. M. Crone
A. Trapp
W. R. Banks
C. H. Bridges
C. H. Carter
W. D. Dagnell
J. F. Craddock
J. L. Shoemaker
G. H. Cartwright
Oscar Sims
J. A. Carrington
A. D. Russom
T. D. Dill

G. C. Hopkins
Gus Bogan
W. S. Hardeman
J. T. Rogers
T. M. Carter
T. H. Cartwright
E. Corbitt
J. A. Harris
J. O. Blackwell
E. Q. Shamburger
A. R. Cruse
R. A. Reinhardt
G. K. McKenzie
FOURTH WEEK
D. L. Burkett
G. A. Azbell
J. H. King
F. M. Fletcher
J. R. Tucker
T. P. Turner
J. A. Cobb
W. N. Barnes
J. L. Highnote
M. L. Stokes
A. S. Kennemer
W. J. Seawright
Q. B. Morris
J. D. Cave
J. A. Daniels

R. A. Harbin
J. E. Dobbs
C. L. Dial
M. Dobbs
W. C. Dodgen
G. J. Howle
J. H. McDougal
H. M. Williams
C. W. L. Taylor
H. T. L. Wilson
Joe Williamson
T. W. Liles
T. J. Pogue

J. H. Howell
J. M. Cagul
W. M. Carnes
J. A. Newton
C. L. Tinney
S. N. Reed
R. H. Jones
J. F. McAfee
W. P. Murphy
E. B. Terry
J. J. Lloyd
W. E. Laminack
T. S. Teddlie
J. W. Glenn
J. V. Attaway

Resolution of Respect

Whereas, Golden Camp has lost one of its true and worthy members, Sov. J. R. Greer . . .

We ask that a copy of this be . . . sent to Walter Greer, Port Arthur, Texas.

J. T. Brown, S. W. Caldwell, J. A. Barnett, Committee.

Fatal Ending of Joke

Playing a joke ended fatally with Frank **Pierce,** a young man about 18 years of age in the Lone Star community, Franklin county, Wednesday of last week. Pierce, who had been married a few months, tried to scare his wife by pretending that he was going to commit suicide. He was standing on a barrel and had fixed a belt tied to a rafter around his neck when the barrel head fell out and he dropped. It was a few minutes before he was cut down and a doctor reached him. He died the following day. — Winnsboro News.

Thursday, August 5, 1915

Special Term of District Court

Nothing but civil cases will be tried this term, and there is no grand jury . . .

. . . case had to be continued on account of the illness of Mr. (Ras) **Young,** whom Judge **McCord** tells us in dangerously sick at his home in Longview.

Among the visiting attorneys in attendance . . . **Campbell, Mansell** and **Harry** of Alba; **Jones,** Jones, **Tharp,** and **Landers** of Mineola; **McMahan,** Greenville; **Beavers, Carlock, Suiter** of Winnsboro.

. . . Seeing Judge (Felix J.) McCord on the bench carried us back twenty-five years ago when Frank **Smart** was Sheriff and Isham **Robbins** Clerk of the Court. . . .

Miss Lottie Vickers

Mrs. C. J. **Smart** received a message Friday announcing the death of her neice, Miss Lottie **Vickers,** which occurred that morning at Alamagordo, N. Mex., where Miss Lottie had been for several months with a hope of regaining her health.

Miss Lottie was born at Hughes Springs. Her father died when she was only two weeks old and her mother came with the other children to the home of Dr. S. C. **Moore,** a brother, with whom they resided for several years. She grew to womanhood in the Pleasant Grove country . . . About ten years ago the mother, with the three younger children, went to Austin, where they resided a few years, later moving to Galveston, where they have since resided. About three years ago Miss Lottie developed tuberculosis and was sent to West Texas and later to Alamagordo . . .

The remains were brought to Hope Well, where on Monday, Aug 2, they were deposited beside those of her father, after funeral services conducted by Rev. W. S. **Hopkins** . . .

Besides the mother, Mrs. M. J. **Wise**, two brothers, Dr. **Vickers** of Winnsboro, and Judge Vickers of Lubbock, two half-brothers, Richard **Gorman** and Joe **Wise**, are left, with a host of other relatives, . . .

In Memoriam

Little James Wishel **Chatman** died July 22 of congestion. He had been ill with diphtheria for two weeks before, but had recovered and was suddenly taken ill with congestion about 3 o'clock p.m. and died at 11 o'clock.

He was born Aug. 5, 1910.

The little body was interred in Sand Springs cemetery, Bro. W. E. **Stagner** officiating.

Stagner News. (By Ione)

Mrs. J. H. **Carlile** left last Tuesday for Texarkana for an operation.

J. A. **Carlile** and wife of near Mineola, are visiting relatives here.

Miss Rosa **Green** of Grand Saline, is visiting her aunt, Mrs. Shirley.

Mr. **Durm** and wife of Grand Saline . . .

Miss Emma **Billings** of Hainesville . . . her sister, Mrs. B. C. **Stagner**.

Mrs. **Reed** of Pine Mills, visited her sister, Mrs. R. S. **Collins** . .

Dr. **Hood** and wife of Rhonesboro . . .

Mrs. B. F. **Dial** of Ft. Worth, visiting her mother, Mrs. G. A. **Collins**.

Miss Minnie **Collins** left for Greenville . . . visit her sister, Mrs. E. **Dial**, . . .

L. G. **Robbins**, postmaster at Hawkins . . .

Wood County Newspapers

Judge Heath Very Low

From Court Stenographer Henry **Mings** . . . we learn that Judge **Heath** is very low and hopes for his recovery have practically been abandoned . . . in Pittsburg . . .

Local and Personal

Prof. E. E. **Ramsey**, who has been employed as principal of the Quitman school for next term, came down from Lone Oak . . .

D. B. **Mills**, the East Point merchant . . . witness the raising of his friend, W. P. **Lawrence**, to the sublime degree of Master Mason.

J. H. **Taylor** was here from Pleasant Grove Monday as a juror but was excused on account of a sick child.

Joe **Sarver** left last Thursday for Herrick, Ill., where he goes to visit his aged parents, his father being now 85 and his mother 83 years of age. . . .

T. J. **Brown** and I. W. **Wilbanks** . . . of the Klondyke community were here . . .

Geo. **Williams** and wife of Alba passed through town early Monday morning en route to Hopewell to attend the funeral of Miss Lottie **Vickers**, a cousin of Mrs. Williams.

Miss Ura **Harrison**, of forrest Hill . . .

Mrs. P. K. **Derr**, of Oak Grove, is visiting her daughter, Mrs. Tobe **Robinson**.

I. M. **Morrow** of Cartwright . . .

Miss Bessie **Ellis** of Mineola is visiting her aunt, Mrs. Jas. D. **Harris** . . .

Dr. J. W. **Hargraves** and family of Alba . . .

. . . W. E. **Laminack** and family near Pine Mills . . .

Rob **Daniels** and wife of Oak Grove . . .

Dan **Graham** and family . . . from Alba . . .

Lee **Wilcox**, wife and children were here from Mineola . . .

J. O. **McCreight** and wife of Yantis . . .

Miss Lila **Rape** of the Oak Grove community . . .

Jim **Bullock** was here from Mineola . . . his brother, Rev. R. J. **Martin**, and family.

Arthur **Cox** and wife of Winnsboro and Milner **Cain** and wife of Alba visited with relatives here Sunday.

Judge J. H. **Beavers** of Winnsboro . . .

Buck **Low** and family were over from Alba . . . his brother, R. W., and family.

Mrs. C. O. **Hooper** of Randlett, Okla., is visiting her parents, Mr. and Mrs. J. D. **Moore**, this week.

Jno. T. **Robinson**, Prof. Shelton **Clark** and the Misses **Dorman** were over from Golden Sunday in the former's Ford.

Mrs. Jno. F. **Smart** and Master Ernest **Frank** left Friday for Texas City for a several weeks' visit with her sister. Jno. F. got lonesome Tuesday and hiked out for Sherman to spend the week with his wife's parents, Mr. and Mrs. **Krueger**.

H. A. **Richburg** . . . from Huntsville to Winnsboro . . .

Miss Alma **Chappell** . . . her uncle, Sam **Benton**, and family . . . her home in Alba . . .

W. J. **Goldsmith** of the Winnsboro country and J. A. **Thompson** of Yantis . . .

Mrs. H. **Hedick** and children returned to their home in Sulphur Springs . . . her sister, Mrs. A. G. **Britton**.

I. N. **Webber** and wife of Enid, Olka., are here visiting Mrs. Webber's mother and brothers, Mrs. **Harris**, T. L., Grover and Elmer.

Walter **Perrett** reports the arrival of a fine girl at his home last Sunday. Mother and babe getting along nicely.

Ex-County Commissioner Zack **Alvis** . . . from Winnsboro . . .

On Way to Commerce

N. R. **Turner**, W. J. **McGuire**, W. N. **Barnes**, John **Whitehead** and John **Hall**, of the Redland country, passed through Quitman Wednesday morning enroute to Commerce with a load of wheat . . .

Check Forger Arrested

Thursday morning of last week Deputy Sheriff **Moore**, assisted by Clarence **Browning**, arrested E. L. **White**, charged with forgery of bank checks in Greenville and other places, and turned him over to

Sheriff **Akers** of Hunt county in the evening, who carried White to Greenville and placed him in jail.

White was formerly a resident of this section but had been away for quite a time. He has relatives living near town, who are hardworking, respectable people . . .

. . . The following was clipped from Saturday's Herald:

"White was reared in Winnsboro and Sulphur Springs and has been traveling for drug concerns for a number of years . . .

White is a married man of middle age, but has been separated from his family for some time." - Winnsboro News.

D. S. Lankford Appointed Postmaster at Mineola

D. S. **Lankford** of this city has been notified by the postal department of his appointment to the postmastership in Mineola to succeed J. A. **Thomas**, deceased.

Mr. Lankford is a veteran businessman of Mineola . . .

- Mineola Monitor

New Blacksmith Shop

G. C. **Higginbotham** of Golden is opening up a new blacksmith and general repair shop in the building being erected next door to the **Jones & Cooley** shop, just west of the postoffice.

[At least two issues torn and tattered - - - difficult to determine date. Some evidence that the first is Sep 1916, second is Vol XXI, possibly another June 1914 - includes an ad for July 4 - 18. -Ed.]

Thursday, September 2, 1915

The Forrest Hill Meeting

. . . Those uniting with the Methodist church were: Willie **Maye**; Sallie, Era and Emmie **Douglas**; J. E. **Brown**; Lois **Wheeler**; A. M. **Horton**; E. M. **Sutton**; Rufus **Sutton**; Bessie and Kyle **Rape**; Irene **Davis**; Harvey **Stroud**; Cecil **McRight**; Novelle **Harbin**; Ethel

Kincaid; T. G. **Brown**; Vernon **May**; A. S. **Green**; Nellie **Sarver** and Hydie **Cannon**.

W. C. **Middleton**, representative in the legislature for Wood and Raines counties . . .

Yantis High School Building
[Photo]

This Magnificent Building Was Recently Erected at a Cost of $4,500.00.

The Faculty for 1915-1916 consists of Prof. B. W. **Edwards**, Principal, Miss Bab **Garvin**, First Assistant, Miss Mattie **Morrow**, Second Assistant, Miss Emmie **Seawright**, Third Assistant, Miss Ruth **Wright**, Music.

In Memory of Mother

In memory of our dear mother, Mary Francis **Lee**, who departed this life August 22, 1915. Mother was born in Georgia February 7, 1843, and moved to Coosa county, Alabama, with her parents when quite young. In 1865 she was married to Joseph C. Lee, and to this union 8 children were born, 5 of whom, with several grandchildren, still live to mourn our great loss. In 1906 she moved to Wood county, near Cartwright, and lived there until father's [torn, unable to read] November 6, 1912 . . .

Mineola Monitor Changes Hands

Mrs. J. A. **Thomas** has bought the interest of L. W. **Rogers** in the Mineola Monitor . . .

Mob Burns Negroes at Sulphur Springs

Sulphur Springs, Texas, Aug. 29. - Two negroes, King and Joe **Richmond**, one of whom had been shot and killed during a battle with officers, were burned at the stake in Buford's Park here about 5 o'clock this afternoon by a mob a several hundred men and boys. . . . search that began early this morning following the killing of Depty Sheriff Nathan A. **Flippin** and the wounding of Sheriff J. B. **Butler**.

Wood County Newspapers

Local and Personal

Jon. **Russell** and wife and Little Sarafrank returned . . . from their auto trip .. .

Ben **Taylor** returned last week from Alabama, and much to the surprise of his friends, he returned alone. . . .

Barnie and Bennie **Giles**, the twins, . . .

H. V. **Johnson** and wife came over from Golden . . .Mrs. Albert **Green** and children . . .

W. S. **Thorne** came up from Hawkins . . .

J. J. **Lloyd** and son Fike were here from Coke . . .

Henry **Green** and wife came down from Winnsboro . . .

Dr. W. M. **Meadows** and family of Coke ...

Mrs. J. A. **Wilson** and Master Giles of Bowie . . .

Mesdames Arthur **Cox** and Forney **Denney** came down from Winnsboro . . .

T. L. **Harris** left Tuesday for his old home in Illinois, where he goes to wind up affairs pertaining to the estate of his father. He went by way of Enid, Olka., to visit his mother, who is with relatives there.

Hood **Moore**, wife and children came down from the Grove . . .

Miss Lela **Allen** of Trenton, who has been visiting her sister, Mrs. **Mangrum** . . .

Tobe **Lindley**, wife and adopted daughter of Aransas Pass, are visiting relatives in the county,

Miss Cora **Moore** of Pleasant Grove . . .

Miss Lois **Ballard**, of Mineola, . . .

Jon. **Russell**, Ase **Horton** and Will **Vickery** were Winnsboro visitors Monday.

Lee **Wilcox** came up from Mineola . . .

County Board in Session

The County Board of Trustees . . . composed of A. B. **Rhodes**, trustee-at-large; A. H. **Hunt**, of Coke; L. B. **Hart**, of Mineola; T. J. **Shaw**, of Hainesville; and M. A. **Richburg**, of Cartwright.

Sheriff **Williams** and his son, Ray, went to Terrell Saturday evening with the unfortunate young man, Bob **Hamilton**, who was adjudged insane by a commission Saturday.

Democrat - 1915

Stagner News (By Ione)
... revival here at Friendship church ... Bro. **Floyd**, our pastor, ...

By letter: Mrs. **Carroll**, Mrs. **Miles**.

By Baptism: Mr. **Miles**, Oscar **Stevens**, Arkie **Wood**, Herndon **Jolley**, Hugh **Jolley**, Dell **Jolley**, Guy **Jolley**, Guy **Long**, Mrs. Rondah **Jolley**, Ella May **Myers**, Minnie **Carroll**.

Mrs. **Long** and daughter, Miss Bonnye, and son, Guy, ...

Mrs. J. A. **Eitel**, of Redland ... her sister, Mrs. M. C. **Long**.

Ben **Bright**, wife and babe and Miss May **Turner** ... the former's parents, Josy Bright and family.

Mrs. Emma **Walker** and children, of Cass county, who has been at the bedside of her mother, Mrs. **Carlile**, ...

Charlie **Blondale**, of Stout, ...

Thursday, September 9, 1915

Habeas Corpus Hearing

The case of Elbert **Lake** was taken up Friday of last week by District Judge R. M. **Smith** ... bail in the sum of $10,000. The J. T. Lake case was referred back to the justice court ... set the bond at $3,000, which was made Friday evening and defendant released.

Great Meeting Closed Last Sunday

The following are those who joined the Baptist church by experience and baptism:

Mrs. H. G. **Willingham**, Georgia **Lipscomb**, Lois **Martin**, Wayman **Reed**, W. R. **Farrow**, Allie **Todd**, G. A. **McCreight**, Annie Wallace **Taylor**, E. J. **Taylor**, Avis **Britton**, Charlie Morris **Lipscomb**, Elsie **Moore**, Alamo **Ivey**, Winona **Martin**, Cliffie **Ramey**, Clyde **Koonce**, Mrs. T. L. **Harris**, Ida **White**, Bessie **Reed**, Bury **Ooldsmith**, Willie **White**, Effie **Stone**, Zula **Ramey**, Mrs. T. O. **Craddock**, Mrs. W. P. **Lawrence**, Tonk **Hamrick**, Grogan **Shoemaker**, Mrs. Sul **Smith**, Effie **Rainwater**, H. H. **Baker**, Beatrice **Taylor**, Mrs. J. F. **Nichols**,

Mrs. Dr. W. T. **Black**, Lexia **McCain**, Fay **Brogden**, Ethel **Todd**, -- -- **Todd**, Annie Ruth **Britton**, Norman **Wright**, May **Harris**.

By letter: Mrs. H. C. **Black**, Mrs. S. T. **Kendrick**, Ben **Taylor**, W. M. **Taylor**, J. L. **Black**, Mrs. J. L. **Black**, Mrs. **Koonce**, Mrs. Tonk **Hamrick**, Mrs. D. F. **Sutherland**, Mrs. C. C. **Ferguson**, Bonnie Maye **Sutherland**.

By restoration: W. H. **Todd**, W. R. **Lawrence** and T. H. **Cooley**.

There were three additions to the Methodist church, Mrs. A. **Murck** by transfer and Euel and Harmon **Horton** by profession of faith.

Resolutions

Wheras on the 17 day of July, 1915, an Alwise Providence, in its wisdom, saw fit to remove from out midst our beloved brother, Robert **Kennedy**, . . .

Robert was a young man 22 years of age . . .

. . . member of the Myrtle Springs Baptist church and a leader in the singing class . . .

V. C. **Blalock**, Willie **White**, Jno. **Blalock**, A. E. **McCreight**, H. G. **Willingham**, Committee.

Obituary

On the morning of August 23 about 4 o'clock the Death Angel visited the home of Mr. and Mrs. Milton **Smart**, who were living with his sister, Mrs. Nealie **Baker**, at Ogburn, and took from that home the loving husband who had been sick and suffered for more than a year with dropsy.

He was born January 6, 1881, near Simpsonville, where he was raised and married to Miss Jimmie **Gaines** November 24, 1910.

He leaves a wife, father and two sisters to mourn . . .

Loses House by Fire

The splendid residence of Newt **Reich**, near Calvary, was burned last Thursday night. The loss was total, no insurance whatever, . . .

Mrs. M. E. **Daniels** and family moved to Alba Tuesday of this week where they will reside in the future. Two of her sons have a

Democrat - 1915

position in the school there and her other son and her daughter will attend the school.

Local and Personal

Mrs. Delbert **Arnold** and two children of Greenville are visiting her uncle, S. J. **Benton** and family this week.

Dr. Frank **McKnight** has been here . . . see his brother-in-law, Charlie **Green**, who has been quite sick.

Jno. L. **Pogue**, of Peach, and Jno. W. **Smart**, of Mineola . . .

J. A. **Mangrum** of Trenton . . .

Jno. A. **Craver** and N. E. **Bullock** were here from Yantis . . .

Ex-County Commissioner, J. M. **Ray** was here . . . Uncle Joe, as we call him, has been in Palo Pinto county for several months . . . about ready to come back . . .

Misses Hallie **McRight** and Vanolie **Wheeler**, of the Forrest Hill community, . . .

District Atty. M. G. **Sanders** was here from Canton . . .

Reuline **Thomas**, the Democrat's nephew, came down from Lone Oak Saturday . . .

R. R. **Alvis** and wife came down from Winnsboro . . . their daughter, Mrs. T. O. **Craddock**.

J. B. **Sorge** . . . on Winnsboro Rt. 6 . ..for several months, suffering from sciatic rheumatism, but is some improved now.

Rev. W. S. **Hopkins** . . . from Yantis . . .

Miss Blanche **Derr** of Oak Grove . . . her sister, Mrs. Tobe **Robinson** . . .

. . . Prof. George **McAllister** and wife had moved to the **Stephens** residence recently vacated by T. L. **Harris**.

B. F. **Allen** . . . of Hawkins, . . .

Miss Willmyrth **Dial**, of Miami, Texas . . .

Golden Meeting

. . . revival meeting with the Baptist church at Golden . .

By letter: J. T. **Williams**, Z. T. **Brittain**, J. T. **Brown**, M. Z. **Zeigler**, D. C. **Cave**, J. S. **Cave**, M. Q. **Zeigler**, Adolphas **Zeigler**, W. C. **Dowell**, S. B. **Pope**. Henry **Dowell**, Ada **Dowell**, Vise **Gamblin**,

M. E. **Pollard**, A. V. **Zeigler**, Bertha **Russell**, Maggie **Brittain**, V. M. **Zeigler**, H. L. **Pollard**, I. C. **Williams**, L. M. **Pollard**, Willie **Williams**.

By Experience and Baptism: E. D. **Pollard**, Emory **Loving**, Hubert **Brown**, Reg **Gamblin**, Mary **Sheppard**, Leila **Northcutt**, H. C. **Brown**, Lillie **Smith**, G. E. **Brown**, Carrilla **Zeigler**, Thelma **Smart**, Margaret **Cave**.

The Hawkins Meeting
... revival ... Baptist church ...

By Baptism: Avis **Pritchett**, J. T. **Green**, Horace **Green**, Dewey **Barnes**, Ernest **Ponder**, Gerald **Toney**, Leslie **Thorn**, Tom **Reese**, Henry **Cobb**, Walter **Lunsford**, Dell **Hamilton**, Cecil **Adams**, Bollie **Hitt**, Barney **Giles**, Will **Crow**, Albert **Wells**, Homer **Bartlett**, Edgar **Hamilton**, John **Smith**, Raymond **Humphries**, Geo. **Lynch**, Will **Parrish**, Mrs. B. C. **Reese**, Mrs. Esta **Preddy**, Avereen **Smith**, Mrs. Annie **Head**, Eliza **Ashley**, Jewell **Davis**, Lorena **Barnes**, Mattie **Giles**, Mrs. Nellie **Green**, Mrs. Estelle **Hitt**, Ella **Wells**, Flora **Smith**, Edna **Wells**, Maggie **Dagnell**, Ella **Dagnell**, Mrs. Ollie **Goodson**, Mrs. **Downing**.

By letter: Mrs. and Mrs. L. H. **Reese**, Mr. and Mrs. Henry **Holmes**, Mr. and Mrs. Barney **Holmes**, John **Green**, Emma **Head**, Mrs. S. C. **Dean**, Mrs. Will **Crow**, Mrs. Carrie **Lynch**, Mr. and Mrs. **Barnes**, Mr. and Mrs. Jim **Landrum**, Dr. and Mrs. **Browning**, Rosa **Barnes**, Elmer **Thomas**, Edwin **Walker**, Jesse **Hartsfield**, Jerry **Murrell**.

By statement: Mrs. **Hart**, Mrs. J. T. **Green**, W. C. **Beach**, Dovie **Stokes**.

Leaves for Celina

C. W. **Vickery** left Tuesday of this week for Celina. His family will follow in a short time.

Wood County Democrat - 1916

Thursday, August 17, 1916

Hand Badly Mashed.
While assisting in moving the large safe of the F. & M. State Bank this morning Frank **Gilbreath** had three of the fingers on his right hand badly mashed. . . .

Caney News

Bob **Whitworth** and family of Oak Grove . . .

Arch **Lyles** and daughter, Miss Eva, of Oklahoma . . . the former's sister, Mrs. Alice **Dean**.

Hoyt **Johnson** and Miss Willie **Beckonridge** of Brashear . . .

Mrs. Tyrtle **Roberson** of Coke visited her sister, Mrs. E. L. **Faulk** . . .

Grandpa **Barnette** of Pleasant Ridge . . .

Wess **Hargroves**, wife and babe visited the former's parents at Pleasant Ridge . . .

Jess **Parrett** and wife of Winnsboro . . .

The following were guests of W. M. **McCreight** and family Sunday: Dr. Will **McCreight** and wife of Kirbyville, G. A. **McCreight** and wife of Quitman, J. O. **McCreight** and wife of Yantis, H. J. **Caldwell** and wife of Pleasant Ridge, S. J. **White** and wife, C. W. **Smith** and family, Jepp **Coleman** and Aunt Liza **McIntosh** . . . this family reunion.

Death of Mrs. Higginbotham

Mrs. G. C. **Higginbotham** died at the family home in Quitman week before last and the remains were carried to the home of her parents at Lockhart, Tex., and were buried there.

Mrs. Higginbotham was a daughter of Mr. and Mrs. E. J. **Watts** and was born and raised at Lockhart. She was 36 years of age and leaves five children, the oldest a girl 14 years of age and the youngest a two weeks old babe.

She had been in poor health for several years but her death was very sudden and unexpected.

Death of D. J. Cobb

After months of suffering the spirit of Mr. D. J. **Cobb**, one of our oldest and most highly respected citizens, died at the family home three miles east of Quitman last Friday afternoon. Interment was had at Ebernezer on Saturday following his death, the Rev. H. B. **Jones**, his pastor, conducting the funeral.

Deceased was the last one of the family to answer the roll call. A sister, Mrs. **Jones**, mother of Dick **Jones**, died a few months ago. . .

Deceased leaves the wife of his youth, three children: Frank and George, sons, and a daughter, Mrs. Albert **Low**, living three miles east of town. He also leaves several grand children and other relatives . .

Death of Another Pioneer.

Rev. W. W. **Jones**, an old and highly respected citizen of Yantis, died at the family home in that town Sunday and was buried in the Yantis cemetery Monday evening under the auspices of the Odd Fellows, the Rev. Wm. **Stone**, of Hopkins county conducting the funeral services.

Local and Personal

W. A. **Worthington** of Winnsboro . . .

S. R. **Precise** is visiting his brother at Fredonia, Texas . .

Charlie **Rider** and wife of Cilmer . . .

Mrs. C. C. **Norton** of Newson, visited her daughter, Mrs. Clough **Robbins** . . .

J. L. **Shoemaker** and wife are moving back to Alba this week.

Mrs. J. W. **Power** and son, Z. H. and daughter, Mrs. Zelma **Carlin** of Alba, spent Sunday with her son, J.T. Power and family.

Miss Ima Lou **Reese** of Dallas, and Misses Charm **Kitchens** and Eunice **Wood** of Mineola.

Floyd **Daniels** wife and babe of Hamlin . . . his mother at Alba . . .

Mrs. Dr. **Taylor** and daughter and Delvert **McIntosh** and sister, Miss Girdie, of Bettie, . .

Reuline **Thomas**, the Democrat man's nephew . . . left for his home at Alto . . .

Mrs. Geo. E. **Alexander** left for her home at Shawnee, Okla. . . . visit with her father, Jno. D. **Jones** . . .

Miss Lila **Jones** returned home Thursday of last week from Shawnee, Okla . . . Miss Lila spent several weeks with J. H. **Jones** and family at Ada Okla., and reports the health of both Mr. and Mrs. Jones as being very bad, . . .

Mrs. S. J. **Benton** . . . her sister Mrs. R. C. **Brittain** at Golden . . . moving Mrs. Brittain to the home of her parents, Mr. and Mrs. L. A. **Jones**, . . .

Prof J. W. **McRight** and family passed through town Tuesday morning enroute to Corinth, Van Zandt county, where Mr. McRight and his daughter Miss Hallie have been employed as teachers. . .

W. M. **Craddock** and wife and Misses Emma and Annie **Seawright** of Yantis . . .

Fine Residence Burned

The magnificent two story residence of Dave **Kitchen** was burned Thursday night of last week at Mineola. Dave and his family were in Quitman at the time attending the reunion.

Thursday, August 24, 1916

Marriage License Issued

. . . during the first sixteen days of [August] the following permits were issued . . .:

B. J. **Brown** and Mrs. D. E. **Frazier**
C. G. **Kimbrell** and Miss Callie **Steed**
Zelma **Murray** and Miss Eula **Terry**
Joe **Holmes** and Miss Bertha **Reese**
J. C. **Snow** and Miss Mary **Minchew**
H. J. **Austin** and Miss Roxie **Meody**

G. H. C. **Dickey** and Miss Katie **Murphy**
Dan **Richardson** and Miss Temer **Williams**
Farris **Roddell** and Miss Effie **Lovin**
George **Rainey** and Miss Laressa **Davis**
E. I **Brannon** and Miss Jessie Ruth **Stokes**

Local and Personal

. . . former townsman, Rev. W. M. **Bass** of Lindale, and Rev. **Swindall** of Alba. . . .

Dr. J. H. **Moore**, wife and babe were here from Hainesville Tuesday . . .

N. B. **Pickett** and family moved to Sulphur Springs last Monday, where Mr. Pickett takes charge of a garage. . . .

Hunter **Macon** and wife of Alba . . .

Mrs. B. F. **Perrin** visited her daughter, Mrs. R. L. **Butler** Saturday.

B. L. **Mills** was over from Golden . . .

J. J. and Robert **Lloyd** of Coke visited their son, J. M. Lloyd and family Tuesday.

Miss Myrtle **McNeill** has returned from an extended visit with relatives at Bowie.

Mrs. Grover **Harris** is visiting with relatives in Illinois.

Kid **Macon** of Comanchee, Texas, spent several days here last week with his parents, Mr. and Mrs. H. H. Macon.

Uncle Bill **Peden** and Buford **Brown** of the East Point country were in Quitman . . .

Mrs. W. R. **Clanton** is visiting her daughter, Mrs. J. R. **Mayo**, . .

W. C. **Russell** and family . . . visiting with relatives at Oak Grove . . . left for their home at Merkell, Texas. . .

Smith's Grocery has moved to the new brick . . .

Mrs. and Mrs. **Willis** of Ginger, and Mr. and Mrs. J. E. **Gilbreath** of Alba . . . Miss Lorene **Bozeman** who with her grandmother, Mrs. Willis, . . .

Mrs. S. J. **Benton** visited her sister, Mrs. R. C. **Brittain**, who is now at the home of her parents, Mr. and Mrs. L. A. **Jones**, six miles west of town . . .

Hainesville Items (Uncle Jake)

Mrs. Barney **Stagner** of the Stagner community. . . her parents, T. J. **Billings** and wife . . .

Miss Stella **Bankston** of Cartwright . . .

T. R. **Shaw** is teaching a singing school at Caddo Mills. . .

Chas. **Blackwell** and family and brother, Sam, who were raised in this county, but now of Oklahoma, have been visiting relatives here . . .

Miss Bonnie **Beavers**, daughter of Dr. Beavers of Fouke . . .

Prominent Tyler Man Dies.

. . .told us of the death of John **Durst**, one of the most prominent men of Tyler . . .

Thursday, August 31, 1916

Infant Dies

The infant of Mr. and Mrs. Clough **Robbins**, born Thursday the 24th, was buried the day following. Mrs. Robbins has been in quite a precarious condition since the birth of the babe. . . doing reasonably well since Monday of this week. Her parents, Mr. and Mrs. **Norton** of Newsome . . .

Mineola Monitor Changes Hands

Hubert **Thomas** has sold the Mineola Monitor to W. S. **Davis**, late of Rockport, Texas . . .

Local and Personal

Walter **Low** and Milner **Cain** of Alba . . .

Mrs. Pearl **Hill** of Georgetown . . .

Walter **Miller** has here from Cartwright . . .

Mrs. G. A. **McCreight** . . . her parents, Mrs. and Mrs. Hiram **Apel**, at Mineola . . .

Uncle Billie **Darden** of Floyd, Hunt county was here . . .

Mrs. Edgar **Goodwin** and Master Doyle . . from Ft. Worth . . her parents, Mr. and Mrs. J. A. **Nixson**.

Mrs. E. L. **Foster** went back to Alba today to take charge of her hotel. Mr. Foster will remain here at least until he completes his brick contracts. Mr. **Guinn**, who has been charge of the hotel, is moving to Houston . . .

Prof J. R. **Clark** and family moved to Quitman Monday and occupy the residence recently vacated by Prof **Ramsey** and family.

Our Methodist preacher brother, I. E. **Thomas**, paster of the Methodist church at Alto, Cherokee county, and his wife and three boys, Reuline, Merle and Lewis . . .

H. P. **Taylor** and family have moved to our town from Elmo county, Tenn. Mr. Taylor is a brother of the Taylor boys here ..

Jas D. **Harris** . . . his wife who has been visiting in Mineola, and Mrs. Harris' two sister, Mrs. **Hobbs** of Grand Saline, and Miss Bessie **Hall** of Mineola . . .

Miss Alamo **Ivey** . . . from Hainesville . . . her cousin, Mrs. Dr. J. H. **Moore** . . .

The Hainesville Meeting

For Baptism: Alto **Puckett**, Milton **Day**, John **Thomas**, Bessie **English**, Falma **Caver**, S. T. **Puckett**, Oquin **Veitch**, Beatrice **McDougald**, Lucian **Day**, Golda **Puckett**, Mrs. Pearl **Moody**, Velma **Reed**, Mrs. **Thomas**, Gib **Laminack**, John **Henderson**, A. D. **McDougald**, Bernard **Moody**, Jack **English**, Claud **Cagul**, Charlie **Busby**, Green **Monroe**, J. Frank **Haines**, Leanard **Reed**, Will **Henderson**, J. J. **Puckett**, Erma **Stewart**, Oscar **Riley**, Emmett **Williams**, Clemmie **McDougald**, Willie **Anders**, Mary **Andres**, Lucile **Puckett**, Orie Lee **Monroe**, Alma **Andres**, Milton **Parrish**, Ethel **Stewart**, Cordie **Moody**, Albert **Lanier**, Henry **Andres**, Oddist **Puckett**, Dessie **Stewart**, Charlie **Blackwell**, G. T. **Shaw**, Herman **Puckett**, Clyde **English**, Homer **Watson**, Robert **Reed**, Ray **Stavens**, Ellis M. **Burkett**, Benson **Andres**, Tom **McBride**, Bennie **Cagul**, Arthur **Puckett**, Ida **Hays**, Alamo **Puckett**, Harold **Blackwell**, Morgan **Vickery**, Bertha **Folmer**, G. W. **Hasten**, Josiah **Hill**, Oliver **Busby**, Mrs. T. J. **Harrell**, Marshall **Goolsby**.

By letter: Mrs. A. F. **Folmer**, Mattie **Ivey**, Green **Monroe**, Mr. and Mrs. **Jeffries**, Mrs. **Russell**, Mr. and Mrs. T. J. **Shaw**, Mr. and Mrs. M. V. **Andres**, Mrs. R. M. **Parrish**, Lalie and Lola **Jeffries**, Ila **Wallen**.

Caney News

J. B. **Price** and children, Roy and Pansy, . . .

Claud **Perrett** and family and mother returned to their home at Laneville Thursday.

John **Setzler** and family of Pleasant Ridge . . .

Will **Perrett** and family of Winnsboro .. .

Miss Myrtle **Black** of Quitman

Golden Items

Bun **Dunbar** is visiting homefolks at Campbell.

Rock Hill News

Jasper **Gilbreath**, who has been sick for some time, is able to be out.

Lightning struck and destroyed Uncle Pink **Posey**'s barn . . .

Mrs. Bell **Snyder** of Hawkins . . .

L. R. **Dial** of Hopkins county visited his brothers, Charley and Ben, the past week.

Bonnie **Bridges** and wife of Picton . . . his brother Robert.

C. L. **Dial** and D. W. **Bird** are each building nice residences.

Turman **Gilbreath** has added another room to his residence.

Thursday, September 7, 1916

Oather Cowan Dead

Oather, the 16 year old son of Mr. and Mrs. J. F. **Cowan**, died at the family home 3 miles east of town Thursday evening of last week after an illness of about 48 hours with black jaundice.

The remains were carried to Hopewell for interment Friday where Bro. **Blackmon** conducted the funeral services.

Central High School Opens

There were nine boarding pupils entered the first day of the term . . .: Misses Elton **Posey** and Grace **Rhodes**, Coke; Miss Josie **Simons**, Stout; Miss Lovie **Deas**, Mrytle Springs; Miss Rubie **Laminack**, Mt. Pisgah; Emmer **Gallaway**, Yantis; Curtis **Kirkland** and Arthur **McCreight**, Myrtle Springs; Jodie **Vickery**, Hainesville.

Socialist Nominees

For Representative - Jobe **Holbrook**
For County Judge - A. J. **Weems**
For Sheriff - O. J. **Blackmon** Jr.
For County Clerk - Claude **Vandiver**
For District Clerk - Charlie **Coleman**
For Tax Assessor - C. T. **Dickson**
For Tax Collector - B. L. **Mills**
For County Treasurer - A. S. **Webb**
For County Surveyor - John **Dorman**
For Commissioner Pre. No. 1 - Sam **Flournoy**
For Commissioner Pre. No. 2 - J. S. **Vandiver**
For Commissioner Pre. No. 3 - T. E. **Hall**
For Commissioner Pre. No. 4 - E. U. **Phillips**
For Cotton Weigher at Winnsboro - Will **Shively**
For Cotton Weigher at Alba - Sam **Goins**
For J. P. Pre. No. 1 - W. H. **Gable**
For J. P. Pre. No. 2 - A. **Perry**
For J. P. Pre. No. 3 - J. Q. **Parkinson**
For J. P. Pre. No. 4 - S. B. **Whitley**
For J. P. Pre. No. 5 - E. W. **Perkins**
For J. P. Pre. No. 7 - John **Charles**
For J. P. Pre. No. 8 - J. D. **McQueen**
For Constable Pre. No. 1 - J. C. **Ford**
For Constable Pre. No. 2 - George **Barnett**
For Constable Pre. No. 3 -J. R. **White**
For Constable Pre. No. 4 - L. T. **Harrison**
For Constable Pre. No. 5 - Cecil **Malone**
For Constable Pre. No. 7 - S. J. **Morris**

Democrat - 1916

For Constable Pre. No. 8 - Floyd **Henry**

Nominees Democratic Party

For Judge, 7th Jud. Dist. J. R. **Warren** of Upshur County
For Dist Atty., 7th Jud. Dist. - D. M. **Maynor**
For Representative - J. B. **Lee**
For County Judge - R. E. **Bozeman**
For County Attorney - Floyd **Henry**
For Sheriff - W. H. (Bill) **Apel**
For District Clerk - J. R. **Taylor**
For County Clerk - G. A. **McCreight**
For Tax Assessor - W. R. **Caldwell**
For Tax Collector - S. J. **Benton**
For Supt. Public Schools - J. R. **Clark**
For County Treasurer - W. R. **Vickery**
For County Commissioner, Prect. 1 - V. C. **Blalock**
For County Commissioner, Prect. 2 - J. C. (Cal) **Russell**
For County Commissioner, Prect. 3 - Earl **Voorhees**
For County Commissioner, Prect. 4 - W. H. **Carter**
For Justice Peace, Precinct No. 1 - B. F. **Smart**
For Justice Peace, Precinct No. 3 - W. **Kitchens**
For Justice of the Peace at Golden - M. J. **Zeigler**
For Constable, Precinct No. 1 - H. G. **Willingham**
For Constable, Precinct No. 6 - Joe **Shields** Jr.
For Constable at Golden - R. W. **Gatewood**

Pine Mills News (By The Boy.)
... enrolled in the school:

Boys	Girls
Jessie **Moore**	Nobia **Wagner**
Joe **Shields**	Aubia **Laminack**
Lester **Hobbs**	Mary **Skiles**
Kuther **Giles**	Lynchie **Lindley**
Lofton **Riddle**	Isla **Dobbs**
Troy **Jaco**	Mary **Sarver**
Ramon **Turvill**	Jessie **Turner**

Alton **Giles**
Johnie **Turner**
Johnie **Tucker**
H. W. **Bartlett**
Floyd **Daniel**
Alvin **Mitchell**
Clay **Sarver**
Harmon **Bartlett**
Clyde **McManus**
Homer **Turvill**
Clifton **Lindley**
Condred **Lindley**
Morgan **Reed**
Clyne **Murphy**
Vernon **Laminack**
Dude **Laminack**
Bennie **Cox**
Sam **LaRue**
J. W. **Powell**
Raymond **Mansell**

Inez **Ashberry**
Mae **Bartlett**
Mrs. J. E. **Burkett**
Lillie **LaRue**
Mae **Mezzles**
Ollie **Pinnington**
Opal **Pinnington**
Lorene **Messles**
Mildred **Connell**
Bertha **Connell**
Lillie **James**
Gladys **Carrington**
Thelma **Mansell**
Bera **Reed**
Charm **Reed**
Ester **Tucker**
Bertha **McManus**
Vera **Carrington**
Jessie **Hollon**
Dartha **Dobbs**
Winnie **Hollon**
Sallie **Hughes**
Gertrude **Reinhardt**
Myrtle **Reinhardt**

Hurt in Auto Wreck

R. L. **Butler** received a phone message from Dallas Tuesday morning stating that his brother, Tom, who resides at Big Sandy, had been seriously injured in an auto wreck near Dallas the night before.

. . . Mr. Butler's knee was torn open, exposing the ends of the bone . . . hopes to save his leg.

Local and Personal

K. D. and Jno. T. **Robinson** were over from Golden . . .
Mrs. **Willis** of Terrell visited her sister, Mrs. **Grogan** . .
Miss Cloe **Moore** of Yantis . . .

Democrat - 1916

A. J. **Keith** of Stout . . .
Sam **Galloway** was over from Yantis . . .
C. Y. **Harrington** and family of Yantis . . .
Jim **Strange** and Joe **McKenzie** of Yantis . . .
Miss Biddie **Collins** . . . her sister, Mrs. Tilden **Kendrick**.
J. R. **Nutt** . . . farm west of town . . .
Dick **Gilbreath** of Yantis . . .
O. A. **Floyd**, the barber, tailor and laundry agent at Yantis.
Mrs. W. H. **Low** and her daughter, Miss Mattie **Morrow** . . .
Misses Jessie and Eva **Green** of Winnsboro . . .their aunt, Mrs. Dr. C. D. **Lipscomb** . . .
Misses Vashtie **Goldsmith** and Mary Joe **Nabors** of Winnsboro .
Misses Carrie **Davis** and Bertha **Pippin** of Point . . .
Senator **Suiter** and Atty. Max **Newsome** were here from Winnsboro . . .

W. L. **Lake** has moved his tailoring shop into the Democrat old building recently vacated by **Smith's** Grocery.

J. R. **Greer**, the Crow merchant, postmaster and ticket agent. . . .

Mrs. J. H. **Jarman** and daughter, Miss Helen, came in from Lindale . . . her daughter, Mrs. D. M. **Maynor**.

Mr. and Mrs. Elmore **Wright** and their son, Prof. Tobe **Wright**, of Cartwright . . .

Hon. R. G. **Andrews** and wife . . . from Winnsboro . . .

Mrs. G. F. **English** and Misses Bera and Ila **Billings** of Hainesville. . .

Jon. **Russell**, wife and daughter, of Winnsboro . . .

L. L. **Lipscomb** and his daughter, Miss Addie Maye . . .

W. H. **Stokes** . . . his daughter, Mrs. E. L. **Brannon**, Arcadia, Fla. His daughter, Miss Jessie Ruth was recently married to Mr. Brannon . . .

Mrs. **McCrary**, mother of W. G. and O. G. McCrary and her daughter moved to our town last week from Coke and occupy the residence recently vacated by . . A. **Mangrum** . . .

Mrs. W. S. **Hopkins** and daughter, Miss Rubie, came over from Alba . . .

Mrs. Earnest **Ashberry** and Mrs. Will **Gorman** and son, Paul, and daughters, Nola May and Ona Kay, of Winnsboro . . .

Mrs. A. C. **Beard** and daughter, Miss Florence, of Coke . . with her daughter, Mrs. W. G. **McCrary** . . .

Misses Eveline **Morris** and Otha **Smith** of Winnsboro, visited the former's brother, R. E. Morris and family. .

Miss Lola **Bass** of Winnsboro . . .

Dr. W. T. **Black** tells us that his uncle, W. J. **McGuire**, of Redland . . .

Sudden Death at Alba

Barnie **Johnson** informs us this morning that Mrs. **Scarborough**, widow of the late Dr. Scarborough, died suddenly at her late home in Alba yesterday, Tuesday. Deceased first husband was Will **Johnson**, a brother of Sam and Vince Johnson and was principally raised in Quitman.

Thursday, September 14, 1916

Caney News. (Delayed from last week.)

George **Blalock** and family have moved to Albert Blalock's vacated house.

Killed in Montague County.

Moody **Russell** fell from a wagon at his home in Montague county Monday and died from the effects of the injuries received that night. The remains were brought to Ebenezer, seven miles east of Quitman, and buried Wednesday morning.

Mr. Russell was a son of R. C. Russell who came to Wood county a few years ago and located near Ebenezer and only lived a few years after coming to this county. The deceased married the youngest daughter of Mr. and Mrs. Z. C. **Cox** of the Ebenezer country and they left this county a few years ago and located in Montaque county near St. Jo.

Democrat - 1916

Local and Personal

M. B. **Dykes** was here from Winnsboro ...
Coolie **Morris** and Tillett **Teddlie** were here from Alba ...
J. C. **Jennings** and wife were down from Winnsboro ...
Mrs. J. B. **Wallace** and son, Henry ...
Mrs. **Chappell** of Alba ... her brother Sam J. **Benton** ...
Miss Lorene **Bozeman** ... visit with relatives at Itasca.
J. A. **Ford** ... home hear Hainesville.
Mrs. C. M. **Browning** of Winnsboro ...
L. F. **Lloyd** was here from Coke ...
J. S. **Sparks**, out on route 6, Quitman ...
Miss Mattie **Brewer** of Oak Grove ...
Miss Era **Shaw** of Hainesville ...
N. R. **Brogden** was down from Cartwright ...
Uncle Cris **Higginbotham**, Tom **Hamm** and S. E. **Dewitt** of Alba.
E. T. **White** out at Anson ...
W. R. **Vickery**, our next county Treasurer, has moved to Quitman with his mother and children in order that he may get his boys in school. They occupy the residence recently vacated by Mrs. S. F. **Green** who moved to the Shoemaker home now owned by Dr. **Goldsmith**.
Mrs. **Sutherland** has traded her home at Winnsboro to W. M. **Taylor** for the new residence recently erected on College street.
"The Enterprise" of Winnsboro, has moved into larger quarters next door to The First National Bank ...
Miss Florene **Germany** of Greenville ...
A. A. **Lindsey** and J. W. **Corley** of Winnsboro ...
G. F. **English** was in from Hainesville ...
Atty. Edgar **Tharp** was up from Mineola ...
R. S. **Thomas** of the Golden country was here ...
Mrs. Nora **Campbell** of Alba, ...
R. C. **Thomas** has moved from the Peach country to Quitman and occupies the Dr. **Goldsmith** residence recently vacated by E. L. **Foster** and family.
Frank **Haines**, Prof. Tom **Shaw**, B. F. **Saxon** and C. E. **Williams** of Hainesville ...

Uncle Bill **Peden** and R. E. **Knowles** of the Ease Point section. . .

Rev. **Whiteside**, pastor, Sulphur Springs Baptist Church, Rev. J. W. **Sailors**, Missionary of the Rehobeth Baptist Association, and Rev. **Ivans** of Mr. Vernon and Rev. **Phillips**, pastor of the Winnsboro Baptist Church, . . . visit with Bro. **Blackmon**.

A. A. **Lindsey** of Winnsboro . . . recent trip to Tennessee where he visited his parents. . . .

J. M. **Anderson** of Mt. Vernon was here last week visiting J. T. **Power**. Mr. Anderson was a neighbor of Mr. Power and wife when they lived in Georgia and later in west Texas. . . .

John **Dowell** was in Quitman Thursday from his farm west of town and told us he had sent his wife to Becton's sanitarium at Greenville . . . his wife would undergo an operation the following day if she was able.

Marriage License Issued

For the week ending Sept. 2, 1916, the following marriage licenses . . .:

Corbett **Marshall** and Miss Dovie **Page**
Farnest **Bellomy** and Miss Bessie **Ezell**
O. M. **Mapes** and Miss Daily **Carter**
W. E. **Reid** and Miss Rena **McMullen**
J. W. **Pollard** and Miss Ellie **Hughes**
C. R. **Gollyhon** and Miss Lucy **Dugger**

Vital Statistics

For the week ending Sept 9, . . .

BIRTHS

Reported by Dr. C. M. **Rayburn**, a girl to Mr. and Mrs. Joe **Rushing**, on August 17, 1916.

Reported by Dr. E. C. **Hutchings**, Alba, a girl to Mrs. and Mrs. Tom **Brown** on Sept. 7, 1916

By Dr. E. C. Hutchings, Alba, a boy to Mr. and Mrs. Jeff **Hukill** Sept. 5, 1916.

Democrat - 1916

DEATHS

Reported by Dr. E. G. **Pritchett**, Hawkins, the six and a half months old babe of Mr. and Mrs. J. F. **Green**, cause of death erysipelas, death occurred March 15, 1916.

Marriage License

For the week ending Sept. 9, . . .
C. B. **Turner** and Miss Ruby **Jackson**
Noble **Nance** and Miss Josie **Davis**
Clifford **Reese** and Miss Eliza **Ashley**
Buster **Folmer** and Miss Nora **Walthal**
One license issued and requested not to publish.

Hawkins Items. (Delayed from last week.)

Miss Birdie **McLain** has been very sick . . . on the road to recovery. Little Virgil **Peacock** has also been quite sick but is improving now.

The Stork left a fine girl at the home of Mr. and Mrs. Milton **Smart** Sunday.

Mrs. **Massey** and daughter of Canton . . . visiting their sister and aunt, Mrs. B. F. **Allen** .

. . . Rev. J. H. **Hays** is our Baptist preacher . . . His home is at Greenville. Rev. **McCrary** is our Methodist preacher. . . . union Sunday school . . . Jas T. **Smith** is Supt., P. A. and Mrs. **Thorn**, Bert **Smith**, Mrs. Bertha **Holmes** and Miss Frankie **Allen** are the teachers. . . .

. . . fine school . . . Prof **Rhodes** as principal, and Misses Ascha **Moseley** and Frankie **Allen** as assistants.

Thursday, September 21, 1916

Death of Tom Conger

A. J. **Conger** received a phone message from Dallas Thursday night of last week, Sept. 14, that his son, Tom Conger, had been found dead in a car of lumber in the Katy Yard at that place. . . . remains were brought to Quitman . . . services . . . Bro. **Blackmon**, assisted by Bro.

Calhoun, were conveyed to the cemetery near by and buried in the family burying lot.

Tom was the youngest son of A. J. (Bud) Conger, and was 29 years of age the 31st day of August past. He was reared in Quitman. His mother died when he was quite small. His father, together with two brothers, Robert and Kleber, or Pat, as he is best known, and three sisters, Mesdames Wiley **Williams**, of Winnsboro, and Elmer **Harris**, of Quitman survive . . .

Death of Fine Boy

News was received by Mrs. C. J. **Smart** Wednesday evening of last week that Joe **Wise**, the baby boy of her sister, Mrs. M. J. Wise, had died that evening at the family home in Galveston, and that remains would be brought to Hope Well for interment in the family burying ground. . . . funeral services were conducted by Bro. **Blackmon** and the mortal remains of this noble boy deposited beside those of his father, who preceded him to the world beyond several years ago.

Joe was an exceptionally bright boy, 15 years of age, and was employed in the offices of the Santa Fe Railway at the time he was stricken with pneomonia which resulted in his death.

Besides his mother he is survived by a half brother, Dr. Claude **Vickers**, of Winnsboro, also two sisters, Mrs. Pnewell **Denney**, of Winnsboro . . .

Alf Morris Elected Cashier of First National Bank

. . . Mr. Alf **Morris** was elected cashier of the bank, succeeding W. B. **Sellers**, who resigned to go to Greenville to enter the cotton business. - Winnsboro News.

Death of Mrs. Mattox

Mrs. J. W. **Mattox** died at the family residence in Winnsboro Wednesday night of last week and was buried in the City cemetery at that place the following day, Thursday.

Mrs. Mattox was the step-mother of Mrs. R. W. **Low** of our town . . .

Democrat - 1916

County Court Jurors

... for the October term of County Court which convenes Monday October 2, 1916:

FIRST WEEK

B. H. **Bright**, Quitman, Rt. 5
G. W. **Duffey**, Peach, Rt. 2
L. M. **Farris**, Quitman, Rt. 5
J. B. **McKee**, Yantis
W. H. **Pittman**, Quitman, Rt. 1
R. H. **Reed**, Mineola, Rt. 6
R. T. **Jones**, Mineola, Rt. 1
H. J. **Hester**, Peach, Rt. 2
A. A. **Petty**, Winnsboro, Rt. 3

M. E. **Day**, Quitman, Rt. 3
L. **Harvey**, Mineola, Rt. 1
F. G. **Estes**, Alba, Rt. 3
Jno. W. **Faulk**, Big Sandy, Rt. 1
T. J. **Pogue**, Peach, Rt. 2
J. M. **McLain**, Hawkins, Rt. 1
W. T. **Harbuck**, Alba, Rt. 3
R. D. **Littleton**, Golden
J. T. **Posey**, Como, Rt. 1

Uncle Dock Robinson Dead.

George **Jones** phones us this Wednesday morning, that Uncle Dock **Robinson** died at this late home in Golden at 8 o'clock last night.

Married in San Antonio

J. T. **Shaw** ... informed us of the marriage of Mr. J. B. **Guin** to a young lady of Beeville. The marriage took place last Sunday at San Antonio.

Death of Infant.

The infant of Mr. and Mrs. Charlie **Clanton**, born Monday morning, died in about six hours after birth. Interment was had at Concord Tuesday.

Local and Personal

Postmaster Shaw D. **Ray** was here from Winnsboro ...
Postmaster D. S. **Lankford** was here from Mineola ...
Postmaster J. D. **Blizzard** and wife were over from Alba ...
Senator W. D. **Suiter** was here from Winnsboro ...
Hon. D. M. **Reedy** was here from Tyler ...
Jess **Hartsfield** visited his week with his brother, Luther at Hawkins ...

Mrs. M. F. **Guinn** and children left Tuesday to join her husband at Witchita Falls which place they will make their future home.

. . . Jno. S. **Daniels** of Mineola . . .

Kyle **Wright** left Saturday for Toyah, Texas, to accept a position in a drug store at that place. His family will follow in a few days and they will reside at that place in the future.

C. F. **Banks** and wife and Mrs. Ben **Dial** of Rock Hill . . .

Walter **Smart** was up from Mineola . . .

John **Sarver** was in from Pine Mills . . .

Miss Clyde **Koonce** of Mineola . . .

Mrs. N. J. **Holcomb** of Celeste, is visiting her daughter, Mrs. Jno. R. **Edmonds** . . .

J. H. **Forter**, of Point, . . .

C. W. and W. R. **Vickery** and their families spent Sunday with Martin **Anders** and family near Hainesville, an uncle of theirs from La. having come for a visit down there and they had never seen him . . .

Mrs. Kate **Roach** of Goodnight, Texas . . . her cousin, J. L. **Black** and family in our town.

Carl **Sutherland** came in Saturday . . . has been at Kamy, Texas, for the past three years engaged in teaching school . . .

Mr. and Mrs. Sam H. **Hart** received a phone message from Dallas latter part of the week that they have a new grand daughter at the home of Mr. and Mrs. A. M. **Billings**.

Mrs. A. J. **Britton** and her brother, C. Y. **Harrington** of Yantis, left Monday for Monument, New Mexico, where they go to visit their father, Y. J. Harrington, who is in a very low state of health. . . .

Hainesville Items (Uncle Jake)

Dr. **Shields** of Pine Mills . . . his daughter, Mrs. E. M. **Burkett**.

Green **Monroe** and Miss Lerna **Hartsfield** were united in the holy bonds of matrimony Sunday . . .

Misses Rubie and Nobie **Hartsfield** of Concord visited their sister, Mrs. Charlie **Lindley**, Sunday.

Mrs. Kidd-Key Dead.

Sherman, Texas, Sept 13. - Mrs. Lucy A. **Kidd-Key** died at her home here after a brief illness at 11:25 o'clock tonight. She is survived by her husband, Bishop Joseph S. **Key**, and daughter and one son. They are Mrs. Louis **Versai** and Edwin Kidd, both children of their first marriage and both of whom live in Sherman.

Mrs. Kidd-Key came to Sherman about thirty years ago and has had charge of the North Texas Female College continuously since that time. She was married to Bishop Key about twenty five years ago.

Hawkins Items

The stork visited the home of Roe **McCleney** and wife and left a young lady.

Born to Sim **Thorn** and wife, a fine boy.

Marion **McClain** will move to Pritchett in a short time for the purpose of getting his children in a High school. Sandale community will surely miss this family . . .

Fred **Ponder**, the peanut King of Hawkins . . .

Golden Items

Lon **Mize** and wife have a fine boy at their home.

Bert **Ussery** and wife are enjoying the company of a fine boy who arrived a few nights ago.

A fine boy arrived at the home of Mr. and Mrs. Bruce **Harbuck** recently.

Marriage License

. . . for the week ending Sept. 16, 1916

G. L. **Monroe** and Miss Lemma **Hartsfield**
Oliver **Edwards** and Miss Susie **Reed**
Albert **Dees** and Miss Jimmie **Setzler**
Harry **McConnell** and Miss Martha **White**
Gregorio **Rodigues** and Miss Salastiana **Saltana**
Rufus **Wesley** and Ethel **Bell**.
T. H. **Waddleton** and Essie **Schluter**

(Note: the Monroe-Hartsfield license were issued the week previous and request made of the County Clerk that same be not published until this week.)

Thursday, September 28, 1916

Local and Personal

. . . Dr. W. R. **Stevenson** was here from Winnsboro . . .

Barnie **Chappell** and wife, Curtis **Hinds** and wife and Mrs. **McCollough** motored over from Alba Sunday.

E. R. **Brown** of the Alba News . . .

Walter **Crofford** has opened up a jewelry repair shop in the **Lipscomb & Morrison** drug store.

. . . Mayor J. N. **Howard** of Alba, and C. W. **Arlitt**, of Austin, . . .

Steve **Precise** is having a new residence erected on the site where his old one stood.

Another Friend Gone

The Democrat is indeed pained to chronicle the death of W. A. (Ab) **Potter**, which sad event occurred at his late home near Sharon Wednesday of last week. . . .

Interment was had at Sharon cemetery Thursday following his death . . .

Concord News

E. T. **Hartsfield** and sons are building a new gin here . . .

Miss Lillie **Hartsfield** is visiting her brother and family at Hawkins.

Mrs. **Monroe** and daughter Miss Ora Lee have gone to Winnsboro to make their home.

Mr. and Mrs. Chas. **Lindley** of Hainesville visited the latter's parents, Mr. and Mrs. E. T. **Hartsfield**.

Mrs. Martha **Tucker** of Golden . . . her daughter, Miss Gertie.

Green **Monroe** and wife have gone to Hillsboro, Texas to make their home.

Essie **Pollard** and wife have moved to Hew Hope where Prof. Essie has charge of the school.

Oscar **Laminack** of near Winnsboro . . . his brother Jess . .

Death of W. J. Robinson

Just before going to press last week the news came to us of the death of W. J. (Dock) **Robinson** of Golden. . . .

Uncle Dock was a pioneer citizen of the county and has lived at Golden for many years, just how long we are unable to say. He was here when we came to the county 39 years ago.

If we are able to do so we will get a biographal sketch of the life of this pioneer and publish it at a later date.

Local and Personal

Mrs. Barnie **Dodgen** and children of Winnsboro . . .

Nig **Craddock**, cashier of the Yantis State Bank . . .

Mr. and Mrs. **Gully** of Winnsboro . . .

Ellie **Reeves** of Mineola . . .

Howard **Braddy**, with the Dewitt Mercantile Co., Alba, . . .

R. W. **Jones** , of Farmersville, La., was here last week visiting his nephews, C. W. and W. R. **Vickery** . . .

County Court Jurors

. . . for the October term of County Court which convenes Monday October 2, 1916:

SECOND WEEK

M. V. **Anders**, Mineola, Rt. 6
W. M. **Harris**, Big Sandy, Rt. 1
J. C. **Futral**, Quitman, Rt. 2
H. L. **Denton**, Quitman, Rt. 1
G. W. **Oxford**, Quitman, Rt. 2
W. L. **Johnson**, Quitman, Rt. 1
C. W. **Burnett**, Ogburn
F. M. **Cherry**, Quitman, Rt. 3
R. A. **Greer**, Crow
J. T. **Shaw**, Mineola, Rt. 1
S. H. **Binford**, Quitman, Star Rt.
J. H. **Favors**, Hawkins, Rt. 1
W. E. **Hood**, Winnsboro, Rt. 2
J. W. **Reese**, Hawkins
B. I. **Whitworth**, Alba, Rt. 3
J. M. **Sarver**, Quitman, Rt. 1
W. C. **Bartlett**, Mineola, Rt. 6
A. T. **Carlile**, Mineola, Rt. 1

THIRD WEEK

C. L. **Bird**, Quitman, Rt. 4
J. W. **Bogan**, Mineola
T. A. **Gilbreath**, Yantis, Rt. 2
J. A. **Lindley**, Mineola, Rt. 6
H. G. **Murphy**, Peach, Rt. 1
M. V. **Sorge**, Winnsboro, Rt. 6
R. D. **Andrews**, Winnsboro, Rt.2
H. P. **Turner**, Hawkins, Rt. 1
S. E. **Galloway**, Yantis
P. M. **Foster**, Winnsboro, Rt. 6
Tobe **Wright**, Winnsboro, Rt. 4
G. W. **Patrick**, Mineola, Rt. 2
M. V. **Hobbs**, Mineola, Rt. 6
R. A. **Gilbreath**, Winnsboro, Rt. 4
P. L. **Ray**, Crow
P. A. **Carrington**, Quitman, Rt. 2
A. G. **Tinney**, Winnsboro, Rt. 6
I. M. **Morrow**, Winnsboro, Rt. 4

Marriage Lincense.

Issued during the week ending Sept. 23, 1916:
Taylor **Lloyd** and Miss Ora **Padgett**
Owen **Hays** and Miss Gertrude **Myers**
O. C. **Shirley** and Miss Tisha Alma **Hawkins**
G. W. **Shirey** and Miss Lenora **Martin**
J. T. **Crofford** and Miss Clara Bell **Martin**
Jas. **Clayton** and Carrie **Bell**
Lige **Tatum** and Sarah **Carter**

Hawkins Items

. . . only two marriages, Cliff **Reese** to Miss Eliza **Ashley** and Charley **Revell** to Miss Viola **Brashear**.

Miss Dewey **Walker** has returned to her home at Branchville, Miss. Dewey has been with her sisters, Mesdames **Cole** and **Fowler** for a year or more . . .

Johnie **Blackstone** of Sandale, . . .

Thursday, October 7, 1916 [sic]

J. L. **Hartsfield**, wife and babe, and Miss Ascha **Moseley** motored over from Hawkins Saturday . . . Miss Lillie Hartsfield, of Concord, . . . her brother, Luther and family, . . .

Democrat - 1916

Box Supper at Golden
Saturday night, Oct. 14, 1916
Welcome address - Coston **Adrain**, Jr.
Response - J. H. **English**
Music - Misses Beatrice **Moore** and Ruby **Evans**
Address - R. E. **Bozeman**
Song - M. T. **Galusha**
Address - T. O. **Craddock**
"What the Democrat Has Done For the Schools of Wood County"
- Quincy **Ziegler**
Response - P. N. **Thomas**
Auctioning of Boxes - J. C. **Russell**

Hawkins Items

... Will **Crow** traded his farm one mile from town to Bert **Smith** for his house and lot.

Tom **Davis** of Shady Grove is making preparations for the building of a blacksmith shop and garage or automobile repair shop, southwest of depot.

Levi **Robbins** has part of the lumber on ground for the building of his residence.

Leslie **Thorn**, who is going to school at Mineola ...

... young folks attended singing at Shady Grove Sunday, Virgil **Pritchett**, Gerald **Toney**, and Leslie **Thorne** ...

Byron **Reese** left Tuesday ... will attend the State University.

... entertainment Saturday evening at the home of Mrs. Fletcher **Parrish**, given in honor of Misses Pauline **Toney**, Averine **Smith** and Lorena **Barnes**.

Mr. and Mrs. Tullie **Gilliam** and Mr. and Mrs. Clifford **Reese** visited relatives at Mr. Sylvan.

Miss Ruby **Davis** left for Dallas Thursday morning, where she has accepted a position.

Miss Lillie **Hartsfield** of Hainesville ...

Miss Stella **Peacock** of Redland, is visiting her brother Edgar and wife ...

Golden Items

Prof C. J. **Brooks** went to Alba Saturday . . .

I. N. **Reneau** and Dr. **Shelton** went to Alba Thursday . . .

Prof. R. C. **Brittian** went to Mineola Friday . . .

Frank **Jones** and family of Alba . . .

J. K. P. **Lankford** and R. A. **Northcutt** went to Quitman . . .

T. M. **Reneau** of Alba . . .

Miss Rosa **Patrick** of Calvary community . . .

Hon. Robert **Carliles** passed through Golden Monday enroute home at Grand Saline.

Jno. T. **Robinson** went to Quitman Monday . . .

The Wide Tire Wagon

The first freight wagon with wide tires was brought to Quitman Thursday by Pat **Conger**. Pat says he believes he can haul 1000 pounds more on this wagon . . .

In Memorial.

W. A. **Potter** was born in Jackson county, Ala., June 10, 1875, and died in Wood county, Texas, Sept. 20, 1916. When 7 years of age he came to Texas with his parents, who settled 6 miles south of Winnsboro, near Stout, and in this settlement Bro. Potter lived until death. March 10, 1895 he was married to Miss Dovie **Moore**, to which union three sons were born, their ages being at this time 10, 18 and 20. The wife of his youth, together with the three boys, his aged parents and three sisters are left to mourn the death of this good and noble man. . . .

The funeral was conducted by his Pastor, Rev. W. E. **Stagner**, assisted by Rev. J. R. **Reid** and Rev. G. W. **Alcorn** . . . laid to rest in the Sharon cemetery . . .

- W. M. **Watkins**, J. H. **Tittsworth**, W. E. **Stagner**, Committee.

Rev. W. E. **Stagner** and John **Harvey** were among our callers Monday and the former informed us of the serious illness of Mrs. **Moore**, who lives near Sharon . . .

Democrat - 1916

County Court in Session.

The criminal docket shows the following:

Elye **Butler**, charge abusive language, plea guilty, fine $5.00.

W. J. **Moore**, charge, carrying a pistol, reconizance forfeited and alias capias ordered for defendant.

Shag **Christian**, charge, carrying pistol, death of defendant suggested and case dismissed.

Alex **Roten**, charge, theft, continued by defendant.

Carlton **Bailey**, charge, aggravated assault, dismissed . . .

Wallace **Smith**, charge, assault continued for term.

Bud **Boatwright**, charge, gambling, dismissed . . .

Griffin **Thomas**, charge, unlawfully carrying pistol and rudely displaying pistol, plea guilty to last count, fine $5.00.

Sam **Hurley**, charge, injuring and defacing a public building, jury trial, verdict guilty, fine $25.00.

Will **Shelton**, charge, violating Sunday law, dismissed . . .

Ocie **Turner**, charge drunkeness, plea guilty, fine $10.00.

T. M. **Miles**, charge, serious threat to take the life of a human being, bond forfeited, alias capias ordered, bond fixed at $300.00.

Jas. L. **Youghn**, charge, assault, dismissed . . .

C. C. **Dodson**, charge, theft, dismissed . . .

E. A. **McCarty**, charge, gambling, plea guilty, fine $10.00.

C. C. **Smith**, charge, dynamiting fresh water for fish, continued for the term.

George **Davis**, charge, assault, bond forfeited, alias capias ordered, bond fixed at $300.00.

Willie **Galloway**, charge, carrying pistol, jury trial, fine $175.00.

Sam **Grammar**, charge, dynamiting fresh water for fish, continued for the term.

Gaudie **Garret**, charge, theft, plea guilty, fine $10.00 and one hour in jail.

Vernon **Moody**, charge, disturbing religious worship, on trial.

Burrell **Thomas**, charge, gambling, attachment ordered for John **Payne**.

R. F. **Richburg**, same charge, same order.

Clem **Jones**, charge, adultry and fornication, plea guilty, fine $50.00.

Oliver **Webb**, charge, rudely displaying pistol, plea guilty, fine $1.00.

Mrs. **Kavanaugh** and her sister left last week for Alexandria, La., to visit their father who is sick.

We are informed that our good friend, Prof. J. U. **Searcy** has returned to Wood county and has located near Golden. . . . Mrs. Searcy, we are told, is in quite a feeble state . . .

Local and Personal

Coolie **Morris** and Howard **Braddy** came over from Alba . . .

L. H. **Tackett**, of Ada, Okla. . . .

Hunter **Macon** and wife are here from Alba . . .

D. W. **Harry** . . . his daughter, Mrs. Ethel **Allman**, at Petersburg, Texas.

A Big First Monday.

. . . We have been publishing the Democrat, all told, 17 years and 2 months . . .

Tom Butler At Home.

. . . left the sanitarium at Dallas latter part of the week, came to the home of his parents, Mr. and Mrs. J. P. **Butler**, three miles south of Quitman Thursday, and then on to Quitman Saturday morning. Tom is able to "get around with a stick" but is still pretty badly crippled. . . .

Death Near Alba

From Zan **Owens**, who was in Monday, we learn of the death of Miss Francis **Franks**, whose death occured Saturday night at the family home near Cottonwood, south of Alba. The young lady was about 17 years of age. She was the eldest daughter of Henry Franks . . . Interment has had at Cottonwood grave yard Sunday evening, the funeral services being conducted by Rev. **Swindall** of Alba.

Guin-Stiles.

J. B. **Guin**, of this city, and Miss Maud **Stiles**, formerly of Beeville, but who has been visiting relatives in Oklahoma the past year, were united in marriage at San Antonio Sunday morning at 9:30 o'clock at the residence of Mrs. **Lackey**, sister of Rev. S. B. **Beall**, pastor of the Methodist church of this city, Rev. Beall reading the ceremony.

The bride formerly made Bee county her home, residing at Tuleta . . .

The groom has for the past six years conducted a photograph studio in this city. . . .

Parents Return to Their Home.

The parents of Rev. R. J. **Blackmon** returned to their home in South Carolina last week . . . . they have other children back in the old State . . .

The Collin county son accompanied them to their home, it being his first visit there in about 20 years.

Thursday, October 12, 1916

Two Sunday Marriages.

Last Sunday evening as Bro. **Blackmon** was on his way to Hainesville to fill his regular appointment at the church there, he was met just after he passed Concord church by two young couples of Hainesville . . . united in marriage Mr. Clyde **English** and Miss Maude **Anders**, and Mr. Virgil **Shaw** and Mess Mays **Veitch**.

Hainesville Items

Mrs. Kate **Fowler** of Smith county is visiting relatives and friends at Hainesville . . .

G. F. **English**, the enterprising merchant of this place . . . J. F. **Haines** our other business man and progressive farmer . . .

Irvin **Cowley** is talking of moving to Mineola in a few days.

Begging Pardon For Use of Transom, Man Hangs Himself

Dallas, Oct. 8. - John **Schneider**, aged about 25, begged the pardon of a Main street druggist for using the transom over his back door for the deed, and then hung himself with a rope tied to the top of it. Schneider had been in ill health for many months.
. . . He was a native of Pennsylvania.   - Ft. Worth Record.

Business Section of Hawkins Destroyed By Fire.

The following report of the fire appeared in Tuesday's Dallas News:

Hawkins, Wood Co., Texas, Oct. 9. - Fire that started about 8 o'clock Sunday night in the building owned by Mrs. Minnie L. **Cobb** destroyed every business building in the town, resulting in the loss of property, the estimated value of which is given at $102,000, only a small part of which was covered by insurance.

The list of losses are as follows:

P. A. **Thorn**, general merchandise, $6,100; no insurance.

B. F. **Allen**, drugs and groceries, $3,100; no insurance.

J. B. **Smith** & Son, general merchandise, $13,000; insurance $5,500.

Parish & Pritchett, drugs, $2,000; no insurance.

N. J. **Doty**, groceries, $500; no insurance.

Bowie **Holmes**, general merchandise, $10,000; insurance $2,500.

Marvin **Pruitt's** feed store, $500; no insurance.

J. L. **Fowler**, general merchandise, $2,000; no insurance.

First National Bank, furniture and fixtures, $1,500; insurance $1,000.

C. A. **Peacock**, general merchandise, $2,000; no insurance.

City barber shop, $300; no insurance

A. **Warn**, restaurant and dwelling, $1,000; no insurance.

J. W. **Davis**, blacksmith, $1,000; no insurance.

Mrs. Minnie L. **Cobb**, building, $6,000.

Democrat - 1916

Local and Personal

J. D. **Moore** and family have moved to the J. B. **Wallace** home, Mr. Moore having bought same. H. C. **Black** and family who have occupied the residence this year, have moved to the Kyle **Wright** residence.

J. W. **Brown** of Coke, has accepted a chair in the **McCrary** barber shop . . .

Constable **Whitter** and J. C. **Jennings** were here from Winnsboro . . .

Dr. R. A. **Harris** of Winnsboro, and his brother, Atty. W. M. Harris of St. Louis . . .

Miss Mamie **Moore** is quite sick with typhoid fever. . . .

Dr. V. E. **Robbins** has bought the **Lipscomb** two story residence now occupied by Bro. **Blackmon,** from Dr. C. D. Lipscomb, consideration $2,500. This is one of the most desirable homes in Quitman.

. . . T. L. **Powell** was in from the Little Hope country . . .

W. M. **Harris** . . . in the Tarrepin Neck country near Hawkins. . .

Mr. and Mrs. Ed **Hood** and babe of near Winnsboro. . .

C. W. **Burnett**, manager of the Cash Grocery at Ogburn . . .

Little Lucy **Hart** was taken seriously sick Monday evening . .

Lofton **King**, who has been employed in Dallas for several years, came in Tuesday and went out to the home of his parents, Mr. and Mrs. S. A. King, near Forrest Hill.

Clarence **Ferguson** was called from Dallas Saturday on account of the serious illness of his wife. . . . improving . . .

J. W. **Brown** has moved with his family from Coke to Quitman and occupy the **Stephens** residence . . .

Concord News.

Miss Biddie **Collins** spent last week with her sister, Mrs. Tilden **Kendrick** of Quitman . . .

Mrs. Mollie **Pollard** and two daughters Messes Letha and Lena . . . with her son and wife, Mr. and Mrs. Essie Pollard, of Hope.

Steve **Tucker** and two daughters Messes Golda and Emmie of the Golden country . . .

Willie **Sullivan** happened to a serious accident Friday morning when he fell from the second story of E. T. **Hartsfield**'s new gin where is was assisting in the carpenters work . . .

Clyde **Cain** and Lewis **Anders** of Lone Star . . .

. . . Mr. and Mrs. Clarance **Davenport** at Mr. Pisgah . . .

Obituary

. . . Miss Frances Bell **Franks**. She was taken sick September 28, and only lived 2 days, passing away Sept. 30, at 9 p.m. . . . Her remains were laid to rest in Cottonwood cemetery Sunday, Oct. 1. . . . If she had lived till Dec 3, 1916, she would have been 17 years old.

Marriage License Issued

. . . for the week ending Oct. 7th:
Clyde **English** and Miss Maude **Anders**
Virgil B. **Shaw** and Miss Maye **Veitch**
Thos. **Jackson** and Miss Pauline **Crow**
Hardee **Gilbreath** and Miss Augusta **Tucker**
T. H. **Jones** and Miss Ollie **Puckett**
Evy **Grant** and Jennie **Spencer**, col.
Nathan **Turner** and Delila **Griffin**, col.
Pim **Russell** and Martella **English**, col.

Vital Statistics

No deaths reported for the week ending Oct. 7th.

BIRTHS

Reported by Dr. J. D. **Jackson**, Peach, Rt. 2, to Robert **Romine** and wife, Oct. 1, a boy.

Reported by Dr. J. M. **Puckett**, Hainesville to Lee **Gallian** and wife, July 30, a boy.

To I. F. **Cowley** and wife, August 6, a girl.

Reported by Dr. V. E. **Robbins**, Quitman, to W. A. **Sutton** and wife, Sept 30, a girl.

Reported by Dr. A. M. **Shelton**, Golden, to Bury **Ussery** and wife, Sept. 11, a boy.

To Lon **Mize** and wife, Sept. 14, a boy.

Democrat - 1916

To Bruce **Harbuck** and wife, Sept. 17, a boy.
To Lon **Mize** and wife, Sept. 28, a girl.

Thursday, October 19, 1916

Prof. C. S. Clark Marries.

We are told that Prof. C. S. **Clark** and Miss Lula **Dorman** were married last Sunday . . .

J. H. **Brewer**, Clerk of Oak Grove Camp, W.O.W. . . .

J. F. **Graves**, a former Wood county citizen but who now lives at Plainview . . . enroute to the Cartwright country to visit his mother. Mr. Graves used to be known as "Fiddling Jim" . .

List of District Court Jurors

. . . for Fall term of District court, which convenes at Quitman, Monday, November 13, 1916.

GRAND JURORS

W. R. **Parrish**	John **Benton**	J. E. **Bass**
Oscar **Reich**	W. B. **Bryant**	B. B. **Raley**
W. C. **DuBose**	Jim D. **Harris**	Judson **Shipp**
W. N. **Baxley**	Lloyd **Patton**	C. W. **Moore**
E. Q. **Shamburger**	A. L. **Moore**	Grover **Wilson**
L. J. **Morris**		

PETIT JURORS, 1ST WEEK

Ed **Holly**	L. P. **Kirbo**	C. H. **Shamburger**
C. R. **White**	C. L. **Gregory**	J. M. **Busby**
W. H. **Barnes**	C. A. **Hurley**	J. R. **Brock**
R. A. **Copeland**	W. A. **Arrington**	O. O. **Wallace**
J. W. **Coker**	Harv **Maddox**	W. A. **Spruel**
F. M. **Benton**	J. W. **McAllister**	J. L. **Massey**
T. U. **Carter**	Tonk **Hamrick**	J. J. **Dickson**
J. R. **Connell**	Earnest **Johnson**	R. S. **Posey**
Jno. T. **Smith**	S. C. **Meadows**	J. H. **Barnett**
C. E. **Arrington**	C. L. **Utley**	A. R. **Cruce**
Dee **Corbitt**	T. J. **Rushing**	Cal **Barton**
H. A. **Benton**	R. A. **Harbin**	W. A. **Byers**

Wood County Newspapers

	PETIT JURORS, 2ND WEEK	
J. O. Gilbreath	Sam Wheat	J. S. Willingham
J. B. Goolsby	Jake Holley	J. H. Brewer
O. M. McCorley	J. A. McGee	J. L. Anderson
C. W. Thacker	A. A. Gaddis	Abner Blalock
J. G. Campbell	Tom Baker	Will M. Harris
H. B. Burns	Claudie King	Jno. F. Smart
W. M. Lloyd Jr.	Jno. R. Blalock	W. C. Wilson
W. W. Smith	C. C. Patten	S. R. McClenny
T. B. Breedlove	S. S. Maddox	J. D. Buchanan
C. W. Guin	Rayburn Douglas	H. H. Roberts
R. F. Conger	I. M. Morrow	M. T. Cain
M. A. McAllister	J. L. Robinson	J. A. Snider
	PETIT JURORS, 3RD WEEK	
J. B. Reese	A. R. McDougal	Geo. Payne
C. T. Eubanks	W. P. Wheeler	J. A. Pinson
S. M. Pugh	P. L. Johnson	W. B. Gilliland
J. R. Carlile	Homer Allen	J. W. French
Wm. Tucker	Red Shinn	J. M. Minchew
J. L. Brown	J. F. Cowley	J. A. Horton
Clifford Cain	G. B. Lynch	L. A. Bryan
C. W. Redding	J. T. Self	B. C. Stagner
W. T. Stout	G. W. Patrick	F. M. Reid
G. W. Cartwright	H. L. Cannady	T. G. Tapley
W. V. Cruce	J. R. Kirby	Claude Bellomy
J. D. Cathey	O. E. Galloway	W. H. Kelley
W. H. Bailey	Tom Wheeler	A. Giles
T. G. Gilbreath	J. A. Wilson	E. E. Wright
W. T. Minchew	W. M. Russom	E. J. Taylor
	PETIT JURORS, 4TH WEEK	
J. A. McKinzie	E. M. Horton	W. L. Mathis
J. G. McDougal	J. H. Carson	H. G. Farr
W. J. French	C. M. Sutton	W. T. Crow
J. T. Green	Geo. T. Powell	J. E. Brown
J. M. Caldwell	H. H. Brewer	Martin Turner
H. A. Barnett	Frank Bryan	J. H. Hornbuckle

Democrat - 1916

W. A. **Rushing**	J. E. **Davis**	J. T. **Smith**
A. J. **Owens**	J. R. **Davis**	H. J. **Caldwell**
W. A. **Hardeman**	J. S. **Vaughn**	W. L. **Crofford**
J. H. **Collins**	M. A. **Whitworth**	J. M. **Laminack**
W. C. **Corbett**	Sid D. **Pope**	J. R. **Scoggins**
W. D. **Black**	Claud **Crumpler**	T. H. **Penix**
R. A. **Swan**, Jr.	W. A. **Boyd**	I. C. **Larue**
H. P. **Turner**	W. T. **Smith**	R. L. **Patrick**
T. J. **Copeland**	C. J. **Roberts**	D. **Dagnell**

In Texas 70 Years

Grandpa **Nash** left Wednesday morning for Winnsboro to spend a few weeks with his daughter, Mrs. Q. B. **Morris** and family. . . . This good man will celebrate his 70th birthday next Saturday, October 14th, and near the end of December he will round out 70 years in the Lone Star State. When the subject of this sketch was two months old his father came to Texas from Northern Louisiana and Texas has been his home ever since.   - Lone Star News.

The County Teachers

. . . with the exception of two, detained at home on account of sickness, every teacher in the county is in attendance.

Quitman - T. O. **Craddock**, B. W. **Edwards**, Miss Myrtle **Black**, Miss Mozelle **Taylor**, Mrs. Olga **Wright**.

Lone Star - Miss Aver **Newman**, Miss Lois **Sims**.

Reinhardt - Geo. **McAllister**.

Clover Hill - Raborn **Douglas**.

Cartwright - Guy E. **Wisener**, Joe **Rhodes**, Lille **Tucker**, Zella **Cain**.

White Oak - W. M. **Wiggins**.

Rock Hill - Lillie **Jackson** and Elton **Posey**.

Forest Home - R. L. **Simmons**, Pearl **Newman**.

Midway - Lora **Harris**.

Chalybeate - Robt. **Womack**, Mrs. Robert **Womack**.

Spring Hill - J. M. **Lawrence**, Kate **Browning**

Pleasant Hill - Holland **Shirey**, Montz **Shirey**.

Coldwater - J. C. **Huff**, Mary E. **Boyd**.
Shady Grove - Mattie Lee **Simons**, Nannie **Bryant**.
Stout - T. J. **Shaw**, Ethel **Robinson**, T. R. **Shaw**.
Crow - J. J. **Puckett**
Lloyd -Mattie **Brewer**, Minnie **Evans**, Martha **Attaway**.
Common Ridge - Ida Mae **Dickson**, Leaths **Pollard**.
Mt. Pisgah - T. A. **Lipscomb**, Lillie **Strickland**, Georgia **Pullen**
Liberty - E. S. **Hartsfield**
Hawkins - G. C. **Rhodes**, Achsa **Moseley**, Frankie **Allen**.
Pleasant Ridge - H. J. **Caldwell**, Ida **White**, Florence **Beard**, Winnie **Head**.
Belle Font - Rosa **Patrick**, Madgie **Dowell**.
Lone Pine -Edith **Vandiver**, Eunice **Vandiver**.
Smith -Ida **Snow**.
Salem - T. S. **Teddlie**, Mrs. T. S. **Teddlie**.
Webster - Maba **Richburg**, Minnie Lee **Browning**.
Vernon - T. C. **Oxford**, Lois **Huckeba**.
Cottonwood - Bessie **Ezell**.
Concord - J. H. **Awtry**, Ola **Sims**.
New Hope - R. H. **Powell**, Mrs. R. H. **Powell**, Vera **Mitchell**.
Mt. Enterprise - R. J. **Martin**.
East Point - Odessa **Cox**.
Caney - Hill **Robbins**, Beuna **Henderson**.
Union Hill - Lucy **Burnett**.
County Line - C. E. **Baxley**, Mrs. Annie Belle **Baxley**.
Gilbreath - A. L. **Taylor**, T. M. **Taylor**.
Merrimac - V. O. **Teddlie**, Kate **Logan**.
Sandale - J. S. **Richburg**, Emma **Snow**.
McGee - M. C. **Shirey**, Mrs. Linnie **Shirey**.
Gamblin - A. E. **McCreight**.
Fouke - Mollie **Veitch**.
Peach - Lillie **Harris**.
Ogburn - Ara **Schrum**, Winona **Sims**.
Wayside - Burnice **Holbrook**.
Honey Creek - J. E. **Green**.
Oak Grove - J. H. **Hurst**, Annie **Caldwell**.

Democrat - 1916

Jones - Alvin **Carrington**, Mrs. Ruth **Robinson**.
Hainesville - J. W. **Truss**, Mrs. Jessie **English**, Fay **Malone**.
Ayer - H. M. **Butts**, Nettie **Dorman**.
Westbrook - V. S. **Scoggins**, Amy **King**.
Stagner - Herman **Puckett**.
Gunter - Lula **Dorman**.
Mill Springs - E. D. **Pollard**.
Stormville - J. F. **Dial**

The following independent districts cooperate with the county teachers' institute.

Pleasant Grove - Harrison **Bullock**, Lula **Huckeba**, Grace **Rhodes**, Libbie **Nichols**.

Yantis - L. M. **Stone**, Terrell **Kitchens**, Annie **Seawright**, Willie Mae **Douglas**.

Golden - C. J. **Brooks**, Willie **White**, Myrtle **Zeigler**, Mrs. Roxie **Austin**.

The three independent districts of Mineola, Winnsboro, and Alba do not affiliate with the county teachers' institute.

Death of Infant.

The many Quitman friends of Mr. and Mrs. J. E. **Gilbreath** of Alba, deeply sympathise with them on account of the death of their infant which occurred Saturday. Interment was had at Pleasant Ridge Sunday evening.

Marriage License Issued.

For the week ending Oct. 14, . . .:
J. H. **Carlile** and Mrs. Josie **Riley**.
D. T. **McWhorter** and Miss Bertie Lee **Green**.
C. S. **Clark** and Miss Lula **Dorman**.
H. D. **Spigner** and Iva **Parker**, col.
Claud **Dean** and Bertha **Garrett**, col.
Loss **Gunter** and Jewel **Session**, col.

Vital Statistics

No deaths reported for the week ending Oct. 14th.

BIRTHS

August 22, to V. **McMillan** and wife, a girl, reported by Dr. J. M. **Puckett** of Hainesville.

October 3rd, to W. R. **Farmer** and wife, a boy, reported by Dr. J. M. **Puckett** of Hainesville.

October 6th, to Dr. and Mrs. A. P. **Buchanan**, a girl, reported by Dr. A. B. **Moody**, of Mineola.

October 4th, to Gordon **Franks** and wife, a girl, reported by Dr. F. V. **McKnight**, of Alba.

Thursday, October 26, 1916

Forrest Hill Dots.

Miss Alma **Junor**, of Cartwright . . .

Lon **Baker** and daughter Jewel, of Oak Grove . . .

Mrs. G. B. **Cook** left last Wednesday for Simsboro, La., to visit her parents.

Rev. J. A. **Wheeler**, of Ector, Texas, visited his mother the past week.

Jack Sparks Dead.

We are pained to learn of the death of Jack **Sparks**, an old and highly respected citizen of the Bellefont community, which sad event occurred the past week. . . .

J. L. Raley Dead.

. . . the death of J. L. **Raley** which occurred at his home near Clover Hill Tuesday evening. . . .

Local and Personal

Mrs. **Nichols**, of Timpson, is visiting . . .

Leonard **Willis** and family of Como, . . .

Miss Blanche **Derr** of Oak Grove, visited her sister, Mrs. Tobe **Robinson**, Sunday.

Morgan **Boozer** and wife spent Sunday with Mrs. Boozer's parents, Mr. and Mrs. W. E. **McNeill** in our town.

Miss Evelyn **Morris**, of Winnsboro, . ..

Misses Pet and Annie Maye **Smith**, of Hawkins, . . .

Nathan **Morris** and his sister, Miss Euna Maye, of Winnsboro, visited their brother, R. E. Morris and family. . .

W. A. **Thomas**, of Dallas, G. N. **Caler**, of Runnels county, and Hubert Thomas were in Quitman Tuesday looking after probate matters pertaining to the estate of the late J. A. Thomas and wife.

Mrs. Jno. R. **Edmonds** returned Monday from Baird, Texas where she was called several days ago on account of the serious illness of her sister, Mrs. H. F. **Phillips**. . . . greatly improved . . .

John **Thomas**, a nephew of the Democrat man, whose home is in Ft. Worth, . . .

Stagner News

Will **McKenzie** returned home from the west Saturday.

A. T. **Carlile** of near Mineola . . .

J. H. **Carlile** of this place and Mrs. **Riley** of near Hainesville were quietly married last Wednesday.

Another Pioneer Gone

. . . the news came that Mrs. A. J. **Vaughn** had passed away at the family home six miles east of Quitman.

The funeral service was held at Ebenezer Saturday at 11:30, and was conducted by Rev. J. C. **Calhoun**. Interment was had immediately following . . . this pure woman was deposited beside . . a former husband, John H. **Malone**, who preceded her to the other side several years ago.

Her second husband, A. J. **Vaughn**, and two sons, Charlie and Jim Malone, with an adopted son, J. E. **McDade**, together with a number of grand and great grand children survive . . .

Vital Statistics

Sept. 3, to Mr. and Mrs. J. T. **Adams**, Yantis, a girl.
Sept. 11, to Mr. and Mrs. Tom **Coker**, Yantis, a girl.
Sept. 15, to Mr. and Mrs. Roy **Thompson**, Yantis, a boy.
Oct. 4, to Mr. and Mrs. Bill **Finkley**, Yantis, a girl.

Oct. 11, to Mr. and Mrs. Geo. **Wyatt**, Yantis, a girl.
Oct. 11, to Mr. and Mrs. Jim **McLaughlin**, Yantis, a boy.
Oct. 12, to Mr. and Mrs. B. J. **Thompson**, Hainesville, a boy.
Oct. 15, to Mr. and Mrs. John **Vaughn**, Yantis, a girl.
Oct. 16, to Mr. and Mrs. H. H. **Cattney**, Yantis, a girl.
No deaths reported for the week ending Oct. 21.

Marriage License Issued

For the week ending Oct. 21, . . .:
A. B. **Craig** and Miss Mattie **Folmer**.
Orin **Smith** and Miss Lula **Allen**.
Uriah **Short** and Miss Audrey **Dickerson**.
Willie **Jones** and Miss Della Lottie **Dale**.
Rufus **Raley** and Miss Maggie **Pugh**.
Charlie **Castleberry** and Mrs. J. L. **Oliver**.

Hainesville Items

A beautiful baby girl is now staying at the home of Varner **Allen** and wife.
Mrs. R. H. **Reed** and daughter Velma . . .
T. J. **Shaw** and son, Theodore, . . .

Hawkins Items

Hugh **Pennal**, of Gladewater, . . .
Alex **Barbier**, helper at the depot left Friday for his home in New Orleans . . .
George **Herbert** and family have moved to the **Sasser** house recently vacated by W. R. **Parrish**.
Rev. **Edmonson**, of Grand Saline, visited his sister, Mrs. **Barnes** . . .

Golden Items

Mrs. Will **Ralinson** and children visited her aunt, Mrs. Will **Butts**, of Calvary, Sunday.

Thursday, November 9, 1916

Marriage License
. . . issued during week ending Nov. 4, 1916:
L. V. **Petrea** and Miss Mattie **Toles**.
W. H. **George** and Miss Stilla **Alexander**.
J. G. **Ussery** and Miss Carlie **Jones**.
R. T. **Webb** and Miss Lura B. **Hammonds**.

Injured in Auto Accident Tuesday
Dr. W. L. **Baber** was the most seriously injured of four occupants of an automobile which turned turtle off a bridge on the Quitman road four miles south of this city Tuesday afternoon. Those in the car were Dr. Baber, and little son, W. L. Jr., Henry **Marshall**, and J. I. **Conner**, the owner and driver of the car. . . .   - Winnsboro Free Press.

Building Fine Residence
Hon. B. F. **Catney** is having erected a fine two-story residence on his farm one and a half miles west of town. . . . E. P. **Ramey** is the contractor . . .

Local and Personal
Jessie **McNeill**, who is now with the Alba News . . .
Charlie **Dewitt** and Will **Lloyd** of Alba . . .
Cashier W. M. **Craddock** of the Yantis State Bank . . .
Mesdames Sallie **Turman** and Lou **Cash** of the Mr. Enterprise community . . .
E. C. **Rogers** and daughter and Mrs. Ben **Dial** of Rock Hill . .
Mesdames C. A. **Peacock** and Jas T. **Smith** of Hawkins . . .
P. K. **Derr**, of Oak Grove . . .
Mrs. Forrest **Acker** came in from Colorado Springs, Col., Tuesday for an extended visit with her father, Jno. D. **Jones** and family. . . .
A. J. **Peddy** was in from Yantis Monday . . .
W. S. **Poe** was in from Ogburn today . . .
Hon. B. A. **Carter** was here from Emory . . .
W. B. **Rogers** was in from Stinson . . .

Hon. A. B. **Rhodes** was in from Coke . . .

Bert **Smith** . . . at Hawkins . . .

Milner **Cain** and wife and Mrs. **Daniels** and daughter, Mrs. Marvin **Moxley**, of Alba visited with relatives and friends here sunday, all returning to their home Sunday afternoon except Mrs. Daniels who will visit with her brother, I. W. **Robbins**, and family here and with her son at Oak Grove before returning home.

Barber Shop Moved

W. H. **Ayer** has moved his barber shop into the concrete building known as the Democrat old stand, Pete **Lake** having moved his tailoring shop into the Nixon building on south side of square next to the picture show house. . . .

Obituary

Mrs. Emily A. **Vaughn**, was born in Alabama, September 22, 1844; died October 20th, 1916.

Married in 1864 to Jno. H. **Malone**. To this union three children were born. C. A. and J. H. Malone, Jr. and Mrs. C. M. **Thompson**, who is deceased.

Mr. Jno. H. Malone and wife moved to Texas in 1867 and remained here until his death, which occurred some fifteen or sixteen years ago.

Mrs. Malone was again married in April 1905 to A. J. Vaughn.

Aunt Em, as she was familiarly called . . .

Cartwright News

Tom **Shelton**, of Winnsboro, and uncle Abb **Harris** and Butler **Turner** of Pleasant Grove, . . .

Ex-Governor Dead.

G. C. **Little**, of Hainesville, was in Monday and handed us a notice of the death of Ex-Governor Little of Ark., which he clipped from the Little Rock Gazette. Gov. Little was a relative of Mr. G. C. Little . . .

Democrat - 1916

"Little Rock, Ark., Oct. 29 - John Sebastian **Little**, ex-governor of Arkansas and ex-congressman, died here today after a lingering illness. He was 64 years old, and was the first white boy born in Sebastian county. He served in Congress from 1894 to 1906. In 1907 he was elected Governor, and served until 1909 when he resigned because of ill health."

Vital Statistics

No deaths reported for week ending Nov. 4.
Births:
Oct. 1 - To Cleve **French** and wife, Quitman Rt. 4, twin boys.
Oct. 9 - To Carl **Armour** and wife, Mineola Rt. 3, a girl.
Oct. 10 - To J. L. **Brumley** and wife, Quitman, a boy.
Oct. 10 - To H. J. **Wilder** and wife, Quitman, a boy.
Oct. 24 - To Charlie C. **Blackmon** and wife, near Mineola, a girl.
Oct. 26 - To Roy **Awtry** and wife, Oak Grove, a boy.
Oct. 26 - To Robert **Daniels** and wife, Oak Grove, twin girls.
Oct. 30 - To Everett **Lee** and wife, Quitman Rt. 4, a girl.
Oct. 30 - Clem **Griffin** and wife, near Mineola, twins, a boy and a girl.
Oct. 31 - To Joe **Lloyd** and wife, Alba, Rt. 2, a boy.
Nov. 1 - To Jess **Marlow** and wife, near Quitman, twins, a boy and a girl.
Nov. 1 - To Walter **Mills** and wife, Alba Rt. 3, a boy.

Hainesville Items

Mrs. Rose **O'Connel** of Marshall is visiting at the home of her brother, Varner **Allen**, and family.
Misses Georgia **Pullen** and Dynchie **Lindley** of Mr. Pisgah . .
Mr. and Mrs. Irving **Cowley** of Mineola . . .

Hawkins Items.

E. R. **Crone** of Como . . .
Bert **Smith** and sisters, Misses Lillie Belle and Flora . . .
Misses Ethel and Mrytle **York** and brother, Mr. York, of Gladewater . . .

Edward **Walker** of Calvert, who has been visiting his sister, Mrs. J. L. **Fowler** . . .

Little Martin **Compton**, babe of Mr. and Mrs. Frank Compton, died at their home in Dallas last Monday. Its body was shipped here for burial Tuesday. Little Martin was about 15 months old.

Local and Personal

Uncle Jake **Benton** and wife were down from their home near Coke last week and spent the night with their son, E. Benton, and family . . .

F. L. **Fowler** and wife, Miss Aileen Reese and Clarence **Ferguson** came down from Dallas.

Shaw **Ray**, Alf **Morris**, Frank **Morris**, Max **Newsome**, and Johny **James** were here Monday from Winnsboro . . .

Thursday, November 16, 1916

Sheriff Elect Apel Moved In.

Sheriff elect W. H. **Apel** and his daughters moved to the jail Tuesday and Sheriff **Williams** and family moved to the **Stephens** residence in the north part of town recently vacated by Garland **McCrary** and his mother, who moved back to Coke the past week.

Goes Back To Hawkins

Walter **Smart** was here Tuesday and tells us he has bought the interest of Luther **Hartsfield** in the First National Bank at Hawkins and will take charge of same next week.

Marriage Licenses.

. . . for the week ending Nov. 11, 1916:

W. E. **Cartwright** and Miss Margarett **Bradley**
C. A. **Spears** and Miss Margie **Kelley**
G. E. **Cofer** and Miss Lillie **Isbell**
T. H. **McAfee** and Miss Lorena **Wade**

Democrat - 1916

Vital Statistics.
BIRTHS
Oct. 12 to Joe **Newsom** and wife, near Quitman, a girl.
Nov. 5 to J. C. **Plocher** and wife, near Quitman, a boy.
Nov. 7 to Boss **Gaddis** and wife, near Quitman, a boy.

Concord News.
Uncle Hugh **Shaw** . . . the guest of his son, J. T. Shaw and family.
Mrs. J. B. **Mount** and two children, Glyn and Charlie Lue, of Quitman, visited her brother, E. T. **Hartsfield** and family Sunday.

Local and Personal
Mrs. M. L. **Moody** and her daughter, Miss Frankie, of Greenville, . . .

Uncle Billie **Blackwell** of the Hainesville community . . .

Jno. F. **Smart** . . . at Sherman . . . visiting with his wife's parents, Mr. and Mrs. **Kruger**, and his sister, Miss Maggie, who is attending Kidd-Key College.

Miss Maude **Low** of Alba . . .

Misses Mary **Daniels** and Maggie **Dixson** of Alba . . .

Mrs. J. T. **Lake** visited her daughter, Mrs. Thurmon **Touchton** at Mineola . . .

Mrs. Emma **Jones** who has been in San Francisco, Cal. for the past eight months, spent a few days with her brothers, G. W. and Dr. C. D. **Lipscomb** here the past week, returning to her home at Mineral Wells Wednesday.

Hainesville Items.
Prof. T. J. **Shaw** and family moved to Stout the past week.

Gordon **Sharman** of Smith Co., is visiting friends (?) and relatives this week.

Mrs. J. E. **Burkett** visited her sister, Mrs. E. M. Burkett Tuesday of last week.

Married Sunday.

Rev. G. W. **Alcorn** writes us that he united in marriage last Sunday Mr. Willie **Jackson** and Miss Ethel **Wheeler**. The marriage occurred at the home of the bride's parents near Ebenezer.

Thursday, November 23, 1916

G. L. Higgins Dead

News reached us Thursday of last week of the death of G. L. **Higgins** which occurred at his late home in Dallas Wednesday night the 15.

Deceased was an employee in the Democrat office for nearly two years . . .

He was buried in Dallas Thursday of last week.

Death of Mrs. Ellis

The many friends of Rev. G. E. **Ellis**, until a few weeks ago pastor of the Mineola Baptist church . . . the death of his wife which occurred at the family old home in Mt. Selman, Texas, Wednesday of last week. Interment was had in the family burrying ground at the home town, Mt. Selman.

Miss Lela Samples

Miss Lela **Samples** died at the home of her sister, Mrs. G. W. **Lipscomb**, Monday night of this week after an illness of several months. Interment was had in Quitman cemetery Tuesday evening at 3 o'clock . . .

Hainesville Items

A tenant house on Dr. **Puckett**'s farm occupied by Charlie **Hill** was destroyed by fire Friday of last week.

Local and Personal

The Democrat received an appreciated visit from Will **Beggs**, the gentlemanly M. K. & T. station agent at Winnsboro . . .

Bob **Edmonds** and wife are rejoicing over the arrival of a fine girl at their home, born Saturday, Nov. 18.

S. J. **Sandifer** . . . paper . . changed to Decatur, to which place he and family have gone to make their home.

Hawkins Items.

Mr. **Odem** left Sunday on the early morning train in response to a telegram announcing the death of his youngest sister, whose home is in Waxahachie.

Hugh **Adams** of Forney. . .
Herbert **Kay** of Big Sandy . . .
Walter **Shaw** of Mineola . . .
Dr. **Pritchett** of Venice . . .

Thursday, December 7, 1916

Barn Burned.

The barn of Mrs. Hattie **Cathey** was destroyed by fire last Saturday night.

Hainesville Items.

Mrs. Haskie **Lindley** visited her mother, Mrs. Tell **Hartsfield**.

Mrs. **Carr**, of Fouke Mill is visiting her daughter, Mrs. Allen **Henderson**.

Cartwright News

John **Cole** of Winnsboro spent Sunday with his sister, Mrs. P. M. **Eakes**.

Golden Items.

Woodie **Caldwell** is smiling over the arrival of a fine boy at his house.

Henry **Brickey** is rejoicing over the arrival of a fine boy at his house.

W. O. **Zeigler**, of Concord, . . . his son, M. J. Zeigler.

Wood County Newspapers

Prominent Young People Wed.

Mr. Jim **Porter**, son of Mr. and Mrs. C. P. Porter, and Miss Lois **Cain**, daughter of Mr. and Mrs. M. K. Cain, were married in Quitman Tuesday Dec. 5th.

. . . both were reared near Cartwright.

Some objection was raised by the father of the bride and it was some time before the marriage license could be secured; however, the scholastic rolls showed Miss Lois to be 18 years on Tuesday, the 5th, and the Clerk finally issued the license.

Local and Personal

W. S. **Hopkins** Sr. of Alba . . .

Mrs. Lee **Wilcox** and children visited her parents, Mrs. and Mrs. Charlie **McCain**, at Mineola. . . .

Atty. Caloway **Calhoun** of Tyler . . . his parents, Rev. and Mrs. J. C. Calhoun in our town.

R. A. **Swan** Sr. and R. A. Swan Jr. . . . their home east of Winnsboro . . .

Mr. and Mrs. **DeLaney**, Mrs. J. L. **Pogue** and Dick **Lindley** came up from Peach . . .

Mrs. Arthur B. **Hobbs**, wife of Editor Hobbs of the Edgewood Enterprise, visited her sister, Mrs. Jas. D. **Harris** . . .

Emmett **Awtry** and family of the Oak Grove community . . . Mrs. Awtry's parents, Mr. and Mrs. J. H. **Williams** at Mineola.

Mack **Kitchen** was down from Yantis . . .

Robert **Gilbreath** who left this county something over a year ago and went to Crosby county is here on a visit with Mrs. Gilbreath's parents, Mr. and Mrs. C. D. **Turner**, and other relatives. . . . write to him at Cone, Texas . . .

Mr. and Mrs. W. F. **Browning** of Merrimac . . . Mrs. Browning has lived in Wood county all her life and Monday was the first time she was ever in Quitman . . .

L. J. **Morris** and two daughters, Misses Rosa and Florence, of Cartwright . . .

Quintis **Beard**, S. S. **Maddox**, J. O. **Whitter**, and A. M. **McAllister**, of the Forrest Home country, . . .

Mrs. R. J. **King**, of Pleasant Grove . . .
T. B. **Turner** was in from his farm near Pine Mills . . .
Mr. and Mrs. O. Y. **Roten**, Winnsboro rt. 6 . . .
Misses Ruby Mae **Lott** and Gladys **Shirey** of Mineola . . .
P. H. **Huckabe** was in from his farm hear Pleasant Grove . . .

Obituary

Mrs. **Isham** was born April the third 1856, and died Nov. 21, 1916, being 62 years and 7 months old. She leaves a husband and 7 children to mourn . . .; 4 girls and three boys living. She has three children who passed over the river to await . . .

Mother was a native of the good old state of Virginia. She was brought to Texas at the age of five . . . She died at her home in Van Zandt County near Edgewood and her remains were carried to Hunt County and burried at old Shiloh cemetery . . .

Oak Grove News.

Will **Cain** and wife have moved to Dallas.

Notice in Probate.

. . . commanded to summon William **Chadwick**, Sarah C. **Horne**, J. L. Chadwick, T. H. Chadwick, O. D. Chadwick, Mrs. Mattie **Moody**, Mrs. Katie **Kennedy**, O. B. Chadwick, Curtis **Arrant**, James A. Chadwick, Veola S. Chadwick, Ruby Chadwick, Walter Chadwick, Grover Chadwick, Margaret **Thornton**, Mattie **Clark** and Sarah **Burgess** . . .answer a petition files in said Court by Mrs. Leon C. **Wilson** et al., heirs of the estate of Mrs. Jane **Stapler**, Deceased .

Thursday, December 14, 1916

Retrospective and Prospective

In the summer of 1893, A. **Paden** came to Quitman, got a few of the most enterprising men of the town to form a joint stock company and . . . went over to Dallas and bought the (Vaughns Ideal hand press, a job press and a few cases of type). August 24, 1893, the first issue of the Democrat made its appearance. Mr. Paden continued in charge of the business until 1896, and about July of that year he gave it up and moved away. . . . a brother-in-law of Mr. Paden who issued it for a few weeks. . . . Walter **Grogan**, Walter and Edwin **Goodwin** got out the remaining issues in August . . .

Arrest is Made.

The Dallas News of Tuesday carried an announcement from Point to the effect that Charles **Carter** living near Point, had been arrested and placed in jail charged with the offense of robbing the Point bank and killing cashier **Glass**. . . .

Man Found Dead.

Sheriff **Apel** was notified Wednesday morning that Jim **Meeks**, who with his wife lived with Grandma **Earls** near East Point, had been missing from his home since Friday of last week. . . . the dead body of Meeks was found by a searching party. Meeks' throat had been cut . . .

Ed **Parrish**, a young man of the neighborhood, was arrested on suspicion and brought to Quitman . . .

Marriage License.

. . . to Monday of this week:
Rhodes **Reynolds** and Mess Bessie **McElyea**.
Ewing **Williams** and Miss Bertha **Perry**.
Jessie **Jackson** and Miss Addie **Carnathan**.
Earl **Turner** and Miss Jewel **Favors**.
Oscar **White** and Miss Effie Mae **Coker**.
Andrew **McCalla** and Miss Maggie **Upchurch**.
Bidy **Cannon** and Miss Froney **Sta__e**.
Jim **Porter** and Miss Lois **Cain**.
Jerome **Forbis** and Miss Myrtle **Oneal**.
J. H. **Johnson** and Miss Lillie **Scruggs**.
J. A. **Waddleton** and Lovie **Mangrum**.
E. G. **Redwine** and Lonie **Smith**.

Cashier Shot and Killed.

Clarence **Glass**, cashier of the First State Bank at Point, Rains county, was shot Thursday night of last week and died from the effects of the wounds received about 4 o'clock Friday morning.

... His father and mother lives at Emory and a wife and one child survive him.

Death of Babe.

The two months old babe of Mr. and Mrs. J. L. **Brumley** died at the family home in north Quitman Monday and was buried the folowing day in Quitman cemetery. ... Pneumonia was the immediate cause of the death ...

Vital Statistics

No deaths reported.
Nov. 6 to Earl **Cain** and wife, Quitman, a boy.
Nov. 8 to Walter **Grice** and wife, Quitman, rt. 4, a boy.
Nov. 9 to Joe **Gilbreath** and wife, Quitman, rt 4, a girl.
Nov. 25 to Jim **Burgess** and wife, Quitman, rt. 3, a boy.
Dec. 2 to Leonard **Ingram** and wife, Rock Hill, a boy.
Dec. 7. to J. A. **Cameron** and wife, Quitman, a boy.

Thursday, December 21, 1916

Mrs. J. H. Jones Dead

Noble **Jones** received a telegram today, Wednesday, stating that Mrs. J. H. Jones died at the family home at Ada, Okla., early this morning.

We called Earl Jones, son of deceased ... he tells us his mother will be brought to Quitman for burial ...

Marriage License.

... week ending Dec. 17 ...
Charlie **Cooper** and Beulah **Hubbard**.
Andrew **Caldwell** and Lois **Jarred**.

Archie **Terrance** and Becca **Crone**.
Callie **Fannin** and Devasker **Whaley**.
Garnie **Brown** and Daisey **McGee**.

George W. English

G. W. **English** was born May 6, 1853 in Homar, Claborn Parrish, La. His father died when he was 18 months old and at the age of five years his mother moved to Mt. Vernon, Franklin County, Texas, where they remained until after the war. He was married to Miss Laura Alice **Harris** near Ridgeway, Texas, in 1874, to which union thirteen children were born, one of whom died at the age of 12 months, the other twelve with the wife and mother survive and were all present at the time of the death of their husband and father. Eight of the children are girls and the other four are boys. The girls are Mesdames J. F. **Haines**, R. W. **Lindley**, J. S. **Vaughn** and J. A. Lindley; Misses Kate, Floy, Grace and Bonnie. The sons are Jack, Fletcher, Wade and Clyde. Five of the children are single, the other seven are married.

Uncle George is the last of a large family of children. He has no near relatives with the exception of three nephews and one neice, only one of them, W. Z. English of Mineola, being present when the end came . . . His death occurred at 2:30 o'clock, Saturday evening Dec. 16, 1916.

A very impressive funeral service was conducted at Concord church house at 3:30 o'clock Sunday evening by Rev. R. J. **Blackmon** . . . the Woodmen of the World, of which deceased was an honored member, took charge of the remains and deposited them in their last resting place in the beautiful cemetery near by.

Uncle George came to Wood county 24 years ago and has resided in the county ever since . . .

Local and Personal

Jim **Thompson** and wife of Pleasant Grove . . . their son, Will **King**, at Dallas . . .

. . . J. D. T. **Reese** of the Golden country . . .

Democrat - 1916

Mrs. J. D. **Garrett**, the good woman who feeds the hungry at Winnsboro and gives a meal worth a dollar for 85 cents . . .

Jury List County Court
JURY LIST, 1ST WEEK

W. B. **Kirby**, Quitman
H. A. **Robinson**, Como
C. O. **Goldsmith**, Quitman
W. T. **Kirkland**, Mineola
O. D. **Nelson**, Alba
G. K. **McKenzie**, Alba
J. M. **Price**, Peach
Clem F. **Corley**, Winnsboro
W. I. **English**, Mineola
H. W. **Gulty**, Winnsboro
J. T. **Brown**, Alba
M. A. **Williams**, Hawkins
H. Y. **Lindley**, Mineola
J. C. **Snow**, Hawkins
W. M. **Carnes**, Winnsboro
S. W. **Caldwell**, Alba
C. M. **Lindsey**, Peach
J. L. **Hartsfield**, Hawkins

JURY LIST, 2ND WEEK

A. L. **Campbell**, Winnsboro
W. M. **Craddock**, Yantis
W. Z. **English**, Mineola
O. F. **Dykes**, Winnsboro
R. W. **Faulk**, Big Sandy
C. P. **Newman**, Winnsboro
R. N. **McCrary**, Como
W. T. **Crow**, Hawkins
R. H. **Bridges**, Quitman
C. M. **Hughes**, Peach
C. C. **Smith**, Mineola
J. N. **Dyess**, Quitman
J. L. **Hill**, Winnsboro
J. B. **Walker**, Quitman
W. C. **Dodgen**, Winnsboro
G. F. **English**, Mineola
J. L. **Shaw**, Mineola
J. A. **Puckett**, Mineola

JURY LIST, 3RD WEEK

G. C. **Little**, Mineola 6
J. L. **Roundtree**, Pickton 2
S. K. **Crenshaw**, Mineola 2
M. T. **Cain**, Alba
J. W. **Turner**, Mineola 6
R. L. **Simons**, Winnsboro 6
W. E. **Furgason**, Thomas 1
J. R. **Lloyd**, Como 1
R. L. **Reinhardt**, Peach 1
J. D. **Harris**, Winnsboro 3
R. R. **McGuire**, Hawkins 1
J. D. **Benton**, Como 1
T. J. **Tuberville**, Mineola 6
J. M. **Kitchens**, Yantis
J. M. **McAfee**, Winnsboro 6
R. M. **Parish**, Mineola 6
G. D. **Bryant**, Yantis 1
Geo. **Britton**, Yantis

Mrs. Luella McCreight

Mrs Luella **McCreight** was born in Elmo county, Ala., Nov 30th, 1863. Came to Texas with her parents at the age of 12 years and has resided in Wood county since that time. Was married to W. M. McCreight in 1882, to which union ten children were born, five boys and five girls. The boys are G. A. McCreight, County Clerk of wood County; Dr. W. F. McCreight, of Kirbyville; Jim McCreight, of Yantis/ Arthur and Newt who are still under the family roof. The girls are Mrs. Sid **White** and Mrs. H. J. **Caldwell** and Misses Alma, Luella, and Vera, who are still under the family roof. Deceased is also survived by her mother, Mrs. **McIntosh**, and one brother, F. J. **Coleman**.

. . . with pneumonia. . . . Friday evening at about 2 o'clock Dec 15, 1916, she quietly passed away . . .

Interment was had at Myrtle Springs Saturday evening . . .

Connally-Smith

Mr. W. M. **Connally** of Big Sandy, and Miss Floy **Smith** of Peach, were married Sunday at the residence of Rev. J. M. **Boyd** near Peach.

Wood County Democrat - 1917

Thursday, January 4, 1917

[This issue is actually dated in error as 1916. Contrary to my usual policy of recording the entries as closely as possible to the original, I have corrected this date to avoid confusion. -Ed.]

The Quitman Fire

Wednesday night, Dec. 20, 1916, will long be remembered by the people of Quitman. The old town has stood here a long time and the only fire that ever visited the town of any consequence was away back yonder when the courthouse burned. Two residences have been burned since our residence of nearly 30 years in the town and some years ago Frank **Smart**'s smokehouse burned. Those fires constitute the property destruction by fire for the past 40 or 50 years or longer, but on Wednesday night, Dec. 20, we had a pretty bad fire. Property loss to something near $60,000 was the result of the fire. The losses being approximately as follows:

S. W. **Gilbreath** on building $5,500.

J. C. **Wright**, stock and fixtures, $4,500.

Dr. W. T. **Black**, office instruments, books, etc., $1,000.

C. W. **Vickery**, law library, etc, $350.

Jno. R. **Edmonds**, law books, etc., $100.

Judge R. M. **Smith**, law books, etc., $100.

Dr. J. D. **Conger**, office, books, etc., $750.

Dr. S. C. **Noble**, loss not known.

W. O. W. and Maccabee lodges all equipments, loss not known.

J. W. **Brown**, barber shop, pressing and cleaning outfit, $500.

Bill **McCrary**, feed stored in rear of pressing shop, $50.

Dr. J. B. **Goldsmith**, building occupied by J. E. **McDade** & Co. $3,000.

Democrat, building, $2,500.

Democrat, plant, $3,000.

Insurance was carried on the property destroyed as follows:

S. W. **Gilbreath**, on building, $2,000. Insurance adjusted and full amount allowed.

J. C. **Wright**, $2,500 on stock and fixtures, adjusted and $2,053.91 allowed.

Dr. J. B. **Goldsmith**, $1,500 on building, loss not yet adjusted.

Democrat, on building $2,250. Adjusted and $1,830 allowed.

Democrat, on plant, $1,500. Adjusted and $1,381 allowed.

J. E. **McDade** & Co., $4,000, on stock, adjusted and $3,500 allowed.

None of the others had any insurance and their loss is total.

Marriage License

... since our report on the 21st of Dec. 1916:

V. J. **Evans** and Myrtle Irene **White**.
Willie **Cagul** and Ola **Mathis**.
Jim **Daniels** and Lela **White**.
Dewitt **Moseley** and Thurza **Neyland**.
J. I. **Newman** and Pearl **Chreitzberg**.
Milton **Day** and Agnes **Cartwright**.
Claud **Lankford** and Dovie **Clayton**.
Will **Russell** and Denora **Dean**.
M. R. **Turner** and Lila **Rape**.
B. **Bailey** and Lizzie **Price**.
Robt. **Montgomery** and Isadore **Russell**.
Loyd **Harris** and Lola **Goolsby**.
Joel **Elledge** and Effie **Gamblin**.
Perry **Blakeley** and Artie **Roten**.

Moves to Winnsboro

One of the most serious losses our little town has had in citizenship in many years was the removal of Ex-Sheriff Floyd **Williams** and his excellent family the past week from our town to Winnsboro ...

Death of Joe Kirkland

The many friends of Joe **Kirkland** will be pained to learn of his death which sad event occured at his late home about five miles north of Quitman of Friday night, Dec. 21, 1916. Joe was taken sick Sunday before his death and the ravages of pheumonia soon carried him away. He was of a stout, and hardy physique and was seldom sick . . .

Joe Kirkland was born in Shelby county 41 years ago and came to Wood county 20 years ago since which time he has lived in what is known as the Myrtle Springs community. He was married several years ago to Miss Artie **McIntosh** to which union five children were born, one girl and four boys, who with the wife survive him. He is also survived by a brother, Newt Kirkland, who resides in the same community, and a number of near kin in Shelby county.

Interment was had in Myrtle Springs cemetery Saturday evening, the 23rd, and the funeral services were conducted by Rev. J. H. **Baker,** . . .

January 11, 1917

Death of H. C. Gibson

We are pained to learn of the death of H. C. (Buck) **Gibson** which sad event occurred at his late home near Golden last Saturday at about the noon hour. Mr. Gibson had only been sick a few days. Meningitis superinduced by pneumonia, is said to have been the cause of death. County Health officer, Dr. V. E. **Robbins**, received a phone message from Dr. A. M. **Shelton**, the attending physician. . . .

Married in Dallas

At 2 o'clock last Saturday evening, Jan. 6, Mr. W. B. **Lillard** and Miss Pearle **Power** were united in marriage at the home of the presiding Minister, Dr. **White**, of Dallas . . .

. . . He holds the responsible position of manager and buyer of the second floor of the Texas Dry Goods Co., which position he has held for years.

. . . She is a daughter of Mr. and Mrs. J. T. Power, being the eldest child of the family . . .

Mr. and Mrs. Lillard will make their home in Dallas. . . .

Brown - Smith

Married at the methodist parsonage Monday night at 7:30 o'clock by Rev. J. C. **Calhoun**, Mr. T. Grady **Brown** and Miss Nellie **Smith**, both of Forrest Hill community. Miss Nellie is the modest and beautiful daughter of Mr. J. T. Smith and Mr. Brown, the son of J. E. Brown . . , engaged in farming . . .

Death of Pioneer

From J. W. **Moore**, of Mineola, who was in Tuesday, we learn of the death of Mrs. W. M. **McCarroll**, whose death occured at the home of Mr. Moore Dec. 1, 1916.

Mrs. McCarroll had been in failing health for several months and for the past few months had been at the home of her daughter, Mrs. Moore. She was 71 years of age and had resided in Wood county since she was five years old. With her husband she has lived most of this time in the Redland community. . . . The remains were carried to the Turner grave yard near Redland for interment.

One daughter, the only child, with the husband of her youth, and one sister, Grandma **Morrison** of Quitman, survive . . .

Concord News

Mr. and Mrs. Chas. **Lindley**, of Hainesville, are the parents of twin girls. Mother doing fine and Mr. E. T. **Hartsfield** is all smiles over the thought of being "Grandpa."

Death of R. W. French

. . . the horrible accident of R. W. **French** which occured last Friday about 10 o'clock a.m. Mr. French was working on the platform of a windmill tower which was being erected for C. T. **Capel** at his home here in town. . . . fell to the ground . . . He was removed to his home soon after the fall. He lived until Sunday evening at 4 o'clock . . .

Richard Webster **French** was 35 years old and the oldest son. He leaves a wife, two children, father, two brothers and five sisters . . . Mrs. D. E. **Minnick**, formerly of this place, is one of the sisters.

. . . buried Monday in the city cemetery with Woodmen honors. A. L. French of Mansfield, La., and J. W. French of Winnsboro, Texas, brothers of the deceased . . . The father, R. I. French, of Cartwright, Texas . . .

R. W. French was reared at Cartwright, but for last ten years had resided at Mathis Texas.

Some Real Estate Deals

Sometime since Jno. R. **Edmonds** traded 230 acres of land on east side of Lake Fork to B. F. **Cathey** for the residence recently erected by Mr. Cathey in Quitman, and which has been occupied since its completion by Jno. D. **Jones** and family. Last week, Mr. Edmonds sold the home to Mr. Jones, the consideration being $1,750. . . .

Another trade consumated the past week was the selling by J. A. **Nixon** the property occupied by W. G. **McCrary** as a livery barn, to Jno. R. Edmonds, the consideration being $2,500. . . .

Arm Shot Off.

Lorane **Neyland**, the 11 year old son of Mr. and Mrs. Frank Neyland, had his right arm shot off Friday.

He was returning from hunting and was in a buggy with two other boys. He was standing in the rear part of the vehicle when he saw a hawk. He pulled his gun with the muzzle towards him, the hammer snapped by being caught on something in the buggy, firing a load of shot into his right arm just below the shoulder. He was hurried to a doctor's office and later home. The last reports say he is doing well.
- Winnsboro News.

The boy who had the misfortune above mentioned was a nephew of Mrs. R. J. **Martin** of our town, his father, Frank Neyland being a brother of Mrs. Martin.

Hainesville News

Mr. **Atwood** of Georgia, and Miss Dora **Blackwell** were married at the home of Rev. **Hamrick** Friday of last week. Miss Dora is the daughter of "Uncle Billie" Blackwell as he is familiarly called . . .

Local and Personal News Items.

Eugene **Conger** wife and baby girl of Vancouver, B.C., came in . . . visit with his parents, Dr. and Mrs. J. D. Conger, . . .

Jno. W. **White**, of Driggs, Ark. was here . . . two of his old friends, J. A. **Dorman** of Golden, and R. H. **Mansell** of Alba.

Rev. and Mrs. F. P. **Langley** of Golden . . . recently moved to Golden from Comanche, Texas.

Grady **White** and wife left Tuesday for Mountain Park, Okla., where they will make their future home. . . .

Mr. L. H. **Tackett** of Ada, Okla., . . . her parents, Mr. and Mrs. J. W. **Baker** at Forrest Hill . .

Mrs. R. E. **Reid** and little son, Charles, of Alba . . .

Henry **Benton** has rented his farm east of town to Mike **Lloyd** and has moved to town. He occupies the residence recently vacated by Floyd **Williams**.

Grand-ma **Day**, who formerly lived in this county near Cartwright and now residing in Hopkins county . . .

In Memorial.

Mrs. Emmie Williams **Jones**, the subject of this sketch, was a daughter of Jno. P. and Sarah **Williams**. She was born November 1, 1867, at Quitman, where she grew to womanhood. She was married June 19th, 1890, to J. H. Jones, to which union four boys were born. The youngest boy, Virgil died May 9th, 1901, being one year and 18 days old. The second boy, Harold, died on the 17th day of March 1915, being 21 years, 2 months and 26 days old at the time of his death. "Miss Emmie," as she was affectionately called by everyone who knew her, after a lingering illness of more than a year, died at the family home in Ada, Okla., on the night of Dec. 19th, 1916, being at the time of her death, 49 years, one month and 18 days old. . . .

About ten years ago the family left Quitman where they had resided ever since their marriage. . . . brought home . . . cemetery at Quitman.

Beside the husband and two boys, Clyde and Earl, one sister, Mrs. H. S. **Douglas**, of Forrest Hill, and one brother, W. T. **Williams**, of our town . . .

January 25, 1917

Death Near Mineola

. . . in Quitman Friday for a coffin for Mr. M. H. **Roberts**, father of L. C. Roberts, who lived near Mineola, and whose death occured the night before. Mr. Roberts had been sick a long time with consumption . . . buried Firday evening at Sand Springs.

Death of a Pioneer

Saturday, January 14, 1917, Mrs. S. E. **Watkins**, one of the oldest and most highly respected women of the county, died at her late home near Clover Hill where she had resided almost continuously for near a half century. Some 20 years ago her husband died . . . The children are one son, J. R., or Bob, as he is familiarly called, who now lives in West Texas and has for several years; three daughters, Mrs. Dewitt **Johnson**, of Ft. Worth, Mrs. John **Weems** and Mrs. Elbert **Scoggins**, who live in this county and near the home of their childhood. . . . funeral which took place Monday, the 15th, at Clover Hill grave yard . . .

Yantis News

Mr. **Pruitt**, living 2 miles east of Yantis, died last Thursday night Jan 12, at 11 p.m. Interment was had in the Yantis cemetery at 3 p.m. Friday.

Mr. Perce **Hooker**, recently from Palo Pinto County, died Sunday afternoon at 6 at his home 3 miles north of Yantis. Interment was had in the Yantis cemetery Monday evening at 4 o'clock.

February 1, 1917

Accidently Shot

T. J. **Goodwin** received a phone message Sunday evening stating that his son, Edgar, had been accidently shot while bird hunting. The shot took effect in one of this arms, tearing away the flesh above the elbow but no bones were broken. . . . he is getting along all right . .

Thrown From Buggy.

A. J. **Conger** was thrown from his buggy Tuesday and was severely hurt. His condition is quite serious. . . . resting reasonably well.

Died From Poison.

Postmaster S. A. **Kendrick** received a phone message Monday morning announcing the death of his son, Jack Kendrick, which occured Sunday night at Spur, Dickens county, Texas from the effect of poison. The only information was that he had been accidentally poisoned, death resulting in a few hours.

Tilden Kendrick and A. J. **Horton** left Monday for Spur to bring the body to Quitman . . . interment will be had in Quitman cemetery.

An Appreciated Friend

Pink **Lawrence** showed us a letter from his brother, Hon. J. A. Lawrence, of Tahlequah, Okla . . . [excerpts of letter]

H. A. Sweeney Dead.

H. A. **Sweeney,** who lived on the Bob **Caldwell** farm near Oak Grove, died at his late home Friday night of last week after a weeks illness with pneumonia . . . the bereaved wife and children, the aged father and other relatives . . ..

Yantis News

Fox **Gloar,** a well known resident of Yantis, died Monday, Jan 22. Interment was had in the Reiley Springs cemetery Tuesday at 3 p.m.

Democrat - 1917

Oak Grove Items

Mr. Henry **Swinney** died last Friday night at 9 o'clock with pheomonia. He was laid to rest in the Ebenezer cemetery Sunday.

J. H. Sherman Dead.

Arthur **Wilder** showed us a letter Saturday that he had received from an Atty. at Rockport announcing the death of J. H. **Sherman** at that place several weeks ago. The Atty. was making inquiry regarding the heirs of deceased, thinking that Mr. Wilder might know something of them, but he does not.

Mr. Sherman lived for several years in and near Quitman and "batched" near the Dr. Wilder home west of Quitman. . . . He is said to have been related to General Sherman of war fame. . . .

Marriage Permits

Since our last report . . .:

J. E. **Sandifer** and Miss Grace **Robinson**.
B. H. **Bolton** and Maggie Lou **Christian**.
A. B. **Patrick** and Miss Evie **Dixon**.
P. M. **Whatley** and Miss Opal **Mayo**.
A. A. **Harris** and Mrs. Annie **Harris**.
Jim **Crofford** and Paralee **Weeker**.
J. **Franklin** and Mrs. Mollie **Gunn**.
S. T. **Teer** and Miss Rozella **Brown**.
Oliver **Kirkpatrick** and Miss Cora **McClelland**.
Manuel **Palononimo** and Aurora **Mercadanti**.
Quince **Griggs** and Ella **Smith**.

Pleasant Grove

Mr. Amos **Harris** and Mrs. A. E. **Harris** were married at Winnsboro Wednesday night. Amos is the son of the late Bolton Harris, while Mrs. Harris is the widow of the late Ame Harris. They will make their home in Winnsboro.

Stout News

Pete **Limley** died of pneumonia Thursday of last week and was burried in the Ebenezer cemetery that afternoon. He leaves a wife and four little boys . . .

Died in Mississippi

J. S. **Way** writes us that his brother, Tom Way, who formerly lived near Mineola and Golden, died in Mississippi on Jan. 19.

John Precise Dead.

. . . the death of our friend John **Precise**, which occured at his late home on Golden at 7:30 Saturday evening. Interment was had at Golden Sunday evening at 4 o'clock after funeral services conducted at the Methodist church by Rev. W. M. **Bass**.

. . . survived by his wife and seven children . . .

Stagner Items.

The Death Angel visited our community again on the 6th inst taking from her loved ones Mrs. Malindy **Stagner**. She had been sick ever since Christmas . . .She leaves a companion and 8 children . .

Death of S. J. Kendrick.

. . . the remains arrived in Quitman via Mineola, being accompanied from Spur by S. T. **Kendrick**, a brother of deceased, and A. J. **Horton**. . . . interment had in Quitman cemetery . . .

Jack, as he was familiarly called and known, was the eldest son of Pastmaster and Mrs. S. A. Kendrick and was born and raised near Quitman. The parents, two brothers and one sister, the latter Mrs. M. L. **Cartwright**, and a son, Henry, together with a number of other relatives survive.

February 15, 1917

Another Mother in Israel Answers the Last Call.

. . . the death of Mrs. M. J. **Robbins**, mother of our fellow townsman, I. W. Robbins, which occurred at the home of her daughter, Mrs. Mary **Cox**, at Little Hope Saturday morning, Feb. 10.

"Grandma" Robbins . . . was in her 82nd year and had lived in Wood county for nearly half a century.

The remains were laid to rest in Little Hope graveyard Sunday evening following her death . . .

Mary B. Goode Dead

Mrs. Mary B. **Goode**, one of the best known and one of the best liked women of our community passed away last Friday afternoon at the home of Mr. and Mrs. J. P. **Smith**, after an illness of three or four weeks.

Mrs. Goode came to Mineola more than thirty years ago to accept a position in the public schools . . .

Mrs. Goode was born in either North or South Carolina more than 70 years ago. . . . Interment was in the city cemetery Saturday morning, February 3rd.   - Mineola Monitor.

John Precise Gone to Rest

John **Precise** breathed his last on Saturday evening, Feb 3 . . . He was born in Jackson County, Alabama, on Sept 11, 1878. His father, also named John . . .

On Jan. 19, 1898, John was united in marriage to Miss Eva **Riddle** also of Jackson county. By this union two girls, one boy and an infant who died soon after birth were born. . . . Miss Ethel is now doing the junior year of work at the Denton State Normal . . . Leila, the other girl is a high school girl . . . while Otis, the boy, is in the grammar school . . .This happy family moved to Golden . . . and Precise bought land from John **Bellomy** on which he built a home. But the mother was not long to enjoy this home. She contracted disease and, desiring to see her native state in the hope of improvement, Precise carried her back to Alabama where she was soon laid to rest.

On May 21, 1906, **Precise** was married to Miss Nora **Riley** of Golden . . . To them four bright and lovable children were born, all of whom survive him. Besides the above named family, Mr. Precise is survived by an only brother, Joe Precise, of Scottsboro, Alabama, a half brother, Jim **Austin**, of the same place, and other relatives. . .

Prominent Citizen of Winnsboro Dies.

T. G. **Carlock**, a prominent citizen of Winnsboro, died at his late home in that city last Saturday and was burried the following day in the Winnsboro cemetery.

Mr. Carlock had lived in Winnsboro for many years . . .

Mr. Carlock is survived by his wife, several sons and daughters and a brother, the Hon. M. D. Carlock of Winnsboro.

February 22, 1917

Death at Greenville

Jno. D. **Jones** received a phone message Saturday night announcing the death of his sister, Mrs. **Conger** at Greenville. . . . The funeral was held at the residence at 10 a.m. Monday and interment made in the Greenville cemetery.

Another Mother Gone

We are pained to chronicle the death of Mrs. S. A. **Kendrick**, wife of postmaster S. A. Kendrick, which occurred at the family home 2 miles east of Quitman Friday of last month at about 9 o'clock in the forenoon.

"Aunt Sue Kendrick" . . . was born in Butts county, Georgia, in 1852, and with her parents, Mr. and Mrs. **Burford**, came to Wood county in 1857. The parents settled on the home where death claimed Aunt Sue Friday of last week. In early life she was married to S. A. Kendrick to which union there are still living three children, Tilden, Horace, and Mrs. M. L. **Cartwright**, all of whom are married and settled in life, Tilden and Mrs. Cartwright living in Quitman and Horace on the old home place. Of her brothers and sisters of which there were five besides herself, a brother, W. G. Burford living on part of the old home place, is the only survivor. Her parents died a number of years ago.

The funeral services were conducted at Ebenezer church Saturday at 12 o'clock by Rev. R. J. **Blackmon**, assisted by Rev. J. C. **Calhoun** . . . Interment was had in the grave yard near by immediately following the funeral service.

Beside the husband, three children and the lone brother, there are seven grand children left to mourn . . .

Marriage License

Since our last report . . .:
W. W. **Wonzer** and Miss Vera **Dodson**.
Emmett **Sims** and Miss Lillie **Harris**.
J. F. **Green** and Mrs. L. A. **Green**.
Roy **Holt** and Miss Kate **Perkins**.
Bee **Stewart** and Carrie **Smith**.
Wallace **Runnels** and Ethel **Redwine**.

In Memory of Silas Lindley.

On last Friday at 3:00 o'clock p.m. little Silas **Lindley** breathed his last. He was born Sept 22nd, 1910, and died Feb 16, 1917, . . .how sad mother, father, Paul and David! . . . Besides the aged grand parents he has left to mourn for him 9 uncles and 9 aunts . . .

Death of Mrs. Veitch.

. . . the death of Mrs. **Veitch**, wife of W. E. Veitch of the Hainesville community, which occurred at the family home Friday evening of last week, pheumonia being the immediate cause of death. Interment was had at Mr. Pisga Saturday evening . . .

With the husband of her youth there is left twelve children to mourn the loss . . .

In Memorial

Mrs. M. J. **Robbins**, nee **Burnett**, was born in Lincoln county, Tennessee, May 6th, 1835. In 1840, when five years of age, she was brought to Texas by her parents, Isham Burnett and wife. They setled in Red River county near where the city of Clarksville is now. During this residence of eleven years in that county her mother died, and in 1851, she with her father and the other children, came to Wood county and settled in what is now known as the Little Hope community. In 1856 she was married to Elias **Robbins**, to which union six children were born, one son and five daughters. One of the girls died in infancy, the other four survive; they being I. W. Robbins of Quitman, Mrs. Mary **Cox** of Little Hope, Mrs. M. E. **Daniels** of Alba, Mrs. W. P. **Murphy** of Little Hope, and Mrs. S. L. **Johnson** of the Myrtle Springs Community. With her husband they settled on a little farm about 3 miles south of the Gunstream mill place. In 1863, her husband died, leaving her to raise the children alone. . . . in March, 1883, she moved to Quitman and made her home with her son until the fall of 1907, when, after the death of her son-in-law, J. D. Cox, she went to live with her widowed daughter at which place she made her home until her death, Feb. 10, 1917. . . .

Grand-ma Robbins was the last of a large family of 8 own brothers, 3 own sisters, and 3 half brothers. With her five children who survive her there are 35 grand-children. . . .

AN OLD LETTER

Among the papers grand-ma **Robbins** preserved and cherished was the following one from that grand old man, Uncle Jessie **Moseley** . . . Uncle Jessie was with the husband when death claimed him . . .

"Anoils Parish, La., June 6, 1863. Mrs. Robbins, Madam:

It is with much regret that I have to this day chronicle the death of our husband, Mr. Elias Robbins, who departed this life yesterday evening about seven o'clock. Mr. Robbins died of Typhoid fever and disease of the lungs. . . . Mr. Robbins died 40 miles below Alexandria, La., and 40 miles from the mouth of Red River. I had him put away as neat as I could under the circumstances. . . . He left only about $4.00 in money, as he had not drawn any more money since he came up with the command. He lost his mule since he stopped here. A soldier stole it and I reckon it is clear gone. . . . There is about $250.00 coming to Mr. Robbins for his services, which Capt. **Thompson** will collect and send to you. . . . a true friend, J. M. Moseley."

March 1, 1917

Death of Mrs. Blalock

After an illness of about a week with pneumonia, Mrs. Sue **Blalock**, wife of M. R. (Uncle Milt) Blalock, died at the family home in the Myrtle Springs community Monday morning of this week. Interment was had at Myrtle Springs Tuesday evening . . .

"Aunt Sue," as she was familiarly and lovingly called by all of her community, was a daughter of the late R. P. **Mayo**, formerly county treasurer of this county. She was born near the place where the death occurred, Oct. 29, 1853, and on Sept. 1, 1881, was married to M. R. Blalock. Several children were born to this union, only one Johny a son, who is now grown and married survived, the others all died when small. One brother, J. R. Mayo of Quitman, and one sister, Mrs. C. D. **Turner** of Myrtle Springs community, survive.

Concord News

Claude **Laminack** of Okla, and Miss Nellie **James** of Hope, both of whom formerly lived in this community and are known by all, were happily married Thursday afternoon at the home of the bride's parents, Mr. and Mrs. Jno. James. . . .

New Engine

J. B. **Mounts** our hustling water works and light plant man, has placed an order with the Southern Engine and Boiler Works of Texas for a 35 h.p. gasoline engine to run the water plant and light plant. Mr. R. G. **Parker** representative of the above firm was here several days . . .

Mrs. Conger Died After Few Hours Illness

Saturday night Mrs. Sarah E. **Conger** died at the home of her daughter, Mrs. J. P. **Germany** on Lee Street, at 10 o'clock after a few hours illness, the result of pneumonia.

The funeral services were conducted this morning at 10 o'clock at the home of Mr. and Mrs. J. P. Germany. The burial took place in East Mount cemetery.

The active pall bearers were: C. W. **Gee**, Douglas **King**, S. E. **Harwell**, N. E. **Peak**, Raymond **Garnett** and Pat **Russell**.

The honorary pall bearers were: W. W. **Sockwell**, William **Pierson**, J. D. **Herndon**, T. D. **Montrose**, B. J. **Mitchell**, B. W. **Shepherd**, W. C. **Poole**, Joe **Wood**, E. W. **Harrison** and L. A. **Clark**.

BIOGRAPHY

Mrs. S. E. **Conger** was born at Indian Springs, Ga.,73 years ago, where she lived until about fourteen years of age. She came to Texas with her parents and the other children and settled in Wood county four and a half miles north-east of Quitman, on the Quitman and Winnsboro road. Here her father died the following year, 1858, at the age of 40 years. She continued to live with the widowed mother until Dec. 21, 1865, when she was married to T. E. Conger. They lived very happily together until Oct. 29, 1885, when the husband died at Quitman while tax collector of Wood county. Her mother who was with her continuously during her husband's last illness, was stricken with pneumonia and died in November, only a few days after her husband's death.

Mr. and Mrs. Conger had born to them four children, two sons and two daughters. Ada, the oldest, died at Quitman while a small girl. Mrs. J. P. **Germany**, (Eloise) at whose home the mother died, now lives in Greenville. Alvin, the youngest child died in young manhood at Mineola.

Mrs. Conger had two sisters and two brothers. Eliza M., who married Capt. W. M. **Giles**, died at Mineola. The oldest brother, Judge W. J. **Jones**, who was for a number of years county judge of Wood county, died at Mineral Wells a few years ago. The other sister married I. C. **Giles** and died at Bowie several years ago, leaving an only brother ex-county clerk, Jno. D. Jones, who now lives in Quitman.

Marriage License Issued

Since last issue of the Democrat . . .
G. W. **Holley** and Mrs. Sallie **Price**.
Cisero **Conger** and Annie **Johnson**.
C. M. **Laminack** and Nellie **James**.
George **McGruder** and Oma **Jobe**.

Railey **Belcher** and Mrs. Mary **Allen**.
W. J. **Reese** and Mrs. L. M. **Champion**.
Jake **Holmes** and Alice **Johnson**.

The New Hawkins

We spent a few hours in Hawkins last Saturday . . . the town was burned out last fall. . . . looked desolate after the fire. Not so now. . .

Leaving the T. & P. depot coming across the street diagonally South, the first business you come to is that of P. A. **Thorn** who handles a line of general merchandise . . . he erected a frame building on the corner, and in addition he erected a handsome brick just west and adjoining his frame building. This building is completed or just about so, and will be occupied by T. J. **Kelly**, of Big Sandy, with a general stock of merchandise.

Just west of the Thorn brick is the Bowie **Holmes** brick which is occupied by Mr. Holmes with a line of general merchandise. The postoffice is also located in the Holmes brick with L. G. **Robbins** and postmaster. Fronting the Holmes brick, and between it and the railroad is the **Pruitt** store with groceries, etc., and west of the Holmes brick is the **Ussery** gin plant where 735 bales of cotton have been ginned this season.

Leaving the Thorn corner coming back south on the corner opposite is the First National Bank building . . . J. W. **Smart** and his brother, Milton, are the accommodating active officers of the bank and are live wires all right.

Adjoining the bank building is the W. P. **Mings** brick which surrounds the bank building south and west . . .

The two brick buildings [portion unreadable] on the south, the first one will be occupied by C. A. **Peacock** with a general merchandise line, the other is now occupied by J. B. **Smith** & Son, with a splendid stock of general merchandise.

The B. F. **Allen** brick adjoins the Smith brick on the south and is nearing completion. Mr. Allen will move his stock of general merchandise, drugs, etc. into the building this week.

Back west of the block of brick buildings last mentioned is J. L. **Fowler** in a frame building with a general stock of merchandise. He says he will build a brick some time soon.

Across the street east of the brick last mentioned is the frame buildings occupied by **Satterwhite** & Son with groceries, confectioneries, etc., and the drug store of **Parrish** and **Pritchett** . .

The **Cobb** brick building which was destroyed by fire has not been rebuilt . . . plans are under way. . . .Just east of the Cobb brick is A. **Warn** with a stock of groceries.

The T. & P. have recently erected a shipping shed near the depot . . .

THE FOUKE LANDS

G. S. **Northcutt** of Mineola has joined the Hawkins boosters and has secured the agency for the large body of land owned by the **Fouke** Lumber Co. and has placed same on the market. . . .

JARVIS CHRISTIAN INSTITUTE

About one mile down the T. & P. track east is located the colored people's Institute, taking the name from Major J. J. **Jarvis**, who formerly lived in Quitman and was known to all our older people here. . . .

Local and Personal News Items.

Sheriff **Apel** went to Abilene last Wednesday with J. D. **Gayle** a patient for the Epileptic Colony, returning Thursday.

Ralph **Curtis**, a young man whose home is at Crystal City but who has been in the Hainesville country for the past year, is dangerously sick with pneumonia at the home of Van **Wood**. Mr. Curtis is a cousin of Mrs. Wood.

Obituary

Sister M. E. **Robinson** was born in Upshur County, Texas, Feb. 4, 1866, being 51 years, 11 months, and 16 days old at the time of her death. Moved with her parents, while young, to Wood county. Was converted at the age of 14. . . . A husband and 6 children survive her, also 2 brothers and 2 sisters, namely, Mrs. J. G. **Mossenton**, Mrs. Mattie **Higginbotham**, and W. M. **Moody** and J. D. Moody.

Democrat - 1917

March 8, 1917

Arm Shot Off

From Wade **Patrick** of the Golden country who was in our office Monday we learn that Louie Patrick, the 15 year old son of Bert Patrick of same community, had the misfortune to lose his right arm a couple of weeks ago by the accidental discharge of a shot gun that he had with him in the field shooting black birds. Louie had fastened the gun to his plow stock to have it convenient when the birds came round and by some means it was discharged . . . the arm amputated just below the elbow.

U. C. V. Meeting

Persuant to call of J. M. **Welch** a few of the ex-Confederates met at the courthouse in Quitman Monday, March 5, 1917, and reorganized the Wood county Camp of U. C. V. The following members were enrolled, I. H. **Huffmaster**, J. M. **Welch**, B. L. **Farr**, O. F. **Swenney**, J. A. **Calloway**, C. H. **Smart**, G. W. **Birchfield**, W. R. **Clanton**, W. R. **Blalock**, G. W. **Lindley**, D. S. **Robinson**, T. J. **Goodwin**, J. M. **Pugh**, S. A. **Kendrick** and S. H. **Hart**.

. . . election of officers . . . J. M. **Welch** captain, and T. J. **Goodwin** adjutant, . . .

In Memory of Mrs. S. E. Watkins

Mrs. S. E. **Watkins** died Jan 14, 1917 at her home six miles east of Quitman.

"Aunt Puss Watkins" as she was lovingly called by most all who knew her, lived nearly seventy two years, being born July 27, 1845.

Her husband has been dead several years. To this union there were born eight children, four of whom were living when death called "Aunt Puss" away.

The children, Bob living in Throckmorton county, Mrs. **Johnston** in Ft. Worth, Mrs. **Weems** about 3 miles north of Quitman and Mrs. Elbert **Scoggins** who is living on the home place where her mother died . . .

J. T. Lankford Dead.

After ten days of terrible suffering uncle Gus **Lankford** succumb to that awful disease, Pneumonia, Feb 22nd, and was buried at Pleasant Grove, Rev. J. C. **Calhoun** preaching the funeral at 1 o'clock Thursday the 23rd.

His youngest son, Jimmie, was too sick with the same dreadful disease, to attend his father's funeral . . .

Mr. Lankford is survived by the widow, five daughters, three married and two single, and two sons.

Citation by Publication
The State of Texas

. . . J. Max **Pierce** is the surviving husband of Mrs. Martha Pierce, deceased . . . appointed . . . as community administrator of the estate of the said Mrs. Pierce. . . Richard S. Pierce, Julius A. Pierce, Jesse Pierce and Mrs. Mildred **Hughes** are the sole surviving children . . . of the said Mrs. Martha Pierce.

Obituary
(By Her Pastor)

Sister Sue **Blalock**, wife of our beloved brother M. R. Blalock was born Oct 29, 1853. Her maiden name was Sue Memphis **Mayo**. . . . her love was won by M. R. Blalock. . . and on Sept 1, 1881, they two were joined together in the Divine rights of matrimony. . . . To this union was born one son who still lives, and other children who died in infancy. . . .

Pneumonia was the cause of Sister Blalock's death. She was taken sick Feb. 17th. . . . on the morning of the 26th of Feb. 1917, Jesus came . . .

Oak Grove Items

The death angel visited the home of Mr. and Mrs. R. M. **Black** last Thursday evening at 4:45 o'clock and took from them their baby boy, little Herman Paul. He was eighteen months of age and had been sick most all of his life.

Democrat - 1917

Stagner Items.

The Stork visited at the home of Pink **Matheson** and wife on the 1st and left a little boy to brighten their home . . .

Tried for Lunacy

Sam **Wilkins** who was sent from this county to the Terrell Asylum some five or six years ago and was released as cured, was tried again on a lunacy charge before Judge **Bozeman** and a Commission Thursday of last week. Sam is an object of pity, and to think that he has to remain in jail on account of there being no room for him in the Asylum, makes it more sad. . . .

Ike Rountree Dead

Through an oversight last week we failed to mention the death of Ike **Rountree** which occured on Saturday a week ago at his late home near Cartwright.

Mrs. O. M. McCorley Dead

After a lingering illness of some three years duration, Mrs. O. M. **McCorley** died at the family home hear Rock Hill Thursday of last week and was buried at Rock Hill grave yard.

Mrs. McCorley was a daughter of Mr. and Mrs. J. V. **White**. She was born in Alabama April 30, 1887. With her parents she came to Texas in 1900, and on July 12, 1903, she was married to O. M. McCorley who with four children survive.

Accidentally Shot.

Lee **Riner** of Yantis was in Monday and from him we learn of the accidental shooting of Dave **King**, 16 year old son of M. E. King living 2 miles east of Yantis. The accident happened Feb. 24. . . . in his hand . . . getting along alright now and able to be out.

Wood County Newspapers

March 15, 1917

A Mother Called Home.

Monday night March 5th, a sweet baby boy came to the home of Mr. and Mrs. J. C. **Russell** near Golden. On Sunday night March 11th, the Death Angel came and claimed the mother leaving the babe to the care of the father.

Mrs. Russell was a daughter of the venerable and upright citizen, Uncle Green **Smith**, who with several brothers and sisters and the husband, County Commissioner J.C. Russell and five children survive.

Interment was had at Sand Springs Monday evening at 1:30.

Death of Mrs. Russom

Mrs. Isham **Russom** died at the family residence near Alba last Saturday evening and the remains were carried to Ebenezer Sunday for interment. . . . Mrs. Russom was a sister of Dr. J. T. **Maxey** and Mrs. J. H. **Gleaton**, and has a large connection, being a daughter of the late Uncle Frank Maxey. An infant babe of deceased died Friday evening and was buried same day.

In Memorial

Ike T. **Rountree** was born in Pike County, Ala., Jan 15, 1866, and died in Wood county, Texas, Feb 23, 1917. He came to Texas when a young man and at the age of 26 was married to Miss Hanala **Stevens** to which union six children were born, all of whom are still living, three of whom are married, viz: Mrs. Viola **Mallory**, Mrs. Sabina **Layton**, and Charlie **Rountree**, the other three boys are still under the family roof.

Feb. 24, the remains of deceased was carried to Hopewell and laid to rest in the beautiful cemetery. . . .

Death Near Mineola

Lawrence **Blackmon**, grandson of O. J. Blackman, died at the home of his grand-father Sunday night and the remains were buried at Sand Springs Monday evening. . . . Lawrence was an orphan boy, his parents having died when he was a mere child. He made his home with his grand parents and with his uncle, O. J. Blackman Jr.

Seventy-Fifth Birthday

Wednesday March 7th, Mr. John W. **Patrick**, better known and familiarly called "Uncle John," who lives one mile north of Golden, was 75 years old and his children prepared a dinner . . .

The following gathered around the festive board at the dinner hour as guest of this venerable couple:

R. L. Patrick, wife and six children.
A. K. Patrick and six children.
H. N. Patrick, wife and five children.
Wade Patrick, wife and four children.
W. J. Patrick, wife and four children.
Mrs. Z. T. **Brittian**.
Mr. and Mrs. L. A. **Jones**.
Mr. and Mrs. T. F. **Dodgen**.
Jack Patrick and wife, Grand Saline.
Mrs. Drew **Green** and babe, Greenville.
Mr. and Mrs. A. J. **Graves**.
Mrs. M. A. **Hudson** and two children.
Newt **Reich** and wife.
R. C. **Brittian** and babe, Marjorielou.
Jim **Johnson**, wife and babe.
Albert **Owens**, wife and babe.
Henry **Brickey**, wife and babe.
Aubrey **Sullivan**, wife and babe.
Ezra **Carter**, wife and babe.
Clebe **Dodgen** and wife.
Uncle Charlie **Smart**.
E. V. **Shinn**, Grand Saline.
Jim **Patrick**, wife and three children.
H. C. **Dodgen**, wife and babe.
Uncle Tom **Shipp**.
T. J. **Smart** and four children.
J. T. **Gray**, wife and two children.

Alfred **Patrick** and wife.
Sam J. **Benton** and wife.
Lester **Patrick**, A. L. **Dunbar**, John **Shipes**, Dr. **Shelton**, Lydia **Vaughn**, Tressie **Willis**, Jack **Leath** and the Democrat man.

March 22, 1917

In Memory of Grand-Ma Reinhardt

Mrs. Nancy J. **Reinhardt** was born Oct. 18, 1846, and died March 3, 1917. She was 70 years, 4 months, and 15 days old at the time of her death.

Grand-ma, as we all called her came to Texas with her parents Mr. and Mrs. **Ussery**, when but a small child, sometime during the fifties. They located on a farm near Quitman. On Jany. 19, 1867 she was married to Michael A. Reinhardt at Quitman. Later they moved to the Little Hope community, and from there to Peach, where she resided at the time of her death.

To his union six children were born, three of whom preceded father and mother to the better land, the other three being, Albert L. of Peach, Robert of Little Hope, and Mrs. Mary **Baker** of East Point. . . .

Fletcher English

Sunday night, March 18th, at 12:45 o'clock, Fletcher **English** passed away at his late home at Hainesville. His health had been failing for some weeks . . .

Fletcher was born Nov. 4, 1886, and has lived all his life in Wood county. . . .

Fletcher was married June 9, 1912, to Miss Jessie, only daughter of Mr. and Mrs. E. M. **Burkett** of Hainesville. Jessie being the only child in the family they never left the home of the parents and Fletcher became, as it were, a son in the home.

Fletcher was buried at Concord Monday evening . . .

H. V. Johnson

Again the news is chronicled that a good man has passed to his reward. Wednesday night March 14th, H. V. **Johnson** died at his late home near Golden after an illness of only a few days. . . . death occurred that night at about 9 o'clock.

. . . Vince Johnson . . . For four years he was tax collector of Wood county. He was born and raised in and near Quitman and has a large connection, the family being a large one. Only one brother and two sisters of the family survive him, they being S. L. Johnson living four miles north of Quitman; Mrs. J. **Rainwater**, of Quitman, and Mrs. J. C. **Rainwater**, of Alba. The wife of his youth together with a number of children and grand children also survive. . . .

Interment was had Friday at Sand Springs . . .

Marriage License

Since our report of two weeks ago . . .
E. P. **Jones** and Ethel **Applegate**.
Zack **Parker** and Juanita **McFarland**.
Bostal **Gulledge** and Lola Maye **Seymore**.
Harmon **Bartlett** and Era **Carrington**.
R. K. **Wren** and Mrs. Martha Ann **James**.
W. C. **Chaddick** and Ina **Green**.
Joe **Russo** and Ruth **Hinds**.
Luther **James** and Lyncha **Lindley**.
Essie **Brumstey** and Louisa **Grace**.
W. S. **Baker** and Mrs. Nellie **Vance**.
Hinkley **Skinner** and Minnie **Wilson**.
Curtis **Conger** and Fessie **Murry**.

Goes to Avinger.

W. L. **Hartsfield** and family left last week for Avinger, Texas, where Mr. Hartsfiled has been elected cashier of the bank at that place. Up to a few months ago Luther, as he is best known, was president of the First National Bank of Hawkins and sold his interest there to Walter **Smart**, since which time he has been engaged in writing insurance at Mineola.

Wood County Newspapers

March 29, 1917

Little Jarroll Franklin.

After ten days illness little Jarroll Franklin, babe of Mr. and Mrs. C. A. **Green** breathed his last at the family home one mile north of Quitman Thursday March 22, 1917, at 3:15, a.m.

Little Jarroll Franklin was born January 28, 1917, . . .

Funeral service was held at the Baptist church Friday evening at 3 o'clock . . . Interment was had in the Quitman cemetery following the funeral service.

In Memory of Mrs. J. C. Russell.

On Sunday evening, March 11, one of Golden's best loved women, Mrs. J. C. **Russell**, breathed her last. This good woman was the wife of our faithful citizen and commissioner, J. C. Russell. She was born in Smith County July 10, 1882, and before she was a year old her father, G. R. **Smith**, moved to the place in the Bellefont community where he now lives.

Miss Bertha, as she was called . . .

Mr. and Mrs. Russell were married on Dec. 25, 1898, and with the exception of about two years, have made their home among us. During one of these years they resided at Ballinger and during the other at Pecos City.

Five children, all of whom are living, were born to Mr. and Mrs. Russell. The oldest, Miss Aliene, is an accomplished young lady who is making proficiency in both her literary and musical studies. The other children are bright little jewels and . . . Miss Bertha is also survived by her father, G. R. **Smith**, three sisters: Mrs. **Bullard** of San Antonio, Mrs. **Wood** of Abilene, Mrs. **Davenport** of Ballinger, and three brothers: Messrs Arthur **Smith** of Okla., Doss **Smith** of the same state, and Charlie **Smith** of the Bellefonte community.

County Court Jurors
. . . for the April term of Court . . .
FIRST WEEK

G. T. **Chapman**	J. H. **Harvey**	J. L. **Gore**
J. Q. **Beard**	G. H. **Music**	L. C. **Dobbs**

J. A. **Puckett**	M. E. **King**	C. W. **Pearson**
L. H. **Patten**	W. M. **Carnes**	J. H. **McDougald**
J. G. **McCoy**	W. D. **Shirey**	J. L. **Corley**
W. C. **Harpole**	W. G. **Crofford**	Geo. W. **Jones**
	SECOND WEEK	
J. D. **Garrett**	E. **Corbett**	P. J. **McManus**
C. E. **Brown**	J. D. **McQueen**	J. W. **Nutt**
V. **Jarrell**	C. O. **Bateman**	R. H. **Bateman**
A. S. **Scott**	W. T. **Warren**	L. M. **Jennings**
J. B. **Harry**	A. W. **Fulcher**	J. G. **Shamburger**
J. D. **Dale**	W. G. **Irby**	C. C. **Acker**

In Memorial.

. . . H. V. **Johnson** . . . On the 14th day of March 1917, Bro Johnson finished his life's work.

Bro. Johnson was born Nov. 1, 1865 . . . January 8th, 1889, he was married to Miss Texas **Strickland**, a neice of the late Mrs. Mary **Lipscomb** who had raised her from a child, her parents having died when she was an infant. . . . To this union eleven children were born, two died in infancy, the other are left to mourn . . .

The living children of Bro. Johnson are as follows: T. W. **Johnson**, Rotan, Texas; Mrs. H. A. **McRight**, Brandenburg, Texas; S. I. **Johnson**, Electra, Texas; J. L. **Johnson**, Dallas, Texas; Mrs. E. K. **Jones**, Alba, Texas; Mrs. J. B. **Mount** Jr., Alba, Texas; J. H. **Johnson**, Mineola, Texas; Mrs. J. L. **Patrick**, Alba, Texas; Miss Corda **Johnson**, Alba, Texas, the latter being the baby girl now 15 years of age and still under the family roof.

His Former Pastor,
J. T. **Williams**.

(Note: In making mention of the death of this good man last week and giving the names of his brothers and sisters, we inadvertantly failed to mention Mrs. J. H. **Patton**, a sister, who resides at Alba. The failure to mention Mrs. Patton was purely an oversight. Ed.)

Grand and Petit Jurors for District Court

. . . Spring term of District Court. . . convenes Monday April 16, 1917

GRAND JURORS

Clem **Wright**, Quitman
Bert **Patrick**, Golden
W. N. **Barnes**, Hawkins
Harvey **Brewer**, Quitman, Rt. 5.
J. T. **Smith**, Hawkins
I. N. **Reneau**, Golden
Wiley **Bartlett**, Mineola Rt 6
P. E. **Cox**, Ogburn
R. H. **McCrary**, Winnsboro
Jumbo **Shoemaker**, Alba
Walter **Harrison**, Quitman, Rt 4.
Ezra **Carter**, Quitman, Rt. 1
Taylor **Greer**, Mineola
Sam **Galloway**, Yantis
Sam **Jarred**, Winnsboro
Chas, **Bellomy**, Winnsboro

PETIT JURORS, 1st week

A. W. **Flournoy**	A. J. **Falkner**	F. A. **Hollis**
R. E. **Faulk**	R. J. **Gaston**	T. L. **Harris**
C. A. **Cain**	A. R. **Cruse**	S. C. **Davenport**
R. F. **Conger**	H. G. **Coats**	J. W. **Goldsmith**
A. F. **Dean**	R. F. **Guin**	W. H. **Low**
F. G. **Estes**	A. T. **Carlile**	G. W. **Atkins**
L. B. **Blackwell**	J. F. **Haines**	W. R. **Butts**
S. C. **Corbett**	W. M. **Harris**	W. D. **Henson**
E. L. **Foster**	E. **Gentry**	T. B. **Breedlove**
R. A. **Copeland**	Bob **Lindley**	Oscar **Gilbreath**
J. L. **Highnote**	W. J. **Hines**	M. V. **Anders**
J. H. **Loyd**	J. W. **Faulk**	

PETIT JURORS, 2nd week

W. B. **Black**	M. D. **Bright**	J. J. **Holbrook**
D. S. **Armstrong**	J. M. **Coursey**	I. C. **Larue**
A. H. **Culpepper**	W. R. **Darby**	H. D. **Ingram**
R. A. **Byrd**	A. W. **Harper**	H. G. **Farris**
J. P. **Gill**	J. W. **Corley**	Dan **Graham**
W. P. **Flowers**	J. F. **Denton**	J. E. **Braziel**
W. P. **Lawrence**	G. N. **Bowling**	G. C. **Henry**
Jack **Lloyd**	J. Q. **Beard**	Arthur **Sims**
J. B. **Howell**	W. N. **Bexley**	J. A. **Hughes**
Geo. D. **Hurdle**	E. F. **Folmer**	W. C. **Barton**
G. D. **Clayton**	J. L. **Jacobs**	W. W. **Myers**
J. A. **Blalock**	J. B. **Mount**	I. W. **Browning**

Democrat - 1917

PETIT JURORS, 3rd week

P. E. Harrison	C. M. Dozier	J. H. Hester
J. E. McDade	J. R. White	J. D. Cade
B. H. Jolly	E. D. Brady	R. E. Carrington
I. P. Gibson	R. P. Knight	W. A. Crumpler
J. H. Dixon	J. E. Gilbreath	A. J. Horton
R. F. Derr	R. W. Galloway	Frank Davis
C. A. Green	C. R. LaForce	B. C. Hollinquest
R. F. Green	W. B. Kirby	H. F. Elledge
J. W. Kennedy	L. M. Gilbreath	A. C. Ayer
W. M. Hartsfield	J. S. Amos	Jon Russell
F. M. Bynum	F. E. Bagby	C. Y. Harrington
H. L. Crosby	A. H. Hunt	C. M. Cain
L. A. Bryant	J. R. Connell	A. L. Cain
C. C. Sisler	P. H. Huckaba	Sam Jones
J. A. Carlile	J. M. Hollinshed	J. C. Caldwell

PETIT JURORS, 4th week

J. G. Cathey	J. R. Fouse	P. A. Carrington
M. T. Galusha	S. H. Craver	J. W. Gilbert
W. J. Bailey	M. A. Hudson	O. P. Hallman
C. L. Dial	J. F. French	M. H. Benton
Verdie Cassel	J. R. Hilburn	R. D. Littleton
J. D. Byrd	B. F. Campbell	J. T. Ivey
H. M. Dunahoe	Doll Alvis	J. H. Hitt
H. L. Cannady	Bob Edmonds	J. K. Deas
W. T. Harbuck	R. S. Collins	C. D. Davis
Jas. Gregory	Claud Bellomy	W. H. Holly
H. F. Downing	Jno. D. Fowler	J. W. Burford
M. A. Farris	B. A. Cox	L. L. Dodgen
J. M. Buckner	E. N. Clower	J. W. Kilburn
J. H. Burgess	B. G. Dickey	Joe Kirkland
H. L. Herring	J. M. Boyd	W. A. Burke

April 5, 1917

Fatal Auto Accident

One of the saddest accidents to occur in our county was that one last Thursday, March 19th, when the ford of Sheriff **Apel**, which was being driven by Miss Willie Mae Apel, went off the bridge between the home of John and Archie **Shamburger** on the Quitman and Winnsboro road, resulting in the death of the babe of Mr. and Mrs. R. L. **Butler** and the injury of practically every occupant of the car.

. . . Misses Willie Mae and Lona Apel, Mrs. R. L. Butler and babe and Miss Bessie Butler, with Miss Willie Mae driving . . .

Little Bennie Bob.

Little Bennie Bob [**Butler**] was born Feb 10th, 1917. . . . After the funeral services the remains were carried to Mrytle Springs grave yard. . . .

Barn Burned.

The large barn, garage, and out buildings of C. A. **Green** one mile north of Quitman, was destroyed by fire Tuesday, about 2 o'clock.

Caught Bootlegger.

Sheriff **Apel** went to Rockwall last week and brought in Sam **Wells** col., who was indicted by the grand jury of this county about three years ago for bootlegging and has been on the scout ever since.

Obituary.

On Feb. 28 the death angel visited the home of O. M. **McCorley** and claimed his darling wife. She was the daughter of Mr. and Mrs. J. V. **White**, who live near Rock Hill. She leaves a husband and four children, father and mother, five sisters and one brother. . . .

Maud, as everyone caller her, had been an invalid for three years. . . .

She was born in Alabama Apr. 30, 1887. In the year 1900 together with her father and mother and sisters and brother she moved to Texas. In 1903 she was married to O. M. McCorley.

Democrat - 1917

Barn Burned.

Albert **Blalock** called at our office the other day and reported that Claude **Bateman** had the misfortune to lose his barn and about 150 bushels of corn by fire one night the past week.

Stagner Items.

D. P. **Cumbie** of Vera, Texas, visited his sister, Mrs. M. L. **Long** and family . . .

County Attorney Weds.

. . . we received the following from Marshall:

"At the home of Mr. and Mrs. W. T. **Dickinson**, Sunday morning at 8 o'clock, Rev. H. H. **Drake** of Pittsburg, Texas, united in marriage, Mr. Floyd **Harry** and Miss Lillie **Jackson** of Quitman, Texas, in the presence of a few friends and relatives. . . . Miss Jackson is a cousin of Mrs. Dickinson . . .

Mr. and Mrs. Harry are spending the week with the bride's mother, Mrs. M. P. Jackson at Oak Grove . . .

Pleasant Grove.

The infant babe of Mr. and Mrs. J. H. **Jackson** died Friday afternoon and was buried Saturday at Hope Well.

Miss Florine Germany.

The following account of the death of Miss Florine **Germany** is taken from the Greenville Morning Herald of March 29:

"Miss Florine Germany died at the family home, 3403 West Lee street, at 8:30 o'clock Wednesday night after an illness of almost three weeks' duration from typhoid fever. . . .

"Miss Florine Germany was born August 13, 1894, in this city and her life was spent in Greenville, with the exception of several months she was studying art elsewhere. . . .

"She is survived by her father and mother and the following brothers and sisters: Edna, who is at Pecos, Texas, and Sibyl, Joe, Frank and Jack, besides numerous other relatives."

Miss Florine was a grand daughter of Mrs. S. E. Conger whose death was reported in these columns some weeks ago.

Wood County Newspapers

Obituary.

The death angel visited the home of our neighbor and friend, Mr. **Russom** on the 10th day of March and took from him his companion, Mrs. Rosabell Russom. . . . The remains were carried to Ebenezer and laid to rest the day following her death. . . . had just passed 30 years of age Feb. 12, 1917. She leaves behind a husband, four children and a host of relatives and friends.

April 12, 1917

"A Good Woman."

. . . on Saturday night at 8:30 the death angel came to the home of I. W. **Robbins** in Quitman and claimed his wife . . .

Mrs. Robbins was born in Georgia, May 11, 1867. She was a daughter of Mr. and Mrs. S. M. Lipscomb and with her parents came to Texas, Quitman and Wood county, in 1884. February 12, 1885, she was married to I. W. Robbins, who was then District Clerk of Wood county. To this union twelve children were born, five of them died in infancy, the other seven with the aged mother, the husband of her youth, two brothers and two sisters survive. The aged mother has been at the Robbins home for several months, one sister, Mrs. **Dickerman**, came from her home at Gainesville, and was here when the end came, the other sister was not able to come on account of being sick. Neither of the brothers were able to be here. The two brothers are J. H. **Lipscomb**, of Mennington, Okla., Prof. M. A. Lipscomb, of Dexter, Texas and the other sister is Mrs. J. L. **King**, of Portland, Oregon.

The surviving children are Dr. Virgil E., Clough, Hill, Misses Lois, Mary and Ella and Master Buster, the baby boy, all of whom are living in Quitman and are all still under the family roof except the two older sons, who are married.

. . . the remains were carried to the family burrying plot in Quitman cemetery . . .

Democrat - 1917

Doings in County Court

Pleas of guilty - J. S. **Warren**, aggravated assault, fine $50.00. Ike **Thomas**, theft, fine $10.00 an one hour in jail. W. **Sinnett**, aggravated assault, fine $25.00.

Jury Trials - Frank **Campbell**, threats to take human life, guilty, fine $100.00. Stafford **Wilson**, gaming, guilty, fine $10.00. Joe **Dodson**, gaming, guilty, fine $10.

Dismissed - Bud **Jackson**, Lorenza **Malone**, Commie **Campbell**, George **McDaniel**, 3 cases, **Wheeler Anderson**.

Marriage Permits.

Since our last report . . . :
F. S. **Robinson** and Emma **Wade**.
Jessie **Session** and Lula **Jackson**.
Frank **Dyess** and Bera **Day**.
Roy **Bartlett** and Hattie **Matheson**.
L. P. **Milner** and Martha **Jackson**.
W. B. **Johnson** and Jessie **Poe**.
Lawrence **Revley** and Mae **Gilliland**.
R. B. **Wood** and E. A. **Wood**.
C. A. **Pierce** and Winnie **Davis**.
Frank **Turner** and Louella **Blake**.

Tuesday's Dallas News had among the list of volunteers the name of Spencer Rudolph **Horton**. . . . it is our Spencer, eldest son of Mr. and Mrs. A. J. Horton of our town . . . he left Tuesday night with the Marine Corps for North Carolina . . . the first Quitman young man to enter the service. . . .

Prominent Alba Couple Wed.

The Democrat has received the following announcement:

"Mr. and Mrs. W. B. **Gilliland** announce the marriage of their daughter Mae to Mr. Lawrence W. **Reavley** at 9 o'clock Wednesday evening, April the fourth, nineteen hundred and seventeen, Alba, Texas."

April 19, 1917

Patriotic Appeal.

The United States has told Texas that a part of her duty in this creat conflict is to feed herself. Indeed, say the authorities, Texas must feed herself or go hungry. . . .

Death of Infant.

The remains of the infant of Mr. and Mrs. Arch **Moore** was carried to Sharon Friday of last week for burial. . . .

An Easter Wedding.
PIERCE - DAVIS

On last Sunday eve Mr. "Cater" **Pierce** of Ogburn drove to the residence of J. N. **Davis** of Peach, and taking Miss Winnie Davis in the buggy, they, with a few others who had been given the "tip," drove to the residence of Rev. J. B. **Boyd** east of town, where that reverend gentleman pronounced the ceremony which made them husband and wife.

Mr. Pierce is the merchant prince of Ogburn, being head of the Pierce Mercantile Co. of Ogburn, Texas. . . .

Miss Winnie is the second eldest daughter of J. N. Davis.

Death of Mrs. Smith.

Mrs. Charlie **Smith** died at the family home near Golden early part of last week and interment was had at Sand Springs the day following her demise.

April 26, 1917

Pleasant Grove

. . . the sudden death of Russell **McDonald**. . . . caused by pneumonia. He is a son of Jim McDonald and is survived by his father and one sister, Mrs. Bob **Kennimer** of Coke. He was 21 years of age . . . buried at Hopewell Saturday afternoon.

Democrat - 1917

Forrest Hill News.
. . . Mr. Dick **Ingram** and Miss Medie **Sutton** were happily married Saturday evening at two o'clock.

Obituary.
Andrew Walter **Morrison** was born in Polk County, Texas, Oct. 28, 1876. . . returned to his mother's home near Mineola, reaching home Saturday, March 24th, and lived till Wednesday of the next week. . . . the death of his Father fourteen years ago, . . .
He leaves his mother, four brothers, and four sisters to mourn . . . his brother Claude passed away on Easter Sunday, less than two weeks after Andrew's death.

May 3, 1917

Sunday Wedding.
At the residence of the bride's father at Peach, Mr. Church **Young** and Miss Dosia **Davis** were united in marriage at 11 o'clock a.m. in the presence of a few relatives and friends. . .
The bride is the youngest of J. N. Davis . . .The groom is formerly of Gilmer . . . agent of the M. & E.T.R.R.
The happy couple . . . will make their home at Peach.

Marriage License.
Dr. C. T. **Vickers** and Nollie Mae **Gorman**.
J. L. **Moreland** and Carrie **Parkerson**.
S. C. **Selby** and Lillian **Maxfield**.
Orman **Bradshaw** and Lizzie **Mills**.
O. W. **Chreitzberg** and Katy **Rodney**.
R. F. **Murdock** and Ione **Holley**.
Jim **Spencer** and Mary **Jones**.
Robert **Patterson** and Emma **Lewis**.
Jerry **Crowl** and Dovie **Spencer**.
Haywood **Spratt** and Lenora **Copeland**.
Homer **Richey** and Gladis **Thompson**.

Notaries Public For Wood County.
Senator Will **Suiter** has furnished the Democrat with the list of Notaries Public for Wood county, . . .

Alvis, Gordon	Winnsboro	**Breen**, Jno. J.	Mineola
Benton, F. M.	Alba	**Britton**, A. J.	Quitman
Burkett, J. E.	Mineola	**Barnett**, J. A.	Golden
Bankston, Miss S. M.	Winnsboro	**Britton**, Geo.	Yantis
Burnett, C. W.	Ogburn	**Cain**, C. M.	Winnsboro
Cowan, Geo. W.	Mineola	**Craddock**, W. M.	Yantis
Campbell, W. W.	Alba	**Carter**, J. L.	Winnsboro
Corley, J. W.	Winnsboro	**Dickey**, B. G.	Winnsboro
Davis, J. N.	Peach	**Dowell**, J. D.	Mineola
Dykes, J. B.	Winnsboro	**Dunbar**, A. L.	Golden
Edelin, J. C.	Mineola	**Eskridge**, Edgar	Winnsboro
Falkner, J. M.	Mineola	**Greer**, Taylor	Mineola
Gaston, R. J.	Mineola	**Giles**, J. D.	Hawkins
Gilbreath, J. E.	Alba	**Howell**, P. B.	Winnsboro
Harris, V. B.	Quitman	**Howard**, J. N.	Alba
Hale, G. W.	Quitman	**Harris**, James D.	Mineola
Harris, T. I.	Quitman	**Hart**, I. B.	Quitman
Hitt, Jno. F.	Winnsboro	**Hitt**, J. O.	Winnsboro
Jones, W. P.	Mineola	**Jones**, W. N.	Mineola
Little, Miss Commye	Mineola	**Landers**, M. H.	Mineola
Landers, J. H.	Mineola	**Laforce**, S. C.	Hawkins
Low, W. H.	Alba	**Lloyd**, L. F.	Quitman
Low, R. W.	Quitman	**Lambert**, J. W.	Quitman
Lloyd, J. M.	Quitman	**Meredith**, H. W.	Mineola
Mansell, M. E.	Mineola	**Morris**, Alf	Winnsboro
Malone, J. H.	Quitman	**Mansell**, B. G.	Alba
Morrison, W. A.	Quitman	**Morris**, R. E.	Quitman
Newsome, T. M.	Winnsboro	**Peacock**, C. A.	Hawkins
Paschal, D. B.	Winnsboro	**Pierson**, L. P.	Winnsboro
Revell, C. E.	Mineola	**Russell**, W. G.	Winnsboro
Reeves, E. A.	Mineola	**Riley**, T. J.	Alba
Ray, Shaw D.	Winnsboro	**Russell**, Jonathan	Winnsboro
Reneau, T. M.	Alba	**Reeves**, Geo. C.	Mineola

Russell, J. C.	Golden	**Shields**, R. S.	Mineola
Shields, Mrs. Lura	Mineola	**Smith**, R. M.	Quitman
Sellers, W. B.	Winnsboro	**Stevenson**, W. C.	Winnsboro
Smart, J. W.	Hawkins	**Shaw**, T. J.	Mineola
Shelton, W. W.	Quitman	**Smart**, Jno. F.	Quitman
Stokes, Ben	Winnsboro	**Tharp**, E. A.	Mineola
Toney, B. H.	Hawkins	**Torrance**, R. J.	Mineola
Tuggle, Lucy	Winnsboro	**Vickery**, C. W.	Quitman
Wilkinson, H. L.	Winnsboro	**Williams**, J. Matt	Mineola
Woods, J. B.	Mineola	**Wright**, Elmore	Winnsboro
Worthington, W. A.	Winnsboro	**Wilson**, W. G.	Quitman

May 10, 1917

Death of Mrs. Harris

We are pained to chronicle the death of Mrs. **Harris**, widow of the late H. B. Harris, which sad event occurred at her home a few miles from Quitman last Saturday night.

Mrs. Harris was a sister of T. F. **Dodgen**, a prominent citizen of the Forrest Home country, and the mother of Prof. R. L. **Simmons**, one of our prominent teachers. A sister, Mrs. J. W. **McRight**, and several other children survive deceased.

Interment was had at Hopewell grave yard Sunday evening, . . .

Child Killed By Auto

About 6:30 Tuesday afternoon, Harold, the 8-year-old child of Mr. and Mrs. H. A. **Wylie**, was run over by an automobile and so badly hurt that he died within an hour and a half.

Death of Mrs. Cameron.

Mrs. **Cameron** died at the family home north of town Saturday night May 5, and was buried at Concord Sunday evening. Mrs. Cameron has been in failing health for some months, tuberculosis being the cause of death.

The husband and children . . .

J. O. Hitt Dead.

J. O **Hitt**, aged 54, died at his home in this city Thursday morning, May 3, at 4:30. . . . laid to rest in the city cemetery.

. . . afflicted with Bright's disease. . . He is survived by his wife and three children, Lorene, Jimmie and Jeless. - Winnsboro News.

Bateman- Posey

Sunday evening, May 6, 1917, Mr. Jesse **Bateman** and Miss Elton **Posey** drove to the Methodist parsonage in Quitman and were united in marriage by Rev. J. C. **Calhoun**.

The young couple live in the Coke country. Miss Elton is the eldest daughter of Mr. and Mrs. J. T. Posey . . .

May 17, 1917

Biography of Mrs. M. A. Harris

Mrs. Marietta A. **Harris** was born in Cobb Co., Georgia Sept. 3rd, 1858. At the age of ten years she came to Texas with her parents and settled near Pleasant Grove. the next year her father and mother died leaving the children to support themselves. At the age of 18 she was married to R. L. **Simmons**. To them eight children were born, two of whom died in infancy. On July 13th, 1891, Mr. Simmons died leaving her with six small children to support, this she did for seven years. On January the 16th, 1898, she was married to H. B. Harris. To them three children were born all of whom died in infancy. . .. On August 19th 1909, Mr. Harris died. . . . no one present at the time of her death but two of her children, Eula and Leon, and a grandson.

Besides her children she is survived by one brother, T. F. **Dodgen** of Pleasant Grove, and two sisters, Mrs. Octavia **Manning** of Hunt Co., and Mrs. J. W. **McRight** of Van Zandt county.

Obituary.

Noah W. **Hillburn** passed over the River of Death April 11, 1917. . . .

Bro. Noah lived at Rotan, Texas, when death claimed him. The remains were brought to Mineola and carried to Sand Springs ..

Marriage License.

Willie **Lee** and Ella **Clay**.
Jess **Bateman** and Elton **Posey**.
Fred **Beck** and Minnie **Chaney**.
Henry **Jackson** and Ursey **Dickey**.
Geo. **Williams** and Zella **Douglas**.
Lemon **Davis** and Ollie **Criner**.

May 24, 1917

Mrs. Hood Moore.

After a lingering illness of more than a year Mrs. Hood **Moore** died at the family home in Winnsboro Sunday night May 20th. The remains were carried to Hope Well Tuesday where interment was had.

Mrs. Moore was formerly Miss Beatrice **Browning**, a daughter of that venerable and good citizen, J. C. Browning, and was reared near Pleasant Grove. She was married to hood Moore several years ago. Three children with the husband and a host of friends survive her.

Aged Mother Dies.

J. C. **Parker** informed us the other day of the death of his mother, Mrs. Rebecca Parker, which occured in Georgia, May 18th. He tells us his mother was 86 years old at the time of her death. there are three sons and three daughters who survive, our friend, J. C. being the oldest of the children.

Isham Hays Dead.

Isham **Hays**, col., for years a prominent figure in political affairs in Wood county, being at one time chairman of the Republican party of this county, died at Ft. Worth last week and was brought to Quitman for burial.

Aged Wife Dies.

Our veteran friend John S. **Daniels** of Mineola, informed us Monday of the death of his wife which occured the past week at the family home in that City.

May 31, 1917

Tommie Ramey Dead.

Tommie **Ramey**, aged 14 years, son of Mrs. Ella Ramey, died at the family home two miles north of Quitman Thursday evening of last week after an illness of only a few days. Interment was had at Myrtle Springs grave yard . . .The bereaved mother, brothers and sisters . . .

In Memory of Mrs. Beatrice Moore.

Mrs. **Moore**'s maiden name was Miss Beatrice **Browning**, she being the eldest daughter of Mr. and Mrs. Jno. C. Browning. She was born April 23, 1882.

In February 1917 [sic] she was married to Mr. J. Hood Moore. To this union there was three children born, two boys and one girl.

She breathed her last about 2 o'clock Monday morning, May 21, 1917 . . .

Deceased leaves to mourn her loss, a loving husband, three children, aged father, a step mother, five brothers, two sisters and two half sisters, only a few of whom were present at the burial, as they are scattered in different parts of the country.

The remains were conveyed to Hopewell on Tuesday . . .

Marriage License Issued.

Since our last report . . .:
Burie **Lawrence** and Myrtle **Harris**.
Willie **Browning** and Jewel **Bogues**.
Ecignio **Cacillas** and Leonot **Mercedauti**.
J. F. **Dial** and Lovie **Deas**.
H. B. **Gilbreath** and Dolly **French**.
Aubrey **Woods** and Flora **James**.
S. P. **Thompson** and Alice McCain.

Democrat - 1917

Walter Russell Married.

Mr. and Mrs. Claude **Scoggins**, of Golden, the latter a sister of Walter **Russell**, passed through Quitman Tuesday morning enroute to Mt. Pleasant where Walter Russell and Miss Nora **Dupree** were to be married Tuesday night of this week

June 7, 1917

W. H. Britton Dead

W. H. **Britton** died at his home in Yantis Monday and was buried in the Yantis cemetery Tuesday evening. . .

Deceased had been a sufferer for years . . .

Carried to Sanitarium

G. W. **Lipscomb** was carried to the Baptist sanitarium at Dallas Saturday night, his brother, Dr. C. D. Lipscomb and his sons, Silas and Lindsey, accompanying him. Mr. Lipscomb has been suffering for some weeks with an infection caused from a rat bite on his leg.

A Correction

In the obituary of Mrs. Hood **Moore** published in last weeks issue of the Democrat a typographical error occurred in the date of deceased's marriage. She was married to Mr. Moore in February 1907, instead of 1917, as it appeared in last weeks paper . . .

Sheriff's Daughter Weds.

When Sheriff **Apel** reached Hainesville last Thursday evening returning from Hawkins, he learned that he had a son-in-law in the person of Bill Oates **Mounts**. Mr. Apel was expecting the marriage to take place sometime in the future, but did not expect it so soon and when on Thursday of last week he left for Hawkins he had no intimation that the event would take place that day, however, after the Sheriff left home his daughter, Miss Willie Mae and Prof. B. O. Mounts dedided to get married. They procured the necessary papers, repaired to the home of Rev. R. J. **Martin** where they were married and when Mr. **Apel** got home they were well on their way to Dallas where they visited the grooms brother and sister until Sunday evening when they returned home and received parental forgiveness and were admitted to "The Jail" where the Sheriff says he will keep them.

. . . Bill Oates as he is familiarly called, is a son of Mr. and Mrs. J. B. **Mounts** . . . Miss Willie Mae is the eldest daughter of Sheriff Apel. . . .

A Pretty Home Wedding

Last Sunday evening at 4:30 Mr. Thomas A. **Lipscomb** and Miss Ila Ben **Billings** were married at the residence of the bride's parents. The attendants being District Clerk J. R. **Taylor** and Miss Bonnie Maye **Sutherland**. Rev. J. C. **Calhoun** officiated at the marriage. Miss Ila is the pretty and charming daughter of Mr. and Mrs. T. J. Billings, living near Hainesville. . . . Tommie, as he is familiarly called, is the eldest sone of Dr. and Mrs. C. D. Lipscomb, of Quitman.

In Memorium.

How our hearts ached with sorrow Thursday morning when the sad message "Tommie **Ramey** is dead" reached us.

He was only sick a few days, but his suffering was intense.

Tommie's body was laid to rest in the Myrtle Springs cemetery Friday afternoon by the side of his father who preceded him several years ago.

June 14, 1917

Craig-Higginbotham.

Mr. Will **Craig** and Miss Ola **Higginbotham** went over to Emory Wednesday morning of last week where they secured marriage license and were married at 10 o'clock, returning home that afternoon.

Marriage License.

. . . since our last report:
Horace **Owens** and Maudie **Haskins**.

Democrat - 1917

S. K. **Van Nostrand** and Clyde **Koonce**.
Edward H. **Skinnell** and Bessie May **Finley**.
W. O. **Mount** and Willie May **Apel**.
W. R. **Wheeler** and Addie **Rhymes**.
L. J. **Reynolds** and Leola **Samples**.
Benjamin E. **Rice** and Ina **Vaughn**.
H. E. **Speights** and Clara **Smith**.
S. L. **Bailey** and Gladys **Harry**.
T. A. **Lipscomb** and Ben I. **Billings**.
Jesse **Patterson** and Ella **Taylor**.

Biographical Sketch.

At the funeral of W. H. **Britton** held at the Baptist church in Yantis Tuesday evening of last week, the following biographical sketch of the life of this pioneer of Wood county, was read by Rev. J. C. **Calhoun**. This sketch was prepared by Andrew J. Britton, a nephew of deceased, who was perhaps as close to deceased as any person living with the possible exception of the wife.

"The deceased, William H. Britton, was 63 years of age at the time of his death; his life work is too well known . . . His father was a confederate soldier and died during the civil war, leaving him a mere child; at the end of the war his mother who was a member of the **Hanson** family of Smith County, moved to Wood County, and to the place where Dick **Gilbreath** now lives, which place she settled with her six orphan boys, John, Jeff, Harvey, George, Bill, and Frank Britton, all of whom are now gone, except Frank.

". . . Deceased was afflicted and handicapped physically; he was on a walking stick practically all his life. . . .

". . . He studdied law under the direction ofthe late Govenor **Hogg**, when he lived in Quitman . . .

"In 1884 he was married to Miss Minnie **McDonald**, and to this union 10 children were born all of whom survive him; deceased was an uncle of George and Andrew Britton . . .

"The children are Jim Britton, Mrytle, wife of Bill **Morgan**, Fannie, wife of Don **Nichols**, Ola, wife of Walter Gilbreath, John, Ben, Maye, ___, Hart, and Ruby.

217

June 21, 1917

[This issue contains lists of the persons registered in Wood County on June 5th, 1917. The list is organized by precinct. The lists are not extracted here. They are lengthy and do not add information about previous generations. -Ed.]

Letter From Soldier Boy.

Mrs. J. A. **Cook** writes us a letter in which she encloses one that she received a few days ago from her son, Gordon Russell Cook, who is now a Norfolk Va. Mrs. Cook is a daughter of our veteran friend, Uncle Gus **Rape**, . . . [Letter follows.]

Committed Suicide.

Justice **Smart** received a phone message this Wednesday morning that a man by the name of **Pilkinton** had committed suicide near Hainesville. . . .

A Good Woman Called to That Home Above.

Tuesday morning the news spread over our little city that Grandma **Smith** had passed away. . . . Her death occurred at the home of her daughter Mrs. J. H. **Farrington**, at 7 o'clock a. m. June 12th.

Grandma Smith had reached the ripe age of 76 years and 8 months. She was the wife of Dr. W. E. Smith, having been married to him about 60 years ago. There were 13 children born to the union, 8 boys and 5 girls. Of this number 5 are still living, two boys and three girls. The children who survive are, Mrs. J. H. **English**, Mrs. Dr. Farrington and Bob Smith, of this city; Mrs. **Scoggins** of Greenville, and a son who lives in West Texas.

Uncle Jim Kirbo Dead.

News was received in Quitman Monday evening of the death of Uncle Jim **Kirbo**, which event occurred at his late home about six miles east of town that day.

Uncle Jim was a pioneer citizen of the county . . .

June 28, 1917

Monitor Changes Hands.

Mr. N. W. **Wade** phones us from Mineola that he has bought the Mineola Monitor from W. S. **Davis** and has taken charge. Mr. Wade is from Atlanta, Ga. and is an experienced newspaper man.

Smith Family Reunion.

According to their yearly practice, the members of the John **Smith** family met at the home of Harvey **Bright** near Oak Grove, Sunday June 17, 1917. This being Mr. Smith's 73rd birthday. At this reunion seven children were present, twenty grand children, four great grand children, . . .

Death of W. C. Puckett.

After a lingering illness, W. C. (Bud) **Puckett** died at his home near Hainesville Thursday morning June 21, 1917, at 10:30. Interment was had a Mr. Pisga Friday morning at 11 o'clock after funeral services had been held in the church house by Revs. H. V. **Hamrick**, J. C. **Calhoun** and J. W. **Truss**.

W. D. Puckett, of "Bud" Puckett as he was best known, was born January 14, 1851, in Cherokee county, Ala., and when seven years of age his parents came to Texas and settled in Wood county, near what is now known as the **Wallace** place on Sandy. His father volunteered his services when the war came on and served for near four years, being killed at Mansfield, or Pleasant Ridge, La. just before the close of the conflict. The death of the father left the widow with four children to fight the battles alone. There were four of the children, Bud, the oldest, a daughter, Miss Josie who later married Pink **Hughes**, J. A. (Asa) and Dr. J. M., the latter two being still with us, the daughter having died several years ago. . . . Sept. 30, 1894, he was married to Miss Maggie **Laminack** to which union ten children were born nine of whom are still living, the eldest a daughter, being now the wife of Irby **Wallin**. His aged mother continued to make her home with him until her death about seven years ago.

Wood County Newspapers

A Fire 68 Years Old.
[Story of old fire in Pennsylvania coal mine.]
Out north of Honey Grove, a few years since, according to one of our most truthful citizens, a tree caught fire and burned for more than a year. . . .   - Honey Grove Signal.

Death of Dr. Lindsey.
A. A. **Lindsey** and Ben **Stokes** were here from Winnsboro Thursday of last week. Mr. Lindsey informed us of the death of his father which occurred some weeks ago in Tennessee. The following account of the deathof Dr. Lindsey is taken from Paris, (Tenn.) Post:
"On Saturday last, at his home near Big Sandy, Go. G. L. A. Lindsey died at the age of 70 years, and was buried with Masonic honors on Monday at the family burying ground. Dr. Lindsey was a consistent member of the Presbyterian Church since boyhood and a very worthy cirizen. His is survived by a wife, four sons and one daughter."

Returns from Alabama.
Uncle Abb **Harris** and his family spent Thursday of last week with his daughter, Mrs. Dr. C. D. **Lipscomb**, . . . he and his wife have recently returned from Troy, Ala., to which place they were called the latter part of May on account of the death of Mrs. Sarah **Davidson**, wife of J. A. Davidson, of Troy, who was a sister of Mrs. Harris. Uncle Abb tells us that Mrs. Davidson's death was caused from getting burned. She was 73 years of age and was sitting in front of the fire making a broom for her daughter when her clothing caught fire and before the flames could be extinguished she was so badly burned that death resulted in about ten hours.

July 5, 1917

Mrs. Lou Leath Dead.
News reached Quitman Sunday of the death of Mrs. Lou **Leath**, which occured at the home of her son, W. B. Leath at Keifer, Okla.,

Sunday morning. The remains reached Quitman Tuesday and burial took place that evening in Quitman cemetery. . .

July 12, 1917

Marriage License.

Since June 8, the following:
Jim **Banks** and Lillie **Meeks**.
Carson **Cornelius** and Willie **Wheeler**.
T. H. **Kennimer** and Dora Lee **McDonald**.
Sam **Woods** and Mattie **Hall**.
Henry **Terry** and Jessie **Griffin**.
Honier **Bush** and Ada **Wallace**.
Joe **Hoard** and Mozelle **Griffin**.
Sid **Sandlin** and Estelle **Hood**.
Thornton **Scott** and Estelle **Russell**.
V. O. **Shropshire** and Estelle **Morrison**.
Richard **Burnett** and Francis **Sorge**.
U. T. **Tucker** and Vera **Mitchell**.
D. D. **Moore** and Sindie **Sutton**.
L. C. **Coats** and Dilmon **McCrary**.
Holland **Shirey** and Edith **Vandiver**.
H. T. **Chappell** and Maude **Beard**.
Big Sye **Holland** and Ellen **Williams**.

Death of J. L. Ross.

The Democrat is pained indeed to hear of the death of J. L. **Ross** which occcured at his late home sunday evening last. . . .

Married Sunday Night.

At the home of Mr. and Mrs. R. W. **Daniel** in this city Sunday night at 8 o'clock, Mr. Carl **Coats** and Miss Dilmon **McCrary** were married, Rev. Jno. E. **Roach** officiating. The bride is a daughter of R. N. McCrary of Coke . . . Mr. Coats is a traveling salesman for a Kansas City hat house, was reared in this section, . . .

July 19, 1917

Dr. Stevenson Dead.

Dr. W. R. **Stevenson** died at the home of W. E. Stevenson Wednesday afternoon at six o'clock. The Doctor was 80 years old, was born in San Augustine, Texas, and moved to Winnsboro in 1884, residing here since that time. He was an ex-Confederate soldier . . remains were laid to rest in the Lee cemetery.   - Winnsboro News.

In Memorium.

Death has called at the home of W. A. **Gilbreath** and took away his beloved wife, Lesta. Her illness was short, her suffering was only a few days. On the 21 day of June, 1917, Lesta finished her life's work. She was born in Wood Co., Oct. 13, 1899. . . .

Lesta's mother departed from this world some years ago leaving her at the ago of nine years to fill her place in taking care of we smaller children. . . . She is a daughter of Lewis **Smith**, having lived in Wood Co. most of her life and under her father's roof until Oct. 9, 1916, when she was married to Wade **Gilbreath**, a son of uncle Joe Gilbreath Sr.

. . . her remains laid to rest in the Rock Hill cemetery June 22, 1917.   - Her sister, Belle Smith

July 26, 1917

Dr. Roy Harris Weds.

Dr. Roy **Harris** of Oak Grove came home sunday with his new bride and is now at home t Oak Grove. The Doctor and Miss Lucille **Todd** were married in Dallas the past week.

August 9, 1917

Another Good Woman Gone

Mention was made last week of the death of Mrs. **Goodwin**, wife of T. J. Goodwin, which sad event occurred at the home of her son, C. M. Goodwin in Dallas, Tuesday night, July 31st, 1917.

Mrs. Mattie C. Goodwin was born in Runnels county, near Garard, Ala., Sept. 23, 1843. In 1880 she was married to T. J. Goodwin to which union three children now living, were born, viz: Edgar, who is a mail clerk running out of Ft. Worth to Parsons, Kansas; Clarence, who is a bookkeeper in Dallas, and a daughter, Mrs. R. A. **Moore** who is now and has been for some months, under the family roof.

A tinge of romance is connected with the marriage of this aged couple. Mrs. Goodwin, whose maiden name was Mattie **Osborne**, was the youthful sweetheart of Mr. Goodwin. They became separated while both were young, Mr. Goodwin married and one child, now Mrs. J. L. **Shoemaker** of Alba, was born to this union. This wife died and Mr. Goodwin was again married and to his union two sons, Rufus and Walter born, when this second wife died. Miss Mattie Osborne had remained single and correspondence began after a time between these two who had been sweethearts in their younger days. This soon culminated in Mr. Goodwin returning to the old Alabama state where they were married and came to Texas where the girl of his youth took the place of mother for the three motherless children of the man whom she had known and loved in her girlhood days. . . .

Negro Drowned.

An eighteen year old son of Pink **Smith** Sr. col., was drowned Wednesday evening of last week in what is known as the Rainwater eddy on Lake Fork. The negro boy was in bathing with some other negroes and got beyond his depth and before assistance could reach him he sank. The body was recovered in a short while and was buried the following day in the grave yard north of town.

Marriage License Issued.

Since our last report . . .:
Irion Jack and Mary Haley.

Boyd **Bolton** and Emma **Lee**.
Rush **Morrison** and Lula **Prather**.
Pink **Wright** and Nellie **Douglas**.
John **Stapler** and Claudie **Neal**.
Henry **Spencer** and Rosa **Coughman**.
Edgar **Kennimer** and Jane **Hollis**.
W. C. **Mills** and Millie **Buck**.
C. O. **Huff** and Carlee **Monroe**.
Silas **Gill** and Maudie **Gilbreath**.
O. S. **Wheeler** and Tempie **Walker**.
Henry **Downing** and Beulah **Smith**.
Lawrence **Sewell** and Mary **Skiles**.
Henry H. **Willett** and Nellie **Seymore**.
Momentus **Gains** and Julia **Banks**.
Marvin **Stagner** and Vera **Sewell**
C. G. **Gunter** and Lila **Jones**.
Two license issued with request not to publish.

A Family History.

Edgar **Goodwin** left an interesting book at our office Friday. The book contains in his own language a history of "One Branch of the Goodwin Family." The history starts with John Goodwin leaving England on the Mayflower in the year 1620. After reaching this country he drifted from Jamestown, Va. to the Carolinas. He was the beginning of the Goodwin family in America.

The history continues with interesting details regarding the family including the war record of his father, T. J. Goodwin, who enlisted in Co. B, 8th Alabama Regiment under Lee.

In reading this history of the Goodwin family we are made to think how very interesting and important it is to keep a record of family history. If more people would do this it would prove of great interest to generations yet unborn.

Edgar is to be commended for his interest in his family history. He has the whole book typewritten, which contains 82 pages bound in leather with gold lettering on the cover with the above emblem.

August 16, 1917

Family Reunion.

The report as given by Uncle Cicero [**Alston**] follows:

"Alba, Texas, August 11, 1917. Mr. P. N. **Thomas**. My long time friend. I must tell you of the reunion of my family This is the first time we have all been together in 17 years. Olin, of Okmulgee, Okla, came to Sulphur, Okla., in his car and got Ella and they came by Collinsville, Texas, and got David, and they all came here for a short visit. They got here Thursday night and will leave Sunday morning for their homes. They joined me with the four boys that live here, which makes the total of seven children, as follows: Mrs. R. E. **Weems**, A. C. Alston, D. A., C. H., C. B., C. T., and O. R. Alston. Six of the above have families with a total of 24 children ranging in age from one year of age to seventeen years of age."

Respectfully, C. F. Alston

A Noble, Good Woman.

Not until after the paper was off the press last week did we learn of the death of Mrs. I. W. **Browning** which sad event occured at the family home near Stout on Sunday August 5th. Interment was had at Sharon Monday, the 6th inst, . . .

Mrs. Browning was a sister of our fellow townman, Arch **Moore** and Will Moore who lives a few miles east of town. She is also survived by two sisters, Mrs. Dovie **Potter** and Mrs. Maude **Bellomy**, and two half sisters, Mrs. Lenora **Smith** and Mrs. Bettie **Graves**, the latter living in Okla., and a half brother, Tim **Sparkman** of the Sharon commjunity, as well as her aged mother, Mrs. Moore who has lived near Sharon church for many years.

Mrs. Browning was 36 years of age and is survived by her husband and eight children, beside the relatives above named. The eldest of the children is a boy who on Sunday after his mother's death, was called to the army, he having enlisted some weeks previous. The next is a daughter about 16 years of age. An infant only about three hours old was left in the home. This was given to the keeping of Mr. and Mrs. Arch Moore who brought it to their home last Sunday . . .

August 23, 1917

L. M. Seat Dead.

Mr. L. M. **Seat** died at the home of Mr. and Mrs. J. V. **Attaway** Tuesday afternoon at 4 o'clock and was burried the following morning. Mr. Seat was 91 years old. He was a resident of this place many years . . . -Winnsboro News.

Man 73 Willing to Go.

Esq. John S. **Daniels** of Mineola, is 73 years old but if needed he is ready to join the forces in the present war. . . . he jotted down the following:

"I went to war at 17 and will go at 73 if needed, . . . I was in all the battles with Brigg's Army from April 7, 1862 to July 20, 1864. I was wounded four times. I was Sheriff four years, arrested many men. I have built over 400 brick chimneys. . . .

August 30, 1917

Barnes-Russell

Friday morning of last week our young friend, Prof. Frank **Barnes** of Redland, stepped into our office with a most beautiful young lady whom he introduced to us as his wife. . . . Frank and Miss Vera **Russell** had been married at Miami, Roberts county, Wednesday August 22, and that Rev. Chas D. **Pitts**, pastor of the Presbyterian church there had tied the nuptial knot. . . .

Hightower & Hightower.

Drs. **Hightower & Hightower**, Dentists of Winnsboro, have opened an office in Quitman over Lipscomb & Morrison's drug store and will be here one week in each month. Dr. J. A. Hightower, whom many of our people know, has been here this week doing dental work.

September 13, 1917

[Map of Wood County Showing Location of Voting Precincts, Courtesy Mineola Monitor. -Ed.]

Marriage License Issued.

Since our last report . . .:
Leroy **Palmer** and Daisey **Jones**.
R. A. **Green** and Eda **Moore**.
L. B. **Lindley** and Hattie **Lynch**.
W. H. **Wesson** and Ruby **Frazier**.
J. G. **Scott** and Bertha **Eubanks**.
S. R. **Irby** and Myrtle **Fitts**.
Robert **Wheeler** and Sedelia **Campbell**.
M. G. **Goldsmith** and Eula **Gilbreath**.
Emmett **Lloyd** and Anna **Brown**.
R. C. **Brunett** and Martha **Neill**.
Virgil **Graham** and A?lie **Todd**.
E. N. **Clower** and Martha **Lee**.
Cloyd **Wright** and Ida **Pope**.
H. D. **Lindley** and Bertha **Turner**.
Robert **Hill** and Stella **Buchanan**.
Marvin **Zimmerman** and Margarett **Pruitt**.
P. **Posey** and Amanda **Skipper**.
C. C. **Smith** and Maude **Hartsfield**.
J. R. **Hartsfield** and Maude **Low**.
John **Shaw** and Oma **Crouch**.

Hartsfield-Low Marriage.

Wednesday evening at 8:30, Sept. 5, 1917, Mr. Jessie R. **Hartsfield** and Miss Maude **Low** were united in marriage at the home of the brides parents, Mr. and Mrs. W. H. Low, at Alba, Rev. W. M. **Bass** performing the marriage ceremony.

Jessie . . . is a son of Mr. and Mrs. W. M. Hartsfield of the Concord community . . .

Maude comes from two of our oldest and best families, being a grand daughter of J. W. Low and the late Capt. C. D. **McKnight**.

Posey-Skipper Marriage.

Mr. P. **Posey** of Coke, and Mrs. Amanda **Skipper** of Winnsboro, were married while sitting in an automobile in front of the residence of W. B. **Kirby** . . . last Thursday morning at 10 o'clock . . .

The two daughters, Mrs. Mary **Benton** of Quitman, and Mrs. Annie **Hayden** of Pickton . . .

September 20, 1917

Double Wedding.

A double wedding was solemnized Monday night at Winnsboro when Mr. Alston **Bexley** and Miss Alamo **Ivey** of Quitman and Mr. Joe Ivey of Quitman and Miss Thelma Bexley of Winnsboro were married. Rev. G. J. **Rousseau**, pastor of the Winnsboro Baptist church, officiating.

September 27, 1917

Smith-Harbin.
(Delayed from last week)

Married in a car driven by C. M. **Smart** last Monday at 3:30 p.m. under the beautiful oaks near Sister **Morrison**'s in Quitman, Mr. James W. **Smith** and Miss Movelle **Harbin**, Rev. J. C. Calhoun officiating.

Mr. Smith, the son of Mr. Jas. T. Smith of Forrest Hill community . . . Miss Novelle the modest and beautiful daughter of A. A. Harbin of Lone Star . . .

October 4, 1917

Permanently Located At Winnsboro

Dr. **Roberts**, specially in the treatment of disorders of the Eye, Ear, Nose and Throat, is permanently located in Winnsboro and has moved his family from Williamson County where he lived for ten years. . .

Killing Near Crow.

Friday night of last week at the home of Bill **Alexander** near Crow, a cutting scrape occured wherein Earl Alexander, Bill **Foster** and Jim **Pruitt** were all severely cut by Bill **Newman**. Foster died from the effects of his wounds Saturday evening and the others are said to be in pretty bad shape.

. . . A young man by the name of Wilson was brought to Quitman by Mr. **Apel** Sunday evening and placed in jail charged with assisting Newman to escape. . . .

Little Upton Stone

Upton, the 18 months old baby boy of Mrs. **Stone**, died at the home of its grand father, W. H. **Todd**, out north of town a mile, Thursday night of last week, and was buried at Pleasant Ridge . .

October 11, 1917

W. H. Wood Dead.

After months of illness most of which time he was confined to his bed, W. H. **Wood** died at his late home in Mineola Saturday a week ago.. . .

Deceased was about 62 years of age and had resided in Wood county for many years, a goodly portion of which time he lived in Quitman. After the death of his first wife he went to Mineola and later was married to Mrs. **Bryan** who, with five sisters, three sons and one daughter survive. He was a son of the lamented W. M. D. L. Wood who lived for years near Lone Star four miles east of Quitman. The surviving sisters are Mesdames N. R. **Brogden**, J. D. **Gilbreath**, T. J.

Warlick, Jno. T. **Smith**, all residing in this county a few miles out from Quitman, and one residing in Grayson county whose name we failed to note. None of the children reside in this county. The daughter has been in California for a number of years, but was with her father at the time of his death. J. C. Wood, a prominent business man of Mineola, is a cousin of deceased.

October 18, 1917

Passing of a Pioneer.

Wednesday evening October 10, 1917, Peyton J. **Hendrix** passed away at his home one mile north of Quitman after a lingering illness of months duration. He was buried Thursday evening in the family grave yard on the old farm beside his parents who years ago passed on to the great beyond, the funeral service being conducted at the residence by Rev. J. C. **Calhoun**.

Uncle Pate Hendrix, as he was familiarly called by everyone who knew him, was born July 25, 1842. More than a half a century ago he was married to Miss Sallie **Carroll** and for all these years he with his wife resided on the same farm where death claimed him on Wednesday of last week. No children ever came to bless that home. Two neices of the wife were taken when small children and were reared by this grand couple, these being Dixie and Emma Carroll. The former when grown to womanhood married Dr. F. V. **McKnight** and the latter married C. A. **Green**. The former died several years ago while the latter with her husband and children reside at the old family home. The wife of his youth survives with an only sister, Mrs. J. P. **Butler**, the latter being the only survivor of the Hendrix family.

. . . He was a faithful Confederate soldier and for four years followed the flag of his country, doing valiant service in Texas and Louisiana. . . .

Golden News.

We were very much pained to learn of the death of Uncle Dave **Robinson**. Undle Dave died suddenly on the morning of the 13th.

Democrat - 1917

Local and Personal News Items.

Bill **Newman**, the party charged with murder in connection with the death of the party killed at or near Crow some weeks ago, and whom the Sheriff got near Dallas last week, has furnished bond and been released to await the action of the grand jury.

Tommie **Lipscomb** and wife have gone to Grand Saline to make their home, Tommie having accepted a position with J. L. **Fail**, druggist of that City. . . .

Bagby-Reinhardt.

At 10 o'clock Sunday morning Oct. 7, at the home of the bride's parents, Mr. Lummie **Bagby** and Miss Myrtle **Reinhardt** were united in marriage by their pastor, R. J. **Martin** of Quitman.

The groom is a promising young farmer of the Little Hope community and the bride is the third eldest daughter of Mr. and Mrs. R. A. Reinhardt of the same community.

October 25, 1917

Mrs. Craver Dies at Yantis.

Mrs. A. R. **Craver** died at the family home near Yantis Monday of this week after a lingering illness of several months. Interment was had at the Yantis cemetery Tuesday evening, the funeral service being conducted by Rev. R. J. **Blackmon**.

Miss Daisy Murphy Dead.

Miss Daisy **Murphy**, daughter of Mr. and Mrs. W. P. Murphy of the Little Hope community, died at the Epileptic Colony, Abilene Wednesday of last week. The remains were brought home and buried at Little Hope community.

Miss Daisy was 37 years of age. She had been aflicted since she was five years of age. For the past 15 years or more she had been at the Colony, only coming home occasionally.

November 1, 1917

A Surprise Wedding.

A wedding which was not wholly unexpected, but which came in the nature of a surprise to their many friends in Alba, was consumated in Kaufman Sunday when Mr. Linnie J. **Howard** of this city was united in marriage to Miss Bessie **Morris** of that city.

. . . Miss Bessie being a daughter of Mr. and Mrs. Ben Morris, who had lived in Alba for several years and only recently moved to Kaufman.

Linnie . . . is a son of Mr. and Mrs. J. N. Howard of this city.

Uncle Hugh Shaw.

The many friends of Uncle Hugh **Shaw** will regret to learn that he has lost his mind and is now confined in the Quitman jail. . .

Uncle Tom Shipp Dead.

We are pained indeed to learn of the death of our veteran friend, Uncle Tom **Shipp**, which occured at his late home near Calvary Thursday of last week. Interment was had Friday at Sand Springs cemetery, Rev. F. P. **Langley** conducting . . .

Passing of a Pioneer.

Mrs. A. R. **Craver** nee Elizabeth **Vickers**, was born in Taledigger [sic] county, Alabama, March 5th, 1842. At the age of five years, the family moved to Ripty county, Miss., and lived there two years and then moved to Harrison county, Texas. At the age of thirteen years she joined the Baptist church and was baptized by Rev. **Gorman**, an old veteran Baptist minister who was a direct relative of the Gorman's at Winnsboro. Her father, Uncle Jack Vickers, joined the church and was baptized when she was. . . . She was married to A. R. Craver February 27, 1868, to which union nine children were born, three boys and six girls. Two boys and two girls are dead, the living children are J. H. Craver, a leading merchant of Yantis, Mrs. Gertrude **Gamblin** of Yantis, Mrs. Laura **Taylor** of Winnsboro, Mrs. Tula **Lindley** of Yantis, and Mrs. W. T. **Smith** of Arbala. One brother, L. M. Vickers

of Como and two sisters, Mrs. Emily **Kimon** of Lamb county and Mrs. J. P. **Thompson** of Mineola also survive her.
. . . Her only living son, J. H. (Bunk) Craver . . .

November 8, 1917

Wood County Negroes Called Into Service.

The first negroes from Wood county to be called into military service left Tuesday morning of last week for Camp Travis. They were:

Oscar **Thomas**, Quitman
Emmet L. **Lloyd**, Mineola
Virgil **Duncan**, Mineola
Walter **McGruder**, Hawkins
Leroy **Young**, Hawkins
Frank **Crawford**, Mineola
Frank **Ellis**, Quitman
Griffin **Thomas**, Mineola
Alvin **Rooney**, Winnsboro
Warren **Hays**, Crow
Harrison **Prince**, Hawkins
Talmadge **Grant**, Quitman
A. D. **Devon**, Mineola
Thailie **Edwards**, Hawkins
Jesse **Reed**, Mineola
Bexley **Dean**, Mineola
Will Levi **Griffin**, Mineola
Henry **Bell**, Mineola
George **Hill**, Mineola
Albert **Washington**, Peach
Libingy **Price**, Winnsboro
Henry **Caldwell**, Mineola
Garnie **Brown**, Quitman
Willie **Hale**, Quitman
Willie D. **Hacher**, Hawkins
Claud **Kelly**, Quitman
Henry A. **Berry**, Quitman
Silas **Jobe**, Hawkins
Jim Boy **Lee**, Winnsboro
Lonnie **Gunter**, Mineola
Henry **Jones**, Mineola
Charlie **Brown**, Mineola
Sam **Perkins**, Big Sandy
Hartie **Boyd**, Crow
Aubrey C. **Shaw**, Mineola

November 15, 1917

Aged Woman Dies.

Mrs. J. M. **Luman** died at the family home six miles east of Quitman Sunday evening at 7:30, and was buried at Concord Tuesday evening. An aged husband and several children survive, a son, Annison, being in Camp Travis training camp.

Passing of a Pioneer.

In the death of W. T. (Uncle Tom) **Shipp**, the county lost one of its most useful and honorable citizens. . . .

Uncle Tom was born in Jackson county, Ala., April 20, 1840, and was therefore 77 years, 5 months and 5 days old at the time of his death which occured at his late home near Golden Thursday October 25, 1917. His father left Jackson county when Uncle Tom was 18 years of age and reached Winnsboro and Wood County Nov. 16, 1858. He lived near Winnsboro, now known as Webster, one year. His father bought the R. **Daniel** survey of land, now known as the Shipp place, and lived there until Uncle Tom was called to the war between the ___ [hole in paper] ___February 5, 1868 Uncle ___ was married to Miss M_____ **Dowell** at the home of I. F. Dowell, the late Rev. A. **Fitzgerald** officiating. To this union eight children were born, five boys and three girls, two of the boys died in infancy and one daughter, Mrs. Alice **Seils**, died some seven years ago. The living children are: W. F. Shipp, an attorney at Emory, Prof. J. W. Shipp of Addington, Okla., Judson Shipp who lives near the old home place, Mrs. J. U. **Searcy** who also lives near the old home and Miss Alice Shipp who is still under the family roof. . . . funeral, which was conducted at Sand Springs cemetery the day following his demist, the Rev. F. P. **Langley** conducting the last sad rites.

An Old Letter.

M. A. **Goldsmith** brought to our office the other day an old letter that was received by his mother during the war 61-65, in which the death of her husband was announced. The letter reads, in part, as follows:

"Line of Battle, Drury Bluff
"August 7, 1864.

"Mrs. E. Goldsmith:

It falls to my duty to inform you that your husband, C. Goldsmith, was killed the 28 of July. . . .

Uncle Hugh Shaw Dead.

Uncle Hugh **Shaw** died at the Terrell Asylum last Sunday morning at 6:30. The remains were brought home and buried Monday evening at Concord grave yard, Rev. W. E. **Stagner** conducting . .

November 22, 1917

Grand-Mother Hall.

After weeks of suffering the gentle spirit of grand-mother **Hall** of Mineola wafted its way "to the God who gave it" at 1 o'clock Friday morning November 16, 1917. Interment was had at the Mineola cemetery Saturday after funeral service conducted at the residence by her pastor, Rev. W. A. **Gill**, Pastor Mineola Baptist church.

Deceased was born in Orion, Ala., in 1849, came to Hunt county, Texas, in 1867, and to Mineola in 1882, where she resided until her death. She was married to M. T. Hall when a girl in her teens to which union five children were born, all girls, namely, Mrs. J. S. **Ellis** of Mineola, Mrs. L. B. **Turman**, of Mineola, Mrs. Arthur **Hobbs**, wife of Editor Hobbs of the Edgewood Enterprise, Miss Bessie Hall of Mineola, and Mrs. Jas. D. **Harris** of Mineola, who together with a step son, Isaac N. Hall of Kingston, Hunt county, survive her. A step daughter, the mother of Frank and Hall **Benton**, preceded her to the other world several years ago, as did her husband, the late M. T. Hall who was a well known citizen of Mineola.

Uncle Dick Clanton.

W. R. **Clanton**, familiarly called "Uncle Dick" was born August 24, 1835, in Pickens county, Ala. Came to Texas when a young man and married a daughter of Judge **Harper** of _____ county. After the death of his first wife he was married to Mrs. Mollie **Edwards**, a daughter of the late W. T. Harris, in 1879. No children were born to the first union. To the last union four children were born. The oldest, Will Clayton, now lives at Tyler. Mrs. J. R. **Mayo**, a daughter, lives in Quitman. Mrs. S. C. **Rhodes**, the other daughter lives in Mineral

Wells, and Edgar, the youngest son, lives on the old home place four miles east of Quitman.

Uncle Dick served through the war between the states and was a gallant Confederate soldier.

His death occcured Nov. 11, at his late home where he had lived for many years. Interment was had at Concord cemetery on the day following his demise . . .

Two Deaths Near Hainesville.

Dr. J. M. **Puckett** informs us of the death of two old citizens of the Hainesville community which occured the past week. Uncle Billie **Duke** and Uncle Billie **Thomas**. Burial took place at Concord.

Uncle Billie Duke had been a sufferer for a long time with cancer which finally culminated in his death, while Uncle Billie Thomas had been a paralitle [sic] for a number of years.

Uncle Hugh Shaw.

Uncle Hugh was born Jan. 20, 1851, and came to Texas in the fall of 1893. He wife preceded him to the other world several years ago. Six children survive. Mrs. G. A. **Free**, who lives in Okla., J. M. **Shaw** of Wichita Falls, W. M. Shaw of Montana, Mrs. Ben **Champion** of Throckmorton, Harold Shaw who is in the Coast Artillery, and J. T. Shaw the oldest son who lives five miles east of Quitman and with whom Uncle Hugh made his home for several years before being stricken.

Married North of Town.

Mr. Daniel **Stanley** of Wood county and Miss Iva **Moore** were married at the home of the bride's parents, Mr. and Mrs. Luther Moore, 3 miles north of Cooper, Wednesday night, Nov. 14, at 9:30.

Eld. Sam P. **Jones** of Cooper performed the ceremony . . .
- Cooper Review

Marriage License.

Since November 1st and up to Sunday night the following. .:
Homer H. **Holley** and Miss Lillie May **Stovall**.
Luther **Banta** and Miss Eula **Chamness**.

J. B. **Pickett** and Mrs. M. A. **Holley**.
J. M. **Wynn** and Miss Lizzie **Dickson**.
Russell **Wilson** and Miss Winnie **Newman**.
Willis P. **Cannady** and Miss Annie __ **Hitt**.
Silas **Rushing** and Miss Lola **Bridges**.
John **Kitchens** and Miss Dema **Robinson**.
H. J. **Whitworth** and Miss Katie **Cornelius**.
Jessie **Posey** and Miss Tootsie **Elledge**.
Aaron **Brown** and Linnie **Russell**, col.
Bingham **Bynum** and Rosa **Brown**, col.
Jim **Cullars** and Malinda **Brown**, col.

D. S. **Robinson**.

The subject of this sketch was born in Gimmet county Ga. 1846. He joined the Confederate army in 1862 under Captain **Peoples** in General Bragg's division, serving to the close of the Civil war and was at Appomattox Courthouse when the surrender came in 1865. He then returned home to take up the pursuits of life. Later was married to Miss G. A. **Whitworth** in Hall county, Ga., Nov. 1868, came to Wood county, Texas in 1876 and remained in said county to the end. He moved from the eastern part of the county to the place that I. A. **Jones** now owns in 1883 and remained in this neighborhood to his death.

Uncle Dave, as he was familiarly called, was the last or perhaps next to the last survivor of a family of ten brothers and sisters. He leaves the wife of his youth and five children . . . He had one son who preceded him a long time ago . . .

On the morning of Oct. 13th, 1917 without a minutes warning the death angel swooped down and cut the brittle thread of life .

November 29, 1917

Moves to Alba.

Wednesday of last week Quitman lost one of its best and noblest of women in the person of Mrs. Lillie **Leath** who with her family moved to Alba where she will make her future home. . .

Mrs. Leath goes to Alba to take charge of the Alba News next week, having bought the plant some weeks ago . . . She has purchased the W. B. **Gilliland** residence on Quitman street and moved to same last week. . . . She will be assisted in the work by her brother, J. T. **Kilgore**, an experienced printer and all round newspaper man himself.

Death of Mrs. M. L. Francis.

From Mrs. W. T. **Williams**, a sister of Mr. M. L. **Francis**, we learn of the death of his wife which occured at Santa Clara, Cal., Nov 14, 1917. The remains were shipped to San Francisco, Cal., to be cremated, and then to Paso Robles, Cal., for burial.

Deceased was 39 years of age. She was married to M. L. Francis in June, 1906, at Princess Anne, Va. to which union four children were born. . . .

December 6, 1917

Married in Dallas

. . . announcement of the marriage of Mr. A. L. **Wilfong** and Miss Willa **Rhone**, which happy event occured in Dallas on Wednesday. They will be home in this city after December 3d.- Winnsboro News

Eskridge-McMimms

. . . Edgar **Eskridge** of Winnsboro and Miss Sunshine **McMimms** were married in Tyler Tuesday of last week. Edgar is one of the promising young attorneys of our county. . . .

Leaves Winnsboro

The Democrat regrets to learn that its good friend Jon. **Russell** has severed his connection with the M. & P. Bank at Winnsboro and left that City and Wood County. He and his estimable family have gone to Mt. Pleasant where he will engage in the wholesale feed and grains business with his brother Walter and S. F. **Nelson**.

Death of Miss Mattie Lankford

On Nov. 25, the death Angel came to the home of Mrs. Maggie **Lankford** and claimed her only daughter at home. Mattie . . . 17 years of age . . . She leaves mother, two brothers and four sisters to mourn her death.

Local and Personal News Items.

Henry **Farris**, one of the oldest citizens of the county, left last week with his family for Mineral Wells where they will reside for a few years. Mr. Farris has lived in Wood county 40 years and says he does not expect to live at Mineral Wells that long. . . .

J. D. **Miller** and family, G. W. **Rink** and family and H. M. **Craig** and family left this week for DeQueen, Ark., at which place they will make their future home.

Chas Pitner Dead.

News reached Quitman Tuesday morning of the death of Chas. **Pitner**, which occured at his home five miles west of Alba that morning at 1 o'clock. Mr. Pitner was a brother-in-law of our fellow townsman, J. T. **Power**, his wife being a sister of Mr. Power. Byron a son of deceased, lived in Quitman for several years . . .

Wood County Newspapers

Wood County Democrat - 1918

January 3, 1918

Marriages.

Rev. R. J. **Smith** reports to the Democrat that he united in marriage the first Sunday he was on his work Mr. Will **Lloyd** and Miss Beulah **Goldsmith**. Will is the son of J. J. Lloyd of Coke, and his bride is a daughter of M. A. Goldsmith of the same community.

Last Sunday he reports haveing united in marriage Mr. Henry **Burford** and Miss Ola **Hale**. Henry is the youngest son of W. G. Burford. Miss Ola is a daughter of W. J. Hale living north of town.

Monday morning of this week Rev. Smith united in marriage Mr. Lee **Morrison** and Miss Fannie **Lanier** both of the Hainesville community . . ., the bride being a daughter of G. W. Lanier.

Bootleggers Go To Pen.

Phil **Red** got five years for bootlegging.

Jim **Smith** got two years for bootlegging.

Lancet **Hill**, a negro boy living in the Browning settlement plead guilty to forgery and got two years.   - Tyler Morning Tribune

Christmas Marriage.

Sunday before Christmas Mr. Hilliard **McAllister** and Miss Blanche **Derr** were married by Rev. R. J. **Blackmon**. Hilliard is the eldest son of H. H. McAllister, while his bride is a daughter of Mr. and Mrs. P. K. Derr of Oak Grove.

Mrs. Morgan Dead.

Mrs. **Morgan**, widow of the late Mack Morgan, died at her late home about eight miles north of Quitman the week before Christmas and was buried at Rock Hill cemetery the day following her death. Mrs. Morgan was a sister to Andy and Dick **Gilbreath** of the Yantis country.

Our District Clerk Weds.

Sunday before Christmas District Clerk Julius R. **Taylor** and Miss Bonnie Maye **Sutherland** . . . hied aways to Texarkana, and upon arrival there they found the Pastor of the First Baptist church, Rev. J. P. **Boone**, who soon said the words that united them as husband and wife. . . . his bride, a daughter of Mrs. D. F. Sutherland . . .

Died at Teague.

Mrs. Fred **Hamilton**, wife of Fred Hamilton of Grand Saline died at Teague, Texas, Monday of this week and the remains were brought to Grand Saline for burial. Mrs. Hamilton was a neice of our fellow townsman, W. E. **McNeill**, and Mr. and Mrs. McNeill, their son Chester and daughter Miss Myrtle, attended the funeral Tuesday . . .

Broke Jail.

Two prisoners confined in the county jail dug a hole through the floor Thursday evening of last week and made their getaway. One of them, J. A. **Hilburn**, is charged with forgery and the other, Willie **Romine**, is charged with raising a $2. bill to a $20. and a $1. bill to a $10. Romine was caught at a saw mill between Hawkins and Big Sandy last Sunday by Sheriff **Apel** and brought back to jail. Hilburn is still at large . . .

January 10, 1918

A Good Woman Gone.

Subject of this sketch was Mrs. Dora **Julian**, wife of our fellow citizen, R. S. Julian.

Mrs. Julian's maiden name was Miss Dora **Spencer**. She was born in Sevier County, Arkansas, of August 22, 1875. She came to Texas when about two years old. she was married to R. S. Julian Dec. 3, 1893, at Leesburg, Texas, and to this union were born five children, three boys and two girls, all of whom are living. Mr. Julian moved to the Pleasant Grove settlement eight years ago . . .

Mrs. Julian paid the last debt on the 7th day of December 1917 . . The remains were laid to rest on the following day at the Hopewell Cemetery . . .

January 17, 1918

In Memory of Mrs. Burford.

Mrs. **Burford** died at the family home two miles east of Quitman, Dec. 17, 1917. Being sick only four days, her death was a great shock to the family and friends.

Mrs. Delila Burford was born December 22, 1858, in Tipper county Miss., and came to Texas 43 years ago. Her maiden name was Miss Delila **Robertson**, and she came to Texas with her uncle Rom **Hays** and her aunt, Miss Lizzie Robertson, they having raised her from an infant two weeks old, her mother having died and left her at that age. They landed here Christmas eve day and moved to Uncle Jessie **Moseley**'s place and from there to S. A. **Kendrick**'s and from there to Jim **Herring**'s place and was living there when she and W. G. Burford were married on Sept. 21, 1877. They were married at the home of S. A. Kendrick and T. J. **Goodwin** performed the ceremony, Jim **Hogg** being present at the marriage. After their marriage they moved to the home where she died. To this union six children were born, three boys and three girls, all being present at time of her death and all married except the baby boy, Henry, who has since married. she leaves to mourn her death the husband of her youth, six children, thirteen grand children . . .

Died at Alba.

M. F. **Davis**, Justice of the Peace at Alba for the past several years, died at his late home in Alba last Saturday and was buried the following day at Pleasant Ridge grave yard . . . Mr. Davis was a member of Woodmen . . .

Mr. Davis married a daughter of E. P. **Ramey** of Quitman several years ago and the wife with two children are left to mourn their loss. . . .

Democrat - 1918

Aged German Dies.

W. M. **Coleman**, who had made his home with Richard **Dykes** near Quitman for the past two years, died at the home of Mr. Dykes Thursday of last week. Mr. Coleman was about 84 years old. He was a native of Germany and was brought to the United States when 3 years of age. He had three children who live in Missouri to which place his body was shipped for burial.

Wilcox-Bagby.

Mr. Wallace **Wilcox** and Miss Minnie **Bagby** were married at the home of groom's brother, Lee Wilcox, last Sunday evening, Esquire B. F. **Smart** performing the ceremony.

January 24, 1918

Uncle Sam Kendrick

We are pained indeed to chronicle the death of Uncle Sam **Kendrick** which occured Wednesday evening at 5 o'clock at the home of his son S. T. Kendrick, in Quitman. . . .

Marriage License Issued.

. . . from January 1 to 19 inclusive:
John J. **Wells** and Miss Tempie **Thompson**.
Altus C. **Smith** and Miss Minnie **Rucker**.
W. F. **Blake** and Miss Eula Estelle **Scruggs**.
Charlie **Tittsworth** and Miss Laura **McWhirter**.
J. H. **Orlds** and Miss Fubie Maye **Lovin**.
Robt E. **Bowling** and Miss Mimie **Burgess**.
G. B. **Starnes** and Miss Aver **Newman**.
Walter **Scott** and Miss Willie **Kennedy**.
Arthur **Holiness** and Miss Ellie **Clark**.
T. C. **Duke** and Miss Annie Blanche **Minick**.
Wallace **Wilcox** and Miss Mildred **Bagby**.
Hiram **Gill** and Miss Florence **Morris**.
Andrew J. **Courrages** and Miss Beatrice **Pitts**.

Jessie **Brown** and Miss Dixie **Darden**.
Raymond **Whaley** and Miss Lexie **Hervey**.
Clifford **Swanner** and Miss Rena Maye **Stevens**.
R. H. **Chaney** and Miss Addie **Dill**.

Mrs. Warlick Dead.

Mrs. **Warlick**, wife of T. J. Warlick, died at the family home Wednesday of last week after a lingering illness with Tubercolosis. The remains were carried to Ebenezer for interment.

January 31, 1918

Death at Winnsboro.

Mr. and Mrs. J. W. **Cox** were called to Winnsboro Saturday on account of the serious illness of Mrs. Cox's mother, Mrs. **Carson**. The mother died Saturday night at 2:15, and the remains were carried to Princeton, Collin county, for burial on Sunday.

Passing of A Veteran.

In the passing away of S. A. **Kendrick**, better known and familiarly called "Uncle Sam Kendrick" our town and county has lost one of its best . . .

Uncle Sam was born in the good old state of Tenessee Sept. 8, 1842, and had passed his 75th mile post last September. At the age of 18 he volunteered and entered the Confederate Army and served until the close of the conflict between the States, having engaged in many of the memorable battles in that great war. Soon after the close of the war he started for Texas, headed for Dallas but when he got to Wood Co. his money gave out and he stopped and hired to the late Col. J. A. **Stinson** for whom he worked four years during which time he met and married Miss Eliza **Burford** and soon after their marriage they moved to the old home two miles east of Quitman where they resided continuously until the death of the wife about a year ago since which time Uncle Sam made his home with his son, Tilden and wife. Six children were born to Uncle Sam and his wife, three of whom have

Democrat - 1918

passed on the three survive him, namely: Tilden and Horace and Mrs. Lucian **Cartwright**, all of whom were present when the end came. Several grand children also survive him. . . .

Interment was had at Ebenezer grave yard on Thursday the 24.

In Remembrance of Dr. J. A. Shields.

Dr. J. A. **Shields** was born at Cartersville Georgia, April the first 1834; died in the Little Hope Community near Pine Mills, Texas, on his farm, January 13, 1918. In his boyhood days he moved from Cartersville Georgia to Cedartown Georgia and there studied medicine under Dr. Prier in 1848 and later finished Medical course at Mobile, Alabama. He was married to Miss Elizabeth **Tolbert** August 31st, 1851 to which union three children were born, Ben Shields, who is a merchant at Pine Mills, Texas; Mrs. Nobia Burkett, wife of James E. Burkett of Pine Mills, and Claud **Burkett**, wife of E. M. Burkett, who reside at Hainesville, Texas. All three of the children were with him when he died. He had seven Grand children and five Great Grand children living, most of whom were at his bed side too. His first wife died March 18, 1886, and he later married Mrs. Amanda J. **Pridgen**, who died at Pine Mills, Texas November 20, 1910.

. . . He moved in his early married life to Cherokee County Alabama and made his home in and around Center for more than 35 years. He moved to Texas in 1888 and practiced his profession in and around Pine Mills for a number of years. . . .

Mrs. T. J. Warlick.

Mrs. T. J. **Warlick** died at family home three miles north east of Quitman Wednesday Jan 16, 1918 after a lingering illness of several months.

Mrs. Warlick was a daughter of the late W. M. D. L. **Wood** and had lived in Wood county since a three year old child. She was born in Mississippi and was 58 years old at the time of her death. She was married at an early age to John **Stroud** to which union two children born are still living, Mrs. Geo. **Mitchell** and Harvey Stroud who were with her at the time of her death. Several years after the death of her first husband, she married T. J. Warlick who survives. Two brothers,

H. Wood of Hopkins county, and S. D. Wood of Hunt county, and four sisters, Mrs. N. R. **Brogden** of Cartwright, and Mrs. J. D. **Gilbreath** of Cartwright, Mrs. Henry **Coke** of Hunt county, and Mrs. Jno. T. **Smith** living near the home where Mrs. Warlick died, also survive her.

February 7, 1918

Mrs. E. E. Wellons Dead.

Mrs. E. E. **Wellons** died at the home of her neice Mrs. R. A. **Northcutt** atGolden, Wednesday of last week. Mrs. Wellons was one of the oldest people in the county and had lived in the county for many years.

Death of Baby Girl.

Rev. R. J. **Blackmon** was called to Hainesville last Thursday to conduct the funeral of the baby girl of W. E. **Veitch** which took place at Mt. Pisga. It will be remembered that Mr. Veitch lost his wife a little less than a year ago . . .

Little Floyd Russom.

The subject of this sketch was born May 26, 1916, died Jan. 26, 1917, being 20 months and one day old. Floyd was the only child of Mr. and Mrs. Dude **Russom**, they having lost their first child two and a half years ago at the age of 18 months.

Little Floyd's remains were laid to rest by the side of his little brother at Pleasant Ridge grave yard the day following his death . . .

In Memory of Little Mone Lee **Veitch**.

Oh! how many hearts were saddened last Tuesday afternoon when the news came that Little Mone Lee was dead. She was born Dec. 6, 1912, died Jan. 29, 1918, was buried at Mt. Pisgah, Bro R. J. **Blackmon** conducting . . .

Death of W. L. Vaughn.

After a lingering illness W. L. **Vaughn** died at the home of L. F. **Johnson** near Concord Thursday of last week and was buried the following day at Concord grave yard, the funeral service being conducted by Rev. W. E. **Stagner**. Mr. Vaughn had been sick for a long time and just a week before his death he was carried from his home in the Klondyke community to the home of Mr. Johnson, and near the old home where he has resided for many years.

Will Vaughn, as he was best known, was born in Georgia in 1852, and came to Texas in 1871. He was first married to miss Susie **Hale** to which union three children still living were born, viz: Miss Ollie, who is still under the family roof, Mrs. G. B. **Vickery** and Mrs. R. N. **Anders**, all of whom still live in the Concord neighborhood. After the death of this first wife he married Miss **Duke** and to this union one child was born, now Mrs. Dock **Harbuck** who lives in the Klondyke community near Golden. His last wife also survives. Two brothers, J. C. and A. J. **Vaughn**, and two sisters, Mrs. **Lambert** and Mrs. G. N. **Collins**, also survive deceased.

February 14, 1918

Mrs. N. A. McKnight.

After a lingering illness of some two weeks duration with lagrippe and pneumonia, Mrs. N. A. **McKnight** died at her late residence in Quitman this Wednesday morning at 5 o'clock. Interment will be had Thursday at 10 o'clock in Quitman cemetery.

Mrs. E. E. Wellons.

The subject of this sketch was born near Knoxville, Dooly county, Georgia, March 5th, 1830. At 2:30 a.m. on January 30, 1918, the Death Angel called her at the home of Mr. and Mrs. R. A. **Northcutt** at which place she had made her home for several years. . . .

Aunt Eliza, as we all called her, was married to M. F. **Wellons** in 1851. They came to Texas in 1870. Her husband died near Mineola in 1876 . . .

Marriage License Issued.

From January 19, to Feb. 9, 1918 . . .:
J. E. **Gamblin** and Miss May **Smith**.
Charlie **Scott** and Mrs. Mary **Clark**.
Joe **Darden** and Mrs. Amy **Jones**.
Jesse **James** and Miss Lorene **Skinner**.
Douglas **Richards** and Miss Lucile **Roberts**.
L. R. **Andress** and Miss Velma **Amason**.
C. L. **Atkins** and Miss Lillian **Post**.
Cottrell **Ragsdale** and Miss Irma **Jones**.
Rufus **Hays** and Miss Emma **Ragsdale**.
Jno. M. **Spigner** and Miss Ella May **Parker**.
Sam **Harp** and Miss Lillie **Murrell**.

R. G. Andrews.

We were shocked Friday morning of last week when the news came to us that R. G. **Andrews** is dead. . . .
Interment was had at Winnsboro Sunday evening.

Died in Ft. Worth.

Dewitt **Johnston** died at his late home in Ft. Worth Friday of last week and the remains were brought to Clover Hill grave yard for burial, and on Saturday were deposited there near the old home where deceased lived for many year.
The wife and children . . .

Baby Dies.

Mr. and Mrs. C. B. **Alston** of Alba . . . death of their babe which occured at the family home near Alba. Just a little over a year ago these parents lost their other babe, . . .

Death At Alba.

Mrs. Neal **McCollum** died at the family home in Alba Monday evening of this week. She leaves the husband of her youth, a number of children . . .

February 21, 1918

James C. Wood, Yantis, Texas.

The name of James C. **Wood** of Yantis will go down in history of this cruel war as the first Wood county boy to give us his life to the enemy. He was on the ill-fated Tuscania that was sunk by the enemy U. Boat on the 5th day of this month.

Death of C. L. Corley.

C. L. **Corley** died at his homoe north of town Wednesday, February 6, after an illness of only a few days. Funeral services were conducted by the W. O. W. at Hopewell cemetery Thursday afternoon. Mr. Corley was born in Alabama April, 1869, and came to Texas when one year old with his parents, and lived in this section of the state until his death. . . . A wife and nine children, three brothers and two sisters survive . .   - Winnsboro News.

Passing of A Pioneer.

In the death of Mrs. N. A. **McKnight** which occured at her late home in Quitman Wednesday morning at 5 o'clock, Feb. 13, another of the pioneers of Wood county passes away.

Mrs. McKnight was born in Warren county, Ga., in May 1842, being a daughter of William and Sarah **Hart**. In 1856 her parents moved to Texas, settled first in Rush county and two years later moved to Wood county where they continued to reside until their death.

During the civil war, in 1863, deceased was married to Capt. C. D. McKnight who was at the time a Captain in the Confederacy, being home on furlough. . . . Capt. McKnight died Feb. 5, 1890, twenty eight years and one week before the companion followed. To the union of this couple seven children were born, five of whom preceded their mother to the other shore. Two living, Dr. Frank V. McKnight, a prominent physician of Alba, and Mrs. Rosa **Low**, wife of A. R. (Buck) Low of Aspermont, Texas. Fourteen grand children and two great grand childred also survive, with two brothers, S. H. Hart of Quitman, and B. B. Hart of Mineola.

Mrs. M. B. Rutledge.

Mrs. M. B. **Rutledge**, wife of M. B. Rutledge of the Golden country, died at the family home Thursday night of last week and was buried the following day at Pleasant Ridge . . .

Deceased leaves the husband with four small children. . . The aged mother with four brothers and two sisters also survive. The brothers are S. W., W. R., E. F. and Sidney **Caldwell**, all of whom reside in the county except the latter who lived in Oklahoma. The sisters are Mrs. M. G. **Leonard** and Mrs. Kittie **Owens** who reside in the community near where the sister died.

Old Time Darkey Dies.

Uncle Allen **Session**, an old time darkey, one respected by both white and black, died at his late home five miles north of Quitman last Wednesday. Uncle Allen had been living in the neighborhood where he died for many years, ever since the civil war and possibly longer.

Mrs. Overton McCrary.

Mrs. **McCrary**, wife of Overton McCrary of Coke, died at the home of his brother, R. C. McCrary in Winnsboro last Saturday night and was buried at Clover Hill grave yard Sunday. [more - microfilm too dim to read. -Ed.]

March 7, 1918

Miss Eva Hyde

Miss Eva **Hyde** was 17 years and 2 months old at the time of her death. She lived in Franklin county near Mr. Vernon when death claimed her. . . . She was taken sick with measels and pneumonia during February and on the 16th of that month death claimed her.

Miss Eva was a daughter of Mr. and Mrs. Mack Hyde who lived in the Rock Hill community for many years. Seven years ago they moved to Red River county where one year later Mr. Hyde died. The widowed mother then moved to Franklin county . . .   - Her Uncle.

Democrat - 1918

Little Nora Higginbotham.

Thursday evening of last week, Frbruary 28, the sweet little daughter of G. C. **Higginbotham** returned to the God who gave it. Little Nora had been sick for about a week with pneumonia. . .

Funeral services was held in the Baptist church Friday evening at 4 o'clock and was conducted by the Pastor, Bro. **Blackmon**. . . . Interment was had in Quitman cemetery following the funeral service.

. . . First his wife was called away leaving a week old infant. The little one lived nearly a year and it was taken, now his sweet little Nora who was his housekeeper since the marriage of his oldest daughter, is taken. It is sad indeed for this lonely man and being left now with his two little children . .

Little Nora was nearly 12 years of age . . .

P. W. Blount

The Democrat is pained indeed to chronicle the death of its veteran friend P. W. **Blount** of the Rock Hill community, which occured at the home of his son-in-law and daughter, Mr. and Mrs. Wiley **Galloway** Wednesday evening of last week. Interment was had at Clover Hill Thursday evening . . .

March 14, 1918

In Memory of Little Nora

Little Nora [**Higginbotham**] was born in Lockhart June 30, 1906, and died February 28, 1918, aged 11 years and 8 months . . .

Mrs. J. P. Vaughn

We regret to learn of the death of Mrs. J. P. **Vaughn** of the Calvery community which occured at the family home Saturday night.

W. A. Boyd

We are pained to learn of the death of our good friend W. A. **Boyd** of the Mt. Enterprise community which occured at his late home Saturday night.

[Will of R. G. Andrews]
[died] the 8th day of Feby, 1918 leaving real and personal property of the estimated value of $75,000.00. . . .
. . .my beloved wife, Maggie N. **Andrews**, . . .[all property and estate]
. . . appoint my said wife as guardian of the estate of our child, Sallie Lucy Andrews . . .
. . . appoint my said wife sole Executrix . . .

76 Last Sunday.

Grand-mother **Power** of Alba, was 76 years of age last Sunday and with her son, Z. H. Power and two daughters, Mrs. Selma **Currin** and Mrs. G. L. **Pitner** came over to Quitman and spent the day with her son, J. T. Power and family. . . .

P. W. Blount

P. W. **Blount** was born in Granite county, Georgia July 1, 1840. He was married to Miss Sarah **Wages** Sept. 1, 1861. Eleven children were born to this union, 8 of whom are still living. He enlisted in the cause of the Confederacy Sept. 9, 1861 and served until the close of the conflict between the States. He came with his family to Texas in 1881 and lived the first year with the late Col. George **Haines**, later buying a farm in the Rock Hill community in which section he resided continuously until his death. His wife died July 14th 1909, since which time he has made his home with his married daughter Mrs. Wiley **Galloway**.

The surviving children are Rus who lives at Rotan, Texas, Bill, who lives at Roby, Texas, Jim, who resides near Rock Hill, Abb and Es, who left this country several years ago and whose residence are unknown to the relatives, George who lives near Terrell, and two daughters, Mrs. Wiley Galloway and Mrs. Grover **Harris** both of whom resides near Rock Hill.

March 21, 1918

N. R. Brogden
[Obviously death notice, but microfilm too dim to read. -Ed.]

March 28, 1918

Little Eveline Alston.
Little Eveline was born Jan. 31, 1918, and died March 17, 1918. . . . - Mrs. C. B. **Alston**, Alba, Texas.

Mrs. J. J. Cathey.
Mrs. J. J. **Cathey** died at the family home near Golden last Saturday and was buried at Sands Springs grave yard Sunday evening at 3 o'clock . . .

Deceased leaves the husband of her youth and a number of children, all of them practically grown . . .

April 4, 1918

Representative J. B. Lee.
It is with profound sorrow that we chronicle the death of Representative John B. **Lee**, which occured at Austin Friday morning of last week from a complication of diseases, typhoid fever, pneumonia and Brights disease. The remains were shipped to Winnsboro arriving there Saturday night and was taken to Clover Hill Sunday evening for burial . . . [more, too dim to read.]

T. J. Hamrick
[Another death notice too dim to read.]

April 11, 1918

Biographical Sketch.

Noah R. **Brogden** was born April 23, 1843, at Swanee, Gwinett county, Georgia. He came to Texas in February 1869 after the close of the civil war and settled in Wood county where he continued to reside until his death. He was first married to Miss Nancy Ellen **Morrow** March 6, 1873, she died January 27, 1874. On Dec. 9, 1875, he was married to Miss Martha Ann **Wood**, who with six children survive him. There were 11 children born to the latter marriage, 4 of whom have passed away. Those living are J. B. Brogden, who lives near the family old homestead near Cartwright, Mrs. Eva **Draw** who resides at Pittsburg, S. E. Brogden who is a teacher to the schools at Snyder, Miss Sallie, who is now with her mother under the family roof, Miss Zollie, a teacher in the Jacksonville schools, and Miss Fay who is attending school at Winnsboro.

Deceased was a member of Co. D, 9th Georgia B.A. and served throughout the memorable conflict of 1861-4. . . .

. . . a demit from the Masonic Lodge in Georgia granted to deceased when he left there for Texas, in January 1869. Soon after arriving in Texas he was made a member of Flora Lodge . . . at Quitman . . .

Wallace Spann Dead.

Mrs. C. O. **Goldsmith** received a message Monday of last week, and that her brother, Wallace **Spann** had died at Roswell, New Mexico . . . The remains were buried in Roswell.

Dr. Smith Dead.

Dr. W. E. **Smith** died at the home of his son, Bob Smith, in Alba, Monday night of this week and was buried with Masonic honors at Pleasant Ridge Tuesday evening.

April 18, 1918

Negro Shot.

Aaron **Baker**, col. living a few miles out from Mineola on the Golden road, was shot Tuesday evening by an unknown white man who with his wife and two small children came by his house and asked for something to eat. While they were at Aaron's home they missed a small package and accused one of Aaron's girls taking it. An argument ensued over the affair and the man shot Aaron with a shot gun, inflicting a serious wound in the shoulder. The wound is serious but Dr. **Reed**, the attending physician says it is not necessary fatal unless complications arise.

Sheriff **Apel** and a posse from Mineola hunted for the man all night Tuesday night but up to hour of going to press had failed to locate him.

Later. After the above had been put in type Jim **Caldwell** came to Quitman this morning and surrendered to officers, admitting that he did the shooting.

Two Children Die.

The Democrat sinerely sympathises with our good friend Wash **Gilliland** and family in the death of two of their children, one occuring first of last week and the other Saturday night of the past week, both caused froom Pheomonia and measles.

Hart-Ellis Marriage.

Willie **Hart,** a son of Prof. and Mrs. L. B. Hart, and Miss Clara **Ellis**, a daughter of Mr. and Mrs. Jim Ellie, were married in Ft. Worth where Willis is employed as ticket salesman at the Byers Theater, Thursday of last week. These young people both reside at Mineola when at home . . .

In Memory of C. H. Dykes.

After three weeks suffering the gentle spirit of Charlie **Dykes** took its flight . . . at 6:30 a.m., March 27th, 1918. His death occured at his home 3 1-2 miles northwest of Winnsboro.

Charlie was born near Pleasant Grove 36 years ago, June the 9th, and has lived hear there most all his life. His suffering was intense. He had measles and pheumonia. . . .

Charlie was married in Dec. 1904 to Miss Ola **Porter**. Two sweet little girls, Thelma aged 11 and Charlene aged 5 were born by the union. . . .

The day following his death he was carried to Hopewell . .

Beside his wife and children he leaves his parents, Mr. and Mrs. M. B. Dykes, four sisters, Mesdames Wallace **Holley**, Jimmie **Thompson**, John **Jones** and Grady **Hill**, and two brothers, Richard and Sylvester Dykes . . .

April 25, 1918

George E. Alexander Jr.

The Democrat has received from Rev. and Mrs. George E. **Alexander** of Hoover, Okla., the following announcement: "Mr. and Mrs. George E. Alexander announce the birth of their son George E. Junior Born the 14th day of April nineteen hundren and eighteen."

Congratulations to the parents on this their first born.

Death of Infant.

Mr. and Mrs. Milner **Cain** have the sympathy of the Democrat in the death of their infant daughter, born Thursday night of last week at the home of Mrs. Cain's mother, Mrs. S. W. **Gilbreath**, only living a short while after birth.

Death of Pioneer.

Not until this week did we learn of the death of Mrs. J. C. **Vaughn** which occured at the family home in the Concord community on the 10th inst. Deceased was a pioneer of Wood county and had resided in the Concord community for many years.

The husband of her youth and several children and grand children survive her . . .

May 2, 1918

Stricken With Paralysis

J. T. **Power** suffered a partial strock of paralysis Thursday of last week while carrying the mail for I. W. **Robbins** on the latter's rural route. When he reached Quitman he was unconscious and remained so until Saturday. His condition is quite serious, but somewhat improved apparently. . . .

Another Veteran Dead

From W. H. **Carter**, who was in yesterday morning, we learn of the death of G. M. **Houston**, an old and highly respected citizen of the Winnsboro country. Squire Houston served as justice of the peace at Winnsboro for a number of years . . .

Mrs. J. C. Vaughn.

Mrs. J. C. **Vaughn**, nee Miss Hannah **Doyle**, was born April 12, 1843, in the State of Mississippi, when 9 or 10 years old came with her parents to Texas, first stopping in Smith county, and in the Fifties came to Wood county and to the community where death claimed her. She was married to J. C. Vaughn March 7, 1870, to which union six children were born, all of whom are still living except one. . . . her death April 10, 1918.

Mrs. Amanda Baxter.

After months of suffering Mrs. Amanda **Baxter** died at the home of her nephew, W. H. **Low**, at Alba Thursday April 25, 1918, at 6 o'clock p.m. The remains were carried to Ebenezer on Friday the day following her death where the funeral seervice was conducted by Rev. R. J. **Blackmon** after which the remains were deposited beside those of her husband and daughter who preceded her to the great beyond several years ago.

Aunt Amanda, as she was lovingly called by those who know her intimately and so long, was near 77 years of age, the day following her burial was her birthday and on that day she would have been 77. . . .

She is survived by one brother, J. W. Low, and two sisters, Mrs. Carrie **Russell** and Mrs. Lizzie **Herring**. The brother and Mrs. Russell were with her when the end came, the other sister, Mrs. Herring, could not be reached, living in west Texas . . .

May 9, 1918

Former Wood County Man Dies.

L. L. **Brown**, who was a citizen of Wood county many years ago, died at his late home in Bowie, Texas, Monday night of this week. . . . Mr. Brown was a brother-in-law to A. J. and Dr. J. D. **Conger** of our town, and an uncle of Ely Brown of Mineola. . . .

Uncle John Patrick.

We are pained indeed to chronicle the death of our venerable friend Uncle John **Patrick** whose death occured at his late home near Golden last Sunday night at 2:30. Interment was had at Sand Springs Monday, . . .

Mrs. J. C. Vaughn

Mrs. Hannah **Vaughn** was born April 12, 1843, in Copiah County, Miss., and when only 4 years of age came with her parents and nine brothers and sisters to Texas, landing in Smith county in 1847. All of the brothers and sisters have passed over the River except her youngest sister, Mrs. Amelia **Doyle** of Alba. Mrs. Vaughn's parents were Peter and Adelia **Shamburger** who were born and reared in N. C., and directly after their marriage moved to Miss.

In 1853, the family moved from Smith county to Wood county and settled in what is now known as the Concord community, the same home where Mrs. Vaughn died. . . . Had this good woman lived until the 12th of April she would have been 75 years old. She left four children, one daughter, Mrs. Harve **Mattox**, and three sons, Pete, Matt and Boss Vaughn, a numver of grand children and three great grand children, together with the husband of her youth to mourn her death.

- A Friend.

(Note. The above corrected notice of the life and death of Mrs. J. C. Vaughn is given this week, as a number of errors appeared in the report given last week. This report is given by her old friend, Capt. J. L. **Ray** of Mineola . . .Ed.)

Uncle Jake Benton Dead.

After months of suffering with tubercolosis Uncle Jake **Benton** died at his late home near Coke Wednesday May 1st and was buried the following day at Clover Hill cemetery . . .

May 16, 1918

Fisher-Robbins.

Last Saturday Mr. Henry **Fisher** of Jamestown, Smith county, accompanied by Mr. and Mrs. **Hicks** of that place drove to Quitman and were joined by Misses Mary **Robbins**, Claude **Power** and Shellye **Horton** and returning to Pruitt, near Jamestown, Mr. Fisher and Miss Mary were united in marriage by Rev. **Davis**.

. . . Miss Mary is a daughter of Mrs. I. W. Robbins and is a native of Quitman. . . .

Uncle John Roberts Dead.

News reached Quitman Tuesday of the death of Uncle John **Roberts** whose death occured at his late home in the Little Hope community Monday night. Uncle John was one of the poineer citizens of Wood county and was here during the reconstruction days and lived at the place where his death occured for more than a half century.

May 23, 1918

Uncle John Patrick.

John William **Patrick** was born March 7th, 1842, in Upshur county, Texas, and at the age of 15 he came with his parents to Wood county where he had since resided except while serving in the civil war. . .

. At the age of 17 he was married to Miss Matilda **Graves** and to this union 11 children were born, 8 boys and 3 girls, of whom 6 boys and 1 girl are living. He wife died in 1879 and he later married Eliza **Shipes** and to this union two children were born one of whom died in infancy the other survives. His second wife died in 1896 and he was later married to Lou **Pain** and this wife survives.

He volunteereed at the beginning of the civil war and was a member of Co. E. under Capt. **Renshaw**. He served throughout the memorable struggle and was a valiant and brave soldier.

His eight living children are: Mrs. T. F. **Dodgen**, of Winnsboro, H.N., A.K., G.W., R.L., J.W., H., and W.J. **Patrick**, and Mrs. Dave **Reese**, all living in the same and adjoining neighborhoods of where Uncle John died, and were all present when the end came. He has 54 grand children living, 31 great grand children, and two brothers, George and Jim Patrick of Winnsboro, who survive him. . . .

"A Good Man Gone."

John T. **Boyd** was born Feb. 23, 1861, in Lamar Co., Ala. Living there until the age of manhood. He was married to Miss Morilla S. **Mahan** in the year of 1880. They moved to Ark. the same year and lived there 4 years, then he came to Texas, in which State he spent the remainder of his days.

He departed this life March 11, 1918, after an illness of only a few days of apoplexy of the brain. He left a wife and eight children to mourn his loss.

The children are Andrew Boyd of Sulphur Springs, Texas, Mrs. Emma **Gayle** of Sherman, Texas, Mrs. Bertie **Downing** of Mineral, Ark., David D. Boyd, of Mineola, Alzy, Goldie, Minnie and Willie of Mineola, who are still with their mother.   -Written by a True Friend.

Residence Burned.

Henry **Chreitzberg** Jr. who lives on one of Dr. **Goldsmith**'s farms west of town, had the misfortune to lose his house and contents by fire Tuesday night of last week. . . .

June 6, 1918

Death of Mr. Dunbar.

The Democrat joins the many Wood county friends of Mr. A. L. **Dunbar** of Golden, in tokens of sympathy to him on the death of his father, Mr. Dunbar of Campbell, which occured the part week.

W. P. Willingham Dead.

From Mr. A. R. **Willingham** of our town we learn of the death of W. P. Willingham, a former Wood county citizen, and formerly a Commissioner of Wood county in precinct No. 3. Deceased had been in failing health for many years and had lived in south Texas for a number of years.

Death of Mrs. Malory.

Mrs. Cintha Ann **Malory** died at the home of her son, Joe Malory at Cartwright June 3, and was buried by Clover Hill grave yard on Tuesday, . . .

Deceased was born in Alabama 77 years ago. Her husband died about 24 years ago since which time Mrs. Malory had made her home with her children in the county and in the old Alabama home county.

Mrs. Malory had been a sufferer for near 40 years with cancer which finally resulted in her death. She was the mother of Mrs. Charlie **McCain** of our town and of Joe Malory of Cartwright.

June 13, 1918

In Memorial.

Wm. **Polk** was born in Arkansas October 29, 1838, and was therefore near his 80th mile post. Uncle Bill, as he was familiarly called, was an ex Confederate soldier. After the war he came to Texas and made this county his home until his death. . . . . He was married in 1877 to Miss Martha **Allen** in Franklin county, Texas, and to this union seven children were born, two of whom preceded him to the world beyond, the mother and companion together with five children are left to mourn his departure.

Uncle Bill passed away on May 26, 1918, at 9 o'clock. The remains were laid to rest on the following day at Hopewell . . .

Arrested On Serious Charge.

Tip **McIntosh**, living six miles north of Quitman, was arrested by Sheriff **Apel** last week charged with an unspeakable crime committed on his own daughter and two of his step daughters, aged about 10, 12 and 14 years. McIntosh was carried to Tyler where District court is in session . . .

Obituary.

On May 7, 1918, the death angel visited the home of Asberry **Bird** and took away his darling wife, Mary.

Deceased was born August 27, 1890, near Coke where she lived all her life.

Deceased was a daughter of J. M. **Lewis** now living near Yantis. Mr. Lewis is one of the early settlers of Texas. Her mother, two sisters and two brothers are also still living. She leaves her husband and five children . . . remains in their last resting place in Rock Hill cemetary.   - A Friend.

Death of Mrs. Bexley.

Mrs. Ada Bell **Bexley**, wife of W. N. Bexley, died at the family home in Winnsboro Wednesday night of last week and was buried Thursday June 6, at Providence near Mr. Vernon, Franklin county, near where deceased was born and raised.

Mrs. Bexley leaves the husband of her youth together with five children to mourn her death. The children are: Alston Bexley of Quitman, Lee Bill, Jack and Joe Dan, and Mrs. Joe **Ivey**, all the latter named being still under the family roof. . . . Her maiden name was Ada Bell **Lee**, and she was married to Mr. Bexley about 26 years ago.

Democrat - 1918

June 27, 1918

J. A. Calloway Killed.

J. A. **Calloway**, who left Mineola several years ago and settled near Snyder, father of L. D. Calloway of Mineola, was killed last week when his team he was driving to a cultivator ran away with him dragging him some distance before he could be released. Deceased was a brother of J. W. Calloway of the Liberty community . . .

July 4, 1918

Another Tie In Heaven.

. . . Saturday morning June 1, when it was reported that Mrs. Ola **Dykes** is dead. . . .

Mrs. Dykes was married in December 1904 to Charley Dykes to which union two children were born, Thalma aged 11 and Charlene aged 6. . . . She was born March 25, 1887, being 31 years, 2 months and 5 days old at the time of her death. . . . She was a daughter of Mr. and Mrs. C. P. **Porter** and was reared near Clover Hill. Since the death of her husband which occured two months and three days before her death, she has made her home with her youngest sister, Mrs. George **Gaddis**.

. . . two sisters, Mrs. W. L. **Miller** and Mrs. George Gaddis, two brothers, Jim and Nathan Porter, who reside at Gladewater. . On Sunday June 2, she was carried to Hopewell . . .

Little Raymond Stokes.

Death has again invaded the home of our friend and neighbors, Mr. and Mrs. D. L. **Stokes**, the took their little babe Raymond. He was born April 6, 1917, and died at 8:45 Wednesday morning June 19, and was buried the following day . . .

Mrs. James T. Jones.

. . . Mrs. Jettie **Jones**, wife of James T. Jones, of Alba. Mrs. Jones died on June 17, at the home of her sister, Mrs. George W. Jones, of Golden. . . .She was laid to rest in the Salem cemetery . . .

Mrs. Jettie was the daughter of Will **Wright** of Alba. She was born in the Salem community on March 14, 1889. Her marriage to James T. Jones took place on August 18, 1907. to them have been born two children: a boy, Chilton, nine years of age; and a girl, Ophelia, seven. . . .

. . . She is also survived by a sister, Mrs. Geo W. Jones, and two brothers, Tommie and Milton. All were with her at the last except Tommie who was in the army training camp.

July 11, 1918

Death of Mrs. Conger.

Mrs. Jimmie **Conger**, wife of Dr. J. D. Conger died at the family home one mile east of Quitman Monday evening after months of untold suffering. The body was embalmed and held awaiting the arrival of the oldest son, Eugene, who had to come from Canada. . . . Interment will be in Quitman cemetery . . .

In Memoriam.

Little Malcom, son of Mr. and Mrs. Grover **Harris**, died at the family home hear Rock Hill May 27, aged 4 years, 5 months.

Death of a Pioneer.

We did not learn until last Saturday of the death of our veteran friend G. M. (Uncle Coot) **Sellers**, which occured at the family home in Winnsboro the 27th of June.

Uncle Boot was born in Pike county, Ala., 64 years ago last June and came to Texas 34 years ago and has lived in the Winnsboro country continuously ever since, Winnsboro being his post-office all this time. He was buried at Hopewell on June 28, the day following his death. . . . Three children with the wife of his youth survive him, the children being J. W. Sellers, a prominent citizen of Winnsboro, being at this time and for several years past engaged in weighing cotton. Two daughters, Mrs. Carl **Williams** of Winnsboro, and Mrs. Ed **Green** who lives at old Connersville in Hopkins county. Uncle Coot and his wife married 42 years ago before coming to Texas.

July 18, 1918

Passing of A Good Woman.

In the death of Mrs. Jimmie **Conger**, wife of Dr. J. D. Conger . .

Miss Jimmie, as she was lovingly and familiarly called, was a daughter of the lamented Col. George W. **Haines** and wife. She was born in this county October 30, 1867, and was reared at the Haines old homestead one mile east of town, and lived the principal part of her life in the brick residence where her death occured on July 8, 1918. Her marriage to Dr. J. D. Conger occured Sept. 30, 1886, to which union three children were born, all of whom are living. Eugene, the oldest, lives in Canada. Reba who married John **Chreitzberg** some years ago, and who with her husband and children has made her home with her mother since her health failed, and Andrew the youngest boy who is still under the family roof. One brother, Francis Haines, who resides in Wyoming, and one sister, Mrs. J. W. **Wilson** who resides near Alba, and an aged uncle, Tom **Flournoy**, together with the husband survive.

THE LETTER CAME TO-LATE

The following letter was received on Wednesday from Mrs. Beulah **Iles**, nee Miss Beulah **Conger**, sister to Dr. Conger, . . :

"Denver, Colo, 7,8, 1918,
2655 West 34th Ave.

"Dear Sister Jimmie. [letter follows]

August 1, 1918

For Sale.

My place in Quitman known as the **McDade** home. Must sell, and the first best offer gets the place. Address R. E. **Wright**, 998, 3rd Ave., Gadsden, Ala.

Wood County Newspapers

Henry Strickland Dead.

J. C. **Parker** received a phone message Monday evening announcing the death of Henry **Strickland** of the Pine Mills country. . . .

Lorraine Rouse Married.

A letter from Rev. W. T. **Rouse** of Vernon, Texas, announces the marriage of his son, Lorriane to Miss Mamie Lou **Baldwin** of Memphis, Texas. The marriage took place July 23rd.

Lorriane is an Aviator . . .Lorraine was born in Quitman while his father was County Atty. of Wood county . . .

Death of Mrs. Colliers.

Mrs. **Colliers** was taken sick at Cottonwood church Thursday night and was carried to the home of Mrs. Ollie **Ezell**. . . . on Saturday morning she passed quietly and peacefully away.

Interment was had at Golden cemetery Sunday evening, Rev. Abb **Terry** conducting the last sad rites. She leaves the husband of her youth, six children, three brothers and three sisters . .

Mrs. Colliers was raised near Golden. Her mother Mrs. **Hardy**, was postmaster at Golden for many years.

Farewell Belle till we meet in heaven.   - A Friend.

August 8, 1918

Obituary.

Mrs. Julia **Phillips** was born in Stuart county, Ga., in May 1852. . .

Mrs. Phillips maiden name was **Cooper**. She was married to Mr. S. I. Phillips on August 8, 1875, to which union nine children were born, four of whom preceded her to the other world.

Mr. and Mrs. Phillips moved from Georgia to Texas 29 years ago and settled in the Pleasant Grove community where they resided until the first of this year when they moved near Winnsboro where she was living at the time of her death. . . . her death on Tuesday night at 11 o'clock. . .

There is left to mourn their loss the husband, five children and three sisters, Mrs. Jim **Gilmore**, Mrs. **Jackson** of Greenville, and Mrs. J. M. **Wilson** of near Winnsboro, all of whom were with her except the oldest son Earnest, who is in west Texas.

The remains were laid to rest at Hopewell cemetery the day following her death . . .

Mrs. Mary D. Black.

The subject of the sketch was born in Catoose county, Ga., Sept. 11, 1838. Her maiden name was **Whitworth**. When the war was raging between the States, her family moved to Hall county. At the close of the war she was married to David **Black**, Dec. 14, 1865. To this union four children were born. Two died in infancy. Two sons, Marion and Berrie Black survive. Together with her family she moved to Texas in 1902. She leaves beside her two sons mentioned, one brother, Jimmie **Whitworth**, and one sister, Mrs. G. A. **Robinson**, .

August 15, 1918

Death of Mrs. J. H. Marable.

. . . the death of Mrs. J. H. **Marable**.

Mrs. Marable was carried to the Becton Sanitarium at Greenville Sunday August 4, for an operation . . . continued to grow weaker until Monday night at 8:30 when death resulted.

The remains were brought to Mineola Tuesday evening on the Katy passenger and carried to the home of her brother, Henry **Willingham**, where funeral services will be held this Wednesday morning and interment will be had at Sand Springs cemetery . . .

August 22, 1918

Wood County Girl Marries New Mexico Man.

Miss Alma **Chappell** of Alba was married to Mr. John E. **Whitmore** at Tucumcari, August 6th . . .

Miss Alma . . . was born and reared near Cartwright, and is a daughter of that lamented and good citizen Charlie Chappell. Her mother who now resides at Alba, is a daughter of that pioneer citizen of the county, "Uncle Frank" **Benton**, and a sister of Tax Collector Sam J. Benton.

[Detailed wedding description from The Tucumcari Sun follows.]

Death of Mrs. Marable.

Mrs. Minnie **Marable**, nee **Perrin**, was born January 17, 1883, near Mineola. Her father died when she was about 11 years of age, and a year later her mother was married to Rev. E. A. **Sharp**, familiarly and affectionately called "Uncle Ed" . . .

Minnie married J. H. Marable in January 1903, to which union two children were born, one died when small, the other, Hallie, a girl, now 15, survives and is with the grand parents with whom Minnie made her home when death claimed her.

Beside the aged parents and daughter there is left to mourn the death of this good woman two brothers and three sisters. The brothers are C. D. and W. H. **Willingham** of Mineola, Mrs. B. F. **Perrin** of Myrtle Springs, Mrs. J. S. **Reese** of Dallas, and Mrs. C. C. **Fergason** of Lake Aylewine, all of whom were present at the funeral.

Minnie died at the Becton sanitarium, at Greenville, Monday evening at 8:30, August 18, . . .

Mrs. N. B. Pickett Dies At Yantis.

. . . Mrs. N. B. **Pickett** . . . her death . . . at the family home in Yantis on Wednesday August 7th, after an illness of several weeks with typhoid fever. Interment was had in Shirley in Hopkins county, on the day following her death . . .

September 19, 1918

Family Reunion.

All the children of those grand old people, Uncle Billie **Blackwell** and wife . . . the first time they had all been together in 30 years.

. . . These children were Mrs. Dock **Clements** of Springfield, Colorado, Mrs. John **Price** of Prescott, Ark., Dr. W. M. and J. O. Blackwell, and Mrs. E. A. **Atwood,** all who live near the family home, and Mrs. C. W. **Vickery** of Quitman.

Dock Chreitzberg Weds.

. . . K. D. (Dock) **Chreitzberg** . . and Miss Claudie **Strickland** were married at the home of the bride's mother near Pine Mills on Sunday Sept. 8th, and are now home at the Chreitzberg residence a mile east of town.

Dock . . . a son of . . . "Uncle Frank" Chreitzberg . . .

Sad Death at Golden.

. . . the death of Miss Ethel **Precise** which occured at the family home at Golden Thursday evening of last week.

September 23, 1918

Uncle John **Stagner** Weds.

Uncle John secured marriage license and repaired to the Hart Hotel where Judge **Bozeman** united him and Mrs. Sallie **Moseley** . . .

October 3, 1918

Biography of Mrs. Grice.

Mrs. E. J. **Grice** (nee Elizabeth J. **Price**) was born in Carroll county, Ga. January 25, 1841. Came to Texas with her parents in 1852, and stopped in Fannin county two years then moved to Wood county in December 1854 and settled about four miles north of Quitman, where she continued to live the remainder of her life with the exception of two years. In 1860 she was married to John T. **Harry** and lived near Oak Grove for two years. Her husband was called to the war and she moved back to the home of her parents. In 1866 her husband returned from the war and they moved on Lake Fork near

Gunter crossing. In 1867 her husband died and she again moved back to the old home. To this union two children, Rena and Mary, were born. Her mother died in 1872, and her father in 1883, and in 1874 she bought a part of the old homestead where she continued to reside, and in December 1874 she was married to W. S. Grice, and to this union four children, Claude, Walter, Anna and Lona, were born. Her three oldest children preceded her to the great beyond, the three youngest together with the aged husband survive. . . .

Miss Ethel Precise Dead.

. . . the death of Miss Ethel **Precise**.

Miss Ethel was the daughter of the late John S. Precise of this place, he having died only a little more than a year ago. Miss Ethel was born in Scottsboro, Alabama, on January 13, 1899. Her parents moved to Golden when she was quite young, and her mother died when she was about five years of age. Her father later married Miss Nora **Riley**, . . . of Golden . . .[long eulogy]

October 10, 1918

Henry Brewer Dead.

News was received in Quitman Monday morning of the death of Henry **Brewer**, a son of Mrs. Brewer of Oak Grove, whose death occured at Camp Dix, New Jersey at 12 o'clock Sunday night. His brother, Harvey Brewer, was with him when the end came . . .

The remains will arrive at Winnsboro today, Wednesday, and will be carried to the family home at Oak Grove. Interment will be at Ebenezer but the date or hour for same has not been determined, . .

October 17, 1918

Spanish Influenza Raging.

The epidemic of Spanish Influenza is raging all over the country. Quitman is coming in for its share. There is doubtless not less than half a hundred cases within a radius of half a mile of the courthouse.

Deaths.

Henry P. **English**, born August 7, 1898, died October 13, 1918, at the home of his parents Mr. and Mrs. J. H. English at Alba. Interment was had at Pleasant Ridge cemetery Monday October 14, at 2 o'clock.

Earnest **Gibson**, son of Frank Gibson, died at the family home at Winnsboro Thursday evening after several days suffering with pneumonia.

L. D. **Calloway**, a prominent citizen of Mineola, died at his late home in that city Monday night. . . .

News reached Quitman today, Tuesday noon, that Charlie **Reeves** of Mineola, is dead. Charlie had lived in Mineola all of his life . . .

October 31, 1918

Another Good Citizen Gone.

The people of Alba were shocked last Monday afternoon when word was phoned in by some one that L. N. **Parish** had been found dead at his home in the Colony community four miles southwest of Alba. Apparently Mr. Parish was in good health and when found by his wife, his body was prostrate between the plow handles where he had fallen while at work in the field. He was buried at Willow Springs Tuesday afternoon.

Uncle Jim Adrian.

Another ex-confederate soldier and old settler has gone . . . This time it is Uncle Jim **Adrian** of near Golden.

Uncle Jim was born in Alabama on April 15, 1832. He came to Longview, Texas, 40 years ago and lived there 2 years, remaining 38 years have been spent in Wood county. He married when a young man and there were born to him and his wife 8 children, seven of whom are still living. Besides these seven children . . ., he is survived by a wife, 27 grand-children, and 7 great-grand-children. He bade adieu to all these and his many friends on Sept. 8, 1918 . . .

. . . He enlisted in the infantry of the Confederate army on March 25, 1861, and left the army at the close of the war with the rank of first lieutenant. . . .

Death of Dr. Roundtree.

We failed week before last to mention the death of Dr. Paul **Roundtree** whose death occured at Ft. Worth the week previous.
. . . He married a former Quitman girl, Miss Pearl **Stephens**, . . .

Death of Mrs. Clanton.

Mrs. S. A. **Clanton** died at her late residence in the Lone Star community Wendesday evening of last week with pheomonia.
A number of children survive her. . . .

Death of Mrs. Wilson.

Friend Grover **Wilson** of Pleasant Grove, has the sympathy of the Democrat in the death of his wife which occcured the past week, . .

Accompanied Body of Comrade Home.

Max **Smart** accompanied the body of his comrade, Eugene **Carter**, who died at Camp Travis the past week, to Winnsboro, the body reaching that City Sunday noon. Eugene was a son of T. M. Carter of the Winnsboro country and was in training at Camp Travis. Pneumonia following a case of influenza was the cause of death. Burial was had at Lee grave yard Sunday evening.

Nephew Kills Uncle.

Tuesday night of last week a difficulty occured between Claude **Blackmon**, a son of O. J. Blackmon Jr. and his uncle Bethel Blackmon in which the latter was shot, death resulting from the shot a few days later. A 38 Smith & Weston pistol was the weapon used. Claude made his get-away and up to this time has not been apprehended.
. . .Bethel Blackmon . . . About eight years ago he married a daughter of Ambrose **Clark** of the Golden country and the wife with five children survive him. . . . had lived in the Sand Springs community for the past 12 years.

November 7, 1918

Two More Wood County Boys Go Down In Action.
First of last week the news came that Harry **Strickland**, a son of the late Henry Strickland of Pine Mills, and a brother of Mrs. K. D. **Chreitzberg**, had been killed in action somewhere in France, and on Saturday the news came that Forrest **Harry**, son of D. W. Harry, and a brother of County Attorney Floyd Harry, had been killed in action on the 26th of September.

Deaths.

MANSELL. N. B. Mansell died Friday of last week at his home near Pine Mills and was buried the following day at Mr. Pisga . .

JONES. Frank Jones died at his late home near Alba Friday of last week and was buried the following day at Pleasant Ridge. Deceased was a brother of Commissioner elect, George Jones of Golden.

WRIGHT. The many friends of Bob Wright, who formerly lived at Alba, and later at Quitman, will be pained to learn of the death of his wife which occured at Gadsden, Ala., on the 16th of October.

BREEDLOVE. . . . the death of E. E. Breedlove, formerly of Alba, but who resided at Seymore at the time of his death. He was a brother of T. B. Breedlove of Alba, . . .

WILLINGHAM. Charles Russell, the two year old baby boy of Mr. and Mrs. J. S. Willingham, died at the family home near Mt. Enterprise Saturday night and was buried Sunday at Clover Hill.

JONES. Mrs. Josie Jones, wife of Rufe Jones, died at the family home near Calvery Sunday evening and was buried the following day at Sand Springs. Deceased was a sister of Will **Butts** of the Calvery community.

ROBINSON. Mrs. Ebb Robinson died at the family home at Coke Thursday of last week and was buried the following day at Pleasant Grove.

BINFORD. Mrs. T. M. Binford died at the family home in Mineola Friday evening of last week and was buried Saturday in Mineola cemetery.

SMITH. . . . the death of "Uncle Tom" Smith which occured at his home hear Coke Tuesday night. Interment will take place at Tock Hill this Wednesday evening.

Sheriff Apel Is Married.

Sheriff [Bill] **Apel** and Miss Ruth **Smart** gave their friends a surprise Sunday evening when they drove to the Methodist Parsonage and were married. Rev. R. J. **Smith** performing the ceremony, the preachers family and Dick **Kennimer** and Grogan **Shoemaker** (The two young men having become wise to the procedure during the evening) being the only witness.

. . .She is the eldest daughter of Mr. and Mrs. B. F. Smart and was born and raised in Quitman. . . .

November 14, 1918

Senator McCollum Dead.

Senator A. R. **McCollum** died at Austin Saturday of last week and was buried at Waco, his late home, on Sunday . . .

Senator McCollum was a first cousin of Mr. E. R. **Brown** of the Democrat force. . . .

Another Wood County Boy Goes Down In Action.

I. W. **Robbins** received . . . telegram: Mr. Isham Robbins, Quitman, Texas. Deeply regret to inform you that private I. C. Robbins infantry is officially reported killed in action on Sept. 30. . .

This is the first boy right out of Quitman that has been reported killed or lost over there.

Clough, as he was best known, was born in Quitman October 15, 1890. He was the second son of I. W. Robbins . . . Some years ago he married Miss Leila **Norton** of Newsome who with one little boy survive. He is also survived by his father, three brothers, Dr. V. E. Robbins, Hill Robbins, who is also somewhere over there, and Buster, the baby brother, and three sisters, Miss Lois, Mrs. Henry **Fisher**, of Smith county, and Miss Ella, the baby sister. . . .

Veteran Passes Away.

W. Q. **Zeigler**, a veteran of the civil war, passed away at the home of his son, W. O. Zeigler 4 miles southeast of Quitman, Wednesday the 6th of November and was buried the following day at Mr. Pisga.

Uncle Quincy Zeigler, as he was familiarly called, was born in Tennessee, November 27th, 1840. He served through the civil war, being a member of Co. H. 43rd Tennessee. He came to Texas in 1887, since which time he has resided in Wood county. . . . Two sons, W. O. Zeigler at whose home he died, and M. J. Zeigler of Golden survive him . . .

A Good Woman Gone.

Mrs. Avelena **Rape** is dead. . .

Mrs. Rape was taken with influenza and pheumonia . . . She leaves seven children, two of whom are married, the other five being still under the family roof.

. . . a daughter of Rev. and Mrs. B. F. **Blalock** of the Redland community.

Beside the aged parents and children, several brothers and sisters are left to mourn . . .

M. B. Whitter Dead.

M. B. **Whitter** died Wednesday morning at 12:25, and was buried in the Lee Cemetery at 3 o'clock in the afternoon. Mr. Whitter was 43 years old and leaves a wife and several children. . . . He was serving as constable of this precinct. . . — Winnsboro News.

Little Earl Armour.

Little Earl **Armour**, the 7 year old son of Mr. and Mrs. J. W. Armour, died at the family home in Mineola Sunday Nov. 10, and was buried Monday at Sand Springs grave yard . . .

Woman Badly Burned.

The wife of Jackson **Russell** col. living two miles east of town, was badly burned Tuesday morning by her clothing catching fire as she stood in front of the fire place.

LATER. We learn the woman died at 2 o'clock this morning.

November 21, 1918

Death of Babe.

County Treasurer Will **Vickery** informs us of the death of the week old babe of Mr. and Mrs. J. W. **Lambert** which occured at the family home at Alba, burial taking place Monday evening at Pleasant Ridge.

Tried On Insanity Charge.

Jim **Coffee** who has resided in the eastern portion of the county for about two years, was tried on a charge on insanity Tuesday of this week. Sheriff Apel brought Mr. Coffee to Quitman latter part of last week. He is abour 45 years of age, and has two little girls, aged 9 and 11. His brother, Karles Coffee, of Muskogee, Okla, and brother-in-law, F. N. **Howell** of Eddy, Texas, came here Sunday, the brother remaining until room can be secured at the Asylum for the patient .

Kennimer-Horton.

Mr. Dick **Kennimer** and Miss Vera **Horton** surprised their friends Sunday be driving to the home of Esq. B. F. **Smart** and getting married, . . .

. . . Miss Vera is the pretty daughter of Mr. and Mrs. E. M. Horton.

November 28, 1918

Arrested On Serious Charge.

S. S. **Martin** who lives near Pine Mills, was arrested Saturday at Greenville, on a complaint filed in Justice **Burkett**'s court at Pine Mills, charging him with an unnamable crime committed on his 15 year old daughter. The daughter is said to be in a delicate situation. Deputy Sheriff Bob **Butler** and Bill **Mount** went to Greenville Sunday and brought Martin to Quitman and he is now in jail.

Democrat - 1918

In Memory of Henry English.

Death entered the home of Mr. and Mrs. J. H. **English** Oct. 13, 1918 and claimed for his own the spirit of their eldest son, Henry, aged 20, for he was born on Aug. 7, 1898.

. . . He was laid to rest in Pleasant Ridge cemetery on Monday afternoon Oct. 14, 1918. .

Mrs. Barnie Denton.

Mrs. Barnie **Denton** died at the family home in Dallas Saturday morning Nov. 23, after a brief illness with influenza and pheomonia. The remains were brought to Winnsboro on the noon train Monday and carried to Hopewell grave yard for burial Monday evening.

Deceased was a daughter of M. A. **Richburg** of Cartwright. She was married to Marnie Denton seven years ago. Two children were born to them, both of whom died in infancy. Two sisters, Miss Lilla, who resides in Colorado, and Miss Bamma who is teaching near Dallas, three brothers, Earnest, who resides at Granger, Dewey who made his home with Barnie and his wife, and Maxey whose whereabouts is not known, together with the husband, the father, and step mother, survive deceased.

Died in Oklahoma.

John W. **Flournoy**, a brother of our friend Asa Flournoy of the Hainesville country, died at his late home in Clinton, Okla. the past week.

John was a step-son of J. H. **Knight** and his death removes all the children of which there were three, except Asa, the other, a sister who married W. L. **Vickery** and who died some years ago. Two half brother, Henry and Shaw Knight, who are now somewhere in France, and a half sister, Mrs. J. W. **Lambert** of Alba, survive.

December 5, 1918

More of Our Boys Fall.

. . . the death of five more Wood county boys has been received from France, two killed action and three died from pneumonia. The two killed in action were Walter **Holley** of Pleasant Grove, and Marion **Galloway** of Coke. The three who died with pneumonia were Earnest **Veitch** of Hainesville, Bethel **Scruggs** of Redland, and Conley **Watson** of Golden.

Walter Holley . . . his father, J. W. Holley . . . His grave lies marked on the hill-side southwest of St. Elienne - Walter M. Holley, No. 3060119.

Conley A. Watson, son of W. T. Watson formerly of Golden, now living at Denison, died Sept. 21, in France with pneumonia. .

. . . Earnest Veitch . . . his father W. E. Veitch at Hainesville. . . .

Bob **Reich** of Crow, we are told, received notice of the death of Bethel Scruggs, his nephew . . .

Marion Galloway was a son of the late Uncle Harve Galloway of Coke . . .

Sunday's Dallas News carried in the casuality list the name of Walter **Holland** of Yantis, as being missing in action, also the name of Elza **Zimmerman** wounded in action. . . .

Elliott Madsen.

Mr. and Mrs. Morris **Madsen** of the Mt. Enterprise community, received a telegram from Muscle Shoals, Ala. stating that their son E. A. Madsen died Nov. 15th.

Elliott left his home Nov. 5th for Ala. to work at a Government job. He was stricken with pneumonia and lived a few days. His remains were shipped to Mineola Wednesday Nov. 20, and was intered the following day at Sand Springs.

Elliott was born in Dallas Nov. 24th, 1894, and was 24 years old at the time of his death.

Little J. C. Gilbert.

Thursday evening Nov. 20, . . . little J. C. **Gilbert** . . . Little J. C. was the only son of Mr. and Mrs. Jim Gilbert. He was one year, one month and 29 days old.

Little J. C. leaves father, mother, little sister, grand parents on both sides . . .

Attended Funeral.

Mr. and Mrs. Charlie **Green** and their two boys were called to Bettie Wednesday of last week to attend the funeral of Mrs. Frank Green, wife of the brother of Charlie. The mother leaves nine children together with the husband. . . .

December 12, 1918

Killed In Action.

Mrs. M. E. **Daniel** of Oak Grove received a telegram . . . her son, Isham M. Daniel had been killed in action somewhere in France on the 5th of November, six days before the armistice was signed.

Uncle Bill Williams Dead.

The Democrat is pained indeed to learn of the death of our veteran friend, Uncle Bill **Williams**, which occured at the home of his daughter, Mrs. Dr. J. A. **Fowler** at Malakoff, Wednesday 27th. . .

The Malakoff News of last week . . .:

Wednesday evening, Nov. 27th, W. F. Williams died at the home of his daughter, Mrs. J. A. Fowler, after a lingering illness of cancer.

Mr. Williams was born in Georgia Dec. 17, 1838 and lacked but a few weeks of reaching his eightieth birthday. When only a mere boy he came to Texas and was for 35 years in the hotel business at Winnsboro. . . . Mrs. Williams preceded him to the better land January 9th, 1905.

He is survived by four children Maynard F. Williams, Pocatello, Idaho; Claude O. Williams, Little Rock, Ark.; Mrs. J. A. Fowler and Miss Ora Williams of Malakoff.

Lost Two Good Men.

Wood county lost two good citizens the past week. Jobe **Holbrook** who lived at the four-mile branch on the Mineola road, left us for Lindale where he will make his home, and L. M. **Crow** of the Rowsey settlement north of town, left for Jacksonville where he will make his home.

Wood County Newspapers

December 19, 1918

Mrs. Rob Gilbreath Dead.

Mrs. Rob **Gilbreath** died at the family home hear Gordon, Texas last Saturday morning and the remains were brought home for burial . . . carried to Myrtle Springs for interment, . . .

Deceased was a daughter of Mr. and Mrs. C. D. **Turner** and was reared near Myrtle Springs. She leaves five children together with the husband and her parents . . .

Mother And Two Children Die.

Mrs. **Gilbreath**, a widow lady living north of town 6 miles, died last Saturday evening. Her son, about grown, died a week previous, and the day before the mother died the 15 year old daughter died. Death was the result of influenza and pneumonia.

Sad, Sad Indeed.

Judge **Cathey**, County Atty. **Harry**, Sheriff **Apel** and County Clerk **Ferguson** went to Golden last week and heard a lunacy case against Mrs. J. M. **Darden**. This good woman has been demented for several months and is said to be in very low state of health. Her aged husband, the venerable and grand old Southern gentleman, Uncle Jimmie Darden, has stayed with her and has exhausted all his worldly effects and in his declining years he is left penniless.

They have a son whose health is also bad, . . .

December 26, 1918

Negro Man Died Friday.

Amos **Houston**, col. who lived about a mile out from Quitman, died Friday night. Amos was born and raised in a near Quitman . .

Aged Negro Dies.

"Aunt Harriet" **Russell**, an old time slave darkey, one that has been in and around Quitman for years, died Thursday. . . .

Miss Gerthie **Gilbreath**.

The subject of this sketch was born May 26, 1892 . . . her death which sad event occured at the family home in the Rock Hill community on Dec. 9, 1918.

She is survived by her father, a step mother, three sisters and four brothers, all of whom were present at the funeral except two brothers, one of whom was sick with influenza and pneumonia, the malady which claimed Gerthia, and the other in the U.S.A. station in New York.

Mrs. Fletch Gamblin Dead.

Mrs. Fletch **Gamblin** died at the family home near Yantis Tuesday of last week, and was buried at the Sharp grave yard the day following her death.

Mrs. Gamblin was a daughter of our venerable friends, Uncle Tom **Stevenson** and wife and was a resident of Quitman for many years.

[Miss Ola] was married several years ago to Gletch Gamblin and he with three children, one a babe two months old, survive her together with the aged parents, two sisters, one of whom is Mrs. J. B. **Wallace** of our town, and two brothers.

Winnsboro Weekly News - 1918

March 15, 1918

Roland G. Andrews.

... Roland G. **Andrews**, the subject of this sketch, was born in Lebanon, Tenn., June 23rd, 1867. He married Miss Maggie **Norris** Dec. 26, 1889.

Immediately they left for Winnsboro, Texas where he embarked in business Jan. 1, 1890.

. ... he was smitten with a stroke of apoplexy. Medical aid was quickly summoned but the call had come and he had answered like the hero he was. This was in the early hours of Friday morning February 8th, 1918. ...

In the beautiful cemetery in the little city he loved, his remains were laid away. ... He leaves a wife and a sweet little daughter, Sally Lucy. ...

Wood County Democrat - 1919

January 9, 1919 [Date assumed. Only portions of pages remain.]

B. W. Herron Dead.

B. W. **Herron**, an old and highly respected citizen of the county, died at the family home 3 miles east of town Sunday night Dec. 29th and was buried the following day at Ebenezer.

Death of E. E. Graham.

Walter **Grice** returned Sunday from Caro, Texas, where he was called to attend the funeral of his brother-in-law, E. E. **Graham** who died the past week. Mr. Graham had been a sufferer for some time with Brights disease which culminated in his death. The wife with three children survive.

Mrs. Alfred Wheeler Dead.

J. R. **Connell** informs us of the death of Mrs. Alfred **Wheeler** which sad event occured at the family home at Pine Mills on Dec. 27th.

Dr. T. N. Skeen Dead.

That veteran and grand old patriot, Dr. T. N. **Skeen** died at his late home in Winnsboro Saturday January 4th, and was buried Sunday at the Winnsboro cemetery.

Barn Patrick Dead.

Barn **Patrick**, a prominent citizen of Winnsboro, died at the family home in that City Friday of last week and was buried the following day at the City cemetery.

January 16, 1919

Alba News Notes.

Jim **Robinson**, who had lived at Alba for many years but for the last two years had lived at Como, Texas, and more recently had moved to Garrison, Texas, died at his late home January 5, and was brought to Alba for interment. He leaves a wife and four children . .

Mrs. Ida **Hopkins**, who formerly lived at Alba, but had moved to Greenville died at that place December the 28th and was buried at Pleasant Ridge January 2nd . . . Mrs. Hopkins leaves three children, one boy and two girls . . . She was a sister of our fellow townsmen J. C. and Loyd **Patten**.

. . . the death of our good friend and pupil, M. C. **Kay**, which sad event came at the close of the day Sunday, January 12.

. . . the death of Miss Lorena **Williams**, daughter of C. P. Williams of this place, which occured atDallas, Texas, Sunday January 12. . . . interment will be had a Pleasant Ridge.

January 23, 1919

Death of Old Citizen

J. B. **Sorge**, one of the oldest and best citizens of the county, died at his late home near Stout the past week, after a protracted spell of influenza-pneumonia.

. . . He leaves the wife of his youth and nine children . .

Married in Dallas

Alvin **Carrington**, the eldest son of Mr. and Mrs. P. A. Carrington, and Miss Crena **Nichols** of the Pleasant Grove community were married in Dallas New Year's day. . . .

Death of Popular Young Lady

Miss Kathleen, the eldest daughter of Dr. and Mrs. W. J. **Coleman**, died at the family residence in Mineola the past week, after a short illness with influenza and pneumonia. . . .

Death Has Claimed Mr. W. F. Browning.

The death Angel has claimed one of the most prominent citizens of Fairview school district five miles south of Wetumka.

Mr. W. F. **Browning** was born January 28, 1876, in Wood County, Texas. He was brought up in this county . . . He moved to Hughes county sometime last year, and lived this year on one of Harry **Diamond**'s places near Fairview. He brought his church letter and that of his wife and daughter with him . . .

(. . . The above notice was sent us some weeks ago by Mr. R. E. **Skeep** of Winnsboro stating that Mrs. Browning desired the article published in the Democrat. . . . Ed.)

Another Landmark Gone

The Death Angel has again visited our community and called froom us our old and much loved neighbor, "Uncle" Charlie **Smart**.

Uncle Charlie was born Feb. 22, 1843. He was married to Miss Sarah **Hartsfield** some 53 or 54 years ago, to which union seven children were born, six of them still living, and were all present when the end came except one, who was prevented on account of illness. His first wife died abour eleven years ago and he later married Mrs. Ora **Banks**. No children were born to this union, but they raised an orphan child from infancy who was with them at time of his death.

. . . He was taken sick December 27th, 1918, with pneumonia. . . .and 2:20 o'clock Monday morning, Jan. 6, 1919, the gentle spirit took its flight . . .

January 30, 1919

Death of W. J. McGuire.

Monday January 20, 1919, at 6 o'clock a.m. our community was saddened by the death of one of our oldest citizens, W. J. **McGuire**.

Mr. McGuire was born October 20, 1848, in Campbell county, Georgia. He served 16 months in the Civil War, and came to Texas in 1871. He was married January 15, 1872 to Miss Josephine M. **Reed**.

When he came to Texas he settled in the Redland community where he resided continuously until his death. The remains were laid to rest in the Pine Mills cemetery Tuesday January 21, at 2 o'clock p.m. . . .

Mr. McGuire is survived by his wife, ten children, two sisters, and twenty-eight grand children. One son, Thurmond, answered his country's call some time ago and is now in Germany. . . .

Death of Good Citizen.

J. W. **Layton**, and old and highly regarded citizen of the county, died at Winnsboro the past week after a lingering illness with paralysis. Interment was had at Ebenezer Thursday, . .

February 6, 1919

Death of Ex-Sheriff Low.

We are pained indeed to chronicle the death of J. W. **Low**, ex-Sheriff of Wood county, which occurred at his late home at Alba Monday night of this week. . . .

Funeral service was held at the home Tuesday evening and interment was had at Pleasant Ridge cemetery at 2:30 o'clock Tuesday evening.

In Memory of Mrs. Shelton.

Mrs. Kate Dempsey **Shelton** was born in Harrisburg, Ill., September 12, 1870, and died in Greenville, Texas, Jan. 18, 1919. She was the daughter of John J. and Mary **Dempsey**. . . . She married Thos F. Shelton February 9[?], 1895. To this union three children were born, two sons, Frank and Mack, and a daughter, Lounene [sp?].

James W. Layton

James W. **Layton** was born in Chattanooga, Ga., July 14th, 1847, and died January 22nd, 1919. He was first married to Miss Sarah **Story** March 26, 1876, to whom eight children were born, five still living -- D. A., J. S., O. T., T. L. and Sallie. His first wife died February 16, 1887.

He was again married to Miss Sarah **Cherry** December 8, 1887, and came to Texas in 1904, where she died June 17, 1911.

Death of Mrs. J. S. Blackmon

Mrs. J. S. **Blackmon** died at the family home in Lancaster, S. D., week before last. Deceased was the mother of Rev. R. J. Blackmon of our town. She was in her 75th year and leaves the husband of her youth, together with six sons and four daughters . .

Another Wood County Boy Goes Down.

Frank **Folmer**, son of E. F. Folmer, died somewhere over in France October 18, 1918 . . . He was 27 years old and had resided at his father's home near Yantis all his life.

Little Edith Bridges

On Friday morning at 2 o'clock Jan. 17, 1919, Death, . . . entered the home of Mr. and Mrs. Lonnie **Bridges** and took from them their sweet little daughter, Edith Mae, aged 11 months and 22 days. . . .

Funeral services were conducted at the home, after which the remains were tenderly laid to rest in the Sand Springs cemetery.

Little Edith leaves a father, mother, four brothers, three little sisters . . .

February 13, 1919

Obituary.

Mrs. Bertha **Brown**, the subject of this sketch, passed peacefully away at the late home near Quitman, on Jan. 12, 1919. She was the wife of Virgil Brown, daughter of Mr. and Mrs. Tom **Pennington** of Haskell, Texas. . . .

In Memory of Dr. Skeen

Dr. Titus Nelson **Skeen**, son of Rev. P. H. Skeen, was born in Palmetto, Georgia, Sept. 19, 1843. He entered the war between the States at the ago of seventeen. He was in Twenty-one battles and was with General Lee when the banner of the Southern Confederacy was furled at Appomattox. He received the Cross of Honor for his services in the war.

Immediately after the surrender he came to Texas and in 1867 he married Mary Lou **Newsome** at Leesburg, Texas. To them six children were born. All died in infancy except one, Eugene Skeen, a promising young man who died at Wichita Falls at the age of twenty-four. Dr. Skeen graduated in the Medical College of Augusta, Georgia in 1875. He was also a post graduate of Tulane University, New Orleans.

Dr. Skeen moved to Winnsboro, Texas, in 1871. He continued the practice of his chosen profession until he was stricken by the dreadful scourge of influenza and pneumonia from which he died January 4, 1919.

. . . His widow by whose side he walked for more than half a century, his half brother, R. E. Skeen, and a brother in Texarkana, Dr. B?r?y Skeen, survive him. . . .

Mrs. J. G. Mossenton Dead.

. . . the death of Mrs. J. G. **Mossenton** which occured at the family home near Golden Tuesday morning at 3 o'clock. Interment was had at Sand Springs grave yard Wednesday.

Children Burned To Death.

Commissioner **Voorhees** tells us that the home of a Mr. **Young** living near the **Jolley** place on the Hawkins road below Pine Mills, was burned Monday of this week and three of the children of the family perished in the flames.

Obituary.

J. D. **Mize**, the little seven year old boy of Mr. and Mrs. J. W. Mize, died at twelve o'clock January 16, 1919, at his home near Golden. . . .

C. B. Kay.

The youngest son of Mr. and Mrs. J. B. **Kay**, was born August 14th, 1892, in Parker county, Texas, and lived there until August 1897, and went to Fannin county where we lived until 1902, when we moved to Wood county, where he has resided ever since until death claimed him. . . . at 6:15 the night of the 12th, death came . . .

The day following his death he was carried by loving hands to Pleasant Ridge cemetery and buried with Masonic honors, . .Mother.

Little Cecil Ingram.

On the 15th of Jan. 1919, the death angel visited the home of Mr. and Mrs. Leanard **Ingram** of the Rock Hill community, and took their little boy, Cecil, aged five years and six months. . . .

A Good Woman Gone.

On Jan. 24, 1919, . . . Mrs. Vicie **Gamblin**. She was the daughter of our friend and neighbor, S. B. **Pope** of Golden. She was born July 16, 1890 . . . She was married to R. Gamblin Dec. 21, 1909, to which union three children were born.

. . . laid the body to rest in the City of the Dead at Sand Springs, . . .

February 27, 1919

Mrs. J. F. Craddock.

Mrs. J. F. **Craddock** died Saturday afternoon at 6 o'clock and was buried in the Simron cemetery the following day. Mrs. Craddock was 40 years of age and leaves a husband and six children . . .

- Winnsboro News.

Would Let Mrs. Richburg Sue State.

Austin, Texas, Feb. 10 - In the Senate today Mr. **Suiter** introduced a bill to permit Mrs. Ethel **Richburg** to sue the State either in Wood or Eastland counties for damage on account of the death of her husband killed by rangers on or about Dec. 24, 1918

- Winnsboro News.

In Memory.

In Flanders field where the lillies of France may blossom over his grave and where little French children lovingly and gratefully lay wreathes over the last resting place of our beloved fallen heroes, now lies the body of our brother Walter Marion **Holly**, born August 2nd, 1893 and who fell in action on the battle field Oct. 4th, 1918. [Long eulogy.]

Obituary.

The Death Angel visited the home of Mr. and Mrs. J. M. **Lewis** on February 11, and called their only son at home, Bud Lewis. . . . He was 30 years of age and had lived with his parents all his life.

. . . He leaves his aged father and mother of Yanis, two sisters and a brother to mourn his death. One sister, Mrs. Mat **Rogers**, lives in the Rock Hill community, one, Mrs. Ollie **Clayton**, lives at Martin Springs, and a brother, Wash Lewis, at Winnsboro.

Mrs. Duffay Mapes Dead.

A letter from Duffay **Mapes** of Wichita Falls announces the death of his wife, which sad event occured at the family home in that City on the 15th. . . .

March 13, 1919

Married in Dallas.

Last Sunday's Dallas News contained the following announcement: "B. C. **Skeen** of Fort Worth and Miss Palmer Mozelle **Taylor** of Quitman were married yesterday afternoon at the home of the Rev. S. H. C. **Burgin**, 2741 Fairmont street, the Rev. Mr. Burgin officiating."

Both these young people were reared at Winnsboro . . . Miss Mozelle has lived in Quitman since the election of her brother, J. R. Taylor as Districk Clerk in 1914. . . .

Bryan Skeen, as he is best known, is a son of R. E. Skeen, the prominent merchant of Winnsboro. . . .

Obituary.

In memory of Mrs. W. D. **Hinson**, familiarly known as Mrs. Jimmie Hinson, who died at the family home near Pleasant Grove on March 6, 1919, at about 7 o'clock in the morning. . .

Mrs. Hinson was a daughter of Mr. and Mrs. S. S. **Moore**. She was reared in the Pleasant Grove community . . . She was born Oct. 23, 1880, and was married to W. D. Hinson in January 1896, to which union seven children were born, one died in infancy, the other six are still living.

Mrs. Hinson leaves to mourn their loss, the husband, six children, her aged parents, six sisters and two brothers, all of whom were present when death came except one brother who is in Arizona.

March 20, 1919

Woman Burned To Death.

Mrs. J. T. **Power** received a phone message from her daughter, Mrs. W. B. **Lillard**, of Dallas, Tuesday of this week stating that the residence where Mrs. Lillard lived was destroyed by fire Monday night and that one of the ladies who was in the house at the time was burned to death. Mrs. Lillard was burned also but not seriously. . ..

March 27, 1919

James M. Chitwood.

James M. **Chitwood**, aged 61 years, died very suddenly Friday afternoon. Mr. Chitwood left his home, 215 West Acheson, after his noon meal, feeling in good health, but soon after reporting for work as a carpenter, he complained of feeling badly, and was taken to his home, where he soon expired.

Surviving is his wife, three sons and three daughters. The daughters are Mrs. Ona **Williams**, Mrs. Beulah **Pugh** and Mrs. Elsie **Little** of Mineola, . . . The sons are Drury and Fred of Denison and C. C. Chitwood of Kansas City, . . . Funeral services will be held at the home at 2 o'clock Sunday afternoon, . . . Interment will be made in Oakwook cemetery.   - Denison Herald.

Death of Mrs. McRea.

Our friend Bud **Lloyd** of near Como, was in Thursday and told us of the death of his wife's mother, Mrs. Allie **McRea**, which occured at the family home near Coke, Sunday March 9th. Burial has had at Hopewell following the day of her death, Rev. A. A. **Kidd** of Winnsboro conducting the funeral service. Deceased was a sister of R. N. **McCrary** and Mrs. F. C. **Wingard** of Coke. Four daughters, Mrs. T. R. **Lloyd**, Mrs. G. A. **Kennimer**, Mrs. M. F. **Wilson** and Mrs. Annie **Johnson**, also two sons, B. D. and P. H. **McRea**, survive.

April 3, 1919

Mrs. Tom Banks Dead

. . . Mrs. Tom **Banks** died at the family home west of Quitman Tuesday evening at 8:30. Interment will be had at Quitman grave yard this evening.

April 10, 1919

In Memory of J. W. Low.

John W. **Low** was born April 13th, 1849, in Troupe county, Georgia. His parents came to Texas in 1854, and settled first in Rusk county, where they resided a short time and then came to Wood county, the elder Low settling east of Quitman about six miles where he lived until death called him., February 6, 1868, deceased was married to Mrs. Letha Angelina **Lee** of Smith county, Texas, and they lived near Starville in that county for about a couple of years when they returned to Wood county and bought a part of the old homestead and lived there until the death of the wife, June 2, 1881. To this union six children were born, William Edward, W. H., R. W., A. R. and twins that died in infancy. The first born died also, the other three still living: W. H. being assistant cashier in the Alba National Bank, having served Wood county four years as Tax Collector, R. W., cashier of the F. & M. Bank of our town, and A. R. who now resides at Aspermont, Texas.

October 28, 1881, deceased was again married to Miss Eliza S. **Braziel**, who became a mother indeed to the three little motherless boys . . .No children came to bless the home of this latter union, and after the three boys were grown and out in the world, a sister of Mrs. Low, Mrs. R. A. **Perdue**, died and the baby boy was carried to the home and has been raised to young manhood by this good couple. Later another sister, Mrs. **Clanton**, died and the baby girl of the home was carried to this home and has been raised to young womanhood, thus making five motherless children this good woman has mothered and raised . . . The two children, Roy and Loraine, were as devoted to "Uncle" as they could have been to their own father.

J. W. Low was elected Sheriff of Wood county in 1890, and served four years. . . Several years ago, he moved to Alba. . .He was a Mason and a Deacon in the Baptist church . . .

April 17, 1919

Two Veterans Pass Away.

The past week two of the greatest men Texas ever had within her borders, passed to their reward, they being Father R. C. **Buckner** founder of the Buckner Orphans Home, and Brother Abe **Mulkey**, founder of the Orphans Home at Corsicana. . . .

Death of L. R. White.

The Democrat is pained indeed to chronicle the death of Mr. L. R. **White**, late Secretary of the Chamber of Commerce of Winnsboro, which sad event occured at the Dr. G. L. **Baber** sanitarium at Winnsboro Saturday night of last week. Interment was had at Lee Cemetery Sunday afternoon . . .

Mr. White was 42 years of age. His only immediate relative in this section of the country was his wife. They had been in Winnsboro a short while, comparatively speaking, . ..

RESULTS OF CYCLONE
The Cyclone That Passed Through Wood County
Wednesday Morning April 9th, 1919, Killed 23,
Wounded 56, Completely Wrecked 71 Homes,
Damaged 55 Others, Wrecked 2 School
Buildings. Estimated Property
Loss Half Million Dollars.

[This issue contains more than a full page of text with detailed descriptions of damage and includes four photographs. - Ed.]

April 24, 1919

[Three additional pictures of Cyclone damage. -Ed.]

Died At Mineola.

Mrs. Cress **Hamilton**, daughter of Atty. J. P. **Hart** of Mineola, died at the family home in Mineola Saturday and the remains were carried to Big Sandy for burial Sunday. Mrs. Hamilton's hunband died the past winter while the epidemic of the Flu was raging.

Biographical and Memorial.
(Delayed From Last Week.)

James T. **Power** was born October 10, 1868, and reared in South Carolina, and came to Texas in May 1892. He was married to Miss Ella **Burroughs** at Commerce, Texas, in 1894, and to this union was born five children, namely Mrs. W. B. **Lillard** of Dallas, Roy, Carl, Claude and Laverne. Carl, the third child, died when small, the other three named are still under the family roof, and with the wife of his youth, his aged mother, Mrs. J. W. Power, of Alba, three brothers and four sisters, survive. The sisters are Mrs. C. L. **Pitner**, Alba, Mrs. Selma **Currie**, Alba, Mrs. S. W. **Sisk**, Emory, and Mrs. Maggie **Wheat**, Gainesville. The brothers are L. B. Power, Emory, A. H. Power, Alba, and Will Power of Baird, all of whom were present at the funeral except the elder brother and Mrs. Maggie Wheat. . . .death came . . on Monday evening at 7:45, April 7, 1919 . . . Burial had in Quitman cemetery . . .

C. S. Hart Dies At Gilmer.

C. S. **Hart**, brother of Mrs. Sam H. Hart of our town, died at the family home in Gilmer Wednesday night of last week and was buried Friday the 18, in Gilmer cemetery. Several brothers, among the number being our former townsman W. A. Hart, and several sisters survive.

June 5, 1919

Mrs. Poland Dead

Mrs. J. D. **Poland** died at the family home six miles north of Quitman, Tuesday morning of this week. . . Interment will be at Concord today, Wednesday.

Well Known Negro Dead

Henry **Murray**, familiarly called "Shad," and who was for a number of year the janitor at the courthouse, died at Denison the past week and the remains were brought to Quitman for burial in the colored folks grave yard, and was buried Wednesday.

July 8, 1919

Alba News Changes Hands.

Last weeks Two-County Times, formerly the Alba News, carried the announcement that W. E. **Reid** has sold the paper to T. N. **Brower** and that Mr. Brower is now in charge of same. . . .

July 17, 1919

Killed by Auto.

Mrs. S. F. **Moxley** was run over by an automobile at Dallas Saturday night and died from the effects of the injuries received a few hours later. The remains were brought to Mineola on the 11 o'clock train Monday and carried to Ebenezer for interment . . .

July 24, 1919

Death of Mrs. Moxley.

Mrs. **Moxley** was born in Alabama August 24th 1848, and came to Texas when a mere girl. She was married to Rev. J. J. Moxley in the year 1878, to which union four children were born, two of whom died when small, the other two survive, they being Marvin Moxley now living in Dallas, and Mrs. Arthur **Sims**, living near Oak Grove. Her husband died in Quitman several years ago.

Mrs. Sims, the daughter, informs us that her mother is the seventh of the family to meet death by accident. . . .

July 31, 1919

Death of Mrs. Johnson.

. . . the death of Mrs. **Johnson**, widow of the late H. V. Johnson, who was for four years tax collector of our county.

Mrs. Johnson was principally reared in Quitman, being a neice of those grand and noble people, D. T. **Lipscomb** and wife, who raised her in their home and at whose home she was given in marriage to the husband who preceded her to the other world some years ago.

. . .Interment was had at Sand Springs grave yard Saturday morning July 26th, at 10 o'clock, her death having occured the evening before.

A large family of children are left to mourn . . .

August 7, 1919

The Britton's Leave Us.

Andrew **Britton** and his family left Quitman Thursday of last week and went to Sulphur Springs where they visited with sisters of Mrs. Britton until Monday of this week and then left Sulphur for Vernon, Wilbarger county, their future home.

A Good Woman Gone.

Mrs. Texas Virginia **Johnson** was born Feb. 17, 1863. Died July 25, 1919. She was married to H. V. Johnson about 41 years ago. To this union 11 children were born, two of them died in infancy. . . .

The following children survive: T. W. Johnson and Mrs. Ida **McRight** of Aspermont, J. L. Johnson and Mrs. Ellen **Mount** of Dallas, S. L. Johnson of Wichita Fallas, J. H. Johnson, Mrs. Cora

Jones, Mrs. Ona **Patrick** and Mrs. Cordie **Nicks**, all living in the Calvery community, and one sister, Mrs. Cora **Weaver** of Waco.

. . . laid the body to rest at Sand Springs . . .

Young Lady Dies Suddenly

Miss Opal **Benton**, daughter of Mr. and Mrs. Jake **White** of the Forrest Hill community, died Tuesday evening after an illness of short duration.

Interment was had at Clover Hill Wednesday morning at 10 o'clock.

August 14, 1919

Death of J. A. Watson.

J. A. (Albert) **Watson** died at his late home near Emory, in Rains county, Saturday, August 2nd, after an illness of several months duration. The remains were brought to Clover Hill grave yard for interment on Sunday the 3rd . . .

Veteran Passes Away.

. . . the death of our veteran friend, J. D. T. **Reese**, which sad event occured at his late home at Golden Tuesday August ?, 1919, after an illness of several weeks. Interment was had at Sand Springs the day following his death.

. . . For years he lived in and near Quitman and was for four years Justice of the Peace of the Quitman precinct. He was serving his first term as Justice of the Peace at Golden at the time of his death. He was an ex-Confederate soldier and a native of Alabama . . .

August 21, 1919

Killed By Train

Bud **Lankford**, a well known citizen of Golden, was run over by a train on the Katy one day last week and killed.

. . . Mr. Lankford being somewhat hard of hearing . . .

Deceased was a brother of J. K. P. Lankford of Golden, and of Postmaster D. S. Lankford of Mineola. He had no family and had lived in and near Golden practically all his life.

Man arrested on Serious Charge.

G. L. **Parker**, 70 years old, of Brownsboro, was arrested late yesterday on an affidavit made by Sheriff **Williams** charging him with rape. . . . Miss Mary **Ingram**, the alleged victim, is only sixteen years of age. She is the daughter of Mr. and Mrs. W. D. Ingram and is of unsound mind . . .

Parker is married and has 18 children. Five years ago he was a candidate for representative from this district on the socialist ticket.

- Athens Review.

August 28, 1919

Obituary.

Mrs. Cora **Baker**, eldest daughter of Bro Hardin **Gilbreath** and wife, was born Dec. 31, 1894. . . . She was married to Lon Baker Dec. 26, 1917, and left this sinful world August 19, 1919.

Her remains were carried to Sharon cemetery and laid to rest. . .

October 9, 1919

Died in New Mexico

Our friend A. A. **Lindsay** of Winnsboro, was in to see us Monday, and informed us of the death of his wife which occured at Alamagordo, N. M., Friday, Sept. 19. The remains were brought to Winnsboro and interment had in the City cemetery Tuesday, the 22nd.

Death of a Pioneer.
Delayed from last week

Not until Monday of this week did we hear of the death of that pioneer citizen of Wood county, John M. **Stagner**. His death occured at 9:30 Saturday morning, September 20th. Interment was had at Mt. Pisga grave yard the day following . . .

"Uncle John Stagner," . . . was 77 years of age at the time of his death. He was born in Pike county, Alabama, and came to Texas about the year 1863, stopping near Starville in Smith county, where he remained one year and then came to Wood county and settled a few miles from Pine Mills, in what is now known as the Stagner community, where he had continuously resided since. . . . Eight of the children survive him, viz: Mrs. Jno. **Reed**, Rev. W. E. Stagner, Mrs. Josie **Bright**, Mrs. Joe **Reed**, Mrs. W. R. **Speights**, Mrs. Bob **Collins**, J. M. Stagner, Jr., and B. C. Stagner, . . .

The wife of his youth preceded him . . . in February, 1916.

October 30, 1919

Death of Dr. Eakes

A telegram to the Masonic Lodge at Quitman was received froom Philadelphia, Miss. Thursday of last week announcing the death of Dr. P. M. **Eakes**, who formerly lived at Cartwright.

W. H. Patton Accidently Killed

Word was received here Thursday of last week that Will **Patten**, formerly of this place but late of Brice, Texas, had been killed in a gin at that place.

Will Patten was the son of J. H. Patten and a brother to Lloyd and J. C., all of this place. . . He leaves a wife, six children, an aged father, one sister and two brothers, besides other relatives.

- Alba Two-County Times.

Death of Good Man.

Not until we received the Winnsboro News last week did we learn of the death of Mr. A. H. **McElroy** of Pleasant Grove . .which occured on the 14th inst . .

. . . He was buried at Hopewell the day following his death. . . . his wife and two children and the brother, Frank McElroy of Winnsboro.

Claud Blackman Arrested.

Claude **Blackman** under indictment in this county for murder in connection with the death of his uncle Bethel Blackman, which occured the past year, was arrested at Idabell, Okla., the past week. . .

November 20, 1919

Census Interpretation of The Word "Farm"

Washington, Nov. 3: - What is a farm?

Seems a foolish question to ask, doesn't it? Almost anyone can tell off-hand just what a farm is and knows one when he sees it.

But do you happen to know the interpretation Uncle Sam places on the word "farm" for census purposes? No? Then read how his Bureau of the Census defines the word.

"A farm for census purposes is all the land which is directly farmed by one person conducting agricultural operations, either by his own labor or with the assistance of members of his household or hired employees."

In further explanation of this definition the Census Bureau points out that the term "agricultural operations" is used as a general term referring to the work of growing crops, producing other agricultural products and raising domestic animals, poultry or bees.

. . . if the garden or chicken yard expands until it covers not less than three acres of ground, or until it requires for its care the continuous services of at least one person, or yields products annually to the value of $250 of more, it comes within the census definition of a farm and will be recognized as such and counted.

Another Good Woman Answers The Final Roll Call.

After several weeks suffering, the gentle spirit of Mrs. Martha **Daniels** answered the final roll call Saturday evening at 3:45 o'clock November 15, 1919. Interment was had at Ebenezer grave yard at 3:30 . . .

Mrs. Daniels was born in the Little Hope community December 29, 1859. She was a daughter of Mr. and Mrs. _____**Robbins**, pioneer citizens of the county. She grew to womanhood in the community of her birth and in December 1882, was married to James Y. Daniels, who preceded her to the other side on July 8, 1910.

Ten children were born to Mr. and Mrs. Daniels, all of them are still living except one son, Isham, who fell in battle in France last October a year ago. The children have attained their majority except the youngest son, Howard, who is still in his teens. Those living are Mrs. W. M. **Pritchett**, living near Mineola, J. F. Daniels, of Winnsboro; John, Rob and Claud of Oak Grove, Arch of Dallas, Mrs. M. F. **Moxley** of Dallas, Miss Mary who is teaching at Bellefont, and Howard, the baby boy who was still under the family roof.

In addition to the children there are ten grand children, three sisters and one brother left . . . The sisters are Mrs. Mary L. **Cox** of the Little Hope community; Mrs. W. P. **Murphy** a twin sis who still lives near the place of their birth; Mrs. S. L. **Johnson** of Myrtle Springs, and brother I. W. **Robbins** of our town.

Oldest Man In Wood County Died Last Week.

J. P. **Cain**, the oldest man in Wood county, died at the home of his son, M. K. Cain, at Cartwright, Thursday evening November 13th, 1919. "Grand-pa" Cain . . . was only sick a few hours.

Interment was had at Ebenezer grave yard . . .

Grand-pa Cain was born in Hall county, Ga., October 11, 1826. When he was seven years of age his parents moved to Catoosa county, Ga. In this county he was married to Miss Elizabeth **Smith** in 1844, and they came to Texas in 1884, settled near Stout in Wood county, where they resided until 1901, when they moved to Alba, and resided in Alba until the death of the wife in 1912, since which time Grand-pa made his home among his children, the home of his son, Joe, being called home, and he would spend weeks with each of his children. There is surviving his eight children, the oldest being now 73 and the youngest 47. The children are: A. S. Cain, Alba, Mrs. E. J. **Gilbreath**, Winnsboro, R. A. Cain, Mathis, J. W. Cain, Winnsboro, J. M. and M. K. Cain, Cartwright, Miss Emily and A. L. Cain of Alba, their ages ranging in the order named, A. S. being the oldest and A. L. the youngest.

November 27, 1919

Death of Mrs. Roten

Mrs. Lillian May **Roten** was born in Kaufman county, Texas, in 1885, moved with her parents to Wood county in her girlhood days. . . . was married to Mr. O. Y. Roten which union was lived in happiness.

. . . death . . occured Friday November 14th 1919, after seven years of continued illness and many painful operations. There being no children born in this home, little Miss Bertha was taken into the home some years ago . . .

Earnest Ussery Is Dead.

. . . death of our young friend, Earnest **Ussery**, which sad event occured at the home of his father, W. J. Ussery in the Myrtle Springs community Friday night of last week.

Interment was had at Enon, near Alba, Saturday evening.

December 11, 1919

I. W. Robbins Is Dead.

. . . at 7:40 Monday morning Dec. 8, he breathed his last.

. . . the funeral . . will be held at the Baptist church at about 2 o'clock this afternoon.

Death of J. H. McGee

. . . death of J. H. **McGee** which occured at his late home in Alba Thursday November 27, 1919 . . .

John . . . was born and raised four miles north of Quitman and resided in the community . . . up to a year ago he moved to Alba.

John was first married to Miss Mattie **Rape**, a Wood county girl, and to them were born two daughters, both of whom are now living and married, one being the wife of Frank **Kirkland** of the Myrtle Springs community and the other the wife of O. L. **Ussery** of Donley county. After the death of the first wife he was married to Miss Maye **Cathey** a sister of Judge B. F. Cathey, and to this union five children were born, three of whom died in infancy, the other two being still under the family roof.

Interment was had at Myrtle Springs Friday evening the 28 . . .

Grand-Mother McIntosh.

At the ripe old age of 79 years, three months and two days . . . the gentle spirit of Mrs. Eliza **McIntosh** wafted its way . . . on Friday November 28, 1919. Interment was had the following day . .

Deceased was born in Georgia July 25, 1840, her maiden name was **Wright**. At an early age her parents moved to Alabama where she was married to F. M. **Coleman** Sept 20, 1860 to which union four children were born, two sons and two daughters. One son, F. J. Coleman, died several years ago, as did the two daughters, Mrs. M. L. **Kirkland** and Mrs. W. M. **McCreight**, the other son, J. L. Coleman, survives. Her husband died in Alabama and the widow came to Texas with her 4 children in 1875. She bought land and settled in the Myrtle Springs community where she continued to reside until her death. . . . She was married the second time to E. **McIntosh** May 15, 1890, and this husband preceded her to the other world several years ago.

December 18, 1919

Isham W. Robbins

Isham **Robbins** was born near Stinson's Mill, now known as Little Hope, on May 1, 1856, and was 63 years, 7 months and 8 days old at the time of his death. He came to Quitman when 25 years of age . .

[Much material too dim to read.]

Mr. Robbins was married to Miss Eugenia Mae **Lipscomb** February 12, 1884, to which union 12 children were born, five of the children died in infancy, and one son, Clough, was killed on the battle fields of France at the age of 28 years. Of the six living, all are under the family roof except the oldest son, Dr. V. E. Robbins, and the second daughter, Mrs. Henry **Fisher**, the latter living in Smith county. The other children are Hill, Lois, Ella, and Buster, the baby boy. . . .

Winnsboro Weekly News - 1919

January 31, 1919

A Tribute

Mrs. Katie **Shelton** departed this life in Greenville, Texas, January 18, 1919 at 5 o'clock, following an operation on Tuesday.

Mrs. Shelton has lived in Winnsboro, Texas, practically all of her married life except a few short years of residence in Texarkana, Ark., and Ardmore, Ok. Moving from Winnsboro in 1905, returning in 1908, where the family permanently located on South Main Street until she was called by the death angel. . . .

Mrs. Katie Shelton was born in Harrisburg, Illinois, April 12, 1870. She was married to T. F. Shelton in Ardmore, Okla., Feb 9th, 1895, to which union three children, all living, were born; Frank, age 21; Loudene, age 19; and Mack, age 17.

Funeral service was conducted Jan. 10th, 1919, 2 p.m. at the M. E. church by Rev. E. L. **Egger** of Greenville, Texas, and Rev. A. A. **Kidd**. Burial was in the city cemetery.

James W. Layton

James W. **Layton** was born in Charranooge, Ga., July 14, 1847, and died January 22nd, 1919. He was first married to Miss Sarah **Story** March 26, 1876, to whom eight children were born, five still living, D. A., J. S., O. T., L. L. and Sallie. His first wife died February 16, 1887.

He was again married to Miss Sarah **Cherry** December 8th, 1887, and came to Texas in 1904 where she died June 17th, 1911.

February 7, 1919

Carl Bradshaw Dead.

Mr. I. J. **Bradshaw** was called to Fort Smith, Ark., on Thursday, January 23rd, on account of the illness of his son, Carl. . . . to grow worse until the following Tuesday, when he passed away. The remains were brought to Winnsboro Thursday and buried in the Shady Grove Cemetery Friday.

Carl Bradshaw was born and reared in the Stout community and left here a few years ago for Fort Smith, out of which place he had run as fireman on the frisco road for quite awhile. About a year ago he quit railroading and engaged in farming near Fort Smith, and was doing well. He was married and besides his wife he leaves four children. . . .

Death of E. L. Spivey.

Earnest Leslie **Spivey** was born Feb. 14th, 1882, and died Dec. 25th, 1918 at his residence in Pleasant Hill Community, 8 miles southeast of Winnsboro. This good citizen leaves a kind and devoted wife, five precious little children . . .[long eulogy]

In Memory of Mattie May Thompson

Little Mattie May **Thompson** died at the home of her parents, Mr. and Mrs. John Thompson, on Jan 11th, 1919. She was born Aug 2, 1915. She was permitted to stay with us a little more than three years. . .The funeral services were held in the home Jan. 12, 1919, by Bro. W. H. **Harrison** and the remains were laid to rest in the Smyrna cemetery. . . .

Gone to Rest.

Little Troy **Wheeler** died of influenza at the home of his parents, Mr. and Mrs. Geo. W. Wheeler, in the Pleasant Hill community, on Dec 26th, 1918.

This little soul was given these fond parents June 19th 1915 . . . [long eulogy]

Married Sunday.

Mr. Walter **Allen** of Mineola and Miss Opal **Gibson** of this city were married Sunday afternoon at 4 o'clock, Rev. C. A. **Loveless** officiating.

C. L. **Martin** went to Greenville Wednesday in response to a message stating that his brother, Jno. W. Martin, was very ill.

J. R. **Hinson**, of near Rhonesboro, was in the city Saturday visiting his father-in-law, J. J. **Rouse** . . .

Former Winnsboro Girl to Wed.

Mr. C. C. **Cranston** announces the engagement of his daughter Olive, now living in Philadelphia, to Lt. Fenton Lee **Neblett** of Petersburg, Va. The wedding will take place in early Spring. They will make their home in Philadelphia.

Wood County Boy Dies from Wounds.

J. J. **Coston** told us Friday that his brother-in-law, Ben A. **Turner**, died in France on January 2nd from wounds received in action on November 2nd, according to a telegram from the War Department which the family received a short time ago. Mr. Coston says there is, however, a mistake somewhere, as a letter was received from Mr. Turner dated and postmarked January 3rd. . . .

February 14, 1919

Unclaimed Letters.

List of unclaimed letters for week ending Feb 5, 1919.

Heart, Cary **Gunn**, Neta **Miller**, Mrs. Carmon
Moore, Emily **O'Marrow**, Mike **Putman**, Ben
Wood, Mrs. Carrie

Unclaimed Letters.

List of unclaimed letters for week ending Feb. 12, 1919.

Bills, Mrs. Eliza, **Russle**, Mack, **Smith**, Jessie,
Tucker, L. A., **Turner**, Catline.

A SHAMBURGER FAMILY HISTORY

[The following family history was provided by Mr. Spinks Lafayette Shamburger in an article printed in the November 19, 1930 issue of the *Wood County Democrat*. Mr. Shamburger would have been age 89 at the time of these memories. -Ed.]

Shamburger Descendants Who Lived Near Raleigh, N. C.

Grandmother and grandfather did not have any daughters, but was the father and mother of ten boys, as follows: Dumas, Joshua, Eliga, John, Thomas, Peter, Absolom, Matthew, and Noah, (who died young). There is one I have forgotten, They were all born in North Carolina. Matthew lived near Hawkins, Wood County, Texas, and was over 80 years old. Dumas and Joshua lived in Western Alabama. John, Eliga, Absolom lived in Lauderdale County, Mississippi. Thomas, Peter, Absolom and Matthew came to Texas. Thomas settled near Palestine. Peter, Absolom and Matthew came to Smith County, Texas.

Uncle Thomas **Shamburger** lived near Palestine, Texas, and to this union were born three girls. His widow married a man by the name of **Moore**.

Uncle Peter Shamburger married Adeline **Brower** and their children were: Matthew married Julia Ann **Shockley**, Sallie married Walsh **Ballard**, Mary married W. D. **Doyle**, Emsley died while a young man, Adelia married O. P. **Payst** of Quitman, Texas; Amelia married Russell **Doyle**, John married Martha **Doyle** and died in Parker County, William died in Confederate War and Hannah married J. W. **Vaughn**.

Uncle Matthew Shamburger married Elizabeth **Brown**, Daniel Brown's daughter and their children were: Edwin married Sallie Allen and one of their first children is E. Q. Shamburger. Dan married Mollie **Brown**, W. J. (Bill) married his own cousin, Thomas Shamburger's daughter; Martha Ann married Harvey **Kay**, Sallie married **Willis** in Raines County, Lizzie married Ben **Tonney** at Hawkins, and Henry and Marshall don't know about their marriage.

My father, Absolom, married Elizabeth Francis **Harrison** in Mississippi. Moved to Texas in 1847, and settled ten miles north of Tyler, Smith County, Texas. Their children were: Spinks Lafayette, Eliga, John Archable, who were born in Mississippi. Eliga, John Archable, who died there while young. Peter Monroe and Elizabeth Cornelia were born in Smith County, Texas. Spinks L. married Mary E. **Morrow**, Peter M. married Love **Fuller** and Elizabeth C. married Geo. W. **Hutchings**. Father moved to Pine Mills, Wood County, in 1853 and died in 1866. He lived to be 59 years old. Mother was 79 years old when she died and lived on the home place near Pine Mills until her death.

I, Spinks Lafayette, was born October 31, 1841, in Lauderdale County, Mississippi. Came to Texas November 4, 1847. Lived in Smith County six years. Came to Wood County, nine miles southwest of Quitman, November 3, 1853. I was married to Mary E. **Morrow**, July 23, 1868. Lived on part of home place 24 years, moved to Cartwright July 4, 1877. To this union were born seven boys and five girls, all in Wood County, who married as follows: Peter M. (Pete) married Mary **Holley**, Robert Lee married Julia **Jackson**, Willie J. H. married Olevia **Ray**, Walter Absolom died at five weeks old, Annie E. married Tom **Mayo** and he died then she married Claude (Bud) **Moseley**, Archie L. married Mattie **Thompson**, Maggie E. married Jake **Holley** now deceased, John G. married Jessie **Sharp**, Nora C. married Walter V. **Cruce**, Minnie Jane (Janie) married D. H. **McAnally**, both deceased, Henry C. married Mabel **Gatlin**, and Mary Leacy married Ben F. **Stinson**.

S. L. **Shamburger**, Winnsboro, Texas. Route 5.

Surname Index

Acker 95, 161, 201
Adair 81
Adams 4, 63, 84, 95, 97, 122, 159, 167
Adrain 50, 65, 145
Adrian 60, 271
Akers 115
Alcorn 146, 166
Alcott 50
Alexander 41, 55, 95, 125, 161, 229, 256
Alford 62
Allen 44, 84, 91, 99, 118, 121, 137, 150, 154, 156, 160, 163, 167, 191, 250, 261, 305, 307
Allman 35, 148
Alpine 94
Alpino 93
Alred 7
Alston 63, 225, 228, 248, 253, 262
Alvis 8, 29, 36-38, 115, 121, 203, 210
Amason 22, 248, 293
Amons 46
Amos 47, 84, 183, 203, 280
Anders 128, 140, 143, 149, 152, 202, 247
Anderson 78, 83, 84, 86-88, 91, 95, 97, 136, 154, 207
Andres 128, 129
Andress 248
Andrews 30, 31, 133, 144, 248, 252, 282
Apel 14, 16, 22, 23, 28, 33, 43, 48, 81, 127, 131, 164, 170, 192, 204, 215-217, 229, 241, 255, 262, 274, 276, 280
Apple 56
Applegate 199
Arlitt 142
Armour 163, 275
Armstrong 35, 94, 202
Arnold 93, 98, 121
Arocah 89
Arochy 78
Arrant 169
Arrington 153
Arthur 84, 111, 114, 118, 128, 130, 168, 174, 183, 200, 202, 235, 243, 296
Asbel 83
Ashberry 31, 70, 132, 133
Ashley 122, 137, 144
Askew 61
Aswell 84
Atkins 60, 202, 248
Attaway 13, 65, 103, 111, 156, 226
Atwood 180, 269
Austin 12, 13, 55, 57, 61, 74, 113, 125, 142, 157, 186, 253, 274, 289
Awtrey 81

Awtry 10, 38, 62, 63, 104, 156, 163, 168
Ayer 32, 109, 157, 162, 203
Ayres 67
Azbell 14, 110, 111
Baber 37, 55, 76, 161, 293
Bagby 63, 203, 231, 243
Baggett 9, 55, 95
Bagley 9
Bailey 5, 84, 87, 110, 147, 154, 176, 203, 217
Baird 17, 29, 159, 294
Baker 36, 38, 60, 63, 68, 84, 95, 108, 119, 120, 154, 158, 177, 180, 198, 199, 255, 298
Ballard 99, 118, 307
Banks 111, 140, 221, 224, 285, 292
Bankston 94, 127, 210
Banta 236
Barbier 160
Barbo 79
Barden 3
Barfield 78, 87
Barker 50
Barnes 74, 94, 109, 111, 115, 122, 145, 153, 160, 202, 226
Barnett 36, 52, 111, 130, 153, 154, 210
Barnette 67, 123
Barnhill 92
Barnwell 83
Barsenas 87
Bartlett 61, 105, 122, 132, 143, 199, 202, 207

Barton 153, 202
Bass 36, 38, 39, 42, 50, 57, 71, 84, 126, 134, 153, 184, 227
Bateman 17, 20, 27, 65, 66, 201, 205, 212, 213
Baxley 153, 156
Baxter 8, 9, 257
Beach 122
Beall 149
Bean 78
Beard 69, 111, 134, 156, 168, 200, 202, 221
Beardon 46
Beaty 95
Beavers 112, 115, 127
Beck 48, 84, 213
Beckham 37
Beckonridge 123
Beeville 85, 139, 149
Beggs 166
Bell 9, 14, 84, 129, 141, 144, 152, 233, 262
Bellefont 60, 158, 200, 301
Bellomy 136, 154, 185, 202, 203, 225
Belt 85, 87, 112
Benard 85
Bender 84
Bentley 62
Benton 14, 16, 24, 37, 39, 41, 42, 50, 52, 53, 59, 61, 64, 65, 67, 68, 70, 73, 76, 94, 97, 105, 115, 121, 125, 126, 131, 135, 153, 164, 173, 180, 198,

203, 210, 228, 235, 259, 268, 297
Berry 14, 31, 80, 85, 91, 93, 233
Bessinger 95
Beulah 33, 54, 95, 171, 224, 240, 265, 291
Bexley 202, 228, 233, 262
Bibb 7
Billard 87
Billings 41, 48, 113, 127, 133, 140, 216, 217
Bills 306
Binford 85, 143, 273
Birch 85
Birchfield 193
Bird 10, 13, 69, 76, 110, 129, 144, 182, 262
Black 28, 29, 35, 38, 39, 45, 51, 54, 56, 58, 63-65, 70, 74, 75, 81, 104, 106, 109, 110, 119, 120, 129, 134, 140, 151, 155, 175, 193, 194, 202, 250, 267
Blackburn 72
Blackman 196, 197, 300
Blackmon 35, 36, 46, 58, 66, 106, 129, 130, 136-138, 149, 151, 163, 172, 187, 196, 231, 240, 246, 251, 257, 272, 287
Blackstock 94, 95
Blackstone 76, 144
Blackwell 57, 110, 111, 127, 128, 165, 180, 202, 268, 269
Blagge 78

Blake 207, 243
Blakeley 176
Blalock 14, 27, 37, 40, 42, 51, 67, 72, 81, 103, 120, 131, 134, 154, 189, 193, 194, 202, 205, 275
Blasingame 17
Blizzard 139
Blount 40, 45, 48, 65, 111, 251, 252
Bluett 58
Blundell 85
Boatwright 147
Bogan 20, 111, 144
Bogues 214
Bolton 183, 224
Boman 46
Bonner 18, 104, 108
Booker 94
Boone 241
Booth 57, 78
Boozer 158
Borger 95
Bowden 85
Bowling 202, 243
Boyd 4-6, 60, 85, 96, 99, 110, 155, 156, 174, 203, 208, 224, 233, 251, 260
Bozeman 33, 50, 52, 55, 58, 61, 64, 66, 68, 77, 82, 107, 109, 126, 131, 135, 145, 195, 269
Braddy 143, 148
Bradford 48
Bradley 164
Bradshaw 64, 81, 103, 209, 304, 305

Brady 203
Brannon 126, 133
Brashear 62, 123, 144
Braziel 202, 292
Breedlove 49, 154, 202, 273
Breen 210
Brewer 38, 54, 77, 87, 89, 97, 105, 135, 153, 154, 156, 202, 270
Brickey 167, 197
Bridges 60, 107, 111, 129, 173, 237, 287
Briggs 41, 49, 50, 80, 101
Bright 119, 138, 139, 186, 200, 202, 219, 299
Brinkley 80, 85
Brittain 22, 35, 50, 57, 66, 121, 122, 125, 126
Brittian 146, 197
Britton 35, 37, 42, 43, 53, 54, 65, 69, 71, 101, 105, 110, 115, 119, 120, 140, 173, 210, 215, 217, 296
Brock 9, 29, 37, 153
Brogden 35, 119, 135, 229, 246, 253, 254
Brooks 46, 60, 89, 92, 95, 96, 98, 99, 146, 157
Brower 295, 307
Brown 6, 9, 14, 44, 46, 72, 78, 85, 111, 114, 116, 121, 122, 125, 126, 136, 142, 151, 154, 172, 173, 175, 178, 183, 201, 227, 233, 237, 244, 258, 274, 287, 307

Browning 35, 37, 48, 65, 82, 85, 94, 101, 103, 108, 115, 122, 135, 155, 156, 168, 202, 213, 214, 225, 240, 285
Bruce 17, 18, 38, 62, 66, 77, 78, 141, 153
Brumley 163, 171
Brummett 55
Brumry 88
Brumstey 199
Brunett 227
Bryan 52, 57, 104, 154, 229, 290
Bryant 61, 85, 153, 156, 173, 203
Buchanan 10, 154, 158, 227
Buck 46, 63, 76, 107, 115, 177, 224, 249
Buckley 99
Buckner 93, 98, 111, 203, 293
Bullard 78, 96, 200
Bullock 65, 73, 114, 121, 157
Burch 88, 95
Burford 73, 186, 203, 240, 242, 244
Burgess 169, 171, 203, 243
Burgin 290
Burke 203
Burkett 17, 37, 47, 109, 111, 128, 132, 140, 165, 198, 210, 245
Burley 85
Burnett 85, 93, 143, 151, 156, 187, 210, 221
Burns 75, 117, 154
Burroughs 294

Surname Index

Burrow 50
Burton 70
Busby 36, 128, 153
Bush 221
Busset 29
Butler 21, 26, 48, 62, 70, 77, 94, 96, 101, 109, 117, 126, 132, 147, 148, 162, 204, 230, 276
Butts 33, 53, 60, 157, 160, 186, 202, 273
Byars 99
Byers 5, 153, 255
Bynum 7, 85, 203, 237
Byrd 85, 202, 203
Byrom 4
Cacillas 214
Cade 37, 81, 203
Cagul 56, 68, 111, 128, 176
Cain 22, 37, 41, 58, 61, 63, 65, 68, 72, 94, 110, 114, 127, 152, 154, 155, 162, 168-171, 173, 202, 203, 210, 256, 301
Calderon 78, 90
Caldron 85
Caldwell 34, 38, 65, 67, 72, 75, 111, 123, 131, 154-156, 167, 171, 173, 174, 182, 203, 233, 250, 255
Caler 159
Calhoun 138, 159, 168, 178, 187, 194, 212, 216, 217, 219, 228, 230
Calloway 73, 193, 263, 271
Cameron 85, 171, 211

Campbell 13, 37, 70, 91, 110-112, 129, 135, 154, 173, 203, 207, 210, 227, 261, 285
Cannady 154, 203, 237
Cannon 14, 46, 98, 117, 170
Cantaloo 85
Capel 178
Carlile 37, 85, 113, 119, 143, 154, 157, 159, 202, 203
Carlin 124
Carlock 64, 112, 186
Carnathan 170
Carnes 111, 173, 201
Carpenter 108, 291
Carrington 65, 76, 111, 132, 144, 157, 199, 203, 284
Carrol 28, 96
Carroll 119, 230, 269
Carson 56, 154, 221, 244
Cartemas 96
Carter 3, 33, 37, 61, 67, 81, 85, 96, 111, 131, 136, 144, 153, 161, 170, 197, 202, 210, 257, 272
Cartwright 37, 39, 43, 48, 57, 65, 68, 69, 72, 76, 80, 96, 111, 114, 117, 118, 127, 133, 135, 153-155, 158, 162, 164, 167, 168, 176, 179, 180, 184, 186, 195, 245, 246, 254, 261, 268, 277, 299, 301, 308
Caruthers 78, 98
Cash 52, 70, 81, 151, 161
Cassel 36, 48, 60, 69, 104, 203
Castleberry 84, 160

Castleman 94
Cate 18, 94, 96
Cater 85, 208
Cathey 42, 52, 54, 56, 57, 61, 103, 110, 154, 167, 179, 203, 253, 280, 302
Catney 161
Cattney 160
Cave 111, 121, 122
Caylor 102
Center 2, 43, 245
Chaddick 199
Chambliss 5
Chamness 236
Champion 191, 236
Chamrod 85
Chandler 85, 97, 98
Chaney 91, 108, 213, 244
Chanman 110
Chapell 39
Chappell 38, 67, 71, 115, 135, 142, 221, 267, 268
Charles 3, 78, 79, 130, 170, 180, 273
Charlton 78
Chatman 113
Chereno 89
Cherino 87, 90
Cherry 38, 143, 286, 304
Childress 43, 85
Chism 85
Chitwood 291
Chreitsberg 57
Chreitzber 37
Chreitzberg 58, 81, 176, 209, 260, 265, 269, 273

Christian 14, 17, 59, 83, 85, 147, 183, 192
Clanton 44, 46, 48, 126, 139, 193, 235, 272, 293
Clark 2-5, 7, 8, 33, 37, 78, 86, 115, 128, 131, 153, 157, 169, 190, 243, 248, 272
Clausell 95
Clay 11, 12, 132, 213
Clayton 14, 43, 95, 144, 176, 202, 235, 290
Clements 268
Cleveland 63, 85, 86
Clinton 104, 277
Clower 203, 227
Coats 14, 111, 202, 221
Cobb 17, 104, 111, 122, 124, 150, 192, 212
Coburn 21
Coffee 12, 276
Cofield 17
Coke 246
Coker 7, 14, 16, 153, 159, 170
Cole 29, 144, 167
Coleman 33, 55, 66, 123, 130, 174, 243, 284, 303
Collier 14
Colliers 266
Collins 7, 76, 113, 133, 151, 155, 203, 247, 299
Color 95
Colquitt 41, 42, 78
Compton 78, 164
Conally 53
Conger 13, 14, 33, 34, 37, 42, 48, 50, 51, 54, 64, 68, 72, 75, 100, 137, 138,

146, 154, 175, 180, 182,
186, 189, 190, 199, 202,
205, 258, 264, 265
Conley 14, 278
Connally 174
Connell 132, 153, 203, 283
Conner 161
Cook 14, 32, 74, 158, 218
Cooke 5, 6
Cooley 116, 120
Cooper 23, 171, 236, 266
Copeland 153, 155, 202, 209
Corbitt 111, 153
Corley 54, 110, 135, 173, 201,
202, 210, 249
Cornelius 221, 237
Coston 145, 306
Coughman 224
Courrages 243
Coursey 202
Covington 110
Cowan 11, 28, 110, 129, 210
Cowley 67, 69, 109, 149, 152,
154, 163
Cox 7, 16, 17, 22, 33, 49, 58,
64, 82, 104, 108, 114,
118, 132, 134, 156, 185,
188, 202, 203, 244, 301
Coy 96
Crabb 86
Craddock 10, 11, 29, 38, 46,
58, 66, 68, 70, 103, 111,
119, 121, 125, 143, 145,
155, 161, 173, 210, 289
Cradick 64
Craig 36, 46, 88, 160, 216, 239
Crandford 86

Crane 96
Cranford 96
Cranston 306
Craver 69, 71, 101, 121, 203,
231-233
Crenshaw 37, 60, 86, 173
Crider 96
Criner 213
Crisman 37
Crofford 55, 70, 86, 88, 91, 92,
94-97, 142, 144, 155,
183, 201
Crone 111, 163, 172
Crosby 31, 94, 168, 203
Cross 66, 288
Crossland 43
Crouch 227
Crow 10, 16, 21, 39, 91, 122,
133, 143-145, 152, 154,
156, 173, 229, 231, 233,
278, 279
Crowl 209
Cruce 103, 153, 154, 308
Crumpler 14, 103, 110, 155,
203
Cruse 111, 202
Culberson 104
Cullars 237
Culpepper 46, 202
Culverhouse 110
Cumbie 205
Cummins 33
Curl 65, 97
Currin 252
Curtis 130, 142, 169, 192, 199
Cyrus 86
Dagnell 111, 122, 155

Dale 160, 201
Daniels 22, 62, 64, 111, 114, 120, 124, 140, 162, 163, 165, 176, 188, 214, 226, 300, 301
Darby 81, 202
Darden 61, 127, 244, 248, 280
Davenport 61, 96, 152, 200, 202
Davidson 220
Davis 4, 5, 14, 21, 77, 86, 89, 96, 116, 122, 126, 127, 133, 137, 145, 147, 150, 155, 203, 207-210, 213, 219, 242, 259
Day 128, 180, 207
Dean 122, 123, 157, 176, 202, 233
Deas 35, 65, 81, 110, 130, 203, 214
Deaton 66
Defee 96
Deharp 19
DeLaney 168
Delapp 86, 89, 93, 95
Dement 96
Dempsey 286
Denney 42, 51, 110, 118, 138
Dennis 6
Denton 34, 38, 40, 53, 68, 69, 75, 77, 81, 82, 143, 185, 202, 277
Derr 114, 121, 158, 161, 203, 240
Derry 86
Despalier 95, 97
Devon 233

Dewitt 86, 108, 135, 143, 161, 176, 181, 248
Dial 84, 111, 113, 121, 129, 140, 157, 161, 203, 214
Dickerman 39, 206
Dickerson 9, 160
Dickey 19, 31, 37, 67, 126, 203, 210, 213
Dickinson 205
Dickson 85, 91, 130, 153, 156, 237
Dill 111, 244
Dillard 21
Dillsworth 78
Dismuke 110
Dixon 37, 108, 183, 203
Dixson 33, 78, 165
Dobbs 111, 131, 132, 200
Dodgen 34, 61, 62, 100, 110, 111, 143, 173, 197, 203, 211, 212, 260
Dodson 37, 147, 187, 207
Dollar 110, 173
Dorman 115, 130, 153, 157, 180
Dorrough 104
Doty 150
Douglas 41, 116, 154, 155, 157, 181, 189, 213, 224, 248
Douglass 16
Dourglas 35
Dove 97
Dowell 10, 11, 17, 37, 53, 86, 121, 136, 156, 210, 234
Downing 122, 203, 224, 260
Doyle 6, 8, 9, 127, 257, 258, 307

Dozier 61, 203
Drake 205
Draw 254
Drennan 3
Drew 21, 22, 197
DuBose 38, 72, 91, 153
Duffey 139
Dugger 136
Duke 236, 243, 247
Dunahoe 203
Dunbar 129, 198, 210, 261
Duncan 2, 14, 17, 66, 233
Duncomby 78
Dupree 215
Durm 113
Durst 127
Dyess 173, 207
Dykes 55, 61, 86, 111, 135, 173, 210, 243, 255, 256, 263
Eakes 167, 299
Earls 170
Eason 28
Eastridge 94
Ecans 86
Eddington 86
Eddins 96
Eddis 96
Edelin 81, 210
Edmonds 45, 46, 49, 52, 81, 105, 140, 159, 166, 175, 179, 203
Edwards 38, 66, 117, 141, 155, 233, 235
Egger 304
Eitel 119
Elder 4, 292, 294

Elledge 92, 176, 203, 237
Ellis 42, 78, 88, 97, 99, 109, 114, 128, 166, 233, 235, 255
Ely 34, 47, 51, 57, 258
Engledow 95, 96, 98
English 78, 81, 89, 94, 95, 97, 110, 128, 133, 135, 145, 149, 152, 157, 172, 173, 198, 218, 271, 277
Epps 78, 84
Eskridge 210, 238
Esparsia 84, 89, 92
Essary 4
Estes 105, 107, 139, 202
Eubanks 154, 227
Evans 86, 87, 90, 91, 96, 98, 145, 156, 176
Ezell 136, 156, 266
Fail 231
Falkner 38, 63, 105, 202, 210
Fannin 47, 86, 102, 172, 269, 288
Farr 154, 193
Farrington 3, 6, 7, 79, 86, 104, 108, 218
Farris 126, 139, 202, 203, 239
Farrow 119
Farthing 7
Faulk 22, 37, 82, 100, 110, 123, 139, 173, 202
Favors 143, 170
Fergason 268
Ferguson 54, 120, 151, 164, 280
Fields 45, 107
Finch 36, 62

Finkley 159
Finley 217
Fisher 92, 259, 274, 303
Fitts 227
Fitzgerald 4, 5, 8, 9, 96, 234
Flannigan 98
Fletcher 27, 96, 111, 145, 172, 198
Flippin 117
Florees 86
Florence 96, 134, 156, 168, 243
Flores 93
Flournoy 3, 7, 10, 11, 25, 130, 202, 265, 277
Flowellen 77, 96
Floyd 34, 43, 66, 71, 86, 119, 124, 127, 131-133, 180, 205, 246, 273
Folmar 96
Folmer 86, 128, 129, 137, 160, 202, 287
Forbis 5, 8, 170
Ford 33, 36, 57, 115, 130, 135, 204
Forman 17
Formby 62
Forter 140
Foster 81, 93, 100, 110, 128, 135, 144, 202, 229
Fouke 127, 156, 167, 192
Four 88
Fouse 203
Fowler 14, 51, 54, 65, 79, 96, 98, 109, 144, 149, 150, 164, 191, 203, 279
Fox 60, 182

Francis 54, 80, 94, 101, 117, 148, 221, 238, 265, 308
Frank 115
Franklin 99, 112, 172, 183, 200, 250, 261, 262
Franks 32, 107, 148, 152, 158
Frazier 125, 227
Free 29, 36, 65, 70, 161, 236
French 50, 57, 62, 81, 86, 110, 154, 163, 178, 179, 203, 214, 289
Frizzell 84
Fry 77
Fulcher 201
Fuller 85, 92, 95, 98, 99, 308
Fulong 87
Furgason 173
Futral 143
Futrell 81
Gable 36, 67, 130
Gaddis 154, 165, 263
Gaines 3-5, 120
Gains 224
Gallaway 130
Gallian 152
Galloway 17, 45, 48, 80, 81, 133, 144, 147, 154, 202, 203, 251, 252, 278
Galoway 62
Galt 11, 69
Galusha 145, 203
Gamblin 121, 122, 156, 176, 232, 248, 281, 289
Garnett 190
Garret 147
Garrett 14, 66, 157, 172, 201
Garrison 87, 100, 284

Garvin 54, 117
Gaston 202, 210
Gatewood 131
Gatlin 308
Gause 97
Gay 91
Gayle 192, 260
Gee 96, 189
Gentry 77, 87, 202
Germany 135, 189, 190, 205, 243, 286
Gibbins 61
Gibbs 9
Gibson 31, 81, 87, 103, 177, 203, 271, 305
Gilbert 2-6, 11, 88, 90, 203, 278
Gilbreath 37, 43, 45, 58, 81, 123, 126, 129, 133, 144, 152, 154, 156, 157, 168, 171, 175, 202, 203, 210, 214, 217, 222, 224, 227, 229, 240, 246, 256, 280, 281, 298, 301
Gilbreth 79
Giles 8, 9, 40, 41, 66, 87, 118, 122, 131, 132, 154, 190, 210
Gill 202, 224, 235, 243
Gilliam 145
Gilliend 37
Gilliland 85, 87, 154, 207, 238, 255
Gillum 86, 87, 92, 98
Gilmore 267
Glass 170, 171
Gleaton 82, 105, 196

Glenn 29, 87, 111
Gloar 182
Goins 130
Goldsmith 22, 23, 61, 62, 66, 76, 103, 107, 109, 110, 115, 133, 135, 173, 175, 176, 202, 227, 234, 240, 254
Gollyhon 136
Gonsales 79
Gonzales 85, 93, 95
Goode 185
Goodloe 108
Goodson 122
Goodwin 11, 22, 33, 34, 42, 50, 72, 74, 104, 105, 127, 170, 182, 193, 223, 224, 242
Goolsby 128, 154, 176
Gore 46, 200
Gorman 70, 113, 133, 209, 232
Goswick 110
Grace 36, 46, 130, 157, 172, 183, 199
Grady 62, 87, 178, 180, 256
Graham 6, 17, 38, 51, 53, 77, 87, 114, 202, 227, 283
Grammar 147, 185
Grant 14, 46, 95, 152, 233
Graves 5, 153, 197, 225, 260
Gravirr 6
Gray 90, 197
Green 29, 37, 39, 45, 46, 58, 68, 76, 87, 96, 106, 113, 116, 118, 121, 122, 128, 129, 133, 135, 137, 140, 142, 154, 156, 157, 187,

196, 197, 199, 200, 203, 204, 227, 230, 264, 279
Greer 2-6, 8, 14, 58, 79, 85, 87, 98, 111, 133, 143, 202, 210
Gregg 2, 99
Gregory 87, 103, 153, 203
Grice 51, 171, 269, 270, 283
Griffin 78, 147, 152, 163, 221, 233
Griggs 183
Grimm 87
Grissett 77
Grogan 4, 8, 9, 27, 33, 45, 57, 119, 132, 170, 274
Gross 85
Guin 38, 139, 149, 154, 202
Guinn 128, 139
Gulledge 199
Gully 143
Gulty 173
Gunn 183, 306
Gunstream 2, 3, 10, 53, 188
Gunter 87, 157, 224, 233, 270
Guy 14, 119, 155
Hacher 233
Hagan 60
Haines 4, 5, 7, 8, 10, 11, 23, 37, 87, 88, 128, 135, 149, 172, 202, 252, 265
Hair 110
Hala 96
Halbrook 71
Hale 35, 210, 233, 240, 247
Haley 223
Hall 7, 47, 50, 53, 54, 70, 77, 79, 82, 87, 94, 96, 115, 128, 130, 221, 235, 237, 267, 301
Hallman 203
Ham 87
Hamby 79
Hamilton 8, 37, 79, 87, 118, 122, 241, 294
Hamm 135
Hammonds 82, 161
Hamrick 36, 56, 61, 65-67, 119, 120, 153, 180, 219, 253
Haney 78
Hansell 95
Hanson 217
Harals 37
Harbin 50, 58, 110, 111, 116, 153, 228
Harbuck 139, 141, 153, 203, 247
Hardcastle 77
Hardeman 88, 111, 155
Hardessale 90
Hardigree 5
Hardy 177, 266
Hargett 97
Hargraves 114
Hargrove 29
Hargroves 123
Haris 85
Harp 61, 248
Harper 41, 202, 235
Harpole 201
Harrington 23, 133, 140, 203
Harris 4, 8-10, 14, 16, 37, 38, 42, 45, 46, 49, 50, 54-58, 61, 62, 69, 70, 75, 76, 79, 81, 82, 88,

Surname Index

96, 97, 110, 111, 114, 115, 118-121, 126, 128, 138, 143, 151, 153-156, 162, 168, 172, 173, 176, 183, 187, 202, 210-212, 214, 220, 222, 235, 252, 264

Harrison 35, 62, 97, 110, 114, 130, 157, 190, 202, 203, 232, 233, 305, 308

Harry 6, 69, 88, 99, 112, 141, 148, 201, 205, 217, 269, 273, 280

Hart 8, 37, 46, 48, 49, 63, 73, 76, 80-83, 118, 122, 140, 151, 193, 210, 217, 249, 255, 269, 294

Hartfield 89

Hartsfield 20, 33, 37, 51, 54, 63, 122, 139-142, 144, 145, 156, 164, 165, 167, 173, 178, 199, 203, 227, 285

Harvey 79, 110, 116, 139, 146, 200, 202, 217, 219, 245, 270, 307

Harwell 190

Haskins 216

Hasten 64, 128

Hathcox 65

Hattaway 92

Hawkins 144

Hay 5, 6, 14, 44

Hayden 228

Haygood 55

Hayney 94

Hays 22, 81, 128, 137, 144, 213, 233, 242, 248

Head 31, 88, 94, 99, 100, 112, 122, 156, 208

Hearn 37

Heart 306

Heath 51, 65, 83, 114

Hedick 105, 115

Hedrick 5

Hemm 88

Hendrix 73, 79, 101, 230

Henry 16, 88, 131, 202

Herbert 160, 167

Herndon 119, 190

Herneger 79

Herniger 94

Herring 22, 203, 258

Herron 283

Hervey 244

Hester 4, 139, 203

Hickman 48, 71, 104

Hickmon 43

Hicks 18, 259

Higginbotham 116, 123, 135, 192, 216, 251

Higgins 38, 39, 49, 50, 53, 57, 69, 166

Highnote 73, 111, 202

Hightower 51, 226

Hilburn 66, 203, 241

Hill 61, 68, 88, 94, 110, 127, 128, 166, 173, 227, 233, 240, 256,

Hillburn 212

Hinds 142, 199

Hines 88, 111, 202

Hinson 37, 38, 41, 46, 61, 290, 291, 306
Hitt 122, 203, 210, 212, 237
Hoard 221
Hobbs 37, 128, 131, 144, 168, 235
Hodges 105
Hogan 88
Hogg 10, 11, 19, 47, 242
Holbert 9
Holbrook 35, 36, 66, 130, 156, 202, 279
Holcomb 81, 140
Holder 88
Holiness 43, 243
Holland 84, 96, 155, 221, 278
Holley 16, 26, 27, 37, 76, 154, 190, 209, 236, 237, 256, 278, 308
Hollinquest 203
Hollinshed 22, 203
Hollon 85, 97, 132
Hollond 66
Holly 104, 153, 203, 290
Holmes 88, 122, 125, 137, 150, 191
Holt 187
Hood 113, 118, 143, 151, 213-215, 221
Hooft 77
Hooker 181
Hooper 115
Hopkins 1, 42, 45, 67, 69, 74, 88, 104, 111, 113, 121, 124, 129, 133, 168, 180, 246, 264, 268, 284
Hornbuckle 154

Horne 169
Horton 37, 39, 41, 51, 53, 56, 67, 73, 101, 105, 116, 118, 120, 154, 182, 184, 203, 207, 259, 276
Houston 6, 33, 78, 79, 94, 128, 257, 280
Howard 13, 14, 17, 38, 88, 97, 104, 109, 142, 143, 148, 210, 232, 301
Howell 17, 18, 46, 111, 202, 210, 276
Howington 79
Howle 111
Hoyle 14
Hubbard 171
Huckaba 203
Huckabe 169
Huckeba 156, 157
Hudson 197, 203
Huff 97, 156, 224
Huffmaster 17, 18, 193
Huggin 14
Huggins 14
Hughes 39, 42, 47, 49, 63, 112, 132, 136, 173, 194, 202, 285
Huie 8, 10, 11
Hukill 136
Humphries 122
Hunt 1, 12, 29, 37, 79, 102, 115, 118, 127, 169, 203, 212, 235, 246
Hurdle 202
Hurley 147, 153
Hurst 156
Hurt 16, 56, 92, 132, 182, 211

Surname Index

Hutchings 136, 308
Hyde 29, 94, 250
Iles 265
Ingram 28, 55, 88, 171, 202, 209, 289, 298
Irby 97, 201, 219, 227
Irving 63, 163
Isbell 164
Isham 112, 169, 187, 196, 213, 274, 279, 301, 303
Ivans 136
Ivey 67, 85, 105, 119, 128, 129, 203, 228, 262
Jack 14, 44, 51, 62, 65, 81, 128, 158, 172, 182, 184, 197, 198, 202, 205, 223, 232, 262
Jackson 8, 20, 27, 88, 99, 137, 146, 152, 155, 166, 170, 185, 205, 207, 213, 234, 267, 275, 308
Jaco 91, 93, 131
Jacobs 202
James 46, 48, 96, 132, 190, 199, 214, 248
Jarman 34, 72, 76, 133
Jarred 22, 171, 202
Jarrell 201
Jarvis 6, 7, 13, 15, 192
Jeffries 129
Jenkins 28
Jennings 17, 135, 151, 201
Jeter 41
Jobe 35, 36, 66, 96, 130, 190, 233, 279
Johnson 17, 21, 32, 35, 37, 39, 52, 54, 55, 61, 64, 65, 72, 74, 75, 81, 82, 88, 92, 94, 95, 104, 105, 108, 118, 123, 134, 143, 153, 154, 170, 181, 188, 190, 191, 197, 199, 201, 207, 247, 292, 296, 301
Johnston 17, 193, 248
Jolley 119, 288
Jolly 203
Jones 9-11, 14, 17, 19, 20, 33, 34, 36, 37, 39, 41, 46, 50, 55, 63, 65, 78, 81, 88, 94, 96, 99, 100, 103, 104, 106, 109, 111, 112, 116, 124-126, 139, 143, 146, 147, 152, 157, 160, 161, 165, 171, 179, 180, 186, 190, 197, 199, 201, 203, 209, 210, 224, 227, 233, 236, 237, 248, 256, 263, 264, 273, 296
Jordan 61, 82, 84, 107
Jorday 35
Joseph 6, 8-10, 36, 79, 117, 141
Julian 241
Junor 158
Justice 2-11, 17, 67, 96, 119, 131, 218, 242, 257, 276, 297
Kavanaugh 148
Kay 21, 31, 54, 60, 61, 134, 167, 284, 288, 307
Keaton 79, 91
Keith 61, 89, 133
Kelley 154, 164
Kelly 46, 191, 233

Kendrick 44, 52, 62, 98, 120, 133, 151, 182, 184, 186, 193, 242-244
Kennedy 10, 11, 53, 105, 120, 169, 203, 243
Kennemer 62, 65, 111
Kennimer 39, 58, 73, 208, 221, 224, 274, 276, 292
Key 141, 165
Kidd 141, 165, 292, 304
Kilburn 203
Kilgore 37, 40, 238
Killough 51
Kilpatrick 88
Kimberlan 97
Kimbrell 81, 125
Kimbro 61
Kimon 233
Kinchelo 14
Kine 17
King 14, 21, 35, 50, 71, 77-79, 85-90, 92-97, 99, 111, 117, 141, 151, 154, 157, 169, 172, 189, 195, 201, 206
Kirbo 153, 218
Kirby 81, 154, 173, 203, 228
Kirkland 37, 40, 42, 130, 173, 177, 203, 302, 303
Kirkpatrick 43, 99, 183
Kitchen 125, 168
Kitchens 60, 61, 124, 131, 157, 173, 237
Knight 29, 48, 82, 88, 93, 97, 203, 277
Knowles 136
Koonce 76, 119, 120, 140, 217
Krueger 115
Kruger 165
Kuykendall 79
Lackey 149
Lacy 2, 93
LaForce 203, 210
Lair 6
Lake 29, 48, 56, 68, 108, 119, 133, 162, 165, 179, 223, 268, 269
Lamb 9, 233
Lambert 107, 210, 247, 276, 277
Laminack 111, 114, 128, 130-132, 143, 155, 189, 190, 219
Lammon 94
Landers 37, 112, 210
Landrum 122
Langham 79
Langley 180, 232, 234
Langston 23
Lanier 128, 240
Lankford 6, 10, 11, 17, 37, 68, 110, 116, 139, 146, 176, 194, 239, 297, 298
Lapp 84
LaRue 132, 155, 202
Lasator 5
Lattimore 88
Lawrence 8, 39, 45, 57, 68, 73, 75, 81, 89, 101, 103, 107, 114, 119, 120, 155, 182, 196, 202, 207, 214, 224
Layman 98
Layton 60, 81, 196, 286, 304

Leanard 53, 69, 128, 289
Leath 66, 101, 198, 220, 238
Ledbetter 81
Lee 4, 14, 17, 36, 37, 43, 46, 61, 68, 69, 72, 74, 77, 79, 81-83, 85, 86, 97, 99, 114, 117, 118, 128, 131, 142, 152, 156, 157, 163, 168, 189, 195, 205, 213, 221, 222, 224, 227, 233, 240, 243, 246, 253, 262, 272, 275, 287, 292, 293, 306, 308
Leibrook 89
Lemon 3, 213
Leonard 61, 102, 158, 171, 250
Lestarjette 16
Letonsty 89
Lewis 38, 89, 128, 152, 209, 222, 262, 290
Liles 60, 111
Lillard 177, 178, 291, 294
Limley 184
Lindley 22, 28, 39, 50, 60, 89, 97, 109, 118, 131, 132, 140, 142, 144, 163, 167, 168, 172, 173, 178, 187, 193, 199, 202, 227, 232
Lindsay 298
Lindsey 94, 97, 108, 135, 136, 173, 215, 220
Linley 14
Lipscomb 11, 23, 48, 50, 52, 53, 56, 58, 73, 106, 119, 133, 142, 151, 156, 165, 166, 201, 206, 215-217, 220, 226, 231, 296, 303

Little 82, 162, 173, 210,
Littleton 139, 203
Lively 6, 7, 12
Lloyd 6, 11, 22, 28, 35, 37, 39, 50, 52, 58, 59, 62, 66, 70, 75, 81, 111, 118, 126, 135, 144, 153, 154, 156, 161, 163, 173, 180, 202, 210, 227, 233, 240, 291, 292, 299
Lockett 89
Logan 156
Long 19, 72, 80, 106, 110, 119, 143, 175, 181, 185, 205, 225, 236, 237, 239, 247, 257
Lott 17, 38, 56, 169
Love 41, 61, 62, 194, 308
Lovelady 89
Loveless 305
Lovin 126, 243
Loving 120, 122, 214, 289
Low 22, 39, 41, 43, 45, 48, 50, 57, 63, 64, 68, 70, 73, 76, 82, 84, 107, 114, 115, 124, 127, 133, 138, 140, 165, 202, 210, 227, 228, 249, 257, 280, 286, 292, 293
Lucy 18, 82, 136, 141, 151, 156, 211, 252, 282
Luman 233
Lumans 22
Lundon 89
Lunsford 122
Lutonsty 89
Lyle 66

Lyles 14, 82, 89, 123
Lynch 122, 154, 227
Mabrey 89
Mabry 17
Macon 49, 52, 55, 58, 64, 80, 126, 148
Macoy 101
Maddox 153, 154, 168
Madison 89
Madsen 278
Mahan 260
Mahon 88
Mallory 196
Malone 130, 157, 159, 162, 207, 210
Malory 261
Mangam 89
Mangrum 105, 118, 121, 133, 170
Manning 212
Mansell 14, 37, 45, 65, 81, 110, 112, 132, 180, 210, 273
Mapes 10, 37, 136, 290
Marable 267, 268
Marler 49
Marlow 57, 101, 163
Marlowe 57, 103
Mars 46
Marshall 35, 50, 54, 128, 136, 161, 163, 205, 308
Martin 21, 29, 37, 40, 44, 49, 50, 52, 55, 73, 75, 81, 87, 104, 110, 114, 119, 140, 144, 154, 156, 164, 179, 215, 231, 276, 290, 305
Masset 37

Massey 43, 137, 153
Matheson 69, 195, 207
Mathews 6, 78
Mathis 63, 154, 176, 179, 301
Mattox 48, 138, 258
Mauney 25
Maxey 196, 277
Maxfield 89, 209
May 13, 28, 36, 46, 63, 66, 116, 119, 120, 134, 135, 172, 180, 185, 187, 206, 209, 211-214, 217, 220, 236, 246, 248, 249, 257-259, 262, 264, 266, 281, 289, 294, 302, 303, 305
Maye 33, 48, 54, 56, 58, 68, 76, 100, 116, 120, 133, 152, 159, 199, 216, 217, 241, 243, 244, 302
Maynor 34, 49, 52, 58, 66, 69, 72, 76, 82, 131, 133
Mayo 16, 48, 70, 90, 104, 108, 126, 183, 189, 194, 235, 308
McAfee 17, 111, 164, 173
McAllister 61, 66, 69, 75, 104, 121, 153-155, 168, 240
McAnally 308
McBride 99, 110, 128
McCain 33, 119, 168, 214, 261
McCalla 170
McCarroll 178
McCarter 23
McCarty 147
McClain 141
McClarin 14

McClelland 183
McClellen 83
McCleney 141
McClenny 154
McCollough 142
McCollum 248, 274
McConnell 141
McCord 5, 6, 112
McCorley 154, 195, 204
McCoy 21, 22, 201
McCrary 29, 35, 37, 54, 62, 69,
    103, 133, 134, 137, 151,
    164, 173, 175, 179, 202,
    221, 250, 292
McCreight 43, 48, 50, 53, 58,
    67, 72, 114, 119, 120,
    123, 127, 130, 131, 156,
    174, 303
McCullough 8
McDade 159, 175, 176, 203,
    265
McDaniel 207
McDonald 62, 85, 89, 94, 108,
    208, 217, 221
McDonel 43
McDougal 111, 154
McDougald 128, 201
McElroy 37, 68, 299
McElyea 170
McFarland 14, 30, 111, 199
McGee 5, 21, 65, 97, 103, 154,
    156, 172, 302
McGrane 80
McGruder 190, 233
McGuire 65, 115, 134, 173,
    285, 286

McIntosh 16, 100, 123, 124,
    174, 177, 262, 303
McKee 42, 139
McKenzie 111, 133, 159, 173
McKern 89
McKey 69
McKinzie 37, 105, 154
McKnight 6, 42, 59, 63, 77, 80,
    100, 107, 121, 158, 228,
    230, 247, 249
McLain 37, 81, 137, 139
McLarty 85, 110
McLaughlin 160
McLendon 25
McLeod 49
McMahan 112
McMahon 86, 93-95
McManus 132, 201
McMillan 158
McMimms 238
McMullen 136
McMurry 17, 102
McNeill 126, 158, 161, 241
McNutt 96
McQueen 130, 201
McRae 65
McRight 116, 121, 125, 201,
    211, 212
McWhirter 243
McWhorter 105, 157
Meadows 118, 153
Meeks 170, 221
Meeser 93
Meody 125
Mercadanti 183
Meredith 210
Meridith 18

Messles 132
Mezzles 132
Middleton 66, 117
Miles 119, 147
Miller 36, 38, 46, 77, 97, 127, 239, 263, 306
Milliron 97
Mills 17, 19, 20, 37, 53, 61, 69, 71, 103, 105, 113, 114, 126, 127, 130, 131, 140, 163, 169, 209, 224, 245, 266, 269, 273, 276, 283, 286, 288, 299, 308
Milner 58, 68, 114, 127, 162, 207, 256
Minchew 125, 154
Mingle 56, 57, 102
Mings 114, 191
Minick 243
Minnick 179
Mitchan 36
Mitchell 89, 97, 103, 132, 156, 190, 221, 245
Mize 141, 152, 153, 288
Molnair 89
Molton 97
Monroe 29, 46, 58, 106, 111, 128, 129, 140-142, 224, 308
Monteith 84
Montgomery 4, 16, 176
Montrose 190
Moody 35, 56, 128, 134, 147, 158, 165, 192
Moore 11, 31, 36-38, 43, 45, 47, 52, 53, 61, 63, 79, 86, 89, 90, 92, 93, 97, 99, 103, 108, 110, 112, 115, 118, 119, 126, 128, 131, 132, 145-147, 151, 153, 178, 208, 213-215, 221, 223, 225, 227, 236, 291, 306, 307
Mooring 111
Moreland 57, 209
Morgan 58, 97, 110, 128, 132, 158, 217, 240
Morris 7, 30, 51, 68, 103, 111, 119, 130, 134, 135, 138, 148, 153, 155, 159, 164, 168, 210, 232, 243, 278
Morrison 10, 11, 16, 17, 19, 27, 77, 142, 178, 209, 210, 221, 224, 240
Morrow 8, 35, 45, 82, 114, 117, 133, 144, 154, 308
Morse 16, 100
Moseley 50, 52, 58, 60, 64, 137, 144, 156, 176, 188, 269, 308
Mosely 22, 77, 89, 97
Mosley 52, 96
Moss 110
Mossenton 192, 288
Mount 11, 12, 46, 67, 68, 73, 100, 101, 165, 189, 201, 202, 217, 276, 296
Mounts 33, 34, 51, 189, 215, 216
Mousell 7
Moxley 162, 295, 296, 301
Mulkey 293
Munzesheimer 17, 21, 26, 94

Murck 33, 35, 55, 57, 69, 80, 120
Murphy 36, 57, 58, 89, 97, 111, 126, 132, 144, 188, 231, 301
Murray 125, 295
Murrell 122, 248
Murry 199
Myers 119, 144, 202
Nabors 133
Nagan 97, 98
Nance 137
Napier 42
Nash 155
Neal 224, 248
Neblett 306
Neeland 50, 55
Neill 18, 69, 86, 91, 93, 97, 227
Nelson 68, 91, 92, 95, 99, 173, 239, 287
Netzorg 97
Newby 81, 100
Newman 21, 22, 61, 103, 155, 173, 176, 229, 231, 237, 243
Newsom 8-10, 165
Newsome 9, 38, 43, 57, 63, 127, 133, 164, 210, 274, 288
Newton 97, 111
Neyland 73-75, 176, 179
Nichols 68, 97, 119, 157, 158, 217, 284
Nicholson 94, 97
Nicks 296
Nixon 24, 51, 162, 179
Nixson 128

Noble 68, 93, 137, 138, 146, 171, 175, 225, 296
Noel 73
Noles 37
Northcut 6, 7
Northcutt 122, 146, 192, 246, 247
Northington 89
Norton 2, 3, 124, 127, 274
Nugent 61
Nunes 98, 99
Nutt 133, 201
O'Connel 163
O'Marrow 306
Odem 167
Odom 97
Ogburn 38, 41, 89, 94, 98, 120, 143, 151, 156, 161, 202, 208, 210
Oliver 67, 97, 128, 141, 148, 160, 183
Oneal 170
Orlds 243
Osborne 223
Oshields 89
Owens 17, 148, 155, 197, 216, 250
Oxford 81, 143, 156
Paden 169, 170
Padgett 72, 144
Page 19, 29, 77, 87, 97, 136, 294
Pain 260
Paine 14
Painter 77
Palmer 77, 227, 290
Palononimo 183

Parish 150, 173, 188, 271
Parker 45, 73, 84, 89, 110, 157, 189, 199, 213, 248, 266, 288, 298, 307
Parkerson 60, 209
Parkinson 67, 130
Parrett 123
Parrish 20, 22, 37, 45, 97, 122, 128, 129, 145, 153, 160, 170, 172, 192
Paschal 81, 83, 90, 110, 210
Pate 51, 101, 230
Patrick 31, 40, 46, 97, 144, 146, 154-156, 183, 193, 197, 198, 201, 202, 258-260, 283, 296
Patten 8, 37, 154, 201, 284, 299
Patton 28, 45, 59, 96, 107, 153, 201, 299
Paul 99, 133, 187, 194
Payne 89, 96, 147, 154
Payst 307
Peacock 45, 54, 60, 137, 145, 150, 161, 191, 210
Peak 190
Peddy 81, 161
Peden 126, 136
Pemberton 67, 77, 78, 80, 93, 94
Penix 81, 155
Pennal 160
Penney 98
Pennington 94, 287
Peoples 237
Peppers 51, 58, 71
Perdue 31, 81, 293
Peret 21

Perkins 37, 130, 187, 233
Perret 22
Perrett 115, 129
Perrin 21, 28, 69, 106, 107, 126, 268
Perritt 46
Perry 41, 62, 67, 130, 170, 176
Petrea 161
Petty 70, 139
Pevler 27
Phillips 35, 45, 61, 62, 67, 89, 90, 130, 136, 159, 266
Pickett 71, 126, 237, 268
Pierce 4, 90, 94, 112, 194, 207, 208
Pierson 40, 68, 190, 210
Pilkinton 218
Pilley 61
Pines 61
Pinnington 132
Pinson 154
Pinto 90, 121, 181
Pippin 133
Pitner 239, 252, 294
Pittman 53, 139
Pitts 226, 243
Plocher 165
Po_ter 80
Poe 161, 207
Pogue 38, 42, 49, 58, 73, 109, 111, 121, 139, 168
Pogues 77
Poland 295
Polk 209, 261
Pollard 46, 122, 136, 143, 151, 156, 157
Pollock 80

Polp 92
Pond 6
Ponder 29, 122, 141
Poole 44, 190
Pope 14, 33, 73, 103, 107, 121, 155, 227, 289
Porter 37, 98, 168, 170, 256, 263
Porterfield 90
Posey 35, 50, 100, 130, 139, 153, 155, 212, 213, 227, 228, 237
Post 2, 58, 220, 244, 248, 261, 264, 288
Potter 142, 146, 225
Powell 32, 90, 96, 132, 151, 154, 156
Power 54, 64, 67, 68, 124, 136, 177, 239, 252, 257, 259, 291, 294
Powers 52
Prather 224
Precise 124, 142, 184-186, 269, 270
Preddy 122
Price 10, 14, 35, 38, 50-52, 59, 105, 129, 173, 176, 190, 233, 269
Pridgen 245
Prince 90, 208, 233
Pritchett 90, 122, 137, 141, 145, 150, 167, 192, 301
Pruitt 90, 181, 191, 227, 229, 259
Puckett 22, 64, 82, 108, 109, 128, 152, 156-158, 173, 201, 219, 236
Pugh 154, 160, 193, 291
Pullen 93, 109, 156, 163
Putman 306
Putnam 79
Pyle 78
Ragsdale 248
Rainey 126
Rainsy 91
Rainwater 7, 10, 28, 50, 51, 81, 99, 119, 199, 223
Raley 37, 81, 153, 158, 160
Ralinson 160
Ramey 27, 38, 106, 107, 119, 161, 214, 216, 242
Ramires 90
Ramond 99
Ramsell 96
Ramsey 99, 106, 114, 128
Rape 37, 71, 114, 116, 176, 218, 275, 298, 302
Ray 6-9, 11, 37, 39, 52, 58, 63, 64, 81, 106, 118, 121, 128, 139, 144, 164, 210, 259, 308
Rayburn 136, 154
Read 17, 217, 250, 253, 300, 303
Reagan 5, 8, 78, 105
Reavley 207
Red 154, 188, 240, 250
Redden 98
Redding 14, 154
Reddy 17
Redwine 170, 187
Reed 8, 11, 88, 91, 111, 113, 119, 128, 132, 139, 141, 160, 233, 255, 285, 299

Reedy 100, 139
Reese 21, 37, 43, 44, 61, 63, 90, 91, 108, 122, 124, 125, 137, 143-145, 154, 164, 172, 191, 260, 268, 297
Reeves 17, 41, 52, 77, 91, 98, 143, 210, 271
Rehorse 87, 89, 91
Reich 120, 153, 197, 278
Reid 37, 44-46, 78, 136, 146, 154, 180, 295
Reinhardt 65, 71, 111, 132, 155, 173, 198, 231
Renderez 92
Reneau 37, 146, 202, 210
Renshaw 260
Rentorez 91
Revell 144, 210
Revelle 18
Revley 207
Reynolds 8, 94, 170, 217
Rheinhart 14
Rhodes 29, 54, 67, 73, 81, 110, 118, 130, 137, 155-157, 162, 170, 235
Rhods 61
Rhone 5, 6, 238
Rhymes 217
Rice 2, 3, 5, 217
Richard 5, 7, 29, 35, 77, 91, 109, 178, 194, 221, 243, 256
Richards 5, 15, 77, 91, 248
Richardson 46, 61, 126
Richburg 37, 80, 98, 115, 118, 147, 156, 277, 289

Richey 4, 91, 209
Riddle 131, 185
Rider 124
Rigley 98
Riley 128, 157, 159, 185, 210, 270
Riner 195
Rink 239
Rippy 43
Rivers 84, 89
Roach 140, 221
Robbins 38, 54, 63, 70, 73, 74, 92, 97, 98, 105, 106, 112, 113, 124, 127, 145, 151, 152, 156, 162, 177, 185, 187, 188, 191, 206, 257, 259, 274, 300-303
Roberson 123
Roberts 25, 37, 38, 76, 91, 104, 110, 154, 155, 181, 226, 229, 248, 259
Robertson 65, 98, 242
Robins 11
Robinson 29, 37, 50, 52, 91, 100, 105, 114, 115, 121, 132, 139, 143, 146, 154, 156-158, 173, 183, 192, 193, 207, 230, 237, 267, 273, 284
Rocher 89
Roddell 126
Rodigues 141
Rodney 209
Roe 141
Rogers 14, 21, 23, 37, 98, 99, 111, 117, 161, 290
Roman 44, 85

Romine 91, 152, 241
Rooney 233
Rose 43, 57, 92, 96, 98, 163
Ross 17, 67, 71, 73, 80, 221
Rotan 48, 98, 201, 212, 252
Roten 46, 147, 169, 176, 302
Roundtree 37, 41, 46, 61, 63, 173, 272
Rouse 27, 28, 61, 76, 266, 306
Rousseau 228
Rowsey 42, 56, 69, 73, 279
Rozell 2, 3, 14
Rucker 72, 77, 104, 243
Rudble 80
Runnels 159, 187, 223
Rushing 8, 67, 91, 136, 153, 155, 237
Rusk 39, 42, 47, 51, 78, 97, 292
Russell 16, 22, 42, 54, 56, 57, 60, 61, 63, 67, 70, 73, 81, 91, 118, 122, 126, 129, 131, 133, 134, 145, 152, 176, 190, 196, 200, 203, 208, 210, 211, 215, 218, 221, 226, 237, 238, 258, 273, 275, 280, 307
Russle 306
Russo 199
Russom 108, 111, 154, 196, 206, 246
Rutledge 82, 250
Sage 57
Sailors 136
Sallas 97
Saltana 141
Samples 166, 217

Sanders 10, 66, 91, 102, 121
Sandifer 167, 183
Sandlin 221
Sanford 56, 91
Sarver 20, 63, 65, 114, 116, 131, 132, 140, 143
Sasser 77, 160
Satterwhite 192
Saxon 37, 71, 135
Sayers 103
Scarborough 98, 134
Schluter 141
Schneider 150
Schrum 156
Schrumm 98
Scoggin 66, 67
Scoggins 28, 29, 155, 157, 181, 193, 215, 218
Scroggins 7
Scruggs 170, 243, 278
Searcy 148, 234
Seat 2, 71, 226
Seawright 43, 111, 117, 125, 157
Selby 209
Self 154
Sellers 61, 138, 211, 264
Sells 99, 105
Sepurest 86
Servantes 78, 90
Session 47, 50, 61, 118, 147, 157, 207, 250, 262
Sessions 91
Setzler 14, 100, 108, 129, 141
Sewell 224
Seymore 47, 76, 199, 224, 273

Shamburger 13-15, 37, 50, 61, 68, 111, 153, 201, 204, 258, 307, 308
Sharigk 98
Sharman 165
Sharp 23, 27, 43, 98, 103, 268, 281, 308
Shaw 39, 63-66, 71, 81, 118, 127-129, 135, 139, 143, 149, 152, 156, 160, 164, 165, 167, 173, 210, 211, 227, 232, 233, 235, 236, 277
Shearer 8
Shelton 29, 33, 66, 72, 75, 109, 115, 146, 147, 152, 162, 177, 198, 211, 286, 304
Sheppard 122
Sherman 34, 86, 87, 95, 96, 98, 115, 141, 165, 183, 260
Shields 11, 131, 140, 211, 245
Shinn 154, 197
Ship 8
Shipes 21, 198
Shipp 153, 197, 232, 234
Shirey 65, 76, 144, 155, 156, 169, 201, 221
Shirley 113, 144, 268
Shirtliff 98
Shively 130
Shockley 307
Shoemaker 39, 44, 50, 110, 111, 119, 124, 135, 202, 223, 274
Shropshire 98, 221
Shuford 6, 7, 9
Simmons 155, 211, 212
Simon 66
Simons 37, 82, 130, 156, 173
Simpkins 84, 86, 88, 93, 94, 96-99
Simpson 15, 16, 40, 41
Sims 21, 82, 91, 105, 107, 111, 155, 156, 187, 202, 296
Singleton 91
Sisk 294
Sisler 203
Skeen 15, 283, 287, 288, 290
Skeep 285
Skiles 131, 224
Skinnell 217
Skinner 199, 248
Skipper 227, 228
Skull 32, 98
Slatter 110
Small 55
Smart 28, 34, 35, 39, 48, 52, 55, 57, 58, 63, 64, 68, 73, 81, 91, 100, 101, 112, 115, 120-122, 131, 138, 140, 154, 164, 165, 191, 193, 197, 199, 211, 218, 228, 243, 272, 274, 276, 285
Smith 14, 16-18, 21, 25, 27, 29, 35-38, 42, 44, 49, 52, 56, 58, 60-62, 64, 65, 69, 75, 77, 79-82, 85, 86, 90, 91, 93, 95, 98, 107-110, 119, 122, 123, 134, 137, 145, 147, 149, 150, 153-156, 159-163, 165, 170, 173-175, 178, 183, 185, 187, 191, 196,

200, 202, 208, 211, 217-219, 222-225, 227, 228, 230, 232, 240, 243, 246, 248, 254, 257-259, 272-274, 292, 299, 301, 303-308
Sneed 95
Snider 154
Snow 60, 70, 103, 111, 125, 156, 173
Snyder 129, 254, 263
Sockwell 190
Somin 66
Sonigas 98
Sorey 91
Sorge 121, 144, 221, 284
Spann 254
Sparkman 92, 98, 225
Sparks 13, 15, 90, 91, 98, 135, 158
Spaulding 98
Spearman 104
Speer 80
Speights 37, 217, 299
Spencer 51, 105, 152, 207, 209, 224, 241
Spigner 157, 248
Spivey 92, 305
Spradling 3, 4, 9
Spratt 209
Spruel 153
Spurlock 17
Stafford 11, 16, 207
Stagner 113, 127, 146, 154, 184, 224, 235, 247, 269, 298, 299
Stamps 36, 65, 66

Stanley 3, 92, 103, 236
Stapler 11, 169, 224
Stapp 83
Stark 88, 91
Starnes 5, 6, 243
Stavens 128
Steed 125
Steele 36, 108
Stennett 92
Stephens 75, 121, 151, 164, 272
Stevens 5, 92, 119, 244
Stevenson 43, 92, 142, 211, 222, 281
Stewart 23, 128, 187
Stiles 149
Still 95
Stinson 29, 37, 57, 105, 161, 244, 308
Stivers 29
Stokes 9, 36, 51, 57, 92, 111, 122, 126, 133, 211, 220, 263
Stone 77, 119, 124, 157, 229
Storms 41
Story 125, 151, 152, 161, 304
Stout 2, 3, 154,
Stovall 67, 236
Strange 65, 133
Strickland 156, 201, 266, 269, 273
Stroud 116, 245
Styres 96
Suddeth 23
Suiter 29, 60, 62, 65, 66, 92, 112, 133, 139, 210, 289
Sullivan 37, 110, 152, 197
Sumerland 94, 98

Sutherland 16, 54, 58, 100, 120, 135, 140, 216, 241
Sutton 92, 116, 152, 154, 209, 221
Swan 155, 168
Swanner 244
Sweeney 182
Sweeten 92
Swenney 193
Swindall 126, 148
Swingle 78
Swinney 183
Sykes 46
Tackett 103, 148, 180
Tapley 154
Tarrant 108
Tarver 98, 108
Tatum 144
Taylor 6, 8, 15, 20, 22, 25, 34, 42, 43, 47, 53, 54, 57, 66, 67, 71, 73, 76, 92, 98, 99, 108-111, 114, 118-120, 124, 128, 131, 135, 144, 154-156, 202, 210, 216, 217, 232, 241, 290
Taytum 77
Tedder 98
Teddlie 59, 111, 135, 156
Tedlie 65, 66
Teer 183
Telaferro 93
Templeton 92
Terrance 172
Terrell 17, 77, 80, 83, 96, 99, 118, 132, 157, 195, 235, 252

Terry 17, 37, 92, 111, 125, 221, 266
Testerman 98
Tezzle 78
Thacker 154
Tharp 37, 104, 112, 135, 211
Thatcher 92
Thedford 92
Thomas 3, 7-9, 17, 56, 57, 61, 63, 64, 67, 70, 74, 79-82, 84, 88, 92, 96, 97, 102, 116, 117, 121, 122, 125, 127, 128, 135, 145, 147, 159, 173, 207, 216, 225, 233, 236, 307
Thompson 8, 17, 19, 37, 53, 59, 61, 92, 99, 110, 115, 159, 160, 162, 172, 188, 209, 214, 233, 243, 256, 305, 308
Thorn 44, 122, 137, 141, 145, 150, 191
Thorne 118, 145
Thrailkill 95
Thurman 92
Tier 80, 85
Tiest 99
Tillery 99
Tinney 111, 144
Tittsworth 146, 243
Tocle 92
Todd 44, 46, 119, 120, 222, 227, 229
Tolbert 245
Toles 161
Tollett 84, 91, 98
Tompson 15

Toney 36, 37, 122, 145, 211
Tonney 308
Torrance 211
Tosrell 90
Touchton 165
Trapp 111
Truss 157, 219
Tuberville 173
Tucker 48, 60, 111, 132, 142, 151, 152, 154, 155, 221, 306
Tuggle 110, 211
Turbeville 110
Turman 5, 27, 129, 161, 235
Turner 29, 30, 36, 39, 49, 61, 75, 82, 105, 111, 115, 119, 131, 132, 137, 144, 147, 152, 154, 155, 162, 168-170, 173, 176, 178, 189, 207, 227, 280, 306
Turvill 131, 132
Underwood 92, 99
Upchurch 99, 170
Urutia 94
Usselton 15
Ussery 71, 87, 89, 92, 106, 141, 152, 161, 191, 198, 302
Utley 153
Van Nostrand 217
Vance 199
Vandiver 36, 37, 52, 66, 130, 156, 221
Vanney 4
Vaughn 99, 155, 159, 160, 162, 172, 198, 217, 247, 251, 256-259, 307
Veach 37

Veasey 95
Vehle 92
Veitch 128, 149, 152, 156, 187, 246, 278
Vendervile 94
Vetan 98
Vickers 37, 43, 69, 112-114, 209, 232
Vickery 57, 58, 64, 68, 70-72, 79, 109, 118, 122, 128, 130, 131, 135, 140, 143, 175, 211, 247, 269, 276, 277
Vincent 6
Vines 60
Vining 95
Virt 92
Voorhees 21, 131, 288
Waddleton 92, 141, 170
Wade 164, 172, 193, 197, 207, 219, 222
Wages 252
Wagoner 110
Waldrop 92
Walker 17, 27, 82, 85, 88, 91, 95, 97, 100, 119, 122, 144, 164, 173, 224
Wallace 20, 42, 54, 64, 79, 100, 119, 135, 147, 151, 153, 187, 219, 221, 243, 254, 256, 281
Wallen 99, 129
Wallin 219
Wallis 42, 57, 64
Walsh 93, 307
Walters 79
Walthal 137

Walton 46, 93
Ward 5, 10, 79, 85, 87, 89, 92, 95, 97
Ware 38
Warlick 230, 244-246
Warn 150, 192
Warren 23, 69, 83, 131, 201, 207, 233, 249
Washington 99, 233, 300
Watkins 36, 40, 146, 181, 193
Watson 7, 88, 93, 128, 278, 297
Watts 5, 123
Way 12, 69, 106, 115, 118, 149, 184, 192, 216, 235, 303
Webb 3, 6, 22, 61, 99, 130, 148, 161
Webber 115
Webster 15, 156, 178, 234
Weeker 183
Weeks 32
Weems 20, 36, 66, 93, 95, 130, 181, 193, 225
Weidman 85, 88, 95
Weise 93
Welch 22, 69, 193
Wellons 246, 247
Wells 6-8, 10, 11, 109, 122, 165, 190, 204, 235, 239, 243
Welse 93
Welsh 67
Werblun 59
Wesley 78, 84, 91, 93, 141
Wesson 227
West 85, 93, 110,
Whaley 172, 244

Whatley 183
Wheat 76, 115, 154, 294
Wheeler 66, 71, 116, 121, 154, 158, 166, 207, 217, 221, 224, 227, 283, 305
Wheelis 103
White 4, 5, 32, 36, 37, 42, 43, 51, 54, 65, 70, 76, 78, 79, 85, 86, 88, 89, 92-95, 98, 107, 115, 116, 119, 120, 123, 130, 135, 141, 153, 155-157, 163, 170, 174, 176, 177, 180, 195, 203, 204, 250, 255, 293, 297
Whitehead 115
Whitehurst 22
Whitley 36, 66, 67, 130
Whitmore 267
Whittaker 79, 96
Whitter 75, 151, 168, 275
Whitus 93
Whitworth 93, 107, 123, 143, 155, 237, 267
Wicker 78
Wier 39
Wiggins 155
Wilbanks 65, 114
Wilburn 93
Wilcox 54, 69, 114, 118, 168, 243
Wilder 33, 35, 73, 163, 183
Wiley 48, 60, 61, 65, 138, 202, 252
Wilfong 238
Wilkins 195
Wilkinson 211

Williams 4, 8-11, 17, 32-34,
   37-41, 44-46, 48, 54, 55,
   57, 61, 63, 64, 66, 71,
   79, 82, 89, 93, 95, 99,
   101, 104, 111, 114, 118,
   121, 122, 126, 128, 135,
   138, 164, 168, 170, 173,
   176, 180, 181, 201, 211,
   213, 221, 238, 264, 279,
   284, 291, 298
Williamson 65, 111, 229
Willingham 5, 15, 24, 72, 81,
   119, 120, 131, 154, 261,
   267, 268, 273
Willis 7, 82, 84, 126, 132, 158,
   198, 237, 255, 308
Wilson 13, 15, 37, 57-59, 62,
   66, 75, 91, 93, 99, 104,
   111, 118, 153, 154, 169,
   199, 207, 211, 229, 237,
   265, 267, 272, 292
Wingard 20, 77, 100, 292
Wingo 93
Winkle 38, 76, 103
Winterbaur 64, 104
Wise 113, 138, 274
Wisener 155
Womack 155
Wonzer 187
Wood 21, 27, 32, 35-37, 54, 56,
   61-63, 78, 88, 93, 119,
   124, 200, 207, 229, 245,
   249, 254, 306
Woodard 30, 98
Woodbury 3, 4, 7
Woodfin 45
Woods 32, 211, 214, 221

Worthington 51, 124, 211
Worthy 9, 10, 111, 220
Wren 11, 21, 46, 93, 199
Wright 4, 5, 7, 10, 11, 25, 33,
   36-39, 41, 42, 54, 62,
   65, 67, 68, 80, 95, 101,
   103, 104, 107, 117, 120,
   133, 140, 144, 151, 154,
   155, 175, 176, 202, 211,
   224, 227, 264, 265, 273,
   303
Wyatt 160
Wyley 93
Wylie 34, 37, 64, 211
Wynn 237
Yandall 66
Yantis 53
Yarborough 77-79, 86
Yarbrough 2-5, 11, 84, 85, 87,
   90, 92, 94
York 163, 281
Young 11, 43, 66, 71, 80, 89,
   93, 112, 209, 233, 288
Zeigler 8, 15, 69, 121, 122,
   131, 157, 167, 275
Zimmerman 227, 278

www.ingramcontent.com/pod-product-compliance
Lightning Source LLC
Chambersburg PA
CBHW060941230426
43665CB00015B/2020